Linux© Troubleshooting for System Administrators and Power Users

Hewlett-Packard® Professional Books

HP-UX

Cooper/Moore	HP-UX 11i Internals
Fernandez	Configuring CDE
Keenan	HP-UX CSE: Official Study Guide and Desk Reference
Madell	Disk and File Management Tasks on HP-UX
Herington/Jacquot	The HP Virtual Server Environment
Poniatowski	HP-UX 11i Virtual Partitions
Poniatowski	HP-UX 11i System Administration Handbook and Toolkit, Second Edition
Poniatowski	The HP-UX 11.x System Administration Handbook and Toolkit
Poniatowski	HP-UX 11.x System Administration "How To" Book
Poniatowski	HP-UX 10.x System Administration "How To" Book
Poniatowski	HP-UX 11i Version 2 System Administration
Poniatowski	HP-UX System Administration Handbook and Toolkit
Poniatowski	Learning the HP-UX Operating System
Rehman	HP-UX CSA: Official Study Guide and Desk Reference
Sauers/Ruemmler/Weygant	HP-UX 11i Tuning and Performance
Weygant	Clusters for High Availability, Second Edition
Wong	HP-UX 11i Security

UNIX, LINUX

Ezolt	Optimizing Linux® Performance
Fink	The Business and Economics of Linux and Open Source
Mosberger/Eranian	IA-64 Linux Kernel
Poniatowski	Linux on HP Integrity Servers

COMPUTER ARCHITECTURE

Carlson/Huck	Itanium Rising
Evans/Trimper	Itanium Architecture for Programmers
Kane	PA-RISC 2.0 Architecture
Wadleigh/Crawford	Software Optimization for High Performance Computers
Weldon/Rogers	HP ProLiant Servers AIS: Official Study Guide and Desk Reference

NETWORKING/COMMUNICATIONS

Blommers	OpenView Network Node Manager
Blommers	Practical Planning for Network Growth
Brans	Mobilize Your Enterprise
Cook	Building Enterprise Information Architecture
Lucke	Designing and Implementing Computer Workgroups
Lund	Integrating UNIX and PC Network Operating Systems
Zitello/Williams/Weber	HP OpenView System Administration Handbook

SECURITY

Bruce	Security in Distributed Computing
Mao	Modern Cryptography: Theory and Practice
Pearson	Trusted Computing Platforms
Pipkin	Halting the Hacker, Second Edition
Pipkin	Information Security

Linux© Troubleshooting for System Administrators and Power Users

James Kirkland, David Carmichael, Christopher L. Tinker, and Gregory L. Tinker

www.hp.com/hpbooks

PRENTICE
HALL

Pearson Education

Upper Saddle River, NJ • Boston • Indianapolis • San Francisco

New York • Toronto • Montreal • London • Munich • Paris • Madrid

Capetown • Sydney • Tokyo • Singapore • Mexico City

Many of the designations used by manufacturers and sellers to distinguish their products are claimed as trademarks. Where those designations appear in this book, and the publisher was aware of a trademark claim, the designations have been printed with initial capital letters or in all capitals.

Novell is a registered trademark of Novell, Inc. SUSE is a registered trademark of SUSE LINUX AG, a Novell business. Red Hat is a registered trademark of Red Hat, Inc. Linux is a registered trademark of Linus Torvalds.

The authors and publisher have taken care in the preparation of this book, but make no expressed or implied warranty of any kind and assume no responsibility for errors or omissions. No liability is assumed for incidental or consequential damages in connection with or arising out of the use of the information or programs contained herein.

The publisher offers excellent discounts on this book when ordered in quantity for bulk purchases or special sales, which may include electronic versions and/or custom covers and content particular to your business, training goals, marketing focus, and branding interests. For more information, please contact:

United States Corporate and Government Sales
(800) 382-3419
corpsales@pearsontechgroup.com

For sales outside the United States, please contact:

International Sales
international@pearsoned.com

 This Book Is Safari Enabled

The Safari® Enabled icon on the cover of your favorite technology book means the book is available through Safari Bookshelf. When you buy this book, you get free access to the online edition for 45 days.

Safari Bookshelf is an electronic reference library that lets you easily search thousands of technical books, find code samples, download chapters, and access technical information whenever and wherever you need it.

To gain 45-day Safari Enabled access to this book:

- Go to http://www.awprofessional.com/safarienabled.
- Complete the brief registration form.
- Enter the coupon code M9GP-CJVI-SCH8-XYIT-L4F9.

If you have difficulty registering on Safari Bookshelf or accessing the online edition, please e-mail customer-service@safaribooksonline.com.

Visit us on the Web: www.prenhallprofessional.com

Library of Congress Cataloging-in-Publication Data

Linux troubleshooting for system administrators and power users / James Kirkland . . . [et al.].

    p. cm.

  ISBN 0-13-185515-8 (pbk. : alk. paper) 1. Linux. 2. Operating systems (Computers) I. Kirkland, James.

  QA76.76.O63L54875 2006

  005.4'32—dc22

2006000036

Copyright© 2006 Hewlett-Packard Development Company, L.P.

Pearson Education, Inc.
Rights and Contracts Department
One Lake Street
Upper Saddle River, NJ 07458
Fax: (201) 236-3290

ISBN 0-13-185515-8

Text printed in the United States on recycled paper at R.R. Donnelley in Crawfordsville, IN.

First printing, May 2006

To Kristine: Without your love and support, this book never would have happened. To my father and mother, for not killing me when I deserved it and loving me when I didn't.

—James

Stephanie, thank you for your effort and sacrifice, which made this book possible. You remind me every day how strong our love is by the things you do. Sarah and Shannon, thanks for being such sweet daughters and understanding when daddy had so much homework. Mom and Dad, thanks for buying me that Vic 20 back in high school to get me started.

—Dave

Bonnie, my love, thank you for your understanding, sacrifice, and "word-smith" brilliance without which I would still be sitting under that tree in the back yard trying to figure out how to make `task_struct` flow into a discussion of threads. Steve, Robert, and Greg, you guys are the best. Mom and Dad, thanks for the love you've shown and the incredible work ethic that you have instilled.

—Chris

Kristen, thank you for giving up so many weekends in order to make this effort successful. I also wish to thank my parents and brothers Robert Jr., Steve, and Chris, for being understanding as I missed several family outings in 2005 while working on this endeavor.

—Greg

—

Table of Contents

Preface

My good friend, James Kirkland, sent me an instant message one day asking if I wanted to write a Linux troubleshooting book with him. James has been heavily involved in Linux at the HP Response Center for several years. While troubleshooting Linux issues for customers, he realized there was not a good troubleshooting reference available. I remember a meeting discussing Linux troubleshooting. Someone asked what the most valuable Linux troubleshooting tool was. The answer was immediate. Google. If you have ever spent time trying to find a solution for a Linux problem, you know what that engineer was talking about. A wealth of great Linux information can be found on the Internet, but you can't always rely on this strategy. Some of the Linux information is outdated. A lot of it can't be understood without a good foundation of subject knowledge, and some of it is incorrect. We wanted to write this book so the Linux administrator will know how Linux works and how to approach and resolve common issues. This book contains the information we wish we had when we started troubleshooting Linux.

Greg and Chris are identical twins and serious Linux hobbyists. They have been Linux advocates within HP for years. Yes, they both run Linux on their laptops. Chris is a member of the Superdome Server team (http://www.hp.com/products1/servers/scalableservers/superdome/index.html). Greg works for the XP storage team (http://h18006.www1.hp.com/storage/xparrays.html). Their Linux knowledge is wide and deep. They have worked through SAN storage issues and troubleshot process hangs, Linux crashes, performance issues, and everything else for our customers, and they have put their experience into the book.

I am a member of the HP escalations team. I've primarily spent my time resolving HPUX issues. I've been a Linux hobbyist for a few years, and I've started working Linux escalations, but I'm definitely newer to Linux than the rest of the team. I try to give the book the perspective of someone who is fairly new to Linux. I tried to remember the questions I had when I first started troubleshooting Linux issues and included them in the book. We sincerely hope our effort is helpful to you.

Dave Carmichael

Chapter Summaries

These chapter summaries will give you an idea of how the book is organized and a bit of an overview of the content of each chapter.

Chapter 1: System Boot, Startup, and Shutdown Issues

Chapter 1 discusses the different subsystems that comprise Linux startup. These include the bootloaders GRUB and LILO, the init process, and the rc startup and shutdown scripts. We explain how GRUB and LILO work along with the important features of each. The reader will learn how to boot when there are problems with the bootloader. There are numerous examples. We explain how init works and what part it plays in starting Linux. The rc scripts are explained in detail as well. The reader will learn how to boot to single user mode, emergency mode, and confirm mode. Examples are included of using a recovery CD when Linux won't boot from disk.

Chapter 2: System Hangs and Panics

This chapter explains interruptible and non-interruptible OS hangs, kernel panics, and IA64 hardware machine checks. A Linux hang takes one of two forms. An interruptible hang is when Linux seems frozen but does respond to some events, such as a ping request. Non-interruptible hangs do not respond to any actions. We show how to use the Magic SysReq keystroke to generate a stack trace to troubleshoot an interruptible hang. We explain how to force a panic when Linux is in a non-interruptible hang. An OS panic is a voluntary shutdown of the kernel in response to something unexpected. We discuss how to obtain a panic dump from Linux. The IA64 architecture dump mechanism is also explained.

Chapter 3: Performance Tools

In Chapter 3, we explain how to use some of the most popular Linux performance tools including `top`, `sar`, `vmstat`, `iostat`, and `free`. The examples show common syntaxes and options. Every system administrator should be familiar with these commands.

Chapter 4: Performance

Chapter 4 discusses different approaches to isolating a performance problem. As with the majority of performance issues, storage always seems to draw significant attention. The goal of this chapter is to provide a quick understanding of how a storage device should perform and easy ways to get a performance measurement without expensive software. In addition to troubleshooting storage performance, we touch on CPU bottlenecks and ways to find such events.

Chapter 5: Adding New Storage via SAN with Reference to PCMCIA and USB

Linux is moving out from under the desk and into the data center. An essential feature of an enterprise computing platform is being able to access storage on the SAN. This chapter provides a detailed walkthrough and examples of installing and configuring Fibre Channel cards. We discuss driver issues, how the device files work, and how to add LUNs.

Chapter 6: Disk Partitions and Filesystems

Master Boot Record (MBR) basics are explained, and examples are shown detailing how bootloader programs such as LILO and GRUB manipulate the MBR. We explain the partition table, and a lot of examples are given so that the reader will understand how the disk is carved up into extended and logical partitions. Many scenarios are provided explaining common disk and filesystem problems and their solutions. After reading this chapter, the reader will understand not only what MBA, LBA, extended partitions, and all the other buzzwords mean, but also how they look on the disk and how to fix problems related to them.

Chapter 7: Device Failure and Replacement

This chapter explains identifying problems with hardware devices and how to fix them. We begin with a discussion of supported devices. Whether a device is supported by the Linux distribution is a good thing to know before spending a lot of time trying to get it working. Next we show where to look for indications of hardware problems. The reader will learn how to decipher the hexadecimal error messages from dmesg and syslog. We explain how to use the lspci tool for troubleshooting. When the error is understood, the next goal is to resolve the device problem. We demonstrate techniques for determining what needs to be done to fix device issues including SAN devices.

Chapter 8: Linux Processes: Structure, Hangs, and Core Dumps

Process management is the heart of the Linux kernel. A system administrator should know what happens when a process is created to troubleshoot process issues. This chapter explains process creation and provides a foundation for troubleshooting. Linux is a multithreading kernel. The reader will learn how multithreading works and what heavyweight and lightweight processes are. The reader also will learn how to troubleshoot a process that seems to be hanging and not doing any work. Core dumps are also covered. We show you how to learn which process dumped core and why. This chapter details how cores are created and how to best utilize them to understand the problem.

Chapter 9: Backup/Recovery

Creating good backups is one of if not the most important tasks a system administrator must perform. This chapter explains the most commonly used backup/recovery commands: tar, cpio, dump/restore, and so on. Tape libraries (autoloaders) are explained along with the commands needed to manipulate them. The reader will learn the uses of different tape device files. There are examples showing how to troubleshoot common issues.

Chapter 10: cron and at

The cron and at commands are familiar to most Linux users. These commands are used to schedule jobs to run at a later time. This chapter explains how the cron/at subsystem works and where to look when jobs don't run. The cron, at, batch, and anacron facilities are explained in detail. The kcron graphical cron interface is discussed. Numerous examples are provided to demonstrate how to resolve the most common problems. The troubleshooting techniques help build good general troubleshooting skills that can be applied to many other Linux problems.

Chapter 11: Printing and Printers

This chapter explains the different print spoolers used in Linux systems. The reader will learn how the spooler works. The examples show how to use the spooler commands such as lpadmin, lpoption, lprm, and others to identify problems. The different page description languages such as PCL and PostScript are explained. Examples demonstrate how to fix remote printing and network printing problems.

Chapter 12: System Security

Security is a concern of every system administrator. Is the box safe because it is behind a firewall? What steps should be taken to secure my system? These questions are answered. Host-based and network-based security are explained. Secure Shell protocol (SSH) is covered in detail: why SSH is secure, encryption with SSH, SSH tunnels, troubleshooting typical SSH problems, and SSH examples are provided. The reader will learn system hardening using netfilter and iptables. netfilter and iptables together make up the standard firewall software for the Linux 2.4 and 2.6 kernels.

Chapter 13: Network Problems

Network issues are a common problem for any system administrator. What should be done when Linux boots and users can't connect? Is the problem with the Linux box or something on the LAN? Has the network interface card failed? We need a systematic way to verify the network hardware and Linux configuration. Chapter 13 provides the information a Linux system administrator needs to troubleshoot network problems. Learn where to look for configuration problems and how to use the commands ethtool, modinfo, mii, and others to diagnose networking problems.

Chapter 14: Login Problems

Chapter 14 explains how the login process works and how to troubleshoot login failures. Password aging is explained. Several examples show the reader how to fix common login problems. The Pluggable Authentication Modules (PAM) subsystem is explained in detail. The examples reinforce the concepts explained and demonstrate how to fix problems encountered with PAM.

Chapter 15: X Windows Problems

GNOME and KDE are client/server applications just like many others that run on Linux, but they can be frustrating to troubleshoot because they are display managers. After reading this chapter, the reader will understand the components of Linux graphical display managers and how to troubleshoot problems. Practical examples are provided to reinforce the concepts, and they can be applied to real-world problems.

Acknowledgments

We would like to extend our sincere gratitude to everyone who made this book possible. We wish to express gratitude to Hewlett-Packard and our HP management as well as the Prentice Hall editorial and production teams.

We also wish to express gratitude to our families for their understanding and support throughout the long road from the initial drafting to the final publication.

About the Authors

JAMES KIRKLAND is a Senior Consultant for Racemi. He was previously a Senior Systems Administrator at Hewlett-Packard. He has been working with UNIX variants for more than ten years. James is a Red Hat Certified engineer, Linux LPIC level one certified, and an HP-UX certified System Administrator. He has been working with Linux for seven years and HP-UX for eight years. He has been a participant at HP World, Linux World, and numerous internal HP forums.

DAVID CARMICHAEL works for Hewlett-Packard as a Technical Problem Manager in Alpharetta, Georgia. He earned a bachelors degree in computer science from West Virginia University in 1987 and has been helping customers resolve their IT problems ever since. David has written articles for HP's IT Resource Center (http://itrc.hp.com) and presented at HP World 2003.

CHRIS and **GREG TINKER** are twin brothers originally from LaFayette, Georgia. Chris began his career in computers while working as a UNIX System Administrator for Lockheed Martin in Marietta, Georgia. Greg began his career while at Bellsouth in Atlanta, Georgia. Both Chris and Greg joined Hewlett-Packard in 1999. Chris's primary role at HP is as a Senior Software Business Recovery Specialist and Greg's primary role is as a Storage Business Recovery Specialist. Both Chris and Greg have participated in HP World, taught several classes in UNIX/Linux and Disk Array technology, and obtained various certifications including certifications in Advanced Clusters, SAN, and Linux. Chris resides with his wife, Bonnie, and Greg resides with his wife, Kristen, in Alpharetta, Georgia.

1

System Boot, Startup, and Shutdown Issues

There is no question that startup issues can really cause anxiety for system administrators. We reboot a box and anxiously wait to see it respond to `ping` so we know it is coming up ok. But what do we do if Linux doesn't boot up? Can we resolve the problem, or is it simpler to just reinstall? Reinstalling Linux is easy if we are properly prepared. Yet we sometimes wonder whether we have good backups and contemplate an evening at work reloading the box. Chapter 9, "Backup/Recovery," helps you prepare for the time when Linux must be reinstalled, but hopefully after reading this chapter, you will be able to resolve Linux startup issues with confidence.

Startup issues are difficult to fix because Linux first must be started somehow so that troubleshooting can begin. You must have a good understanding of the Linux three-part boot process to troubleshoot startup problems. The following key topics are discussed in this chapter:

* The bootloaders GRUB and LILO
* The `init` process
* The startup and shutdown scripts
* Fixing problems with the root filesystem

The bootloader is the first software to execute from disk at boot time. The purpose of the bootloader is to start the Linux kernel. GRUB and LILO are the most common bootloaders, and this chapter only discusses these. Both make it easy to configure boot menu choices of different kernels and boot disks.

The init process is the first process started by the Linux kernel during boot. The init process is responsible for starting processes during boot up and when changing runlevels. The rc subsystem is run by init at each runlevel to start and stop the processes for that runlevel. We examine the concept of runlevels in this chapter. init is the parent of every other process.

Linux starts a lot of services at boot up. Networking services, cron, and syslog are just a few. The rc subsystem starts these services. We look at how the rc scripts work and how to troubleshoot them in this chapter.

This chapter explains all these topics in detail. The examples provided demonstrate solutions for common Linux boot problems. In addition, this chapter covers creating rescue CDs and fixing common problems with the root filesystem that prevent Linux from starting.

Bootloaders

The bootloader displays the boot menu that appears during Linux startup. Bootloaders are not unique to Linux. They are the bridge between the BIOS and an operating system, whether it is Linux, Windows, or UNIX.

The bootloader loads the Linux kernel and initial ram disk[1] and then executes the kernel. The BIOS determines which source (hard disk, floppy, CD, etc.) to boot from. The Master Boot Record (MBR) is then loaded, and the bootloader is executed from the selected device.

The operating system load programs or bootloaders covered in this chapter are the GRand Unified Bootloader (GRUB) and LInux LOader (LILO), and we concentrate on the Red Hat and SUSE distributions. This section explains how the bootloaders work, what parts they have, and how to fix common problems with them. This section also discusses how to boot when the bootloader fails.

GRUB

GRUB is the bootloader most commonly used to start installed Linux systems. GRUB identifies the Linux kernel that should be used to boot the system and loads and then executes the kernel. If you installed Linux recently, there is a good chance that GRUB was installed too and serves as the bootloader.

This section examines the features of GRUB and how to fix problems with GRUB. We start with an overview of how GRUB works. Next, we demonstrate the features used for troubleshooting and resolving boot problems. We include examples to show how to boot to single user mode, how to correct a bad GRUB configuration, and how to repair the MBR when it is overwritten or corrupted. GRUB has rich configuration features that are covered well in the GRUB info manual. We won't try to duplicate that information here.

Before discussing GRUB, we need to briefly explain the MBR. The MBR of a hard disk is located in the first sector and is used to load and start the operating system. The MBR contains the partition table and an extremely small program called the bootloader. More information about the MBR can be found in Chapter 6, "Disk Partitions and Filesystems."

GRUB is a two-stage bootloader:

1. Stage 1 is installed in the MBR and is 446 bytes in length. Stage 1's only job is to load and execute Stage 2, although it may use an intermediate step called Stage 1.5 if filesystem support is needed.

2. Stage 2 loads and executes the kernel. It displays the boot menu and provides a shell environment that can be used to specify a kernel location. Stage 2 is normally located in /boot/grub. The GRUB boot menu is displayed on the console after the hardware BIOS messages. The menu contains a list of kernels that can be booted with the default kernel highlighted. Figure 1-1 shows a typical GRUB boot menu. This example has two Linux boot disks. One disk contains Red Hat Linux with three different kernel choices available, and the other disk contains SUSE Linux. One SUSE kernel choice is listed on the menu.

The menu choices are from an ASCII configuration file named /boot/grub/grub.conf for Red Hat and /boot/grub/menu.lst for SUSE. The GRUB configuration file can be edited as needed. Figure 1-1 shows a GRUB configuration with two Linux installations. Each has a /boot partition and a grub.conf or menu.lst configuration file. Whichever Linux install wrote the MBR is the one whose /boot is used at startup. The GRUB menu can be customized using different backgrounds and colors. The screenshots in this chapter show GRUB output from a serial console window. Typically, there is a graphical menu of kernels to boot. Each menu choice has a group of lines consisting of a

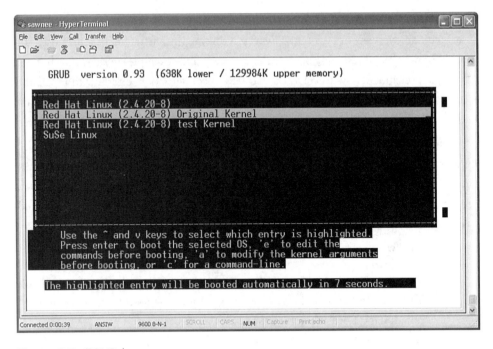

Figure 1-1 GRUB boot menu

menu item title and the kernel location for this choice. The highlighted Red Hat entry in Figure 1-1 consists of the following lines in grub.conf.

```
title Red Hat Linux (2.4.20-8) Original Kernel
        root (hd0,0)
        kernel /vmlinuz-2.4.20-8 ro root=LABEL=/
        initrd /initrd-2.4.20-8.img
```

This is an example of a very simple kernel definition in grub.conf. Each grub.conf line begins with a keyword. The keywords used in Figure 1-1 are:

* title—Begins a new menu choice. The text following the title keyword is displayed on the GRUB menu at boot up.

* root—Specifies the partition where the boot directory is located.

* kernel—Specifies the path to the kernel to boot along with the options to pass.

* initrd—Sets up a ram disk.

note

All the GRUB options are identified in the GRUB info file.

Please notice the disk partition (hd0,0) that is identified as the location of the boot partition. With GRUB, the disks are numbered starting from zero, as are the partitions. The second disk would be hd1, the third hd2, and so on. The root partition in the previous example is the first partition on the first hard disk. Floppy disks are identified as fd rather than hd.

A complete sample grub.conf file is shown here:

```
# Set up the serial terminal, first of all.
serial --unit=0 --speed=9600 --word=8 --parity=no --stop=1
terminal --timeout=10 serial console


# Set default kernel selection. Numbering starts at 0.
default=1


# 10 second delay before autoboot
timeout=10


# Comment out graphical menu
# splashimage=(hd0,0)/grub/splash.xpm.gz


title Red Hat Linux (2.4.20-8)
        root (hd0,0)
        kernel /bzImage ro root=LABEL=/
        initrd /initrd-2.4.20-8.img


title Red Hat Linux (2.4.20-8) Original Kernel
        root (hd0,0)
        kernel /vmlinuz-2.4.20-8 ro root=LABEL=/
        initrd /initrd-2.4.20-8.img
title Red Hat Linux (2.4.20-8) test Kernel
        root (hd0,0)
        kernel /vmlinuz.tset ro root=LABEL=/
        initrd /initrd-2.4.20-8.img
title SuSe Linux
    kernel (hd1,0)/vmlinuz root=/dev/hdb3 splash=silent text desktop \
    showopts
    initrd (hd1,0)/initrd
```

The focus of this chapter is on troubleshooting, not on thoroughly explaining how GRUB works. That information is already available. GRUB has an excellent user manual that explains all the different options and syntax. Visit http://www.gnu.org/software/grub/ to obtain the manual and get the latest GRUB news.

GRUB provides a whole lot more than just the capability to select different kernels from a menu. GRUB allows the menu choices to be modified and even allows a shell-like command interface to boot from kernels not listed on the menu. GRUB makes it easy to correct problems that keep Linux from booting.

Editing the Menu Choices with GRUB

GRUB allows the boot menu choices to be edited by pressing e. GRUB enables users to edit the configuration of the menu choices. This means users can correct problems with grub.conf that prevent Linux from starting. Figure 1-2 shows a GRUB screen after pressing e.

Let's see how this feature can help us resolve a boot problem.

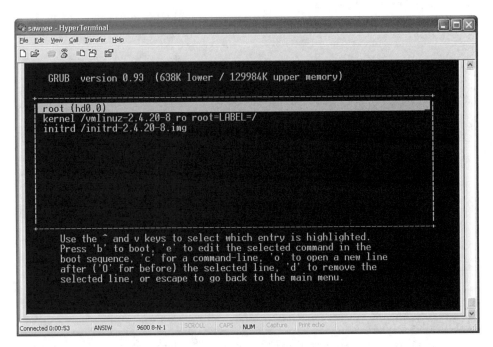

Figure 1-2 GRUB menu edit screen

Figure 1-3 is a console message that no system administrator wants to see. Pressing the space bar just brings up the GRUB menu again. The timer might be restarted too. GRUB tries to boot the same kernel again when the timer expires. If this attempt fails, the screen is displayed again without the timer.

The `Error 15` tells us that the kernel specified in `grub.conf` can't be found. Fortunately, GRUB permits editing the configuration. Pressing e gets the commands for the selected boot entry, as shown in Figure 1-4.

If we arrow down to the `kernel` line and press e, we get the edit screen shown in Figure 1-5.

We can use the arrow keys and Backspace to make changes just like the BASH shell. Press Enter when done to return to the previous screen. Press Esc to exit to the previous screen without keeping changes. We fix the typo by changing `vmlinuz.tset` to `vmlinuz.test` and press Enter. Now, the menu choice in Figure 1-6 looks better.

Press b to boot. Hopefully it works and Linux starts. If it still doesn't work, GRUB lets us try again. The kernel line can also be used to boot Linux to single user or emergency mode.

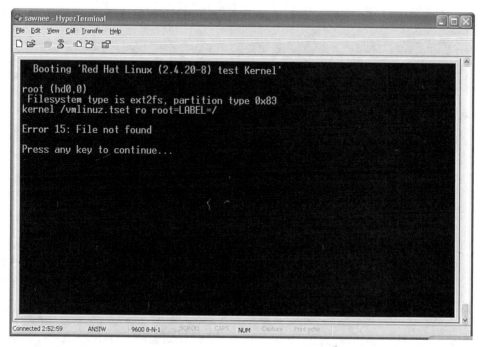

Figure 1-3 GRUB boot error message

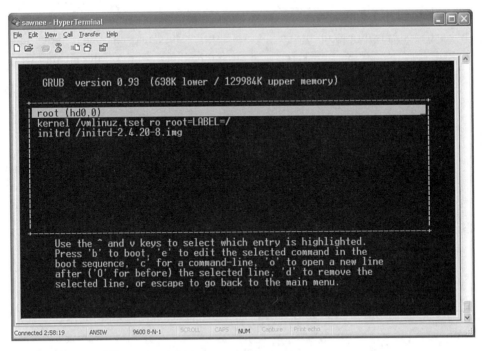

Figure 1-4 GRUB kernel configuration editing

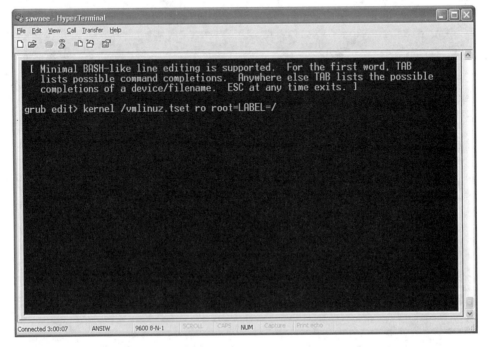

Figure 1-5 GRUB shell interface

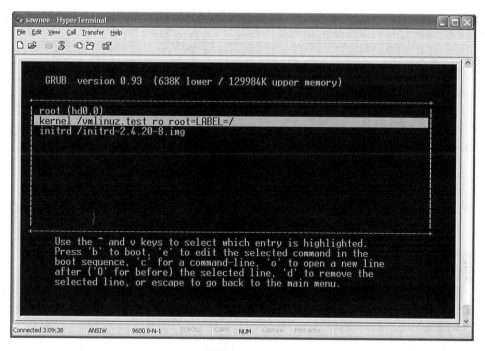

Figure 1-6 GRUB kernel configuration editing

Booting to Single User Mode and Emergency Mode

Occasionally it is necessary to perform system maintenance in a minimalist environment. Linux provides single user mode for this purpose. In single user mode (runlevel 1), Linux boots to a root shell. Networking is disabled, and few processes are running. Single user mode can be used to restore configuration files, move user data, fix filesystem corruption, and so on. It is important to know how to boot Linux to single user mode for the times when the boot to multiuser mode fails. Figure 1-7 is a typical SUSE console screen when booting to single user mode.

Note that SUSE requires the root password in single user mode. Red Hat, however, does not, which makes it easy to change the root password if it is lost. We explain later in this chapter how to reset a lost root password with a rescue CD-ROM.

If Linux boots from the kernel but then hangs, encounters errors during the startup scripts, or cannot boot to multiuser mode for some other reason, try single user mode. Just interrupt the GRUB auto boot, edit the kernel line, and add `single` to the end. Figure 1-8 is a screenshot of a Red Hat single user mode boot.

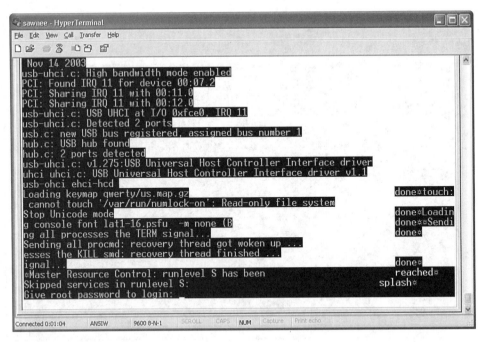

Figure 1-7 SUSE single user mode boot console output

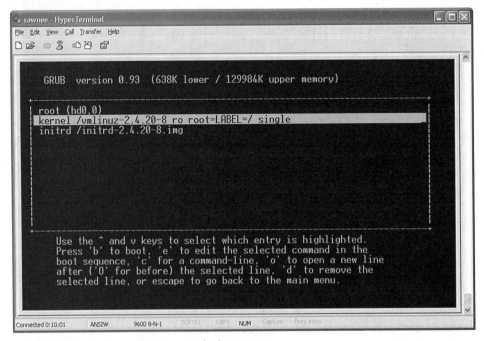

Figure 1-8 GRUB single user mode boot

Booting to emergency mode is accomplished by adding emergency to the end of the command line. Emergency mode is a minimalist environment. The root filesystem is mounted in read-only mode, no other filesystems are mounted, and init is not started. Figure 1-9 shows a Red Hat emergency mode boot.

What if we want to boot a kernel that is not on the menu? The next section looks at the editor features provided with GRUB.

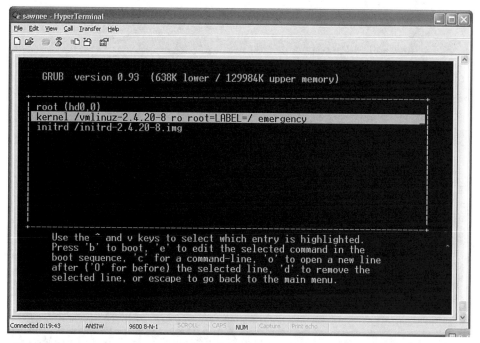

Figure 1-9 GRUB emergency mode boot

Command-Line Editing with GRUB

The GRUB command line can be invoked by pressing c, and it can be used to boot a kernel that is not on the menu. Users can enter their own root, kernel, and initrd lines. Press c and you get

```
grub>
```

GRUB supports tab line completion to list matches for device files and kernels. The previous Red Hat menu example can be used as a template for commands that could be used to boot the system from the GRUB command line.

For example, press Tab after typing the following, and GRUB completes the device if only one choice is available or lists all the matches if multiple matches exist:

```
grub> root (h
```

For a single-disk Linux installation with one IDE drive, GRUB fills in

```
grub> root (hd0,
```

Complete the rest of the root definition so that the line reads

```
grub> root (hd0,0)
```

Press Enter, and GRUB responds

```
Filesystem type is ext2fs, partition type 0x83
```

Now choose a kernel. Enter the following and press Tab:

```
grub> kernel /v
```

GRUB responds by filling in the rest of the unique characters (vmlinu) and showing the matches:

```
Possible files are: vmlinuz vmlinux-2.4.20-8 vmlinuz-2.4.20-8
vmlinuz.good vmlinuz-2.4.20-dave

grub> kernel /vmlinu
```

note

All the kernels in /boot do not necessarily have entries in the grub.conf file.

Tab completion makes it easy to boot a kernel even when the exact spelling isn't known. After the commands are entered, just type boot to boot Linux. This technique can also be used if the grub.conf file was renamed or erased.

Problems with the MBR

We mentioned earlier that GRUB inserts its stage1 file in the MBR. It is important to know how to restore the MBR if it becomes corrupted.

Reinstall MBR with GRUB stage1

Creating a dual-boot Linux system such as the Red Hat/ SUSE example in Figure 1-1 is a nice way to create a fallback position for system changes and to test a new Linux distribution. A small downside is that the GRUB `stage1` information in the MBR can be overwritten by the second install. In our example, Red Hat is installed on the first disk, and SUSE is installed on the second. After SUSE is installed, however, the SUSE GRUB menu is displayed instead of the Red Hat menu that we are used to and that has been customized for our installation. An easy way exists to fix the MBR, though. In Figure 1-10, we've reinstalled the GRUB `stage1` file to the MBR following the instructions in the GRUB manual, which is available at http://www.gnu.org/software/grub/manual/.

The `root (hd0,0)` command sets the `(hd0,0)` partition as the location of the boot directory. This command tells GRUB in which partition the `stage2` and `grub.conf` or `menu.lst` files are located.

The `find /boot/grub/stage1` command in Figure 1-10 returned the first `stage1` entry it found. Both disks should have this file. In this instance, GRUB shows the `stage1` file from the second disk. Because we want GRUB to format the MBR on the first disk, `/dev/hd0` is used.

The `setup (hd0)` command writes the MBR of the selected disk or partition.

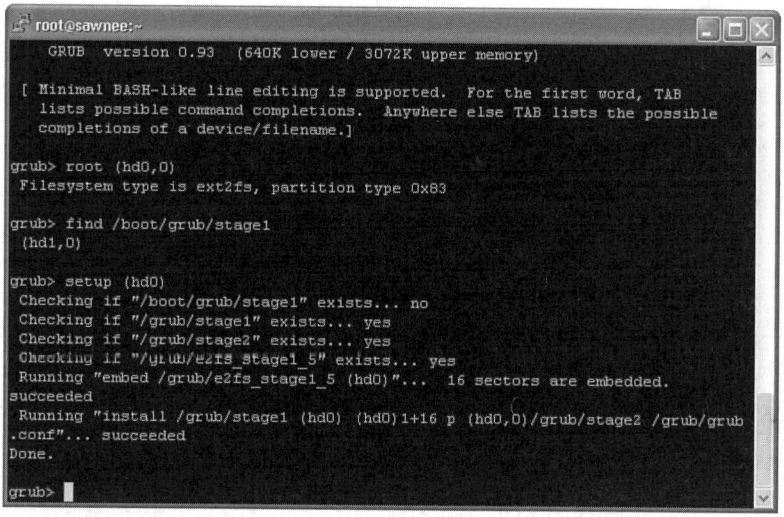

Figure 1-10 Installing GRUB

Using a Boot Floppy to Repair the MBR

It is a good idea to create a GRUB boot floppy or CD and print or archive the GRUB configuration file (/boot/grub/grub.conf for Red Hat and /boot/grub/menu.1st for SUSE) for use when GRUB won't start or won't display the GRUB menu. The following code illustrates how to create the boot floppy, as explained in Section 3.1 of the GRUB manual (http://www.gnu.org/software/grub/manual/grub.pdf):

```
cd /usr/share/grub/i386-pc
# dd if=stage1 of=/dev/fd0 bs=512 count=1
 1+0 records in
 1+0 records out
# dd if=stage2 of=/dev/fd0 bs=512 seek=1
 153+1 records in
 153+1 records out
#
```

The dd if=stage1 of=/dev/fd0 bs=512 count=1 command copies the GRUB MBR file (stage1) to the beginning of the floppy to make it bootable. The command dd if=stage2 of=/dev/fd0 bs=512 seek=1 skips one 512-byte block from the beginning of the floppy and writes the stage2 file.

If GRUB fails to run when the computer is started, you can use this floppy to boot to the GRUB prompt. Enter the commands from the grub.conf file at the GRUB command line to boot Linux. Use tab completion to find a good kernel if there is no grub.conf archive to which to refer.

Creating a boot CD is just as easy. Section 3.4 of the GRUB manual contains the instructions for making a GRUB boot CD. Here are the instructions (without the comments):

```
$ mkdir iso
$ mkdir -p iso/boot/grub
$ cp /usr/lib/grub/i386-pc/stage2_eltorito iso/boot/grub
$ mkisofs -R -b boot/grub/stage2_eltorito -no-emul-boot \
-boot-load-size 4 -boot-info-table -o grub.iso iso
```

Now just burn the grub.iso file created by mkisofs to a CD. The instructions are for GRUB version 0.97. If an earlier version of GRUB is installed on your Linux system, the

/usr/lib/grub/i386-pc/stage2_eltorito file might not exist. In that case, download version 0.97 of GRUB from http://www.gnu.org/software/grub/ and follow the INSTALL file instructions for running configure and make, which produces the stage2_eltorito file. Running configure and make does not affect the version of GRUB installed in /boot on your Linux system.

LILO

The LILO bootloader is similar to GRUB in that it provides menu-based kernel selection. LILO is a two-stage bootloader. Both Stage 1 and Stage 2 are kept in one file, usually /boot/boot.b. The first stage of the LILO bootloader occupies the boot sector, usually the MBR. It relies on the BIOS to load the following:

- The boot sector (second stage)
- The message to be displayed at boot up
- The kernels that can be selected for booting
- The boot sectors of all other operating systems that LILO boots
- The location of all the previous files (map file)

The key to LILO is the map file (/boot/map). This file is created by the /sbin/lilo command. LILO does not understand filesystems. The physical location of the files is stored in the map file. Thus, if the files move, /sbin/lilo must be run. If a new kernel is built, /sbin/lilo must be run to map the new location and size. Because this information is encoded in the map file, LILO doesn't provide a shell-like environment as GRUB does to manually enter kernel location information at boot time. The /sbin/lilo command reinstalls LILO because it writes the MBR.

The /etc/lilo.conf configuration file specifies kernel locations and LILO configuration. The following is a very basic /etc/lilo.conf file for a two-disk configuration with Red Hat on the first disk and SUSE on the second:

```
prompt
serial=0,9600

# wait 10 seconds to autoboot
timeout=100
```

```
# location of boot sector to write
boot=/dev/hda

# location to write map file
map=/boot/map

# identify bootloader location
install=/boot/boot.b

linear

# set default kernel for autoboot
default=SuSE

# RedHat

image=/boot/vmlinuz-2.4.20-8
        label=RedHat
        initrd=/boot/initrd-2.4.20-8.img
        read-only
        append="root=LABEL=/ console=ttyS0,9600"

# SuSE

image=/suse_root_hdb/boot/vmlinuz
        label=SuSE
        initrd=/suse_root_hdb/boot/initrd
        append="root=/dev/hdb3 splash=silent text desktop showopts \
          console=ttyS0,9600"
```

The /etc/lilo.conf file has many options, which are explained in the lilo.conf(5) man page. Lines starting with # are comments and are ignored by /sbin/lilo. Table 1-1 provides a description of the global entries used in this file.

Table 1-1   `/etc/lilo.conf` Global Keywords Definitions

Option	Meaning
prompt	Display boot prompt without requiring a prior keystroke to interrupt boot process.
serial	Display LILO input/output on serial console as well as standard console.
timeout	Timeout value specified in tenths of a second. 100 gives the user 10 seconds to interrupt the boot process before LILO autoboots the default kernel.
boot	The disk whose boot sector will be updated by `/sbin/lilo`. If not specified, the current root partition is used.
map	Location of map file.
install	The stage1 and stage2 bootloader.
linear	Addresses will be linear sector addresses instead of sector, head, cylinder addresses.
image	The first line of a group of lines defining a boot entry.
initrd	File to be used as a ram disk.
append	A string to be appended to the parameter line passed to the kernel.
label	Name of the boot entry to be displayed. If no label entry exists, the boot entry name is the filename from the image parameter.

Many more keywords exist, and explaining them all is beyond the scope of this chapter. Our goal is to show how LILO works and how to fix problems. LILO is well documented in the `lilo.conf(5)` and `lilo(8)` man pages, as well as the excellent LILO README supplied with the LILO package.

Most LILO installations display a nice graphical menu at boot that lists all the kernels from `/etc/lilo.conf`. The kernels are listed by using the `message` option:

```
message=/boot/message
```

The examples we use are from the text LILO output from a serial console. Figure 1-11 shows what the normal boot screen looks like if the message line is not included in /etc/lilo.conf.

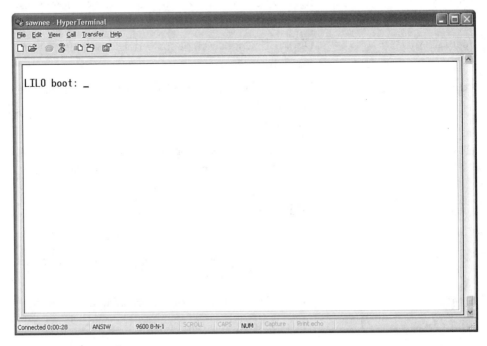

Figure 1-11 LILO boot screen

If no keys are pressed, LILO boots the default entry from /etc/lilo.conf. If the default variable is not set, the first image entry in /etc/lilo.conf is booted. Press Tab to interrupt autoboot and see the list of boot entries. Figure 1-12 shows the display after Tab is pressed.

It is easy to pick a different kernel. Just type the name of the entry and press Enter. The SUSE kernel is chosen in Figure 1-13.

We can append parameters to the kernel command line too. Figure 1-14 demonstrates how to boot to single user mode (init runlevel 1).

Booting to emergency mode is achieved the same way. Just add emergency to the command line. As we stated earlier, emergency mode is a minimalist environment. The root filesystem is mounted in read-only mode, no other filesystems are mounted, and init is not started.

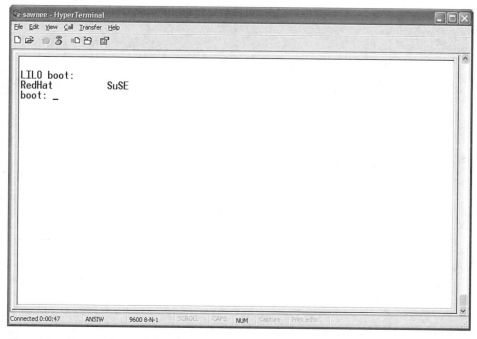

Figure 1-12 LILO boot choices

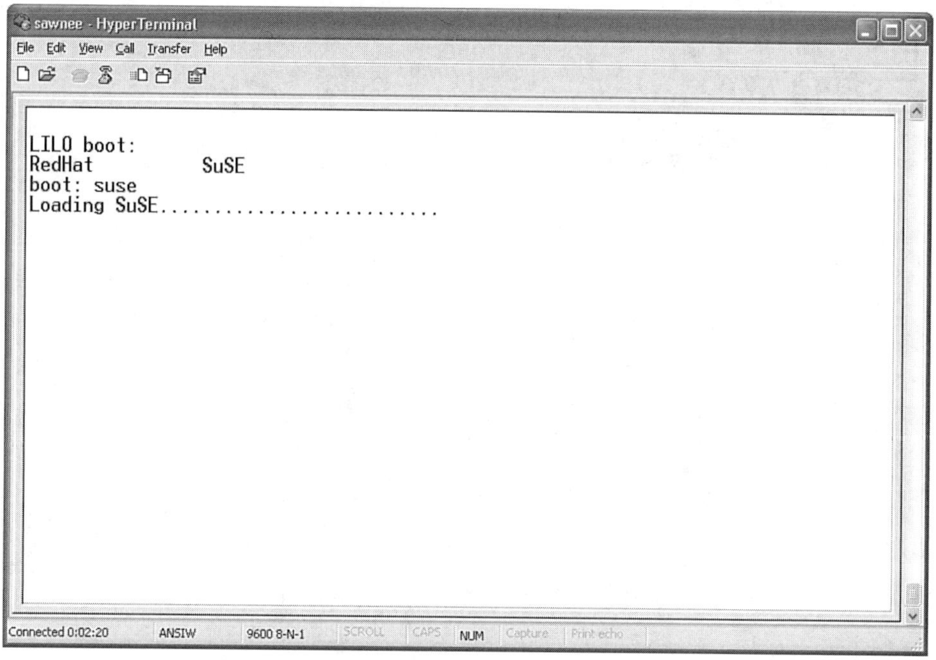

Figure 1-13 Selecting a kernel to boot with LILO

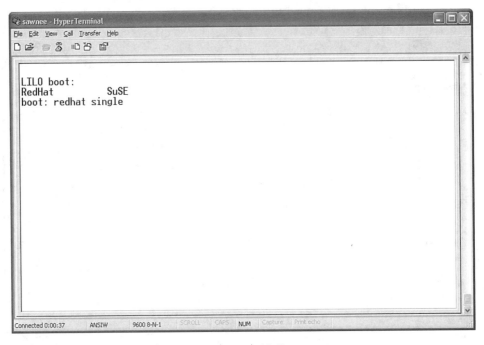

Figure 1-14 Booting single user mode with LILO

Booting When GRUB or LILO Doesn't Work

A boot floppy can be created to boot a Linux box when the /boot filesystem is damaged or missing files.

Red Hat provides the command mkbootdisk[2] to create a bootable floppy. The root filesystem that is mounted when booting from this floppy is specified in /etc/fstab. Thus, the root filesystem must be in good condition. Otherwise, the box starts to boot but then fails when trying to mount /. This is not a rescue utilities disk. It is just a way to boot Linux when /boot is missing files or is damaged. See the mkbootdisk(8) man page for full details. This command works with both LILO and GRUB bootloaders.

Here is an example of making the boot floppy:

```
# mkbootdisk --device /dev/fd0 -v 2.4.20-8
Insert a disk in /dev/fd0. Any information on the disk will be lost.
```

```
Press <Enter> to continue or ^C to abort:
Formatting /tmp/mkbootdisk.zRbsi0... done.
Copying /boot/vmlinuz-2.4.20-8... done.
Copying /boot/initrd-2.4.20-8.img... done.
Configuring bootloader... done.
20+0 records in
20+0 records out
```

Here is what the console shows when booting from this floppy:

```
SYSLINUX 2.00 2002-10-25  Copyright (C) 1994-2002 H. Peter Anvin


Press <return> (or wait 10 seconds) to boot your Red Hat Linux system
from /dev/hda2. You may override the default linux kernel parameters by
typing "linux <params>", followed by <return> if you like.
boot:
```

Boot to single user mode by appending `single` to the `boot` command like this:

```
boot: linux single
```

The `mkbootdisk` floppy makes repairing /boot easy. For example, suppose LILO displays only the following during boot:

```
LI
```

This result means LILO encountered a problem while starting. During boot, LILO displays `L  I  L  O` one letter at a time to indicate its progress. The meaning of each is described in Chapter 6. When only `LI` is displayed, the first stage bootloader could not execute the second stage loader. Maybe the file was moved or deleted. What now? We can use the `mkbootdisk` floppy. The floppy boots Linux, mounts / from the hard disk, and Linux runs normally. After fixing the problem in /boot, don't forget to run `lilo -v` to update the MBR.

A `mkbootdisk` floppy is a good recovery tool. We discuss recovery CDs later in this chapter.

The init Process and/etc/inittab File

When a Linux system is booted, the first process that the kernel starts is /sbin/init. It is always process id (PID) 1 and has a parent process id (PPID) of 0. The init process is always running.

```
root         1    0  0 14:05 ?         00:00:08 init [3]
```

The /etc/inittab file is the configuration file for /sbin/init. /etc/inittab identifies the processes that init starts, and it can be customized as desired. Few environment variables are set when a process is started by init. The inittab lines have four colon-separated fields:

```
<id>:<runlevels>:<action>:<command>
```

Let's look at the meaning of each.

- id—The inittab *id* consists of one to four characters that identify the inittab line. The *id* must be unique.
- *runlevels*—The *runlevels* field contains one or more characters, usually numbers identifying the runlevels for which this process is started. Table 1-2 lists the runlevel meanings.

Table 1-2 Runlevels

Run Level	Meaning
0	System halt
1	Single user mode
2	Local multiuser without remote network (e.g., NFS)
3	Multiuser with network
4	Not used
5	Multiuser with network and xdm
6	System reboot

- *action*—The keyword in this field tells init what action to take. The more common keywords are shown in Table 1-3.
- *command*—This field specifies the path of the command that init executes.

Table 1-3   inittab Keywords for the action Field

Keyword	Usage
respawn	Command is restarted whenever it terminates.
wait	Command is run once. init waits for it to terminate before continuing.
once	Command is run once.
boot	Command is run during boot up. The runlevels field is ignored.
bootwait	Command is run during boot up, and the runlevels field is ignored. init waits for the process to terminate before continuing.
initdefault	Specifies default runlevel of the Linux system
powerwait	Command is run when the power fails. init waits for the process to terminate before continuing.
powerfail	Command is run when the power fails. init does not wait for the process to terminate before continuing.
powerokwait	Command is run when power is restored. init waits for the process to terminate before continuing.
powerfailnow	Command is run when UPS signals that its battery is almost dead.

See the inittab(8) man page for the complete list of inittab action keywords and a more detailed example of the /etc/inittab file. The following is a typical /etc/inittab file from a SUSE 9.0 system. The lines controlling startup and shutdown are bolded.

```
#
# /etc/inittab
#
```

```
# Copyright (c) 1996-2002 SuSE Linux AG, Nuernberg, Germany. All rights
# reserved.
#
# Author: Florian La Roche, 1996
# Please send feedback to http://www.suse.de/feedback
#
# This is the main configuration file of /sbin/init, which
# is executed by the kernel on startup. It describes what
# scripts are used for the different runlevels.
#
# All scripts for runlevel changes are in /etc/init.d/.
#
# This file may be modified by SuSEconfig unless CHECK_INITTAB
# in /etc/sysconfig/suseconfig is set to "no"
#

# The default runlevel is defined here
id:5:initdefault:

# First script to be executed, if not booting in emergency (-b) mode
si::bootwait:/etc/init.d/boot

# /etc/init.d/rc takes care of runlevel handling
#
# runlevel 0  is  System halt   (Do not use this for initdefault!)
# runlevel 1  is  Single user mode
# runlevel 2  is  Local multiuser without remote network (e.g. NFS)
# runlevel 3  is  Full multiuser with network
# runlevel 4  is  Not used
# runlevel 5  is  Full multiuser with network and xdm
# runlevel 6  is  System reboot (Do not use this for initdefault!)
#
l0:0:wait:/etc/init.d/rc 0
l1:1:wait:/etc/init.d/rc 1
l2:2:wait:/etc/init.d/rc 2
```

```
l3:3:wait:/etc/init.d/rc 3
#14:4:wait:/etc/init.d/rc 4
15:5:wait:/etc/init.d/rc 5
16:6:wait:/etc/init.d/rc 6


# what to do in single-user mode
ls:S:wait:/etc/init.d/rc S
~~:S:respawn:/sbin/sulogin


# what to do when CTRL-ALT-DEL is pressed
ca::ctrlaltdel:/sbin/shutdown -r -t 4 now


# special keyboard request (Alt-UpArrow)
# look into the kbd-0.90 docs for this
kb::kbrequest:/bin/echo "Keyboard Request -- edit /etc/inittab to let
this work."


# what to do when power fails/returns
pf::powerwait:/etc/init.d/powerfail start
pn::powerfailnow:/etc/init.d/powerfail now
#pn::powerfail:/etc/init.d/powerfail now
po::powerokwait:/etc/init.d/powerfail stop


# for ARGO UPS
sh:12345:powerfail:/sbin/shutdown -h now THE POWER IS FAILING


# getty-programs for the normal runlevels
# <id>:<runlevels>:<action>:<process>
# The "id" field  MUST be the same as the last
# characters of the device (after "tty").
1:2345:respawn:/sbin/mingetty --noclear tty1
2:2345:respawn:/sbin/mingetty tty2
3:2345:respawn:/sbin/mingetty tty3
4:2345:respawn:/sbin/mingetty tty4
5:2345:respawn:/sbin/mingetty tty5
```

```
6:2345:respawn:/sbin/mingetty tty6
co:2345:respawn:/sbin/agetty -h -t 60 ttyS0 9600 vt102
#
#S0:12345:respawn:/sbin/agetty -L 9600 ttyS0 vt102


#
#  Note: Do not use tty7 in runlevel 3, this virtual line
#  is occupied by the programm xdm.
#


#  This is for the package xdmsc; after installing and
#  and configuration you should remove the comment character
#  from the following line:
#7:3:respawn:+/etc/init.d/rx tty7

# modem getty.
# mo:235:respawn:/usr/sbin/mgetty -s 38400 modem

# fax getty (hylafax)
# mo:35:respawn:/usr/lib/fax/faxgetty /dev/modem

# vbox (voice box) getty
# I6:35:respawn:/usr/sbin/vboxgetty -d /dev/ttyI6
# I7:35:respawn:/usr/sbin/vboxgetty -d /dev/ttyI7

# end of /etc/inittab
Up2p::respawn:/opt/uptime2/bin/uptime2+
Up2r::respawn:/opt/uptime2/lbin/Uptime2+.Restart
```

Startup in Multiuser Mode

Let's look at the inittab lines that affect startup in multiuser mode. The first non-comment line in inittab tells init the runlevel to move the system to at boot up. For example:

```
id:5:initdefault:
```

If the `initdefault` line is missing, the boot process pauses with a console prompt asking for the runlevel to be specified before continuing. The `inittdefault` line typically specifies runlevel 3 or 5.

The second non-comment line in `inittab` is probably the system initialization script or boot script. This script sets up the console, mounts filesystems, sets kernel parameters, and so on. In Red Hat 9.0, the line is:

```
si::sysinit:/etc/rc.d/rc.sysinit
```

For SUSE 9.0, it is:

```
si::bootwait:/etc/init.d/boot
```

The Red Hat boot script, `/etc/rc.d/rc.sysinit`, is a top-down script compared to SUSE's `/etc/init.d/boot` script. The SUSE script executes the scripts in `/etc/init.d/boot.d/` to set up most system needs. You can get an idea of what gets done by looking at a listing of the `boot.d` directory. The `boot.d` directory consists of symbolic links to scripts in `/etc/init.d`.

```
#ll /etc/init.d/boot.d
total 9
lrwxrwxrwx    1 root      root             12 Jul  6 12:19 S01boot.proc ->
../boot.proc
lrwxrwxrwx    1 root      root             12 Jul  6 12:20 S01setserial ->
../setserial
lrwxrwxrwx    1 root      root             10 Jul  6 12:20 S03boot.md ->
../boot.md
lrwxrwxrwx    1 root      root             11 Jul  6 12:20 S04boot.lvm ->
../boot.lvm
lrwxrwxrwx    1 root      root             15 Jul  6 12:20 S05boot.localfs ->
../boot.localfs
lrwxrwxrwx    1 root      root             14 Jul  6 12:20 S06boot.crypto ->
../boot.crypto
lrwxrwxrwx    1 root      root             19 Jul  6 12:20
S07boot.loadmodules -> ../boot.loadmodules
lrwxrwxrwx    1 root      root             27 Jul  6 12:20
S07boot.restore_permissions -> ../boot.restore_permissions
lrwxrwxrwx    1 root      root             12 Jul  6 12:20 S07boot.scpm ->
../boot.scpm
```

```
lrwxrwxrwx    1 root     root             12 Jul  6 12:20 S07boot.swap ->
../boot.swap
lrwxrwxrwx    1 root     root             13 Jul  6 12:20 S08boot.clock ->
../boot.clock
lrwxrwxrwx    1 root     root             14 Jul  6 12:20 S08boot.idedma ->
../boot.idedma
lrwxrwxrwx    1 root     root             16 Jul  6 12:20 S09boot.ldconfig ->
../boot.ldconfig
lrwxrwxrwx    1 root     root             14 Jul  6 12:20 S10boot.isapnp ->
../boot.isapnp
lrwxrwxrwx    1 root     root             16 Jul  6 12:20 S10boot.localnet ->
../boot.localnet
lrwxrwxrwx    1 root     root             13 Jul  6 12:20 S10boot.sched ->
../boot.sched
lrwxrwxrwx    1 root     root             16 Jul  6 12:20 S11boot.ipconfig ->
../boot.ipconfig
lrwxrwxrwx    1 root     root             12 Jul  6 12:20 S11boot.klog ->
../boot.klog
```

If you have a SUSE distribution, you should read /etc/init.d/README, which further explains the SUSE boot strategy.

The runlevels consist of a set of processes that start at each runlevel. The processes are started by the /etc/rc.d/rc script. In SUSE, the rc.d directory is a symbolic link to /etc/init.d. The rc script is explained further in the next section.

The /etc/inittab file includes lines similar to the following to start the services for runlevels 0 through 6. Remember, the second field specifies the runlevel at which the line is executed. The following is from a Red Hat 9.0 system:

```
l0:0:wait:/etc/rc.d/rc 0
l1:1:wait:/etc/rc.d/rc 1
l2:2:wait:/etc/rc.d/rc 2
l3:3:wait:/etc/rc.d/rc 3
l4:4:wait:/etc/rc.d/rc 4
l5:5:wait:/etc/rc.d/rc 5
l6:6:wait:/etc/rc.d/rc 6
```

After the rc scripts finishes, the Linux startup is complete. The /etc/inittab file includes other lines to run getty processes, handle the powerfail condition, and so on.

The lines that affect system startup and shutdown are those that run the /etc/rc.d/rc script.

The runlevel can be changed after boot up as well. The root user can move Linux to a different runlevel. The telinit command can be used to tell init to move to a new runlevel. For example, the command telinit 5 tells init to move to runlevel 5. The telinit command is just a link to init:

```
#ls -al /sbin/telinit
lrwxrwxrwx    1 root      root         4 Nov  6  2003 /sbin/telinit -> init
```

Looking at the previous /etc/inittab entries, we can see that the command telinit 5 causes init to execute /etc/rc.d/rc 5. The 5 argument tells /etc/rc.d(or init.d)/rc what runlevel scripts to execute.

The telinit command can also make init look for changes in /etc/inittab. The syntax is telinit q. See the telinit(8) man page for further details.

init errors

If the console shows errors such as the following, init has detected a problem while running a command from /etc/inittab.

```
INIT: Id "db" respawning too fast: disabled for 5 minutes
```

In this example, the message corresponds to the following line in /etc/inittab:

```
db:345:respawn:/usr/local/bin/dbmon
```

Remember that the respawn keyword in /etc/inittab means that init restarts any command whose process terminates. The previous message means init ran the command ten times, but the command keeps terminating, so init is giving up.

After the problem with the command is fixed, run telinit u to make init try again, or run telinit q if changes have been made to /etc/inittab. The init process logs its messages using the syslog facility,[3] and by default you can find init messages in the /var/log/messages file. The following is a sample message:

```
Dec 30 10:40:29 sawnee init: Re-reading inittab
```

rc Scripts

The rc script is not a big, monolithic script that starts all the processes needed for Linux services such as sshd, syslog, xinetd, and so on. Rather, rc runs a small script in /etc/init.d for each required Linux service. Each service script both starts and stops the service. Here is an example of the cron service script:

```
-rwxr-xr-x   1 root    root       1297 Mar  3  2005 /etc/rc.d/init.d/crond
```

The rc script knows which service scripts to start or stop for each runlevel by using directories populated with links to the /etc/init.d startup and shutdown service scripts. These directories could be /etc/init.d/rc#.d or /etc/rc.d/rc#.d, where # is the runlevel to execute. Runlevels are defined by the service scripts that start or stop services at that level. This example shows all the cron startup and shutdown links:

```
lrwxr-xr-x   1 root    root         15 Feb  9  2005
/etc/rc.d/rc0.d/K60crond -> ../init.d/crond
lrwxr-xr-x   1 root    root         15 Feb  9  2005
/etc/rc.d/rc1.d/K60crond -> ../init.d/crond
lrwxr-xr-x   1 root    root         15 Feb  9  2005
/etc/rc.d/rc2.d/S90crond -> ../init.d/crond
lrwxr-xr-x   1 root    root         15 Feb  9  2005
/etc/rc.d/rc3.d/S90crond -> ../init.d/crond
lrwxr-xr-x   1 root    root         15 Feb  9  2005
/etc/rc.d/rc4.d/S90crond -> ../init.d/crond
lrwxr-xr-x   1 root    root         15 Feb  9  2005
/etc/rc.d/rc5.d/S90crond -> ../init.d/crond
lrwxr-xr-x   1 root    root         15 Feb  9  2005
/etc/rc.d/rc6.d/K60crond -> ../init.d/crond
```

The rc script (/etc/rc.d/rc or /etc/init.d/rc) links to service scripts starting with S in either /etc/init.d/rc#.d or /etc/rc.d/rc#.d. For the syntax /etc/rc.d/rc 5, all the /etc/init.d/rc5.d/S* or /etc/rc.d/rc5.d/S* service scripts are executed. The following is from a Red Hat 9.0 system[4]:

```
#ls -al /etc/rc.d
total 76
drwxr-xr-x   10 root    root       4096 Dec 12 15:18 .
```

```
drwxr-xr-x  70 root     root       8192 Dec 16 04:08 ..
drwxr-xr-x   2 root     root       4096 Dec 12 15:52 init.d
-rwxr-xr-x   1 root     root       2338 Feb 18  2003 rc
drwxr-xr-x   2 root     root       4096 May 18  2004 rc0.d
drwxr-xr-x   2 root     root       4096 May 18  2004 rc1.d
drwxr-xr-x   2 root     root       4096 May 18  2004 rc2.d
drwxr-xr-x   2 root     root       4096 Aug 20 08:53 rc3.d
drwxr-xr-x   2 root     root       4096 May 18  2004 rc4.d
drwxr-xr-x   2 root     root       4096 Aug 20 08:53 rc5.d
drwxr-xr-x   2 root     root       4096 May 18  2004 rc6.d
-rwxr-xr-x   1 root     root        220 Jul 10  2001 rc.local
-rwxr-xr-x   1 root     root      23299 Feb 24  2003 rc.sysinit
```

The entries in rc#.d are symbolic links. The actual scripts are in /etc/init.d. These links begin with either K or S. The S links are for startup scripts, and the K links are for shutdown scripts. The numbers following the S or K are used to order the execution of the scripts. When moving to a new runlevel, the shutdown scripts are run, followed by the startup scripts. Let's look more closely at the startup scripts in rc5.d:

```
# ls -al /etc/rc.d/rc5.d/S*

lrwxrwxrwx   1 root     root         15 May 18  2004
/etc/rc.d/rc5.d/S05kudzu
 -> ../init.d/kudzu
lrwxrwxrwx   1 root     root         18 May 18  2004
/etc/rc.d/rc5.d/S08iptables ->
../init.d/iptables
lrwxrwxrwx   1 root     root         17 May 18  2004
/etc/rc.d/rc5.d/S10network ->
../init.d/network
lrwxrwxrwx   1 root     root         16 May 18  2004
/etc/rc.d/rc5.d/S12syslog ->
../init.d/syslog
lrwxrwxrwx   1 root     root         17 May 18  2004
/etc/rc.d/rc5.d/S13portmap ->
../init.d/portmap
```

```
lrwxrwxrwx    1 root     root              17 May 18  2004
/etc/rc.d/rc5.d/S14nfslock ->
../init.d/nfslock


... (rest omitted)
```

The script name is the same as the link name without the leading S or K and numbers.

```
#ls -al /etc/init.d
lrwxrwxrwx    1 root     root              11 Nov  6  2003 /etc/init.d ->
rc.d/init.d


#ls /etc/rc.d/init.d
aep1000   firstboot  isdn       network    random      squid      xinetd
anacron   FreeWnn    kdcrotate  nfs        rawdevices  sshd       ypbind
apmd      functions  keytable   nfslock    rhnsd       syslog     yppasswdd
atd       gpm        killall    nscd       saslauthd   tux        ypserv
autofs    halt       kudzu      ntpd       sendmail    vncserver  ypxfrd
bcm5820   httpd      linuxcoe   pcmcia     single      vsftpd
canna     innd       lisa       portmap    smb         webmin
crond     iptables   named      postgresql snmpd       winbind
cups      irda       netfs      pxe        snmptrapd   xfs
```

For Red Hat, the initlog command is called to run the individual service startup scripts and log the output using syslogd. The /etc/initlog.conf file defines local7 as the syslog facility for the messages. Looking at this /etc/syslog.conf excerpt, we can see that the boot messages are sent to /var/log/messages and boot.log:

```
# Log anything (except mail) of level info or higher.
# Don't log private authentication messages!
*.info;mail.none;news.none;authpriv.none;cron.none      /var/log/messages


... (lines omitted)


# Save boot messages also to boot.log
local7.*                                                /var/log/boot.log
```

The initlog(8) and syslogd(8) man pages have further details.

For SUSE, the blogger command sends messages to /var/log/boot.msg. See the blogger(8) man page for details.

It would be cumbersome to manage all the symbolic links needed for an rc start or stop script. Let's look at crond as an example. It runs at runlevels 2 through 5, so it has a start script for each runlevel. It does not run at levels 0, 1, and 6, so it has kill scripts for these levels. That makes seven symbolic links for just crond.

```
#find /etc/rc.d -name *crond
/etc/rc.d/init.d/crond
/etc/rc.d/rc0.d/K60crond
/etc/rc.d/rc1.d/K60crond
/etc/rc.d/rc2.d/S90crond
/etc/rc.d/rc3.d/S90crond
/etc/rc.d/rc4.d/S90crond
/etc/rc.d/rc5.d/S90crond
/etc/rc.d/rc6.d/K60crond
```

Fortunately, the chkconfig command is provided to add and remove the links as needed. The chkconfig(8) man page lists all the options, but the most useful options are provided in Table 1-4.

As an example, let's manipulate crond. First we determine what the current settings are:

```
#chkconfig --list crond
crond           0:off   1:off   2:on    3:on    4:on    5:on    6:off
```

Next we turn off crond at runlevel 2:

```
#chkconfig --level 2 crond off
#chkconfig --list crond
crond           0:off   1:off   2:off   3:on    4:on    5:on    6:off
```

Table 1-4   chkconfig Syntax

Option	Purpose
chkconfig --list	Lists all rc scripts and their runlevels
chkconfig --list <script name>	Lists a single script and its runlevel
chkconfig --level <levels> <script name> <on or off>	Turns a script on or off at specified levels
chkconfig <script> reset	Sets the configuration for a script to defaults

Now we look at the symbolic links to see whether anything changed:

```
#find /etc/rc.d -name *crond
/etc/rc.d/init.d/crond
/etc/rc.d/rc0.d/K60crond
/etc/rc.d/rc1.d/K60crond
/etc/rc.d/rc2.d/K60crond
/etc/rc.d/rc3.d/S90crond
/etc/rc.d/rc4.d/S90crond
/etc/rc.d/rc5.d/S90crond
/etc/rc.d/rc6.d/K60crond
```

We can see that rc2.d has the K60crond stop script instead of the S90crond start script. We can return the crond configuration to the default values:

```
#chkconfig crond reset
#chkconfig --list crond
crond         0:off   1:off   2:on    3:on    4:on    5:on    6:off
```

The chkconfig command uses the following line in /etc/rc.d/init.d/crond to determine the default values and link names:

```
# chkconfig: 2345 90 60
```

Linux distributions use different methods to encode the default runlevel values in startup and shutdown scripts. The previous example was from a Red Hat 9.0 crond script. A SUSE 9.0 cron script has the following:

```
### BEGIN INIT INFO
# Provides:        cron
# Required-Start: $remote_fs $syslog $time
# X-UnitedLinux-Should-Start: sendmail postfix
# Required-Stop:  $remote_fs $syslog
# Default-Start:  2 3 5
# Default-Stop:   0 1 6
# Description:    Cron job service
### END INIT INFO
```

We must mention one more directory. The /etc/sysconfig directory contains configuration files for the rc scripts. Here is a typical listing:

```
ls /etc/sysconfig
```

apmd	grub	mouse	redhat-config-securitylevel
apm-scripts	harddisks	named	redhat-config-users
authconfig	hwconf	netdump	redhat-logviewer
autofs	i18n	netdump_id_dsa	rhn
clock	init	netdump_id_dsa.pub	samba
console	installinfo	network	sendmail
desktop	ip6tables-config	networking	squid
devlabel	iptables-config	network-scripts	syslog
dhcpd	irda	ntpd	tux
dhcrelay	irqbalance	pcmcia	vncservers
firstboot	keyboard	prelink	xinetd
gpm	kudzu	rawdevices	yppasswdd

These configuration files contain variables for the rc scripts. The configuration files are sourced by the rc scripts from which they get their name. As we can see, /etc/sysconfig includes some directories, such as the network directory. The /etc/sysconfig files are small. The sendmail script, for example, consists of only two lines:

```
# cat sendmail
DAEMON=yes
QUEUE=1h
```

Red Hat provides the `ntsysv` command to manipulate startup/shutdown script configuration. It is not as powerful as chkconfig, but it is easier to use.

Linux gives us a way to control what scripts run at boot time. Sure, a system administrator can use `chkconfig` to configure which scripts run and which don't, but wouldn't it be nice to pick and choose during boot up? The Linux confirm mode provides this feature.

Confirm Mode

You can use the `rc` script to prompt whether each script should be run during startup. This feature is useful when one or more scripts need to be skipped for whatever reason.

To run `rc` in confirm mode, add the keyword `confirm` to the kernel command line, just as you would add the keyword `single` to boot to single user mode. This can be done from the bootloader, as Figure 1-15 shows.

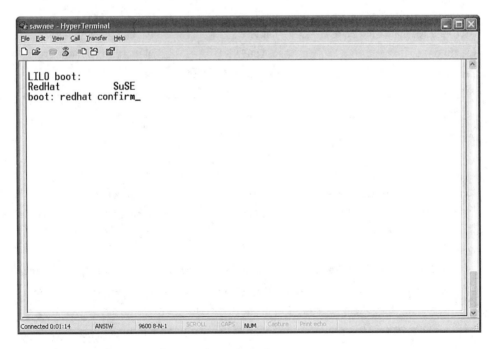

Figure 1-15 Booting confirm mode with LILO

Figure 1-16 shows how the Ethernet rc script hangs if the LAN card is configured to get an IP address through DHCP but is not connected to the network. The user must sit and wait for the timeout from DHCP.

```
[  OK  ]
Remounting root filesystem in read-write mode:  [  OK  ]
Activating swap partitions:  [  OK  ]
Finding module dependencies:  [  OK  ]
Checking filesystems
/boot: clean, 51/18960 files, 13688/75568 blocks
Reiserfs super block in block 16 on 0x343 of format 3.6 with standard journal
Blocks (total/free): 3208983/2389461 by 4096 bytes
Filesystem is cleanly umounted
/dev/hdb1: clean, 43/4016 files, 4853/16032 blocks
Checking all file systems.
[/sbin/fsck.ext3 (1) -- /boot] fsck.ext3 -a /dev/hda1
[/sbin/fsck.reiserfs (1) -- /suse_root_hdb] fsck.reiserfs -a /dev/hdb3
[/sbin/fsck.ext2 (1) -- /suse_root_hdb/boot] fsck.ext2 -a /dev/hdb1
[  OK  ]
Mounting local filesystems:  [  OK  ]
Enabling local filesystem quotas:  [  OK  ]
Enabling swap space:  [  OK  ]
INIT: Entering runlevel: 5
Entering non-interactive startup
Setting network parameters:  [  OK  ]
Bringing up loopback interface:  [  OK  ]
Bringing up interface eth0:  [  OK  ]
Bringing up interface eth1:
```

Figure 1-16 Boot hanging at eth1 configuration

If Linux is started in confirm mode, the script can be skipped. Press y to run the script, or press n to skip it. Press c to run the script and all the following scripts. This is a nice way to skip a script and not have to change the configuration. Figure 1-17 shows how this looks.

Startup Problems in rc Scripts

Problems with startup scripts can be difficult to troubleshoot because many files are involved. The problem could be with the rc script, one of the scripts rc is trying to run, or any command or script rc relies on. Figure 1-18 demonstrates a typical example, in which the Linux kernel boots and then displays some errors.

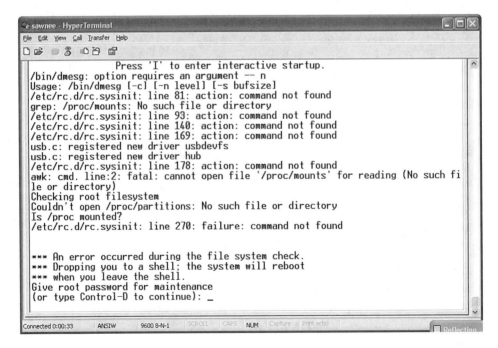

```
sawnee - HyperTerminal
File  Edit  View  Call  Transfer  Help

Blocks (total/free): 3208983/2389461 by 4096 bytes
Filesystem is cleanly umounted
/dev/hdb1: clean, 43/4016 files, 4853/16032 blocks
Checking all file systems.
[/sbin/fsck.ext3 (1) -- /boot] fsck.ext3 -a /dev/hda1
[/sbin/fsck.reiserfs (1) -- /suse_root_hdb] fsck.reiserfs -a /dev/hdb3
[/sbin/fsck.ext2 (1) -- /suse_root_hdb/boot] fsck.ext2 -a /dev/hdb1
[  OK  ]
Mounting local filesystems: [  OK  ]
Enabling local filesystem quotas: [  OK  ]
Enabling swap space: [  OK  ]
INIT: Entering runlevel: 5
Entering interactive startup
Start service iptables (Y)es/(N)o/(C)ontinue? [Y]
Start service network (Y)es/(N)o/(C)ontinue? [Y]
Setting network parameters: [  OK  ]
Bringing up loopback interface: [  OK  ]
Start service eth0 (Y)es/(N)o/(C)ontinue? [Y]
Bringing up interface eth0: [  OK  ]
Start service eth1 (Y)es/(N)o/(C)ontinue? [Y] n
Start service syslog (Y)es/(N)o/(C)ontinue? [Y] c
Starting system logger: [  OK  ]
Starting kernel logger: [  OK  ]
Starting portmapper: _

Connected 0:01:18    ANSIW    9600 8-N-1    SCROLL   CAPS   NUM   Capture   Print echo
```

Figure 1-17 Skipping eth1 configuration in confirm mode

```
sawnee - HyperTerminal
File  Edit  View  Call  Transfer  Help

          Press 'I' to enter interactive startup.
/bin/dmesg: option requires an argument -- n
Usage: /bin/dmesg [-c] [-n level] [-s bufsize]
/etc/rc.d/rc.sysinit: line 81: action: command not found
grep: /proc/mounts: No such file or directory
/etc/rc.d/rc.sysinit: line 93: action: command not found
/etc/rc.d/rc.sysinit: line 140: action: command not found
/etc/rc.d/rc.sysinit: line 169: action: command not found
usb.c: registered new driver usbdevfs
usb.c: registered new driver hub
/etc/rc.d/rc.sysinit: line 178: action: command not found
awk: cmd. line:2: fatal: cannot open file '/proc/mounts' for reading (No such fi
le or directory)
Checking root filesystem
Couldn't open /proc/partitions: No such file or directory
Is /proc mounted?
/etc/rc.d/rc.sysinit: line 270: failure: command not found


*** An error occurred during the file system check.
*** Dropping you to a shell; the system will reboot
*** when you leave the shell.
Give root password for maintenance
(or type Control-D to continue): _

Connected 0:00:33    ANSIW    9600 8-N-1    SCROLL   CAPS   NUM   Capture   Print echo
```

Figure 1-18 Boot error from rc

It is a good idea to stop and write down all the messages and errors before they scroll off the screen. We have a limited opportunity to fix problems with Linux in this state because / is mounted as read-only. However, we can troubleshoot and hopefully find the problem.

The following command not found errors from Figure 1-18 stand out:

```
/etc/rc.d/rc.sysinit: line 81: action: command not found
grep: /proc/mounts: No such file or directory
/etc/rc.d/rc.sysinit: line 93: action: command not found
/etc/rc.d/rc.sysinit: line 140: action: command not found
/etc/rc.d/rc.sysinit: line 169: action: command not found
```

We edit the file with vi just to check the line numbers:

```
*** An error occurred during the file system check.
*** Dropping you to a shell; the system will reboot
*** when you leave the shell.
Give root password for maintenance
(or type Control-D to continue):
(Repair filesystem) 1 # vi /etc/rc.d/rc.sysinit
```

Enter :se nu to turn on line numbers. Enter :81G to go to line 81. In Figure 1-19, you can see that the rc.sysinit script is calling the subroutine named action. The other line numbers call action as well.

We could look around to see where the action subroutine is located, but it might have been removed. Let's verify that the startup script files are all in place and the correct size. We can use rpm, but we need to determine what package to verify. We use the rpm command to learn what delivered the rc script:

```
(Repair filesystem) 2 #  rpm -q -f /etc/rc.d/rc
initscripts-7.14-1
```

Now we verify that the initscripts-7.14-1 rpm is intact:

```
(Repair filesystem) 3 # rpm -V initscripts-7.14-1
S.5....T c /etc/inittab
S.5....T c /etc/rc.d/init.d/functions
```

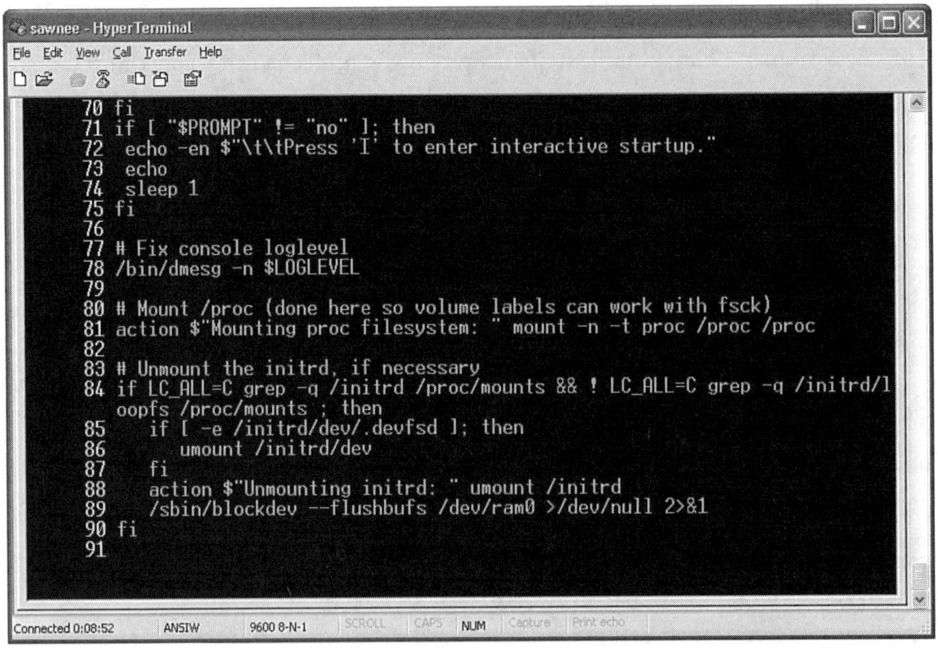

```
70 fi
71 if [ "$PROMPT" != "no" ]; then
72   echo -en $"\t\tPress 'I' to enter interactive startup."
73   echo
74   sleep 1
75 fi
76
77 # Fix console loglevel
78 /bin/dmesg -n $LOGLEVEL
79
80 # Mount /proc (done here so volume labels can work with fsck)
81 action $"Mounting proc filesystem: " mount -n -t proc /proc /proc
82
83 # Unmount the initrd, if necessary
84 if LC_ALL=C grep -q /initrd /proc/mounts && ! LC_ALL=C grep -q /initrd/l
   oopfs /proc/mounts ; then
85    if [ -e /initrd/dev/.devfsd ]; then
86       umount /initrd/dev
87    fi
88    action $"Unmounting initrd: " umount /initrd
89    /sbin/blockdev --flushbufs /dev/ram0 >/dev/null 2>&1
90 fi
91
```

Connected 0:08:52   ANSIW   9600 8-N-1   SCROLL   CAPS   NUM   Capture   Print echo

Figure 1-19 Editing /etc/rc.d/rc.sysinit

The output looks pretty cryptic, but the rpm(8) man page[5] gives a good explanation:

```
The format of the output is a string of 8 characters, a possible "c"
denoting a configuration file, and then the file name. Each of the 8
characters denotes the result of a comparison of attribute(s) of the file
to the value of those attribute(s) recorded in the database. A single "."
(period) means the test passed, while a single "?" indicates the test
could not be performed (e.g. file permissions  prevent reading).
Otherwise, the (mnemonically emboldened) character denotes failure of the
corresponding --verify test:

    S file Size differs

    M Mode differs (includes permissions and file type)

    5 MD5 sum differs

    D Device major/minor number mis-match
```

```
L readLink(2) path mis-match

U User ownership differs

G Group ownership differs

T mTime differs
```

So, the output means the size and timestamp of the `inittab` and `functions` files have changed since the files were delivered. This can be expected for `inittab`, but why for `functions`? Let's look:

```
(Repair filesystem) 5 # ls -al /etc/inittab
-rw-r--r--   1 root     root        1807 Dec 17 15:52 /etc/inittab
(Repair filesystem) 6 # ls -al /etc/rc.d/init.d/functions
-rwxr-xr-x   1 root     root           0 Dec 21 14:39
/etc/rc.d/init.d/functions
```

It looks like `function` was zeroed out. We need to restore this file. Because / is mounted as read-only, the box should be booted from a different source. We can use a rescue CD, rescue disk, or second boot disk. When Linux is up, we just mount / to a temporary mount point and restore the `functions` file. Rescue disks are explained in the next section.

Fixing Problems with the Root Filesystem

Here is a simple example demonstrating a problem with the root filesystem. The cause is a typo in `/etc/fstab`. The fix is easy if we can figure out how to boot Linux. Attempting to boot Linux results in the following:

```
Initializing USB keyboard:                              [  OK  ]
Initializing USB mouse:                                 [  OK  ]
Checking root filesystem
LBEL=/:
The superblock could not be read or does not describe a correct ext2
filesystem. If the device is valid and it really contains an ext2
```

```
filesystem (and not swap or ufs or something else), then the superblock
is corrupt, and you might try running e2fsck with an alternate
superblock:
      e2fsck -b 8193 <device>

fsck.ext3: No such file or directory while trying to open LBEL=/
                                                        [FAILED]


*** An error occurred during the file system check.
*** Dropping you to a shell; the system will reboot
*** when you leave the shell.
Give root password for maintenance
(or type Control-D to continue):
```

Booting from the `mkbootdisk` floppy gives the same result. The problem isn't with `/boot`—it is with `/`. We need a way to get the system up to fix or restore `/`.

There are three common ways to boot when the Linux boot fails:

* Boot from another hard disk
* Boot from a rescue CD
* Boot from a floppy rescue disk

Booting from a Second Hard Disk

The box we have been using in the examples is a dual-boot system with Red Hat on one disk and SUSE on the other. Repairing a damaged Red Hat root filesystem is easy in this configuration. We can just boot SUSE, mount the Red Hat root filesystem to some temporary mount point, and fix the problem.

Booting from a Rescue CD

A convenient method of repairing the root filesystem is to use a bootable Linux CD. We will use the Knoppix distribution (http://www.knoppix.net/), but there are many choices, and the most popular are listed at the end of this section. A rescue disk might have been provided with your Linux distribution CDs that can serve the same purpose.

You will probably need to modify the BIOS settings to boot from the CD-ROM or DVD drive before the hard disks. After that is done, restart the computer with the Knoppix CD in the drive. After the Knoppix CD boots, log into KDE. There is no password. Open a terminal window and run df to see what is mounted. The following listing shows that no disk filesystems are mounted.

```
knoppix@ttyp0[knoppix]$ su - root
root@ttyp0[~]# df
Filesystem 1K-blocks Used Available Use% Mounted on
/dev/root 3471 1113 2358 33% /
/dev/scd0 716308 716308 0 100% /cdrom
/dev/cloop 1943588 1943588 0 100% /KNOPPIX
/ramdisk 95948 2020 93928 3% /ramdisk
root@ttyp0[~]#
```

The hard disks are not mounted, but we can see that they are in /etc/fstab. It is easy enough to mount them, as you can see here:

```
root@ttyp0[~]# cat /etc/fstab
/proc /proc proc defaults 0 0
/sys /sys sysfs noauto 0 0
/dev/pts /dev/pts devpts mode=0622 0 0
/dev/fd0 /mnt/auto/floppy auto user,noauto,exec,umask=000 0 /dev/cdrom
/mnt/auto/cdrom auto user,noauto,exec,ro 0 0
# Added by KNOPPIX
/dev/hda1 /mnt/hda1 ext3 noauto,users,exec 0 0
# Added by KNOPPIX
/dev/hda2 /mnt/hda2 ext3 noauto,users,exec 0 0
# Added by KNOPPIX
/dev/hda3 none swap defaults 0 0
# Added by KNOPPIX
/dev/hdb1 /mnt/hdb1 ext2 noauto,users,exec 0 0
# Added by KNOPPIX
/dev/hdb2 none swap defaults 0 0
# Added by KNOPPIX
/dev/hdb3 /mnt/hdb3 reiserfs noauto,users,exec 0 0
```

```
root@ttyp0[~]# mount /mnt/hda2
root@ttyp0[~]#
```

We can see in the following listing that a typo is keeping our Linux box from booting. The fstab has a typo: LBEL=/ should be LABEL=/ instead.

```
root@ttyp0[~]# cd /mnt/hda2
root@ttyp0[hda2]# ls
bin etc lib opt quota.group suse_root_hdb usr
boot fd lost+found original quota.user swapfile var
cdrom home misc proc root tftpboot web
dev initrd mnt prod_serv sbin tmp
root@ttyp0[hda2]# cat etc/fstab
LBEL=/ / ext3 defaults LABEL=/boot /boot ext3 defaults none /dev/pts
devpts gid=5,mode=none /proc proc defaults none /dev/shm tmpfs defaults
/dev/hda3 swap swap defaults /dev/cdrom /mnt/cdrom udf,iso9660
noauto,ro 0 0
/dev/fd0 /mnt/floppy auto noauto,owner,/swapfile none swap pri=2
/dev/hdb3 /suse_root_hdb reiserfs defaults /dev/hdb1
/suse_root_hdb/boot ext2 defaults root@ttyp0[hda2]#
```

Now just fix fstab, unmount the repaired root filesystem, and reboot from the hard disk. The following shows the corrected fstab.

```
root@ttyp0[hda2]# cat etc/fstab
LABEL=/ / ext3 defaults LABEL=/boot /boot ext3 defaults none /dev/pts
devpts gid=5,mode=none /proc proc defaults none /dev/shm tmpfs defaults
/dev/hda3 swap swap defaults /dev/cdrom /mnt/cdrom udf,iso9660
noauto,ro 0 0
/dev/fd0 /mnt/floppy auto noauto,owner,/swapfile none swap pri=2
/dev/hdb3 /suse_root_hdb reiserfs defaults /dev/hdb1
/suse_root_hdb/boot ext2 defaults root@ttyp0[hda2]# cd
root@ttyp0[~]# umount /mnt/hda2
root@ttyp0[~]#
```

note

Many different "Linux on a CD" distributions are available. Here is a list of some of the most popular:

- Knoppix (http://www.knoppix.net/)
- LNX-BBC (http://lnxbbc.org/)
- SystemRescueCd (http://www.sysresccd.org/)
- Timo's Rescue CD Set (http://rescuecd.sourceforge.net/)
- SuperRescue (http://freshmeat.net/projects/superrescue)

We don't endorse any particular rescue CD distribution, and we list several so that you can evaluate them and choose the best method for your situation.

Reset Lost Root Password Using a Knoppix CD

If the root password is lost, there is no way to log in at multiuser mode. Red Hat doesn't require a password in single user mode, though, which makes it easy to reset the password. Just reboot to single user mode and run passwd. But what about distributions such as SUSE that require a password in single user mode? It is just a bit more complicated to resolve in this case.

The solution is to boot from the Knoppix CD or whatever rescue disk you use. When the box is booted, mount the SUSE root filesystem to some temporary mount point such as /mnt/hdb3. If you are using Knoppix, be sure to change the mount option to defaults in /etc/fstab first, or else device file access won't work. When the filesystem is mounted, just run chroot /mnt/hdb3 and passwd as root to reset the SUSE password. The chroot command is used to start a new shell with an effective root directory of the root partition on the problem disk. In other words, after running chroot /mnt/hdb3, the command ls/ shows the files and directories from the /mnt/hdb3 directory. See the chroot(1) man page for further details.

Reinstall GRUB Using Knoppix CD

The process to reinstall GRUB when booted from Knoppix is very similar to resetting the SUSE root password. We again use chroot. In this example, GRUB is written to the MBR of /dev/hda. First, we change fstab to mount the boot partition under /boot and change the options to defaults for both /dev/hda1 and /dev/hda2. /dev/hda1 is /boot, and /dev/hda2 is /. /dev/hda3 is swap, so we leave it alone. The next listing shows the original fstab that Knoppix gives us:

```
knoppix@ttyp1[knoppix]$ su - root
root@ttyp1[~]# cat /etc/fstab
/proc /proc proc defaults 0 0
/sys /sys sysfs noauto 0 0
/dev/pts /dev/pts devpts mode=0622 0 0
/dev/fd0 /mnt/auto/floppy auto user,noauto,exec,umask=000 0 /dev/cdrom
/mnt/auto/cdrom auto user,noauto,exec,ro 0 0
# Added by KNOPPIX
/dev/hda1 /mnt/hda1 ext3 noauto,users,exec 0 0
# Added by KNOPPIX
/dev/hda2 /mnt/hda2 ext3 noauto,users,exec 0 0
# Added by KNOPPIX
/dev/hda3 none swap defaults 0 0
# Added by KNOPPIX
/dev/hdb1 /mnt/hdb1 ext2 noauto,users,exec 0 0
# Added by KNOPPIX
/dev/hdb2 none swap defaults 0 0
# Added by KNOPPIX
/dev/hdb3 /mnt/hdb3 reiserfs noauto,users,exec 0 0
root@ttyp1[~]#
```

The following listing shows fstab after we change the /dev/hda1 and /dev/hda2 lines:

```
root@ttyp1[~]# cat /etc/fstab
/proc /proc proc defaults 0 0
/sys /sys sysfs noauto 0 0
```

```
/dev/pts /dev/pts devpts mode=0622 0 0
/dev/fd0 /mnt/auto/floppy auto user,noauto,exec,umask=000 0 /dev/cdrom
/mnt/auto/cdrom auto user,noauto,exec,ro 0 0
# Added by KNOPPIX
/dev/hda1 /mnt/hda2/boot ext3 defaults 0 0
# Added by KNOPPIX
/dev/hda2 /mnt/hda2 ext3 defaults 0 0
# Added by KNOPPIX
/dev/hda3 none swap defaults 0 0
# Added by KNOPPIX
/dev/hdb1 /mnt/hdb1 ext2 noauto,users,exec 0 0
# Added by KNOPPIX
/dev/hdb2 none swap defaults 0 0
# Added by KNOPPIX
/dev/hdb3 /mnt
```

Now we mount the disk filesystems so that we can reinstall GRUB:

```
mount /dev/hda2
mount /dev/hda1
```

Next, we run chroot /mnt/hda2 to make /mnt/hda2 the effective / for the following
GRUB work. The commands in the following listing are the same as the previous GRUB
reinstallation example.

```
grub> root (hd0,0)
grub> find /boot/grub/stage1
grub> setup (hd0)
 >>

grub>
root (hd0,0)
Filesystem type is ext2fs, partition type 0x83
grub>
find /boot/grub/stage1
(hd1,0)
grub>
```

```
setup (hd0)
Checking if "/boot/grub/stage1" exists... no
Checking if "/grub/stage1" exists... yes
Checking if "/grub/stage2" exists... yes
Checking if "/grub/e2fs_stage1_5" exists... yes
Running "embed /grub/e2fs_stage1_5 (hd0)"... 16 sectors are embedded.
succeeded
Running "install /grub/stage1 (hd0) (hd0)1+16 p (hd0,0)/grub/stage2
b.conf"... succeeded
Done.
grub>
```

After this is done, we can just quit the GRUB shell and exit the chroot shell. We then unmount /dev/hda1 and /dev/hda2 and reboot.

Booting from a Floppy Rescue Disk

A 3.5-inch floppy disk doesn't have room for a full Linux system. However, you can make a bootable rescue disk that includes critical utilities needed to recover a system. We recommend using Knoppix, SystemRescueCd, or some other CD-based solution because they are full Linux distributions and have all the commands and utilities you are used to. If a CD-ROM is not available on the Linux server, then a rescue floppy is a good solution.

Check tomsrtbt (http://www.toms.net/rb/) for a good floppy disk distribution. Tom Fawcett has an excellent article explaining how to build a rescue disk on the Linux Documentation Project Web site at http://www.tldp.org/HOWTO/Bootdisk-HOWTO/.

Whatever method you decide to use, be sure to verify that it will boot all your Linux boxes before you need it to resolve a problem.

Summary

The intent of this chapter is to give the reader a good understanding of the Linux boot process. If you know how the startup and shutdown processes work, you probably have a good idea of how to troubleshoot problems. The examples are intended to demonstrate the skills needed to resolve common problems.

Hopefully, you now feel more confident booting from a rescue CD, repairing MBR problems, and fixing other problems.

Endnotes

1. Refer to `initrd(4)` for more information about the initial ram disk.

2. I was trying to limit the bootloader discussion to just GRUB and LILO, but you can see I failed. The `mkbootdisk` floppy uses `SYSLINUX` as its bootloader. More information on `SYSLINUX` (floppy bootloader) and `ISOLINUX` (CD bootloader) is available at http://syslinux.zytor.com/.

3. Look at the `syslog.conf(5)` man page to understand `syslog` routing. `init` uses the daemon facility.

4. The `crond` file listing was created on a Red Hat 3.0ES system with

   `find /etc/rc.d -name *crond -exec ls -al {} \;`

5. `RPM` man page taken from a Red Hat 9.0 system.

2

System Hangs and Panics

Anyone with any system administration experience has been there. You are in the middle of some production cycle or are just working on the desktop when the computer, for some mysterious reason, hangs or displays some elaborate screen message with a lot of HEX addresses and perhaps a stack of an offending NULL dereference.

What to do? In this chapter, we hope to provide an answer as we discuss kernel panics, oops, hangs, and hardware faults. We examine what the system does in these situations and discuss the tools required for initial analysis. We begin by discussing OS hangs. We then discuss kernel panics and oops panics. Finally, we conclude with hardware machine checks.

It is important to identify whether you are encountering a panic, a hang, or a hardware fault to know how to remedy the problem. Panics are easy to detect because they consist of the kernel voluntarily shutting down. Hangs can be more difficult to detect because the kernel has gone into some unknown state and the driver has ceased to respond for some reason, preventing the processes from being scheduled. Hardware faults occur at a lower level, independent of and beneath the OS, and are observed through firmware logs.

When you encounter a hang, panic, or hardware fault, determine whether it is easily reproducible. This information helps to identify whether the underlying problem is a hardware or software problem. If it is easily reproducible on different machines, chances are that the problem is software-related. If it is reproducible on only one machine, focus on ruling out a problem with supported hardware.

One final important point before we begin discussing hangs: Whether you are dealing with an OS hang or panic, you must confirm that the hardware involved is supported by the Linux distribution before proceeding. Make sure the manufacturer supports the Linux kernel and hardware configuration used. Contact the manufacturer or consult its documentation or official Web site. This step is so important because when the hardware is supported, the manufacturer has already contributed vast resources to ensure compatibility and operability with the Linux kernel. Conversely, if it is not supported, you will not have the benefit of this expertise, even if you can find the bug, and either the manufacturer would have to implement your fix, or you would have to modify the open source driver yourself. However, even if the hardware is not supported, you may find this chapter to be a helpful learning tool because we highlight why the driver, kernel module, application, and hardware are behaving as they are.

OS Hangs

OS hangs come in two types: *interruptible* and *non-interruptible*. The first step to remedying a hang is to identify the type of hang. We know we have an interruptible hang when it responds to an external interrupt. Conversely, we know we have a non-interruptible hang when it does not.

To determine whether the hang responds to an external interrupt, attempt a ping test, checking for a response. If a keyboard is attached, perform a test by simply pressing the Caps Lock key to see whether the Caps Lock light cycles. If you have console access, determine whether the console gives you line returns when you press the Enter key. If one or more of these yields the sought response, you know you have an interruptible hang.

note

> Any time an OS hangs, one or more offending processes are usually responsible for the hang. This is true whether software or hardware is ultimately to blame for the OS hang. Even when a hardware problem exists, a process has made a request of the hardware that the hardware could not fulfill, so processes stack up as a result.

Troubleshooting Interruptible Hangs

The first step in troubleshooting an interruptible hang is obtaining a stack trace of the offending process or processes by using the *Magic SysRq* keystroke. Some Linux distributions have this functionality enabled by default, whereas others do not. We recommend always having this functionality enabled. The following example shows how to enable it.

Check whether the Magic SysRq is enabled:

```
# cat /proc/sys/kernel/sysrq
0
( 0 = disabled  1 = enabled)
```

Because it is not enabled, enable it:

```
# echo 1 > /proc/sys/kernel/sysrq
# cat /proc/sys/kernel/sysrq
1
```

Alternatively, we can use the `sysctl` command:

```
# sysctl -n kernel.sysrq
0
# sysctl -w kernel.sysrq=1
# sysctl -n kernel.sysrq
1
```

To make this setting persistent, just put an entry into the configuration file:

```
# /etc/sysctl.conf
kernel.sysrq=1
```

When the functionality is enabled, a stack trace can be obtained by sending a Break+t to the console. Unfortunately, this can be more difficult than it first appears. With a standard VGA console, this is accomplished with the Alt+sysrq+t keystroke combination; however, the keystroke combination is different for other console emulators, in which case you would need to determine the required key sequence by contacting the particular manufacturer. For example, if a Windows user utilizes emulation software, such as Reflections, key mapping can be an issue. Linux distributions sometimes provide tools such as cu and minicom, which do not affect the key mapping by default.

With the latest 2.4 kernel releases, a new file is introduced in /proc called sysrq-trigger. By simply echoing a predefined character to this file, the administrator avoids the need to send a break to the console. However, if the terminal window is hung, the break sequence is the only way. The following example shows how to use the functionality to obtain a stack trace.

Using a serial console or virtual console (/dev/ttyS0 or /dev/vc/1), press Alt+sysrq+h.

After this key combination is entered and sysrq is enabled, the output on the screen is as follows:

```
kernel: SysRq : HELP : loglevel0-8 reBoot tErm kIll saK showMem Off
showPc unRaw Sync showTasks Unmount
```

The following is a description of each parameter:

- loglevel—Sets the console logging level.
- reBoot—Resets the processor so that the system starts booting.
- tErm—Sends SIGTERM to all processes except init.
- kIll—Sends SIGKILL to all processes except init.
- saK—Kills all process in virtual console: Secure Access Keys. This ensures that the login prompt is init's and not some third-party application.
- showMem—Shows system memory report.
- Off—Shuts machine down.
- showPc—Dumps registers: Includes PID of running process, instruction pointers, and control registers.
- unRaw—Turns off keyboard RAW mode and sets it to ASCII (XLATE).
- Sync—Syncs filesystems.
- showTasks—Dumps all tasks and their info.
- Unmount—Attempts to remount all mounted filesystems as read-only.
- shoWcpus—Shows stacks for each CPU by "walking" each CPU (smp kernel).

With the latest kernels, it is possible to test the "Magic SysRq" functionality by writing a "key" character from the previous list to the /proc/sysrq-trigger file. The following example causes the CPU stacks to be written to the kernel ring buffer:

```
# echo w > /proc/sysrq-trigger
```

To view the processor stacks, simply execute the dmesg command or view the syslog.

```
# dmesg
...
SysRq : Show CPUs
CPU1:

Call Trace: [<e000000004415860>] sp=0xe0000040fc96fca0
bsp=0xe0000040fc969498 show_stack [kernel] 0x80
[<e000000004653d30>] sp=0xe0000040fc96fe60 bsp=0xe0000040fc969480
showacpu [kernel] 0x90
[<e000000004653d80>] sp=0xe0000040fc96fe60 bsp=0xe0000040fc969470
sysrq_handle_showcpus [kernel] 0x20
[<e000000004654380>] sp=0xe0000040fc96fe60 bsp=0xe0000040fc969428
__handle_sysrq_nolock [kernel] 0x120
[<e000000004654230>] sp=0xe0000040fc96fe60 bsp=0xe0000040fc9693f0
handle_sysrq [kernel] 0x70
[<e00000000458a930>] sp=0xe0000040fc96fe60 bsp=0xe0000040fc9693c8
write_sysrq_trigger [kernel] 0xf0
[<e0000000045167a0>] sp=0xe0000040fc96fe60 bsp=0xe0000040fc969348
sys_write [kernel] 0x1c0
[<e00000000440e900>] sp=0xe0000040fc96fe60 bsp=0xe0000040fc969348
ia64_ret_from_syscall [kernel] 0x0
CPU0:

Call Trace: [<e000000004415860>] sp=0xe0000040fbe07ac0
bsp=0xe0000040fbe01518 show_stack [kernel] 0x80
[<e000000004653d30>] sp=0xe0000040fbe07c80 bsp=0xe0000040fbe01500
showacpu [kernel] 0x90
[<e000000004446980>] sp=0xe0000040fbe07c80 bsp=0xe0000040fbe014a0
handle_IPI [kernel] 0x200
```

```
[<e000000004412500>] sp=0xe0000040fbe07c80 bsp=0xe0000040fbe01460
handle_IRQ_event [kernel] 0x100
[<e000000004412be0>] sp=0xe0000040fbe07c80 bsp=0xe0000040fbe01418
do_IRQ [kernel] 0x160
[<e000000004414e20>] sp=0xe0000040fbe07c80 bsp=0xe0000040fbe013d0
ia64_handle_irq [kernel] 0xc0
[<e00000000440e920>] sp=0xe0000040fbe07c80 bsp=0xe0000040fbe013d0
ia64_leave_kernel [kernel] 0x0
[<e00000000447b9b0>] sp=0xe0000040fbe07e20 bsp=0xe0000040fbe012c8
schedule [kernel] 0xa70
[<e000000004486ce0>] sp=0xe0000040fbe07e30 bsp=0xe0000040fbe01288
do_syslog [kernel] 0x460
[<e0000000045876f0>] sp=0xe0000040fbe07e60 bsp=0xe0000040fbe01260
kmsg_read [kernel] 0x30
[<e000000004516400>] sp=0xe0000040fbe07e60 bsp=0xe0000040fbe011d8
sys_read [kernel] 0x1c0
[<e00000000440e900>] sp=0xe0000040fbe07e60 bsp=0xe0000040fbe011d8
ia64_ret_from_syscall [kernel] 0x0
CPU3:

Call Trace: [<e000000004415860>] sp=0xe000004083e87b00
bsp=0xe000004083e81318 show_stack [kernel] 0x80
[<e000000004653d30>] sp=0xe000004083e87cc0 bsp=0xe000004083e81300
showacpu [kernel] 0x90
[<e000000004446980>] sp=0xe000004083e87cc0 bsp=0xe000004083e812a0
handle_IPI [kernel] 0x200
[<e000000004412500>] sp=0xe000004083e87cc0 bsp=0xe000004083e81260
handle_IRQ_event [kernel] 0x100
[<e000000004412be0>] sp=0xe000004083e87cc0 bsp=0xe000004083e81218
do_IRQ [kernel] 0x160
[<e000000004414e20>] sp=0xe000004083e87cc0 bsp=0xe000004083e811d0
ia64_handle_irq [kernel] 0xc0
[<e00000000440e920>] sp=0xe000004083e87cc0 bsp=0xe000004083e811d0
ia64_leave_kernel [kernel] 0x0
[<e0000000044160c0>] sp=0xe000004083e87e60 bsp=0xe000004083e811d0
default_idle [kernel] 0x0
[<e0000000044161e0>] sp=0xe000004083e87e60 bsp=0xe000004083e81160
cpu_idle [kernel] 0x100
```

```
[<e00000000499c380>]  sp=0xe000004083e87e60 bsp=0xe000004083e81150
start_secondary [kernel] 0x80

[<e0000000044080c0>]  sp=0xe000004083e87e60 bsp=0xe000004083e81150
start_ap [kernel] 0x1a0

CPU2:


Call Trace: [<e000000004415860>] sp=0xe0000040fdc77b00
bsp=0xe0000040fdc71318 show_stack [kernel] 0x80

[<e000000004653d30>]  sp=0xe0000040fdc77cc0 bsp=0xe0000040fdc71300
showacpu [kernel] 0x90

[<e000000004446980>]  sp=0xe0000040fdc77cc0 bsp=0xe0000040fdc712a0
handle_IPI [kernel] 0x200

[<e000000004412500>]  sp=0xe0000040fdc77cc0 bsp=0xe0000040fdc71260
handle_IRQ_event [kernel] 0x100

[<e000000004412be0>]  sp=0xe0000040fdc77cc0 bsp=0xe0000040fdc71218
do_IRQ [kernel] 0x160

[<e000000004414e20>]  sp=0xe0000040fdc77cc0 bsp=0xe0000040fdc711d0
ia64_handle_irq [kernel] 0xc0

[<e00000000440e920>]  sp=0xe0000040fdc77cc0 bsp=0xe0000040fdc711d0
ia64_leave_kernel [kernel] 0x0

[<e0000000044161d0>]  sp=0xe0000040fdc77e60 bsp=0xe0000040fdc71160
cpu_idle [kernel] 0xf0

[<e00000000499c380>]  sp=0xe0000040fdc77e60 bsp=0xe0000040fdc71150
start_secondary [kernel] 0x80

[<e0000000044080c0>]  sp=0xe0000040fdc77e60 bsp=0xe0000040fdc71150
start_ap [kernel] 0x1a0
```

Scenario 2-1: Hanging OS

In this scenario, the OS hangs, but the user is unable to determine why. The way to start troubleshooting is to gather stacks and logs.

Because the OS is not responding to telnet, ssh, or any attempt to log in, we must resort to another log collection method. In this case, we test the keyboard to see whether the system still responds to interrupts. As mentioned at the start of this section, an easy test is to press the Caps Lock key and see whether the Caps Lock light toggles on and off. If not, the hang is considered non-interruptible, which we discuss later. If the light does toggle and the Magic SysRq keys are enabled, gather the system registers by pressing the Alt+sysrq+p key combination.

The following is output from the register dump:

```
SysRq: Show Regs (showPc)

Process:0,{               swapper}
kernel 2.4.9-e.3smp
EIP: 0010:[<c010542e>] CPU: 0EIP is at default_idle [kernel] 0x2e
  EFLAGS: 00000246 Not Tainted
EAX 00000000 EBX: c030a000 ECX: c030a000 EDX: 00000000
ESI: c0105400 EDI: c030a000 EBP: ffffe000 DS: 0018 ES:0018
CR0: 8005003b CR2: 0819d038 CR3: 1544c000 CR4: 000006d0


Call Trace: [<c0105492>] cpu_idle [kernel] 0x32
[<c0105000>] stext [kernel] 0x0
[<c02405e0>]  .rodata.str1.32 [kernel] 0x560


../drivers/char/sysrq.c
...
static struct sysrq_key_op sysrq_showregs_op = {
        .handler       = sysrq_handle_showregs,
        .help_msg      = "showPc",
        .action_msg    = "Show Regs",
};
```

Referring to the register dump output, we can assume the machine is in an idle loop because the kernel is in the default_idle function and the machine is no longer responding. This message also informs us that the kernel is not "tainted." The latest source code provides us with the various tainted kernel states, as shown in the following code snippet.

```
linux/kernel/panic.c
...
/**
 *   print_tainted - return a string to represent the kernel taint state.
 *
 *   'P' - Proprietary module has been loaded.
```

```
 *       'F'  - Module has been forcibly loaded.
 *       'S'  - SMP with CPUs not designed for SMP.
 *       'U'  - Unsupported modules loaded.
 *       'X'  - Modules with external support loaded.
 *
 *       The string is overwritten by the next call to print_taint().
 */

const char *print_tainted(void)
{
        static char buf[20];
        if (tainted) {
                snprintf(buf, sizeof(buf), "Tainted: %c%c%c%c%c%c",
                        tainted & TAINT_MACHINE_CHECK ? 'M' : ' ',
                        tainted & TAINT_PROPRIETARY_MODULE ? 'P' : 'G',
                        tainted & TAINT_FORCED_MODULE ? 'F' : ' ',
                        tainted & TAINT_UNSAFE_SMP ? 'S' : ' ',
                        tainted & TAINT_NO_SUPPORT ? 'U' :
                                (tainted & TAINT_EXTERNAL_SUPPORT ? 'X' :
' '));
        }
        else
                snprintf(buf, sizeof(buf), "Not tainted");
        return(buf);
}
```

In most cases, if the kernel were in a tainted state, a tech support organization would suggest that you remove the "unsupported" kernel module that is tainting the kernel before proceeding to troubleshoot the issue. In this case, the kernel is not tainted, so we proceed along our original path.

Reviewing the register dump tells us the offset location for the instruction pointer. In this case, the offset is at default_idle+46 (0x2e hex = 46 dec). With this new information, we can use GDB to obtain the instruction details.

```
gdb vmlinux-2.4.9-e.3smp
(gdb) disassemble default_idle
```

```
Dump of assembler code for function default_idle:
0xc0105400 <default_idle>:          mov     $0xffffe000,%ecx
0xc0105405 <default_idle+5>:        and     %esp,%ecx
0xc0105407 <default_idle+7>:        mov     0x20(%ecx),%edx
0xc010540a <default_idle+10>:       mov     %edx,%eax
0xc010540c <default_idle+12>:       shl     $0x5,%eax
0xc010540f <default_idle+15>:       add     %edx,%eax
0xc0105411 <default_idle+17>:       cmpb    $0x0,0xc0366985(,%eax,4)
0xc0105419 <default_idle+25>:       je      0xc0105431 <default_idle+49>
0xc010541b <default_idle+27>:       mov     0xc0365208,%eax
0xc0105420 <default_idle+32>:       test    %eax,%eax
0xc0105422 <default_idle+34>:       jne     0xc0105431 <default_idle+49>
0xc0105424 <default_idle+36>:       cli
0xc0105425 <default_idle+37>:       mov     0x14(%ecx),%eax
0xc0105428 <default_idle+40>:       test    %eax,%eax
0xc010542a <default_idle+42>:       jne     0xc0105430 <default_idle+48>
0xc010542c <default_idle+44>:       sti
0xc010542d <default_idle+45>:       hlt
0xc010542e <default_idle+46>:       ret     ← Our offset!
0xc010542f <default_idle+47>:       nop
0xc0105430 <default_idle+48>:       sti
0xc0105431 <default_idle+49>:       ret
0xc0105432 <default_idle+50>:       lea     0x0(%esi,1),%esi
```

Now we know that the OS is hung on a return to caller. At this point, we are stuck because this return could have been caused by some other instruction that had already taken place.

Solution 2-1: Update the Kernel

The problem was solved when we updated the kernel to the latest supported patch release. Before spending considerable time and resources tracking down what appears to be a bug, or "feature," as we sometimes say, confirm that the kernel and all the relevant applications have been patched or updated to their latest revisions. In this case, after the kernel was patched, the hang was no longer reproducible.

The Magic SysRq is logged in three places: the kernel message ring buffer (read by dmesg), the syslog, and the console. The package responsible for this is sysklogd, which provides klogd and syslogd. Of course, not all events are logged to the console. Event levels control whether something is logged to the console. To enable all messages to be printed on the console, set the log level to 8 through dmesg -n 8 or klogd -c 8. If you are already on the console, you can use the SysRq keys to indicate the log level by pressing Alt+sysrq+*level*, where *level* is a number from 0 to 8. More details on these commands can be found in the dmesg and klogd man pages and of course in the source code.

Reviewing the source, we can see that not all the keyboard characters are used.

```
See:   /drivers/char/sysrq.c
...
static struct sysrq_key_op *sysrq_key_table[SYSRQ_KEY_TABLE_LENGTH] = {
/* 0 */ &sysrq_loglevel_op,
/* 1 */ &sysrq_loglevel_op,
/* 2 */ &sysrq_loglevel_op,
/* 3 */ &sysrq_loglevel_op,
/* 4 */ &sysrq_loglevel_op,
/* 5 */ &sysrq_loglevel_op,
/* 6 */ &sysrq_loglevel_op,
/* 7 */ &sysrq_loglevel_op,
/* 8 */ &sysrq_loglevel_op,
/* 9 */ &sysrq_loglevel_op,
/* a */ NULL, /* Don't use for system provided sysrqs,
                  it is handled specially on the spark
                  and will never arrive */
/* b */ &sysrq_reboot_op,
/* c */ &sysrq_crash_op,
/* d */ NULL,
/* e */ &sysrq_term_op,
/* f */ NULL,
/* g */ NULL,
/* h */ NULL,
/* i */ &sysrq_kill_op,
/* j */ NULL,
```

```
#ifdef CONFIG_VT
/* k */ &sysrq_SAK_op,
#else
/* k */ NULL,
#endif
/* l */ NULL,
/* m */ &sysrq_showmem_op,
/* n */ NULL,
/* o */ NULL, /* This will often be registered
                  as 'Off' at init time */
/* p */ &sysrq_showregs_op,
/* q */ NULL,
/* r */ &sysrq_unraw_op,
/* s */ &sysrq_sync_op,
/* t */ &sysrq_showstate_op,
/* u */ &sysrq_mountro_op,
/* v */ NULL,
/* w */ &sysrq_showcpus_op,
/* x */ NULL,
/* w */ NULL,
/* z */ NULL
};
...
```

Collecting the dump is more difficult if the machine is not set up properly. In the case of an interruptible hang, the `syslog` daemon might not be able to write to its message file. In this case, we have to rely on the console to collect the dump messages. If the only console on the machine is a Graphics console, you must write the dump out by hand. Note that the dump messages are written only to the virtual console, not to X Windows. The Linux kernel addresses this panic scenario by making the LEDs on the keyboard blink, notifying the administrator that this is not an OS hang but rather an OS panic.

The following 2.4 series source code illustrates this LED-blinking feature that is used when the Linux kernel pulls a panic. Notice that we start with the `kernel/panic.c` source to determine which functions are called and to see whether anything relating to blinking is referenced.

```
# linux/kernel/panic.c
...

      for(;;) {
#if defined(CONFIG_X86) && defined(CONFIG_VT)
                extern void panic_blink(void);
                panic_blink();
#endif

                CHECK_EMERGENCY_SYNC
      }
...
```

We tracked down the `panic_blink()` function in the following source:

```
# linux/drivers/char/pc_keyb.c
...
static int blink_frequency = HZ/2;

/* Tell the user who may be running in X and not see the console that
   we have panicked. This is to distinguish panics from "real" lockups.
   Could in theory send the panic message as Morse, but that is left as
   an exercise for the reader.  */
void panic_blink(void)
{
        static unsigned long last_jiffie;
        static char led;
        /* Roughly 1/2s frequency. KDB uses about 1s. Make sure it is
           different. */
        if (!blink_frequency)
                return;
        if (jiffies - last_jiffie > blink_frequency) {
                led ^= 0x01 | 0x04;
                while (kbd_read_status() & KBD_STAT_IBF) mdelay(1);
                kbd_write_output(KBD_CMD_SET_LEDS);
                mdelay(1);
                while (kbd_read_status() & KBD_STAT_IBF) mdelay(1);
```

```
                mdelay(1);
                kbd_write_output(led);
                last_jiffie = jiffies;

        }
}


static int __init panicblink_setup(char *str)
{
    int par;
    if (get_option(&str,&par))
            blink_frequency = par*(1000/HZ);
    return 1;
}


/* panicblink=0 disables the blinking as it caused problems with some
   console switches. Otherwise argument is ms of a blink period. */
__setup("panicblink=", panicblink_setup);
```

By default, the 2.6 kernel release does not include the panic_blink() function. It was later added through a patch.

Even though this source informs the user that the machine has pulled a panic, it does not give us the stack or even the kernel state. Maybe, if we were lucky, klogd was able to write it to the syslog, but if we were lucky, the machine would not have panicked. For this reason, we recommend configuring a serial console so that you can collect the panic message if a panic takes place. Refer to Scenario 2-3 for an illustration.

Troubleshooting Non-Interruptible Hangs

The non-interruptible hang is the worst kind of hang because the standard troubleshooting techniques mentioned previously do not work, so correcting the problem is substantially more difficult. Again, the first step is to confirm that the hardware is supported and that all the drivers have been tested with this configuration. Keep in mind that hardware vendors and OS distributions spend vast resources confirming the supported configurations. Therefore, if the machine you are troubleshooting is outside of the supported configuration, it would be considered a best effort by those in the Linux community. It would be best to remove the unsupported hardware or software and see whether the problem persists.

Try to determine what the OS was doing before the hang. Ask these questions: Does the hang occur frequently? What application(s) are spawned at the time of the hang? What, if any, hardware is being accessed (for example, tape, disk, CD, DVD, and so on)? What software or hardware changes have been made on the system since the hangs began?

The answers to these questions provide "reference points" and establish an overall direction for troubleshooting the hang. For example, an application using a third-party driver module might have caused a crash that left CPU spinlocks (hardware locks) in place. In this case, it is probably not a coincidence that the machine hung every time when the user loaded his or her new driver module.

You should attempt to isolate the application or hardware interfaces being used. This might be futile, though, because the needed information might not be contained within the logs. Chances are, the CPU is looping in some type of spinlock, or the kernel attempts to crash, but the bus is in a compromised state, preventing the kernel from proceeding with the crash handler.

When the kernel has gotten into a non-interruptible hang, the goal is to get the kernel to pull a panic, save state, and create a dump. Linux achieves this goal on some platforms with a boot option to the kernel, enabling non-maskable interrupts (nmi_watchdog). More detailed information can be found in `linux/Documentation/nmi_watchdog.txt`. In short, the kernel sends an interrupt to the CPU every five seconds. As long as the CPU responds, the kernel stays up. When the interrupt does not return, the NMI handler generates an oops, which can be used to debug the hang. However, as with interruptible hangs, we must be able to collect the kernel dump, and this is where the serial console plays a role. If `panic_on_oops` is enabled, the kernel pulls a `panic()`, enabling other dump collection mechanisms, which are discussed later in this chapter.

We recommend getting the hardware and distribution vendors involved. As stated earlier, they have already put vast resources into confirming the hardware and software operability.

Thus, the most effective ways to troubleshoot a non-interruptible hang can be obvious. For example, sometimes it is important to take out all unnecessary hardware and drivers, leaving the machine in a "bare bones" state. It might also be important to confirm that the OS kernel is fully up-to-date on any patches. In addition, stop all unnecessary software.

Scenario 2-2: Linux 2.4.9-e.27 Kernel

In this scenario, the user added new fiber cards to an existing database system, and now the machine hangs intermittently, always at night when peak loads are down. Nothing of note seems to trigger it, although the user is running an outdated kernel. The user tried gathering a sysrq+p for each processor on the system, which requires two keystrokes for each processor. With newer kernels, sysrq+w performs a "walk" of all the CPUs with one keystroke. The user then tries gathering sysrq+m and sysrq+t. Unfortunately, the console is hung and does not accept break sequences.

The next step is to disable all unnecessary drivers and to enable a forced kernel panic. The user set up nmi-watchdog so that he could get a forced oops panic. Additionally, all hardware monitors were disabled, and unnecessary driver modules were unloaded. After disabling the hardware monitors, the user noticed that the hangs stopped occurring.

Solution 2-2: Update the Hardware Monitor Driver

We provided the configuration and troubleshooting methodology (action plan) to the hardware vendor so that its staff could offer a solution. The fact that this symptom only took place when running their monitor was enough ammunition. The hardware event lab was aware of such events and already had released a newer monitor. While the administrator was waiting on the newer monitor module to be available, he removed the old one, preventing the kernel from experiencing hangs.

If the kernel hang persists and the combination of these tools does not lead to an answer, enabling kernel debugging might be the way to go. Directions on how to use KDB can be found at http://oss.sgi.com/projects/kdb/.

OS Panics

An OS panic is caused by some unexpected condition or kernel state that results in a voluntary kernel shutdown. In this case, we are not talking about the OS shutdown command, but rather a condition where the code finds itself calling panic().

Because the panic is a voluntary kernel shutdown, a reboot is necessary before troubleshooting can begin. By default, Linux does not reboot when encountering a `panic()`. Automatic system reboots can be set by entering the number of seconds to wait in `/proc/sys/kernel/panic`. `0` is the default for most Linux distributions, meaning that the system will not reboot and will remain in a hung state. Otherwise, a hardware-forced reset can be used.

Troubleshooting OS Panics

To troubleshoot an OS panic, first try to obtain a dump. Consult the console, which contains the panic string. The panic string leads us to the source of the panic. From there, we can determine the function calls that were made at the time of the panic. Sometimes the console data is not enough. If more data is required, a dump utility must be enabled. When the kernel pulls `panic()`, the crash dump takes control and writes the kernel memory to a dump device. To date, this feature is not in `kernel.org`.

Several competing technologies are available for obtaining a dump. For example, the Linux distributions SGI, SUSE, and HP Telco use LKCD (Linux Kernel Crash Dump). Red Hat offers `netdump` and its alternative `diskdump` (similar to `lkcd`). Again, these mechanisms get triggered as a result of a kernel `panic()` and depend on the dump driver supporting the underlying hardware. That being said, if the system's state is unstable (for example, spinlocks, bus state compromised, and CPU interrupt state), these utilities might not be able to save a kernel dump.

Unlike other flavors of Unix, the Linux kernel does not have a native dump mechanism. Rather, in Linux, a kernel dump is the result of a panic in which one of the aforementioned capabilities is enabled.

Scenario 2-3: Users Experience Multiple OS Panics

In this case, the system administrator has a machine that has been in service for some time. This is her primary production machine, and she needs to add a new PCI host bus adapter (HBA). Instead of confirming that the kernel is at the supported patch level or, for that matter, confirming that the machine boots properly after having just installed 250 package updates two weeks earlier, she decides to simply shut down the system and install the new card. Because this will affect production, management has allotted 30 minutes to perform hardware addition, and then the machine must be back online.

After shutting down the system and adding the hardware, the system administrator gets the machine to boot with no errors. After a few minutes pass, however, the system administrator notices that the machine is no longer responding, and the console shows that the machine has panicked. Because production has been impacted, managers become involved, and the system administrator is under pressure to get the machine stabilized.

Because the machine was not booted since the last package updates were installed, it is very difficult to determine whether the PCI card is causing the problem. The first step is to review the stack trace in an attempt to isolate the code section that triggered the panic.

```
Stack traces appear like this:     Bad slab found on cache free list
    slab 0xf53d8580:
      next 0xf7f7a0b0, prev 0xf7f7a0b0, mem 0xf43ef000
      colouroff 0x0000, inuse 0xfffffffe3, free 0x0000
    cache 0xf7f7a0a0 ("names_cache"):
      full    0xf7f788a0 <-> 0xf53d85a0
      partial 0xf7f7a0a8 <-> 0xf7f7a0a8
      free    0xf53d8580 <-> 0xf53d8580
      next    0xf7f7a200 <-> 0xf7f7bf38
      objsize 0x1000, flags 0x12000, num 0x0001, batchcount 0x001e
      order 0, gfp 0x0000, colour 0x0000:0x0020:0x0000
      slabcache 0xf7f7c060, growing 0, dflags 0x0001, failures 0


  kernel BUG at slab.c:2010!
  invalid operand: 0000
  Kernel 2.4.9-e.49smp
  CPU:     1
  EIP:     0010:[<c0138d95>]    Tainted: P
  EFLAGS: 00010082
  EIP is at proc_getdata [kernel] 0x145
  eax: 0000001e   ebx: f53d8580   ecx: c02f8b24   edx: 000054df
  esi: f7f7a0a0   edi: 0000085e   ebp: 00000013   esp: f42ffef8
  ds: 0018   es: 0018     ss: 0018
  Process bgscollect (pid: 2933, stackpage=f42ff000)
  Stack: c0267dfb 000007da 00000000 00000013 f42fff68 f8982000 00000c00
  00000000
```

```
    c0138eec f8982000 f42fff68 00000000 00000c00 f8982000 00000c00
00000000
    c0169e8a f8982000 f42fff68 00000000 00000c00 f42fff64 00000000
f42fe000
Call Trace: [<c0267dfb>] .rodata.str1.1 [kernel] 0x2c16 (0xf42ffef8)
[<c0138eec>] slabinfo_read_proc [kernel] 0x1c (0xf42fff18)
[<c0169e8a>] proc_file_read [kernel] 0xda (0xf42fff38)
[<c0146296>] sys_read [kernel] 0x96 (0xf42fff7c)
[<c01073e3>] system_call [kernel] 0x33 (0xf42fffc0)
```

Immediately, we can see that this is a tainted kernel and that the module that has tainted the kernel is proprietary in nature. This module might be the culprit. However, because the machine has been in production for a while, it would be difficult to blame the panic on the driver module. However, the panic occurred because of memory corruption, which could be hardware or software related.

Continuing with troubleshooting, we note that additional stack traces from the console appear like this:

```
 2:40:50: ds: 0018   es: 0018   ss: 0018
12:40:50: Process kswapd (pid: 10, stackpage=f7f29000)
12:40:50: Stack: c0267dfb 00000722 00000000 f7f7a0b0 f7f7a0a8 c0137c13
c5121760 00000005
12:40:50:      00000000 00000000 00000000 00000018 000000c0 00000000
0008e000 c013ca6f
12:40:51:      000000c0 00000000 00000001 00000000 c013cb83 000000c0
00000000 c0105000
12:40:51: Call Trace: [<c0267dfb>] .rodata.str1.1 [kernel] 0x2c16
(0xf7f29f78)
12:40:51: [<c0137c13>] kmem_cache_shrink_nr [kernel] 0x53 (0xf7f29f8c)
12:40:51: [<c013ca6f>] do_try_to_free_pages [kernel] 0x7f (0xf7f29fb4)
12:40:51: [<c013cb83>] kswapd [kernel] 0x103 (0xf7f29fc8)
12:40:51: [<c0105000>] stext [kernel] 0x0 (0xf7f29fd4)
12:40:51: [<c0105000>] stext [kernel] 0x0 (0xf7f29fec)
12:40:51: [<c0105856>] arch_kernel_thread [kernel] 0x26 (0xf7f29ff0)
12:40:51: [<c013ca80>] kswapd [kernel] 0x0 (0xf7f29ff8)
```

```
12:40:51:
12:40:51:
12:40:51: Code: 0f 0b 58 5a 8b 03 45 39 f8 75 dd 8b 4e 2c 89 ea 8b 7e 4c d3
12:40:51:   <0>Kernel panic: not continuing
12:40:51: Uhhuh. NMI received for unknown reason 30.
12:51:30: Dazed and confused, but trying to continue.
12:51:30: Do you have a strange power saving mode enabled?
```

It is difficult to identify exactly what is causing the problem here; however, because NMI caused the panic, the problem is probably hardware related. The kernel error message, "NMI received for unknown reason," informs us that the system administrator has set up NMI in case of a hardware hang. Looking through the source, we find this message mentioned in linux/arch/i386/kernel/traps.c.

The following is a snapshot of the source:

```
...
static void unknown_nmi_error(unsigned char reason, struct pt_regs *
regs)
{
#ifdef CONFIG_MCA
        /* Might actually be able to figure out what the guilty party
        * is. */
        if( MCA_bus ) {
                mca_handle_nmi();
                return;
        }
#endif
        printk("Uhhuh. NMI received for unknown reason %02x.\n", reason);
        printk("Dazed and confused, but trying to continue\n");
        printk("Do you have a strange power saving mode enabled?\n");
}
...
```

Solution 2-3: Replace the PC Card

Because the HBA was new to the environment, and because replacing it was easier and faster than digging through the stacks and debugging each crash, we suggested that the administrator simply replace the card with a new HBA. After obtaining a new replacement for the PCI card, the kernel no longer experienced panics.

Troubleshooting Panics Resulting from Oops

It is possible for an oops to cause an OS panic. Sometimes applications attempt to use invalid pointers. As a result, the kernel identifies and kills the process that called into the kernel and lists its stack, memory address, and kernel register values. This scenario is known as a kernel oops. Usually the result of bad code, the oops is debugged with the `ksymoops` command. In today's Linux distributions, `klogd` uses the kernel's symbols to decode the oops and pass it off to the `syslog` daemon, which in turn writes the oops to the message file (normally `/var/log/messages`).

If the kernel, in killing the offending process, does not kill the interrupt handler, the OS does not panic. However, this does not mean that the kernel is safe to use. It is possible that the program just made a bad code reference; however, it is also possible for the application to put the kernel in such a state that more oops follow. If this occurs, focus on the first oops rather than subsequent ones. To avoid running the machine in this relatively unstable state, enable the "panic on oops" option, controlled by the file `/proc/sys/kernel/panic_on_oops`. Of course, the next time the kernel encounters any kind of oops (whether or not it is the interrupt handler), it panics. If the dump utilities are enabled, a dump that can be analyzed occurs.

Scenario 2-4: Oops Causes Frequent System Panics

In this scenario, an application has been performing many NULL pointer dereferences (oops), and because the system administrator has the kernel configured to panic on oops, each oops results in a panic. The oops only seems to take place when the system is under a heavy load. The heavy load is caused by an application called VMware. This product creates a virtual machine of another OS type. In this case, the system administrator is running several virtual machines under the Linux kernel.

We gather the VMware version from the customer along with the kernel version (also noted in the oops). The next step is to review the logs and screen dumps. The dump details are as follows:

```
Unable to handle kernel NULL pointer dereference at virtual address
00000084
*pde = 20ffd001
Oops: 0000
Kernel 2.4.9-e.38enterprise
CPU:    4
EIP:    0010:[<c0138692>]    Tainted: PF
EFLAGS: 00013002
EIP is at do_ccupdate_local [kernel] 0x22
eax: 00000000    ebx: 00000004    ecx: f7f15efc    edx: c9cc8000
esi: 00000080    edi: c9cc8000    ebp: c0105420    esp: c9cc9f60
ds: 0018    es: 0018    ss: 0018
Process swapper (pid: 0, stackpage=c9cc9000)
Stack: c9cc8000 c9cc8000 c9cc8000 c0113bef f7f15ef8 c0105420 c02476da
c0105420
      c9cc8000 00000004 c9cc8000 c9cc8000 c0105420 00000000 c9cc0018
c9cc0018
      fffffffa c010544e 00000010 00003246 c01054b2 0402080c 00000000
00000000
Call Trace: [<c0113bef>] smp_call_function_interrupt [kernel] 0x2f
(0xc9cc9f6c)
[<c0105420>] default_idle [kernel] 0x0 (0xc9cc9f74)
[<c02476da>] call_call_function_interrupt [kernel] 0x5 (0xc9cc9f78)
[<c0105420>] default_idle [kernel] 0x0 (0xc9cc9f7c)
[<c0105420>] default_idle [kernel] 0x0 (0xc9cc9f90)
[<c010544e>] default_idle [kernel] 0x2e (0xc9cc9fa4)
[<c01054b2>] cpu_idle [kernel] 0x32 (0xc9cc9fb0)
[<c011ceb8>] printk [kernel] 0xd8 (0xc9cc9fd0)
[<c0265e4a>] .rodata.str1.1 [kernel] 0xd25 (0xc9cc9fe4)

Code: 8b 3c 1e 89 04 1e 8b 42 20 89 3c 81 5b 5e 5f c3 8d b4 26 00
LLT:10035: timer not called for 122 ticks
```

```
Kernel panic: not continuing
In idle task - not syncing
```

Interesting—"oops" in the swapper code. This does not sound right because we know that virtually no Linux machines panic because of swapper. So, in this case, we assume that some other software bundle or hardware exception is causing the anomaly. Notice that this kernel is tainted because it has a proprietary module that has been forcibly loaded.

While we are researching the traces and studying the source, the machine panics again. The details of the subsequent kernel panic follow:

```
Unable to handle kernel NULL pointer dereference at virtual address
00000074
*pde = 24c6b001
Oops: 0000
Kernel 2.4.9-e.38enterprise
CPU:    0
EIP:    0010:[<c0138692>]      Tainted: PF
EFLAGS: 00013002
EIP is at do_ccupdate_local [kernel] 0x22
eax: 00000000   ebx: 00000004   ecx: c9cedefc   edx: e7998000
esi: 00000070   edi: 0000013b   ebp: e7999f90   esp: e7999df8
ds: 0018   es: 0018   ss: 0018
Process vmware (pid: 9131, stackpage=e7999000)
Stack: e7998000 e7998000 0000013b c0113bef c9cedef8 00000000 c02476da
00000000
        efa1fca0 c0335000 e7998000 0000013b e7999f90 00000000 e7990018
f90c0018
        fffffffa f90cc2a2 00000010 00003286 00003002 ca212014 00000001
e6643180
Call Trace: [<c0113bef>] smp_call_function_interrupt [kernel] 0x2f
(0xe7999e04)
[<c02476da>] call_call_function_interrupt [kernel] 0x5 (0xe7999e10)
[<f90cc2a2>] .text.lock [vmmon] 0x86 (0xe7999e3c)
[<c0119af2>] __wake_up [kernel] 0x42 (0xe7999e5c)
[<c01da9a9>] sock_def_readable [kernel] 0x39 (0xe7999e84)
```

```
[<c021e0ad>] unix_stream_sendmsg [kernel] 0x27d (0xe7999ea0)
[<c01d7a21>] sock_recvmsg [kernel] 0x31 (0xe7999ed0)
[<c01d79cc>] sock_sendmsg [kernel] 0x6c (0xe7999ee4)
[<c01d7bf7>] sock_write [kernel] 0xa7 (0xe7999f38)
[<c0146d36>] sys_write [kernel] 0x96 (0xe7999f7c)
[<c0156877>] sys_ioctl [kernel] 0x257 (0xe7999f94)
[<c01073e3>] system_call [kernel] 0x33 (0xe7999fc0)


Code: 8b 3c 1e 89 04 1e 8b 42 20 89 3c 81 5b 5e 5f c3 8d b4 26 00
 <4>rtc: lost some interrupts at 256Hz.
Kernel panic: not continuing [Tue Jul 27
LLT:10035: timer not called for 150 ticks
```

The second panic reveals that the machine was in VMware code and on a different CPU.

Solution 2-4: Install a Patch

It took the combined efforts of many engineers to isolate and provide a fix for this scenario. The problem was found to reside in the smp_call_function() in the Red Hat Advanced Server 2.1 release, which used the 2.4.9 kernel. It turns out that the Linux kernel available on http://www.kernel.org did not contain the bug, so no other distributions experienced the issue. The Red Hat team, with the assistance of the VMware software team, provided a fix for the condition and resolved the oops panics.

Hardware Machine Checks

Finally, let us briefly discuss the IPF's IA64 hardware aborts and interrupts. Whereas hangs and panics are normally associated with how the kernel handles the scenario, the firmware is in control during a Machine Check Abort (MCA) or INIT.

Work is under way for the IA64 kernel to handle INITs. An INIT is a Processor Abstraction Layer (PAL)-based interrupt where in essence a transfer of control has taken place from the OS to the hardware. This interrupt is serviced by PAL firmware, system firmware, or in some cases the OS. During an INIT, the System Abstraction Layer (SAL) checks for an OS INIT handler; if one is not present, a soft reset takes place. Some of the current Linux kernel releases have built-in support for the INIT handler, and if a dump utility is enabled, the kernel will perform a panic and create a memory dump. In addition to the dump, we can extract the processor registers from the Extensible Firmware Interface (EFI), which can enable us to determine the code of execution at the time of the INIT.

A hardware abort, better known on the IA64 platform as an MCA, tells the processors to save state and perform a hardware reset. Hardware normally is the cause; however, software can be the cause as well. Examples of such an abort would be any sort of double bit error (whether it be in memory bus, I/O bus, or CPU bus). The current kernel releases do not show any console output when the IA64 platform experiences an MCA; however, work is under way to remedy this issue.

The kernel is essentially independent of a hardware machine check. Other tools must be used to collect the savestate registers and isolate the hardware at fault. At the EFI prompt, the command errordump is used to collect savestate registers. At this point, the hardware vendor must be contacted to decode the dump and processor registers.

Summary

When encountering a kernel hang, panic, oops, or MCA (IA-64 only), remember that troubleshooting each condition involves key steps. In the event of an OS hang, you must decide whether it is an interruptible hang. After you determine this, you can proceed with troubleshooting. The goal with any hang, panic, oops, or MCA is to obtain a stack trace. This information is necessary early in the troubleshooting process to guide us to the source of the problem. Let us recap the key points of each type of scenario and the steps to troubleshooting them.

- **Interruptible hangs**

  1. Use the Magic SysRq keys to attempt to gather stack of processor and offending processes.
  2. Check the registers: Alt+sysrq+p.
  3. Gather process stacks: Alt+sysrq+t.
  4. If SMP kernel, gather all processor stack: Alt+sysrq+w.

5. Synchronize filesystems: Alt+sysrq+s.

6. Reboot (soft reset) the system to clear the hang: Alt+sysrq+b.

7. After system is booted, review all the logs.

8. A serial console may be required to capture output of the sysrq keys.

Non-interruptible hangs

1. Set up dump utility in case a panic is taking place. Recommended dump utilities include `diskdump` and `lkcd`. If running on an IPF system, a dump can be achieved by issuing a TOC, forcing a hardware INIT. The System Abstraction Layer then sees that the OS has an INIT handler. If the functionality is in place, the kernel handles the INIT and pulls `panic()`, utilizing the aforementioned dump utilities to create a dump. (SUSE Linux Enterprise Server 9 (ia64) - Kernel 2.6.5-7.97 uses `lkcd` and has this feature enabled by default.)

2. On IA-32 x86 systems, the nmi_watchdog timer can be helpful in troubleshooting a hang. See `linux/Documentation/nmi_watchdog.txt`.

3. As with interruptible hangs, review system logs.

Panics

1. Collect the panic string.

2. Review hardware and software logs.

3. If problem cannot be identified through the console, the dump utilities must be enabled.

Oops

1. Review the stack trace of the oops with `ksymoops` (no longer needed with the latest `klogd` and kernel releases).

2. Locate the line that states `Unable to handle kernel NULL pointer`.

3. Locate the line showing the instruction pointer (IP).

4. Use `gdb` to look at the surrounding code.

- **MCA**

  At the EFI shell (IA64 only), collect the CPU registers by performing the following steps:

  1. `shell> errdump mca > mca.out.`
  2. `shell> errdump init > init.out.`
  3. Send to hardware vendor for review.

Although these are the key conditions and steps to remember, every troubleshooting process is unique and should be evaluated individually to determine the ideal troubleshooting path. Of course, before consuming vast resources troubleshooting a problem, confirm that you are running on the latest supported kernel and that all software/hardware combinations are in their vendor-supported configurations.

3

Performance Tools

This chapter explains how to use the wealth of performance tools available for Linux. We also explain what the information from each tool means. Even if you are already using top or sar, you can probably learn some things from this chapter.

You should make a habit of using these tools if you are not already doing so. You need to know how to troubleshoot a performance problem, of course, but you should also regularly look for changes in the key metrics that can indicate a problem. You can use these tools to measure the performance impact of a new application. Just like looking at the temperature gauge in a car, you need to keep an eye on the performance metrics of your Linux systems. The tools we cover are:

- top
- sar
- vmstat
- iostat
- free

These tools can be run as a normal user. They all take advantage of the /proc filesystem to obtain their data. These performance tools are delivered with a few rpms. The procps rpm supplies top, free, and vmstat. The sysstat rpm provides sar and iostat.

The top command is a great interactive utility for monitoring performance. It provides a few summary lines of overall Linux performance, but reporting process information is where top shines. The process display can be customized extensively. You can add fields, sort the list of processes by different metrics, and even kill processes from top.

The sar utility offers the capability to monitor just about everything. It has over 15 separate reporting categories including CPU, disk, networking, process, swap, and more.

The vmstat command reports extensive information about memory and swap usage. It also reports CPU and a bit of I/O information. As you might guess, iostat reports storage input/output (I/O) statistics.

These commands cover a lot of the same ground. We discuss how to use the commands, and we explain the reports that each command generates. We don't discuss all 15 sar syntaxes, but we cover the most common ones.

top

The top command is one of the most familiar performance tools. Most system administrators run top to see how their Linux and UNIX systems are performing. The top utility provides a great way to monitor the performance of processes and Linux as a whole. It is more accurate to call Linux processes tasks, but in this chapter we call them processes because that is what the tools call them.[1] top can be run as a normal user as well as root. Figure 3-1 shows typical top output from an idle system.

```
 dave@fisher:~
16:28:44  up 16 days,  7:33,  2 users,  load average: 0.67, 0.21, 0.07
73 processes: 72 sleeping, 1 running, 0 zombie, 0 stopped
CPU states:  cpu    user    nice  system    irq  softirq  iowait    idle
             total  60.7%   0.0%    6.2%   0.0%    0.0%    0.0%    33.0%
Mem:   511996k av,   499028k used,    12968k free,        0k shrd,    59672k buff
                     387556k actv,    68492k in_d,     9508k in_c
Swap:  105832k av,     2500k used,   103332k free                   343048k cached

  PID USER     PRI  NI  SIZE  RSS SHARE STAT %CPU %MEM   TIME CPU COMMAND
 9979 dave      16   0  1120 1120   896 R    0.9  0.2   0:01   0 top
10105 root      23   0   568  568   492 S    0.3  0.1   0:00   0 sleep
    1 root      15   0   512  512   452 S    0.0  0.1   0:04   0 init
    2 root      15   0     0    0     0 SW   0.0  0.0   0:02   0 keventd
    3 root      15   0     0    0     0 SW   0.0  0.0   0:00   0 kapmd
    4 root      34  19     0    0     0 SWN  0.0  0.0   0:00   0 ksoftirqd/0
    7 root      15   0     0    0     0 SW   0.0  0.0   0:01   0 bdflush
    5 root      15   0     0    0     0 SW   0.0  0.0   3:15   0 kswapd
    6 root      15   0     0    0     0 SW   0.0  0.0   3:45   0 kscand
    8 root      15   0     0    0     0 SW   0.0  0.0   0:00   0 kupdated
    9 root      25   0     0    0     0 SW   0.0  0.0   0:00   0 mdrecoveryd
   13 root      15   0     0    0     0 SW   0.0  0.0   3:21   0 kjournald
   72 root      25   0     0    0     0 SW   0.0  0.0   0:00   0 khubd
  704 root      15   0     0    0     0 SW   0.0  0.0   0:00   0 kjournald
 1071 root      15   0   576  576   492 S    0.0  0.1   0:31   0 syslogd
```

Figure 3-1 top output

The top display has two parts. The first third or so shows information about Linux as a whole. The remaining lines are filled with individual process information. If the window is stretched, more processes are shown to fill the screen.

Much general Linux information can be obtained by using several other commands instead of top. It is nice to have it all on one screen from one command, though. The first line shows the load average for the last one, five, and fifteen minutes. Load average indicates how many processes are running on a CPU or waiting to run. The uptime command can be used to display load averages as well. Next comes process information, followed by CPU, memory, and swap. The memory and swap information is similar to the free command output. After we determine memory and CPU usage, the next question is, which processes are using it?

Most of the process information can be obtained from the ps command too, but top provides a nicer format that is easier to read. The most useful interactive top command is h for help, which lists top's other interactive commands.

Adding and Removing Fields

Fields can be added or removed from the display. The process output can be sorted by CPU, memory, or other metric. This is a great way to see what process is hogging memory. The top syntax and interactive options differ among Linux distributions. The help command quickly lists what commands are available. Many interactive options are available. Spend some time trying them out.

Figure 3-2 shows a Red Hat Enterprise Linux ES release 3 help screen.

The f command adds or removes fields from the top output. Figure 3-3 is a Red Hat Enterprise Linux ES release 3 help screen showing what fields can be added.

Figure 3-4 shows a SUSE Linux 9.0 top help screen. You can see that the commands they offer differ greatly.

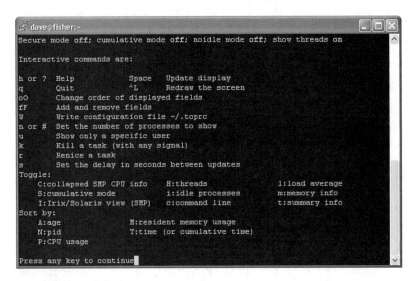

Figure 3-2 top help screen

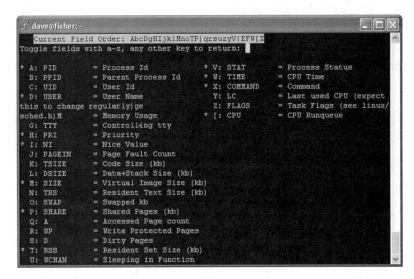

Figure 3-3 top add/remove fields screen

```
 dave@sawnee:~                                                      _ □ X
Help for Interactive Commands - procps version 3.1.11
Window 1:Def: Cumulative mode Off.  System: Delay 3.0 secs; Secure mode Off.

  Z,B        Global: 'Z' change color mappings; 'B' disable/enable bold
  l,t,m      Toggle Summaries: 'l' load avg; 't' task/cpu stats; 'm' mem info
  1,I        Toggle SMP view: '1' single/separate states; 'I' Irix/Solaris mode

  f,o     .  Fields/Columns: 'f' add or remove; 'o' change display order
  F or O  .  Select sort field
  <,>     .  Move sort field: '<' next col left; '>' next col right
  R       .  Toggle normal/reverse sort
  c,i,S   .  Toggle: 'c' cmd name/line; 'i' idle tasks; 'S' cumulative time
  x,y     .  Toggle highlights: 'x' sort field; 'y' running tasks
  z,b     .  Toggle: 'z' color/mono; 'b' bold/reverse (only if 'x' or 'y')
  u       .  Show specific user only
  n or #  .  Set maximum tasks displayed

  k,r        Manipulate tasks: 'k' kill; 'r' renice
  d or s     Set update interval
  W          Write configuration file
  q          Quit
             ( commands shown with '.' require a visible task display window )
Press 'h' or '?' for help with Windows,
any other key to continue █
```

Figure 3-4 SUSE top help screen

Output Explained

Let's take a look at what the information from top means. We'll use the following output from top as an example:

```
16:30:30  up 16 days,  7:35,  2 users,  load average: 0.54, 0.30, 0.11
73 processes: 72 sleeping, 1 running, 0 zombie, 0 stopped
CPU states:  cpu     user    nice   system    irq  softirq  iowait    idle
            total    13.3%   0.0%   20.9%    0.0%   0.0%    0.0%    65.7%
Mem:   511996k av,  498828k used,   13168k free,  0k shrd,  59712k buff
                    387576k actv,   68516k in_d,  9508k in_c
Swap:  105832k av,    2500k used,  103332k free            343056k cached


  PID USER     PRI  NI   SIZE   RSS SHARE STAT %CPU %MEM    TIME CPU COMMAND
10250 dave      20   0   1104  1104   800 R     3.8  0.2   0:00   0 top
10252 root      23   0    568   568   492 S     0.9  0.1   0:00   0 sleep
    1 root      15   0    512   512   452 S     0.0  0.1   0:04   0 init
```

The first line from top displays the load average information:

```
16:30:30  up 16 days,  7:35,  2 users,  load average: 0.54, 0.30, 0.11
```

This output is similar to the output from uptime. You can see how long Linux has been up, the time, and the number of users. The 1-, 5-, and 15-minute load averages are displayed as well. Next, the process summary is displayed:

```
73 processes: 72 sleeping, 1 running, 0 zombie, 0 stopped
```

We see 73 total processes. Of those, 72 are sleeping, and one is running. There are no zombies or stopped processes. A process becomes a zombie when it exits and its parent has not waited for it with the wait(2) or waitpid(2) functions. This often happens because the parent process exits before its children. Zombies don't take up resources other than the entry in the process table. Stopped processes are processes that have been sent the STOP signal. See the signal(7) man page for more information.

Next up is the CPU information:

```
CPU states:  cpu     user    nice  system    irq  softirq  iowait     idle
             total   13.3%    0.0%   20.9%   0.0%     0.0%    0.0%    65.7%
```

The CPU lines describe how the CPUs spend their time. The top command reports the percentage of CPU time spent in user or kernel mode, running niced processes, and in idleness. The iowait column shows the percentage of time that the processor was waiting for I/O to complete while no process was executing on the CPU. The irq and softirq columns indicate time spent serving hardware and software interrupts. Linux kernels earlier than 2.6 don't report irq, softirq, and iowait.

The memory information is next:

```
Mem:    511996k av, 498828k used,   13168k free,     0k shrd,    59712k buff
               387576k actv,  68516k in_d,    9508k in_c
```

The first three metrics give a summary of memory usage. They list total usable memory, used memory, and free memory. These are all you need to determine whether Linux is low on memory.

The next five metrics identify how the used memory is allocated. The shrd field shows shared memory usage and buff is memory used in buffers. Memory that has been allocated to the kernel or user processes can be in three different states: active, inactive dirty, and inactive clean. Active, actv in top, indicates that the memory has been used recently. Inactive dirty, in_d in top, indicates that the memory has not been used recently and may be reclaimed. In order for the memory to be reclaimed, its contents must be written to disk. This process is called "laundering" and can be called a fourth temporary state for memory. Once laundered, the inactive dirty memory becomes inactive clean, in_c in top. Available at the time of this writing is an excellent white paper by Norm Murray and Neil Horman titled "Understanding Virtual Memory in Red Hat Enterprise Linux 3" at http://people.redhat.com/nhorman/papers/rhel3_vm.pdf.

The swap information is next:

```
Swap:   105832k av,     2500k used,   103332k free          343056k cached
```

The av field is the total amount of swap that is available for use, followed by the amount used and amount free. Last is the amount of memory used for cache by the kernel.

The rest of the top display is process information:

```
  PID USER      PRI  NI  SIZE  RSS SHARE STAT %CPU %MEM   TIME CPU COMMAND
10250 dave       20   0  1104 1104   888 R     3.8  0.2   0:00   0 top
10252 root       23   0   568  568   492 S     0.9  0.1   0:00   0 sleep
    1 root       15   0   512  512   452 S     0.0  0.1   0:04   0 init
```

top shows as many processes as can fit on the screen. The field descriptions are described well in the top(1) man page. Table 3-1 provides a summary of the fields.

Saving Customization

A very nice top feature is the capability to save the current configuration. Change the display as you please using the interactive commands and then press w to save the view.

Table 3-1 top Process Fields

Field	Description
PID	Process id number
USER	User name of the process owner
PRI	Priority of the process
SIZE	The size in kilobytes of the process including its code, stack, and data area
RSS	Total amount of memory in kilobytes used by the process
SHARE	The amount of shared memory used by the process
STAT	State of the process, normally R for running or S for sleeping
%CPU	Percentage of CPU this process has used since the last screen update
%MEM	Percentage of memory this process uses
TIME	Amount of CPU time this process has used since the process started
CPU	The CPU where the process last executed
COMMAND	The command being executed

top writes a .toprc file in the user's home directory that saves the configuration. The next time this user starts top, the same display options are used.

top also looks for a default configuration file, /etc/toprc. This file is a global configuration file and is read by top when any user runs the utility. This file can be used to cause top to run in secure mode and also to set the refresh delay. Secure mode prevents non-root users from killing or changing the nice value of processes. It also prevents non-root users from changing the refresh value of top. A sample /etc/toprc file for our Red Hat Enterprise Linux ES release 3 looks like the following:

```
$ cat /etc/toprc
s3
```

The s indicates secure mode, and the 3 specifies three-second refresh intervals. Other distributions may have different formats for /etc/toprc. The capability to kill processes is a pretty nice feature. If some user has a runaway process, the top command makes it easy to find and kill. Run top, show all the processes for a user with the u command, and then use k to kill it. top not only is a good performance monitoring tool, but it can also be used to improve performance by killing those offensive processes.

Batch Mode

top can also be run in batch mode. Try running the following command:

```
$ top -n 1 -b >/tmp/top.out
```

The -n 1 tells top to only show one iteration, and the -b option indicates that the output should be in text suitable for writing to a file or piping to another program such as less. Something like the following two-line script would make a nice cron job:

```
# cat /home/dave/top_metrics.sh
echo "**** " 'date' " ****" >> /var/log/top/top.'date +%d'.out
/usr/bin/top -n 1 -b >> /var/log/top/top.'date +%d'.out
```

We could add it to crontab and collect output every 15 minutes.

```
# crontab -l
*/15 * * * * /home/dave/top_metrics.sh
```

The batch output makes it easy to take a thorough look at what is running while enjoying a good cup of coffee. All the processes are listed, and the output isn't refreshing every five seconds. If a .toprc configuration file exists in the user's home directory, it is used to format the display. The following output came from the top batch mode running on a multi-CPU Linux server. Note that we don't show all 258 processes from the top output.

```
10:17:21  up 125 days, 10:10,  4 users,  load average: 3.60, 3.46, 3.73
258 processes: 252 sleeping, 6 running, 0 zombie, 0 stopped
CPU states:  cpu    user   nice  system   irq  softirq  iowait    idle
             total  41.0%  0.0%   21.4%  0.4%    0.4%    0.0%    36.5%
             cpu00  36.7%  0.0%   22.6%  1.8%    0.0%    0.0%    38.6%
             cpu01  46.2%  0.0%   17.9%  0.0%    0.9%    0.0%    34.9%
             cpu02  32.0%  0.0%   28.3%  0.0%    0.0%    0.0%    39.6%
             cpu03  49.0%  0.0%   16.9%  0.0%    0.9%    0.0%    33.0%
Mem:  4357776k av, 4321156k used,   36620k free,      0k shrd,  43860k buff
               3261592k actv,  625088k in_d,   80324k in_c
Swap: 1048536k av,  191848k used,  856688k free          3920940k cached
```

PID	USER	PRI	NI	SIZE	RSS	SHARE	STAT	%CPU	%MEM	TIME	CPU	COMMAND
17599	wwrmn	21	0	9160	6900	1740	R	12.2	0.1	0:01	1	logsw
1003	coedev	15	-10	71128	65M	66200	S <	8.0	1.5	414:42	2	vmware-vmx
17471	wwrmn	15	0	10116	7868	1740	S	6.8	0.1	0:12	2	logsw
17594	wwrmn	18	0	9616	7356	1740	R	4.4	0.1	0:01	0	logsw
6498	coedev	25	0	43108	36M	33840	R	4.0	0.8	9981m	1	vmware-vmx
17595	wwrmn	17	0	8892	6632	1740	S	3.0	0.1	0:01	3	logsw
17446	wwrmn	15	0	10196	7960	1740	S	2.8	0.1	0:13	3	logsw
17473	wwrmn	15	0	9196	6948	1740	S	2.8	0.1	0:02	1	logsw
17477	wwrmn	15	0	9700	7452	1740	S	2.3	0.1	0:04	2	logsw
958	coedev	15	-10	71128	65M	66200	S <	2.1	1.5	93:53	3	vmware-vmx
7828	coedev	15	-10	38144	33M	33524	S <	1.8	0.7	4056m	1	vmware-vmx
6505	coedev	25	0	0	0	0	RW	1.8	0.0	3933m	1	vmware-rtc
7821	coedev	15	-10	38144	33M	33524	S <	1.6	0.7	6766m	1	vmware-vmx
6478	coedev	15	-10	43108	36M	33840	S <	1.6	0.8	6224m	0	vmware-vmx
17449	wwrmn	15	0	9820	7572	1740	S	1.6	0.1	0:07	3	logsw
7783	coedev	15	0	47420	15M	1632	S	1.4	0.3	1232m	3	vmware
6497	coedev	15	-10	43108	36M	33840	S <	0.9	0.8	3905m	1	vmware-vmx
1002	coedev	15	-10	71128	65M	66200	S <	0.9	1.5	59:54	2	vmware-vmx
17600	jtk	20	0	1276	1276	884	R	0.9	0.0	0:00	2	top
7829	coedev	25	0	38144	33M	33524	R	0.7	0.7	6688m	0	vmware-vmx
1	root	15	0	256	228	200	S	0.0	0.0	2:25	0	init

By now you can see why top is such a popular performance tool. The interactive nature of top and the ability to easily customize the output makes it a great resource for identifying problems.

sar

sar is a great general performance monitoring tool. sar can output data for almost everything Linux does. The sar command is delivered in the sysstat rpm. We use sysstat version 5.0.5 in our examples. This is one of the more recent versions listed as stable. Look at the sysstat home page at http://perso.wanadoo.fr/sebastien.godard/ for release information and downloads.

sar can display performance data for CPU, run queue, disk I/O, paging (swap), memory, CPU interrupts, networking, and more. The most important sar feature is the capability to create a data file. Every Linux system should collect sar data from cron jobs. The sar data file provides a system administrator with historical performance information. This feature is very important, and it separates sar from the other performance tools. If a nightly batch job runs twice as long as normal, you won't find out until the next morning (unless you get paged). You need the ability to look at performance data from 12 hours ago. The sar data collector provides this ability. Many reporting syntaxes exist, but let's look at data collection first.

sar Data Collector

sar data collection is done with a binary executable and two scripts in /usr/lib/sa. The sar data collector is a binary executable located at /usr/lib/sa/sadc. The job of sadc is to write to the data collection file /var/log/sa/. Several options can be supplied to sadc. A common syntax is:

/usr/lib/sa/sadc *interval iterations file name*

interval is the number of seconds between sampling. iterations is the number of samples to take. file name specifies the output file. A simple sadc syntax is /usr/lib/sa/sadc 360 5 /tmp/sadc.out. This command takes five samples at five-minute intervals and stores them in /tmp/sadc.out. We should collect the samples on a regular basis, so we need a script to be run by cron. We should put the samples in a place that makes sense, like we did with the top script from the previous section. Fortunately, the sysstat rpm provides the /usr/lib/sa/sa1 script to do all this.

The sa1(8) man page is much longer than the sa1 script itself. /usr/lib/sa/sa1 is a very simple script that runs sadc with the syntax sadc -F -L 1 1 /var/log/sa/sa## where ## is the day of the month. Older versions of sa1 use the output from date +.%Y_%m_%d as the file suffix. The -F option causes sadc to force creation of the output file if necessary. The -L locks the output file before writing to it to prevent corrupting the file when two sadc processes are running at the same time. Older versions of sadc didn't have the -L option, so the sa1 script performed manual locking. The only options for the sa1 script are the interval between samples and the number of iterations to sample. A cron file (/etc/cron.d/sysstat) is supplied with sysstat. It differs between sysstat versions. The following are the entries for the version 5.0.5 of sysstat:

```
# cat /etc/cron.d/sysstat
# run system activity accounting tool every 10 minutes
*/10 * * * * root /usr/lib/sa/sa1 1 1
# generate a daily summary of process accounting at 23:53
53 23 * * * root /usr/lib/sa/sa2 -A
```

You can see that after the sysstat rpm is installed, sadc begins taking samples. The sysstat home page is http://perso.wanadoo.fr/sebastien.godard/.[2] The documentation link offers the following crontab suggestions as of January 14, 2006:

```
# 8am-7pm activity reports every 10 minutes during weekdays.
0 8-18 * * 1-5 /usr/lib/sa/sa1 600 6 &

# 7pm-8am activity reports every an hour during weekdays.
0 19-7 * * 1-5 /usr/lib/sa/sa1 &

# Activity reports every an hour on Saturday and Sunday.
0 * * * 0,6 /usr/lib/sa/sa1 &

# Daily summary prepared at 19:05
5 19 * * * /usr/lib/sa/sa2 -A &
```

The crontab example in Sebastien Godard's Web site suggests taking a sample every 10 minutes from 8 a.m. to 6 p.m. weekdays and every hour otherwise. (Note: The crontab comment says 7pm but 18:00 is 6pm.) If disk space in /var is sufficient, you may want to sample every 10 minutes every hour of the day. If the weekend backups are slower, then an hourly sadc sample may not be very helpful.

Now let's look at the more popular reporting syntaxes.

CPU Statistics

The `sar -u` output shows CPU information. The `-u` option is the default for `sar`. The output shows CPU utilization as a percentage. Table 3-2 explains the output.

Table 3-2 `sar -u` Fields

Field	Description
CPU	CPU number
%user	Time spent running processes in user mode
%nice	Time spent running niced processes
%system	Time spent running processes in kernel mode (system)
%iowait	Time during which the processor was waiting for I/O to complete while no process was executing on the CPU
%idle	Time during which no process was executing on the CPU

This should look familiar. It is the same CPU information as in top reports. The following shows the output format:

```
[root@fisher dave]# sar 5 10
Linux 2.4.21-27.EL (fisher)    04/30/2005
```

	CPU	%user	%nice	%system	%iowait	%idle
02:03:20 PM						
02:03:25 PM	all	36.80	0.00	4.20	0.00	59.00
02:03:30 PM	all	37.80	0.00	5.20	2.20	54.80
02:03:35 PM	all	55.40	0.00	4.40	3.00	37.20
02:03:40 PM	all	53.60	0.00	6.20	0.00	40.20
02:03:45 PM	all	37.20	0.00	6.60	1.00	55.20
02:03:50 PM	all	36.00	0.00	4.40	2.20	56.80
02:03:55 PM	all	51.00	0.00	4.20	1.00	43.80
02:04:00 PM	all	55.60	0.00	4.20	0.00	40.20
02:04:05 PM	all	40.60	0.00	8.00	1.20	50.20
02:04:10 PM	all	36.60	0.00	4.20	2.20	57.00
Average:	all	44.12	0.00	5.16	1.28	49.44

The 5 10 causes sar to take 10 samples at 5-second intervals. The first column of any sar report is a timestamp.

We could have looked at the file created with sadc by using the -f option. This sar syntax shows the output from sar -f /var/log/sa/sa21:

```
[dave@fisher dave]$ sar -f /var/log/sa/sa21|head -n 20
Linux 2.4.21-20.EL (fisher)   04/21/2005
```

12:00:00 AM	CPU	%user	%nice	%system	%iowait	%idle
12:10:00 AM	all	0.23	0.00	0.23	0.02	99.52
12:20:00 AM	all	0.22	0.00	0.20	0.01	99.57
12:30:01 AM	all	0.21	0.00	0.19	0.01	99.59
12:40:00 AM	all	0.23	0.00	0.22	0.02	99.54
12:50:01 AM	all	0.19	0.00	0.28	0.01	99.52
01:00:00 AM	all	0.22	0.00	0.18	0.01	99.59
01:10:00 AM	all	0.40	0.00	0.25	0.02	99.34
01:20:00 AM	all	0.20	0.00	0.25	0.01	99.53
01:30:00 AM	all	0.20	0.00	0.23	0.01	99.56
01:40:00 AM	all	0.22	0.00	0.21	0.02	99.56
01:50:00 AM	all	0.22	0.00	0.20	0.02	99.56
02:00:00 AM	all	0.22	0.00	0.19	0.01	99.58
02:10:00 AM	all	0.23	0.00	0.24	0.02	99.50
02:20:01 AM	all	0.22	0.00	0.25	0.01	99.52
02:30:00 AM	all	0.19	0.00	0.22	0.01	99.57
02:40:00 AM	all	0.22	0.00	0.22	0.01	99.55
02:50:00 AM	all	0.21	0.00	0.21	0.01	99.56

The sar command can break down this information for each CPU in a multi-CPU Linux box too, as the following sar -u -P ALL 5 5 output demonstrates:

```
Linux 2.4.21-20.ELsmp (doughboy)      04/13/2005
```

10:17:56 AM	CPU	%user	%nice	%system	%iowait	%idle
10:18:01 AM	all	26.41	0.00	23.46	0.00	50.13
10:18:01 AM	0	23.20	0.00	32.80	0.00	44.00
10:18:01 AM	1	26.60	0.00	20.80	0.00	52.60
10:18:01 AM	2	25.80	0.00	21.00	0.00	53.20
10:18:01 AM	3	30.06	0.00	19.24	0.00	50.70

10:18:01 AM	CPU	%user	%nice	%system	%iowait	%idle
10:18:06 AM	all	17.70	0.00	24.15	0.00	58.15
10:18:06 AM	0	22.40	0.00	26.40	0.00	51.20
10:18:06 AM	1	15.20	0.00	24.60	0.00	60.20
10:18:06 AM	2	19.00	0.00	20.00	0.00	61.00
10:18:06 AM	3	14.20	0.00	25.60	0.00	60.20
10:18:06 AM	CPU	%user	%nice	%system	%iowait	%idle
10:18:11 AM	all	13.69	0.00	23.74	0.05	62.52
10:18:11 AM	0	9.00	0.00	27.40	0.00	63.60
10:18:11 AM	1	19.40	0.00	20.40	0.20	60.00
10:18:11 AM	2	13.20	0.00	21.00	0.00	65.80
10:18:11 AM	3	13.17	0.00	26.15	0.00	60.68
10:18:11 AM	CPU	%user	%nice	%system	%iowait	%idle
10:18:16 AM	all	16.40	0.00	23.00	0.00	60.60
10:18:16 AM	0	16.60	0.00	18.00	0.00	65.40
10:18:16 AM	1	15.00	0.00	23.00	0.00	62.00
10:18:16 AM	2	19.40	0.00	19.80	0.00	60.80
10:18:16 AM	3	14.60	0.00	31.20	0.00	54.20
10:18:16 AM	CPU	%user	%nice	%system	%iowait	%idle
10:18:21 AM	all	32.60	0.00	22.10	0.00	45.30
10:18:21 AM	0	30.80	0.00	24.40	0.00	44.80
10:18:21 AM	1	34.80	0.00	24.00	0.00	41.20
10:18:21 AM	2	32.00	0.00	20.20	0.00	47.80
10:18:21 AM	3	32.80	0.00	19.80	0.00	47.40
Average:	CPU	%user	%nice	%system	%iowait	%idle
Average:	all	21.36	0.00	23.29	0.01	55.34
Average:	0	20.40	0.00	25.80	0.00	53.80
Average:	1	22.20	0.00	22.56	0.04	55.20
Average:	2	21.88	0.00	20.40	0.00	57.72
Average:	3	20.96	0.00	24.40	0.00	54.64

Disk I/O Statistics

sar is a good tool for looking at disk I/O. The following shows a sample of sar disk I/O output.

```
[dave@fisher dave]$ sar -d 5 2
Linux 2.4.21-27.EL (fisher)      04/29/2005


04:22:03 PM        DEV       tps    rd_sec/s   wr_sec/s
04:22:08 PM      dev3-0      1.40      0.00     784.00
04:22:08 PM      dev3-1      0.00      0.00       0.00
04:22:08 PM      dev3-2      1.40      0.00     784.00
04:22:08 PM      dev3-3      0.00      0.00       0.00
04:22:08 PM      dev3-64     0.00      0.00       0.00
04:22:08 PM      dev3-65     0.00      0.00       0.00


04:22:08 PM        DEV       tps    rd_sec/s   wr_sec/s
04:22:13 PM      dev3-0     34.60      0.00    4219.20
04:22:13 PM      dev3-1      0.00      0.00       0.00
04:22:13 PM      dev3-2     34.60      0.00    4219.20
04:22:13 PM      dev3-3      0.00      0.00       0.00
04:22:13 PM      dev3-64     0.00      0.00       0.00
04:22:13 PM      dev3-65     0.00      0.00       0.00


Average:           DEV       tps    rd_sec/s   wr_sec/s
Average:         dev3-0     18.00      0.00    2501.60
Average:         dev3-1      0.00      0.00       0.00
Average:         dev3-2     18.00      0.00    2501.60
Average:         dev3-3      0.00      0.00       0.00
Average:         dev3-64     0.00      0.00       0.00
Average:         dev3-65     0.00      0.00       0.00
```

The -d shows disk I/O information. The 5 2 options are interval and iterations, just like the sar data collector. Table 3-3 lists the fields and descriptions.

Table 3-3 sar -d Fields

Field	Description
DEV	Disk device
tps	Transfers per second (or IOs per second)
rd_sec/s	512-byte reads per second
wr_sec/s	512-byte writes per second

512 is just a unit of measure. It doesn't imply that all disk I/O is in 512-byte chunks. The DEV column is the disk device in the format dev#-#, where the first # is a device major number, and the second # is a minor or sequential number. sar uses the minor number with kernels greater than 2.5. For example, we saw dev3-0 and dev3-1 in the sar -d output. These correspond to /dev/hda and /dev/hda1. Look at the following entries in /dev:

```
brw-rw----   1 root     disk      3,   0 Jun 24  2004 hda
brw-rw----   1 root     disk      3,   1 Jun 24  2004 hda1
```

/dev/hda has major number 3 and minor number 0. hda1 has a major number of 3 and a minor number of 1.

Networking Statistics

sar offers four different syntax options to display networking information. The -n option takes four different switches: DEV, EDEV, SOCK, and FULL. DEV displays networking interface information, EDEV shows statistics about network errors, SOCK shows socket information, and FULL shows all three switches. They can be used separately or together. Table 3-4 shows the fields reported with the -n DEV option.

Table 3-4   sar -n DEV Fields

Field	Description
IFACE	LAN interface
rxpck/s	Packets received per second
txpck/s	Packets transmitted per second
rxbyt/s	Bytes received per second
txbyt/s	Bytes transmitted per second
rxcmp/s	Compressed packets received per second
txcmp/s	Compressed packets transmitted per second
rxmcst/s	Multicast packets received per second

The following is the sar output using the -n DEV option:

```
# sar -n DEV 5 3
Linux 2.4.21-20.EL (fisher)      04/20/2005


03:39:18 AM    IFACE  rxpck/s   txpck/s   rxbyt/s   txbyt/s   rxcmp/s
txcmp/
s   rxmcst/s
03:39:23 AM      lo    0.00      0.00      0.00      0.00      0.00
0.0
0      0.00
03:39:23 AM    eth0   36.80      0.00   8412.20     10.80      0.00
0.0
0      0.00
03:39:23 AM    IFACE  rxpck/s   txpck/s   rxbyt/s   txbyt/s   rxcmp/s
txcmp/
s   rxmcst/s
03:39:28 AM      lo    0.00      0.00      0.00      0.00      0.00
0.0
0      0.00
03:39:28 AM    eth0   50.20      1.80   9798.20    526.60      0.00
0.0
0      0.00
```

```
03:39:28 AM      IFACE    rxpck/s   txpck/s   rxbyt/s   txbyt/s   rxcmp/s
txcmp/
s   rxmcst/s
03:39:33 AM        lo     0.00      0.00      0.00      0.00      0.00
0.0
0      0.00
03:39:33 AM       eth0    38.20     1.80      8882.60   400.80    0.00
0.0
0      0.00


Average:         IFACE    rxpck/s   txpck/s   rxbyt/s   txbyt/s   rxcmp/s
txcmp/
s   rxmcst/s
Average:           lo     0.00      0.00      0.00      0.00      0.00
0.0
0      0.00
Average:          eth0    41.73     1.20      9031.00   312.73    0.00
0.0
0      0.00
```

Information about networking errors can be displayed with sar -n EDEV. Table 3-5 lists the fields displayed.

```
# sar -n EDEV 5 3
Linux 2.4.21-20.EL (fisher)     04/17/2005


10:41:44 AM      IFACE    rxerr/s   txerr/s    coll/s   rxdrop/s  txdrop/s
txcarr/s  rxfram/s  rxfifo/s  txfifo/s
10:41:49 AM        lo     0.00      0.00       0.00      0.00      0.00
0.00      0.00      0.00      0.00
10:41:49 AM       eth0    0.00      0.00       0.00      0.00      0.00
0.00      0.00      0.00      0.00


10:41:49 AM      IFACE    rxerr/s   txerr/s    coll/s   rxdrop/s  txdrop/s
txcarr/s  rxfram/s  rxfifo/s  txfifo/s
10:41:54 AM        lo     0.00      0.00       0.00      0.00      0.00
0.00      0.00      0.00      0.00
10:41:54 AM       eth0    0.00      0.00       0.00      0.00      0.00
0.00      0.00      0.00      0.00
```

```
10:41:54 AM      IFACE   rxerr/s   txerr/s   coll/s  rxdrop/s  txdrop/s
txcarr/s  rxfram/s  rxfifo/s  txfifo/s
10:41:59 AM        lo      0.00      0.00     0.00      0.00      0.00
0.00      0.00      0.00      0.00
10:41:59 AM      eth0      0.00      0.00     0.00      0.00      0.00
0.00      0.00      0.00      0.00

Average:         IFACE   rxerr/s   txerr/s   coll/s  rxdrop/s  txdrop/s
txcarr/s  rxfram/s  rxfifo/s  txfifo/s
Average:           lo      0.00      0.00     0.00      0.00      0.00
0.00      0.00      0.00      0.00
Average:         eth0      0.00      0.00     0.00      0.00      0.00
0.00      0.00      0.00      0.00
```

Table 3-5 sar -n EDEV Fields

Field	Description
IFACE	LAN interface
rxerr/s	Bad packets received per second
txerr/s	Bad packets transmitted per second
coll/s	Collisions per second
rxdrop/s	Received packets dropped per second because buffers were full
txdrop/s	Transmitted packets dropped per second because buffers were full
txcarr/s	Carrier errors per second while transmitting packets
rxfram/s	Frame alignment errors on received packets per second
rxfifo/s	FIFO overrun errors per second on received packets
txfifo/s	FIFO overrun errors per second on transmitted packets

The SOCK argument displays IPCS socket information. Table 3-6 lists the fields displayed and their meanings.

Table 3-6 sar -n SOCK Fields

Field	Description
totsck	Total number of sockets used
tcpsck	Number of TCP sockets used
udpsck	Number of UDP sockets used
rawsck	Number of raw sockets used
ip-frag	Number of IP fragments used

```
# sar -n SOCK 5 3
Linux 2.4.21-144-default (sawnee)        04/17/05

16:00:56        totsck    tcpsck    udpsck    rawsck    ip-frag
16:01:01          117        11         8         0          0
16:01:06          117        11         8         0          0
16:01:11          117        11         8         0          0
Average:          117        11         8         0          0
```

sar can generate many other reports. It is worth reading through the sar(1) man page to see whether there are any others you want to start using.

vmstat

The vmstat command is yet another way to show Linux performance metrics. vmstat reports a lot of information, and it can be difficult to understand what it is telling you.

The output is separated into six categories: process, memory, swap, I/O, system, and CPU. Like iostat, the first sample is an average since the last reboot. Here is a typical vmstat output:

```
# vmstat -m 5 3
procs                   memory      swap        io      system        cpu
 r  b  swpd  free buff  cache   si   so   bi  bo   in    cs us sy wa id
 3  0   185    23  136   3679    0    0    9  10    0     4  8 18 10 17
 1  0   185    22  136   3676    0    0  285  76 2671 28571 18 19  0 63
 1  0   185    22  136   3670    0    0  333  41 2876 24252 36 17  0 46
```

The -m option causes the memory fields to be shown in megabytes. vmstat takes the sample interval and count parameters as many of the other performance commands do.

The process (procs) information has two columns. The r column is the number of runable processes. The b column is the number of blocked processes.

The memory section has four fields reporting how virtual memory is used. Table 3-7 lists them along with their meaning.

Table 3-7 vmstat memory Fields

Field	Description
swpd	Amount of used swap space
free	Amount of free RAM
buff	Amount of RAM used for buffers
cache	Amount of RAM used for filesystem cache

Next up are the swap metrics. Swap is an obsolete term but one that apparently won't go away. A swap involves paging all the memory consumed by a process to or from disk at one time. What a performance hit this would be. What Linux does instead is page to and from disk as needed in small chunks. Thus, we should probably stop saying memory swapped to disk and start saying memory paged to disk. Either way, Table 3-8 explains the fields.

Table 3-8 `vmstat swap` Fields

Field	Description
si	Amount paged from disk to memory
so	Amount paged to disk from memory

After swap are the two I/O fields. This section provides a short summary to help you determine whether Linux is busy doing a lot of disk I/O. `vmstat` only provides two fields showing the volume of data moving to and from disk (see Table 3-9).

Table 3-9 `vmstat io` Fields

Field	Description
bi	Blocks in from disk
bo	Blocks out to disk

The system fields provide a summary of how busy the Linux kernel is performing process management. Interrupts and context switches are listed (see Table 3-10). A context switch is the moving of a process off of or onto a CPU.

Table 3-10 `vmstat system` Fields

Field	Description
in	System interrupts
cs	Process context switches

Lastly, CPU state information is expressed as a percentage of total CPU time, as shown in Table 3-11.

Table 3-11 vmstat cpu Fields

Field	Description
us	User mode
sy	Kernel mode
wa	Waiting on I/O
id	Idle

iostat

The iostat command is another tool for looking at disk throughput. Just like sar, iostat can be given the interval and count arguments. The output for the first interval contains metrics for the entire time Linux has been running. This is probably the most unique feature of iostat compared to other performance commands. The following output, from a system that is mostly idle, is a good example. You can see that the hda device has read about 9158MB (18755572*512/1024/1024) since boot up. The Blk columns are 512-byte blocks.

```
# iostat 5 3
Linux 2.4.21-27.EL (fisher)     04/24/2005

avg-cpu:  %user    %nice    %sys %iowait    %idle
          0.47    12.72     2.18    1.16    83.47

Device:            tps  Blk_read/s  Blk_wrtn/s   Blk_read   Blk_wrtn
hda               6.61       93.98      238.64   18755572   47627302
hda1              0.00        0.06        0.00      11394         78
hda2              6.60       93.83      238.53   18726682   47604696
hda3              0.01        0.09        0.11      17176      22528
hdb               0.65       66.86        0.22   13344250      44336
hdb1              0.65       66.86        0.22   13344130      44336
```

```
avg-cpu:   %user    %nice    %sys %iowait    %idle
            0.00     0.00     0.20   0.00    99.80
```

Device:	tps	Blk_read/s	Blk_wrtn/s	Blk_read	Blk_wrtn
hda	0.40	0.00	20.80	0	104
hda1	0.00	0.00	0.00	0	0
hda2	0.40	0.00	20.80	0	104
hda3	0.00	0.00	0.00	0	0
hdb	0.00	0.00	0.00	0	0
hdb1	0.00	0.00	0.00	0	0

```
avg-cpu:   %user    %nice    %sys %iowait    %idle
            0.00     0.00     0.00   0.00   100.00
```

Device:	tps	Blk_read/s	Blk_wrtn/s	Blk_read	Blk_wrtn
hda	0.40	0.00	8.00	0	40
hda1	0.00	0.00	0.00	0	0
hda2	0.40	0.00	8.00	0	40
hda3	0.00	0.00	0.00	0	0
hdb	0.00	0.00	0.00	0	0
hdb1	0.00	0.00	0.00	0	0

With no options, iostat only shows one set of metrics that cover the entire time since boot up.

The CPU information contains basically the same fields as top. The iostat CPU output shows the percentage of time the CPU was executing in user mode, executing niced processes, executing in kernel (system) mode, idle with processes waiting for an I/O to complete, and idle with no processes waiting. The CPU line is a summary for all CPUs.

The disk information is similar to what sar -d provides. The output contains the number of transfers per second (tps), 512-byte block reads per second (Blk_read/s), 512-byte block writes per second (Blk_wrtn/s), and the total number of 512-byte blocks read (Blk_read) and written (Blk_wrtn).

`iostat` offers several switches to tailor output. Some of the most useful are:

-c   Display only CPU line

-d   Display disk lines

-k   Display disk output in kilobytes

-t   Include timestamp in output

-x   Include extended disk metrics in output

These options can be combined. The output from `iostat -tk 5 2` is:

```
# iostat -tk 5 2
Linux 2.4.21-27.EL (fisher)     04/24/2005


Time: 04:34:19 PM
avg-cpu:  %user    %nice    %sys  %iowait    %idle
          0.46    12.67    2.17     1.16    83.53


Device:            tps   kB_read/s   kB_wrtn/s   kB_read     kB_wrtn
hda               6.59       46.81      118.90   9377806    23822991
hda1              0.00        0.03        0.00      5697          39
hda2              6.58       46.73      118.85   9363361    23811688
hda3              0.01        0.04        0.06      8588       11264
hdb               0.65       33.30        0.11   6672125       22168
hdb1              0.65       33.30        0.11   6672065       22168

Time: 04:34:24 PM
avg-cpu:  %user    %nice    %sys  %iowait    %idle
          0.00     0.00    0.20     0.00    99.80


Device:            tps   kB_read/s   kB_wrtn/s   kB_read     kB_wrtn
hda               0.40        0.00       10.40         0          52
hda1              0.00        0.00        0.00         0           0
hda2              0.40        0.00       10.40         0          52
hda3              0.00        0.00        0.00         0           0
hdb               0.00        0.00        0.00         0           0
hdb1              0.00        0.00        0.00         0           0
```

free

The free command outputs memory and swap information, much as the top command does. With no options, free shows the information in kilobytes:

```
# free
             total      used       free     shared    buffers     cached
Mem:        511996    501616      10380          0      60224     359336
-/+ buffers/cache:     82056     429940
Swap:       105832       884     104948
```

The free command has a handful of options. We recommend -mt. The -m switch causes the output to be in megabytes, and the -t switch provides a total line:

```
# free -mt
             total      used       free     shared    buffers     cached
Mem:           499       489         10          0         58        350
-/+ buffers/cache:        80        419
Swap:          103         0        102
Total:         603       490        112
```

Summary

As this chapter shows, the performance tools available in Linux overlap a lot in the information they provide. Memory information can be displayed with top, vmstat, free, and sar, for example. A system administrator doesn't need to be an expert in all the tools. However, it is important to know how to find and interpret all the performance information you need, no matter which tools you decide to use. Thus, we recommend spending a lot of time getting familiar with the tools and their output.

Endnotes

1. The terms processes and tasks are used interchangeably. See Chapter 8, "Linux Processes: Structures, Hangs, and Core Dumps," for more information.

2. The cron lines are taken from http://perso.wanadoo.fr/sebastien.godard/use_en.html.

4

Performance

As a general discussion, performance is much too broad for a single book, let alone a single chapter. However, in this chapter we narrow the focus of performance to a single subject: I/O on a SCSI bus within a storage area network (SAN). SANs are growing in popularity because they assist with storage consolidation and simplification. The main discussion point within the computing industry with regards to storage consolidation is, as it has always been, performance.

In this chapter, we cover basic concepts of SCSI over Fibre Channel Protocol (FCP) using raw/block device files and volume managers. In addition, we cover block size, multipath I/O drivers, and striping with a volume manager, and we conclude our discussion with filesystem performance and CPU loading. We include examples of each topic throughout the chapter.

Start Troubleshooting at the Lowest Layer Possible

A majority of the time, performance issues are related to I/O. However, assuming that a given performance problem is I/O-based is grossly oversimplifying the problem. With any filesystem I/O, there are middle-layer tasks that require resources which may be the source of an I/O contention, such as the volume manager, the volume manager's striping, the filesystem, a multipath I/O driver, or something similar. When troubleshooting a performance problem, always try to simplify the problem by removing as many middle layers as possible. For example, if a particular filesystem is slow, focus your attention first on the disk block or character device performance before considering the volume manager and filesystem performance.

Dissecting a volume with respect to physical device (aka LUN) or lvol into its simplest form is absolutely required when preparing to run any performance test or find a performance concern. In this section, we test the raw speed of a storage device by bypassing the filesystem and volume management layers. We bypass as many layers as possible by using a raw device, better known as a character device. A character device must be bound to a block device through the raw command. To describe "raw" with more detail would include the physical access to a block device bypassing the kernel's block buffer cache. Our first test performs a simple sequential read of a Logical Unit Number (LUN), which resides on a set of spindles, through a single path after we bind the block device to the character. We create a (LUN) character device because we want to test the speed of the disk, not the buffer cache.

note

Today's large arrays define a data storage device in many ways. However, the best description is Logical Device (LDEV). When an LDEV is presented to a host, the device changes names and is referred to as a Logical Unit Number (LUN).

The components used throughout this chapter for examples and scenarios include:

* HP IA64 Superdome (hostname is atlorca2 in this chapter) running SUSE Linux Enterprise Server 9.0 (SLES 9.0)
* 2 Gig Fibre Channel Emulex LP9802 Host Bus Adapter (HBA)
* McData 6064 Fibre Switch with 2Gbps UPMs
* HP XP128 Storage array with 10K RPM RAID 5

The tools for examining the hardware layout and adding and removing LUNs are discussed in Chapter 5, "Adding New Storage via SAN with Reference to PCMCIA and USB." Performance tools were fully discussed in Chapter 3, "Performance Tools," and are used in examples but not explained in detail in this chapter. As stated previously, this chapter's focus is strictly on performance through a system's I/O SCSI bus connected to SAN. Let's look at how to find and bind a block device to a character device using the raw command.

Binding a Raw Device to a Block Device Using the raw Command

The LUN, hereafter called disk, used throughout this example is /dev/sdj, also referred to as /dev/scsi/sdh6-0c0i012. Determine the capacity of the disk through the fdisk command:

```
atlorca2:~ # fdisk -l
Disk /dev/sdj: 250.2 GB, 250219069440 bytes
255 heads, 63 sectors/track, 30420 cylinders
Units = cylinders of 16065 * 512 = 8225280 bytes


   Device Boot      Start         End      Blocks   Id  System
/dev/sdj1               1       30421   244354559+  ee  EFI GPT
```

Use lshw (an open source tool explained in more detail in Chapter 5) to show the device detail:

```
atlorca2:~ # lshw
~~Focus only on single disk test run~~~~
        *-disk:2
                description: SCSI Disk
                product: OPEN-V*4
                vendor: HP
                physical id: 0.0.2
                bus info: scsi@6.0:0.2
                logical name: /dev/sdj
                version: 2111
                size: 233GB
                capacity: 233GB
                capabilities. 5400rpm ### <- just the drivers attempt to
                guess the speed via the standard scsi lun interface...
                Take this at face value.
                configuration: ansiversion=2
```

Linux does not allow raw access to a storage device by default. To remedy this problem, bind the device's block device file to a /dev/raw/rawX character device file to enable I/O to bypass the host buffer cache and achieve a true measurement of device speed through the host's PCI bus (or other bus architecture). This binding can be done by using the raw command. Look at the block device for /dev/sdj:

```
atlorca2:~ # ls -al /dev/sdj
brw-rw----  1 root disk 8, 144 Jun 30  2004 /dev/sdj
```

Take note of the permissions set on the device file brw-rw----. The b means block device, which has a major number 8, which refers to the particular driver in control. The minor number 144 represents the device's location in the scan plus the partition number. Refer to man pages on sd for more info. Continuing with our example, the next step is to bind the /dev/sdj to a raw character device, as depicted in the following:

```
atlorca2:~ # raw /dev/raw/raw8 /dev/sdj
/dev/raw/raw8:  bound to major 8, minor 144
```

Now, issue one of the following commands to view the binding parameters:

```
atlorca2:~ # raw -qa
/dev/raw/raw8:  bound to major 8, minor 144
```

or

```
atlorca2:~ # raw -q /dev/raw/raw8
/dev/raw/raw8:  bound to major 8, minor 144
```

Raw Device Performance

Now that we have bound a block device to a character device, we can measure a read by bypassing the block device, which in turn bypasses the host buffer cache. Recall that our primary objective is to measure performance from the storage device, not from our host cache.

disclaimer

Throughout this chapter, we use a sequential read test provided by the dd command. By no means are we implying that this is the best performance benchmark tool. Every array has certain strengths with regards to I/O size and patterns of sequential versus random, so for benchmarks, we like IOzone (refer to http://www.iozone.org) for a nice benchmark tool. One must be aware that some arrays suffer during heavy, large sequential reads, whereas other arrays thrive in these situations, and the same is true for particular HBAs. In addition, those arrays that suffer on sequential read/writes usually excel at random read/writes, whereas the reverse can be said about the arrays that perform well under sequential read/write operations. In addition, hdparm impacts performance with respect to direct memory access (DMA) and read-ahead along with other parameters. In this chapter, we use the default settings of hdparm. So to reiterate, this chapter uses a simple sequential read/write test to help isolate a performance problem by comparison, and many examples are illustrated.

Our next step requires that we measure a sequential read and calculate time required for the predetermined data allotment. Throughout this chapter, our goal is to determine what factors dictate proper performance of a given device. We focus on average service time, reads per second, writes per second, read sectors per second, average request size, average queue size, and average wait time to evaluate performance. In addition, we discuss the I/Os per second with regard to payload "block" size. For now, we start with a simple sequential read to get our baseline.

Though a filesystem may reside on the device in question, as shown previously in the fdisk-l output, the filesystem cannot be mounted for the test run. If mounted, raw access is denied. Proceed with the following action as illustrated in the next section.

Using the dd Command to Determine Sequential I/O Speed

The dd command provides a simple way to measure sequential I/O performance. The following shows a sequential read of 1GB (1024MB). There are 1024 1MB (1024KB) reads:

```
atlorca2:~ # time -p dd if=/dev/raw/raw8 of=/dev/null bs=1024k
count=1024
```

```
1024+0 records in
1024+0 records out
real 6.77
user 0.00
sys  0.04
```

The megabytes per second can be calculated as follows:

```
1GB/6.77 sec = 151.25MBps
```

For those who are unfamiliar with high-speed enterprise servers and disk storage arrays, 151MBps may seem extremely fast. However, higher speeds can be achieved with proper striping and tuning of the filesystem across multiple spindles. Though we discuss some of those tuning options later, we first need to reduce the previous test to its simplest form. Let us begin with calculating MBps, proceeding with the blocking factors on each I/O frame and discussing service time for each round trip for a given I/O.

In the previous example, we saw 1024 I/Os, where each I/O is defined to have a boundary set to a block size of 1MB, thanks to the bs option on the dd command. Calculating MBps simply takes an arithmetic quotient of 1024MB/6.77 seconds, providing a speedy 151MB/sec. In our testing, cache on the array is clear, providing a nice 151MBps, which is not bad for a single LUN/LDEV on a single path. However, determining whether the bus was saturated and whether the service time for each I/O was within specifications are valid concerns. Each question requires more scrutiny.

note

> Different arrays require special tools to confirm that cache within the array is flushed so that a true spindle read is measured. For example, HP's largest storage arrays can have well over 100GB of cache on the controller in which a read/write may be responding, thereby appearing to provide higher average reads/writes than the spindle can truly provide. Minimum cache space should be configured when running performance measurements with respect to design layout.

Using sar and iostat to Measure Disk Performance

Continuing with the dd command, we repeat the test but focus only on the data yielded by the sar command to depict service time and other traits, as per the following.

```
atlorca2:~ # sar -d 1 100
Linux 2.6.5-7.97-default (atlorca2)      05/09/05


14:19:23            DEV       tps   rd_sec/s  wr_sec/s
14:19:48         dev8-144    0.00       0.00      0.00
14:19:49         dev8-144    0.00       0.00      0.00
14:19:50         dev8-144  178.00  182272.00      0.00
14:19:51         dev8-144  303.00  311296.00      0.00
14:19:52         dev8-144  300.00  307200.00      0.00
14:19:53         dev8-144  303.00  309248.00      0.00
14:19:54         dev8-144  301.00  309248.00      0.00
14:19:55         dev8-144  303.00  311296.00      0.00
14:19:56         dev8-144  302.00  309248.00      0.00
```

This sar output shows that the total number of transfers per second (TPS) holds around 300. rd_sec/s measures the number of read sectors per second, and each sector is 512 bytes. Divide the rd_sec/s by the tps, and you have the number of sectors in each transfer. In this case, the average is 1024 sectors at 512 bytes each. This puts the average SCSI block size at 512KB. This is a very important discovery; because the dd command requests a block size of 1MB, the SCSI driver blocks the request into 512 byte blocks, so two physical I/Os complete for every logical I/O requested. Different operating systems have this value hard coded at the SCSI driver at different block sizes, so be aware of this issue when troubleshooting.

As always, more than one way exists to capture I/O stats. In this case, iostat may suit your needs. This example uses iostat rather than sar to evaluate the dd run.

```
atlorca2:~ # iostat
Linux 2.6.5-7.97-default (atlorca2)      05/09/05


avg-cpu:  %user   %nice    %sys %iowait    %idle
           0.00    0.01    0.02    0.08    99.89


Device:           tps  Blk_read/s  Blk_wrtn/s  Blk_read  Blk_wrtn
```

sdj	0.06	57.76	0.00	15222123	72
sdj	0.00	0.00	0.00	0	0
sdj	0.00	0.00	0.00	0	0
sdj	98.00	102400.00	0.00	102400	0
sdj	298.00	305152.00	0.00	305152	0
sdj	303.00	309248.00	0.00	309248	0
sdj	303.00	311296.00	0.00	311296	0
sdj	301.00	307200.00	0.00	307200	0
sdj	302.00	309248.00	0.00	309248	0
sdj	302.00	309248.00	0.00	309248	0
sdj	141.00	143360.00	0.00	143360	0

Calculating MBps from iostat can be achieved by calculating KB from blocks read per second (Blk_read/s) and multiplying them by the transactions per second (TPS). In the previous example, 311296 Blk_read/s / (303 tps) = 1027.3 blocks × 512 bytes/block = 526018 bytes / 1024 bytes/KB = 513KB avg.

Before we explain the importance of the blocking size based on a given driver, let us demonstrate the same test results with a different block size. Again, we move 1GB of data through a raw character device using a much smaller block size. It is very important to understand that the exact same 1GB of data is being read by dd and written to /dev/null.

Understanding the Importance of I/O Block Size When Testing Performance

The I/O block size can impact performance. By reducing the dd read block size from 1024k to 2k, the FCP payload of 2k and the SCSI disk (sd) driver can deliver about 1/16 of the performance. Additionally, the I/O rate increases dramatically as the block size of each request drops to that of the FCP limit. In the first example, the sd driver was blocking on 512k, which put the I/O rate around 300 per second. In the world of speed, 300 I/O per second is rather dismal; however, we must keep that number in perspective because we were moving large data files at over 100 MBps. Though the I/O rate was low, the MBps was enormous.

Most applications use an 8K block size. In the following demonstration, we use a 2K block size to illustrate the impact of I/O payload (I/O size).

```
atlorca2:~ # time -p dd if=/dev/raw/raw8 of=/dev/null bs=2k \
 count=524288
524288+0 records in
524288+0 records out
real 95.98
user 0.29
sys 8.78
```

You can easily see that by simply changing the block size of a data stream from 1024k to 2k, the time it takes to move large amounts of data changes drastically. The time to transfer 1GB of data has increased 13 times from less than 7 seconds to almost 96 seconds, which should highlight the importance of block size to any bean counter.

We can use sar to determine the average I/O size (payload).

```
atlorca2:~ # sar -d 1 100¦ grep dev8-144
14:46:50     dev8-144    5458.00   21832.00     0.00
14:46:51     dev8-144    5478.00   21912.00     0.00
14:46:52     dev8-144    5446.00   21784.00     0.00
14:46:53     dev8-144    5445.00   21780.00     0.00
14:46:54     dev8-144    5464.00   21856.00     0.00
14:46:55     dev8-144    5475.00   21900.00     0.00
14:46:56     dev8-144    5481.00   21924.00     0.00
14:46:57     dev8-144    5467.00   21868.00     0.00
```

From the sar output, we can determine that 21868 rd_sec/s transpires, while we incur a tps of 5467. The quotient of 21868/5467 provides four sectors in a transaction, which equates to 2048 bytes, or 2K. This calculation shows that we are moving much smaller chunks of data but at an extremely high I/O rate of 5500 I/O per second. Circumstances do exist where I/O rates are the sole concern, as with the access rates of a company's Web site. However, changing perspective from something as simple as a Web transaction to backing up the entire corporate database puts sharp focus on the fact that block size matters. Remember, backup utilities use large block I/O, usually 64k.

With the understanding that small block I/O impedes large data movements, note that filesystem fragmentation and sparse file fragmentation can cause an application's request to be broken into very small I/O. In other words, even though a dd if=/file system/file_name of=/tmp/out_file bs=128k is requesting a read with 128k block

I/O, sparse file or filesystem fragmentation can force the read to be broken into much smaller block sizes. So, as we continue to dive into performance troubleshooting throughout this chapter, always stay focused on the type of measurement needed: I/O, payload, or block size. In addition to considering I/O, payload, and block size, time is an important factor.

Importance of Time

Continuing with our example, we must focus on I/O round-trip time and bus saturation using the same performance test as earlier. In the next few examples, we use `iostat` to illustrate average wait time, service time, and percent of utilization of our test device.

The following `iostat` display is from the previous sequential read test but with block size set to 4096k, or 4MBs, illustrating time usage and device saturation.

```
atlorca2:~ # dd if=/dev/raw/raw8 of=/dev/null bs=4096k &

atlorca2:~ # iostat -t -d -x 1 100

Device:     rrqm/s wrqm/s   r/s   w/s rsec/s  wsec/s      rkB/s      wkB/s \
avgrq-sz avgqu-sz   await  svctm  %util

sdj            0.00   0.00 308.00  0.00 319488.00    0.00 159744.00         \
0.00  1037.30    4.48  14.49   3.24  99.80
sdj            0.00   0.00 311.00  0.00 319488.00    0.00 159744.00         \
0.00  1027.29    4.53  14.66   3.21  99.70
```

In this `iostat` output, we see that the device utilization is pegged at 100%. When device utilization reaches 100%, device saturation has been achieved. This value indicates not only saturation but also the percentage of CPU time for which an I/O request was issued. In addition to eating up CPU cycles with pending I/O waits, notice that the round-trip time (service time) required for each I/O request increased.

Service time, the time required for a request to be completed on any given device, holds around 3.2ms. Before we go into detail about all the items that must be completed within that 3.2ms, which are discussed later in this chapter, we need to recap the initial test parameters. Recall that the previous `iostat` data was collected while using the `dd` command with a block size of 4096k. Running the same test with block size set to 1024k yields identical block counts in iostat, as you can see in this example:

```
atlorca2:~ # dd if=/dev/raw/raw8 of=/dev/null bs=1024k &

atlorca2:~ # iostat -t -d -x 1 100

Device:     rrqm/s wrqm/s   r/s   w/s rsec/s  wsec/s    rkB/s    wkB/s \
avgrq-sz avgqu-sz   await  svctm  %util

sdj          0.00   0.00 303.00  0.00 309248.00   0.00 154624.00      \
0.00  1020.62    1.51   4.96  3.29  99.80
sdj          0.00   0.00 303.00  0.00 311296.00   0.00 155648.00      \
0.00  1027.38    1.51   4.98  3.29  99.70
sdj          0.00   0.00 304.00  0.00 311296.00   0.00 155648.00      \
0.00  1024.00    1.50   4.95  3.26  99.00
sdj          0.00   0.00 303.00  0.00 309248.00   0.00 154624.00      \
0.00  1020.62    1.50   4.93  3.28  99.40
sdj          0.00   0.00 304.00  0.00 311296.00   0.00 155648.00      \
0.00  1024.00    1.50   4.93  3.28  99.60
```

Determining Block Size

As we have illustrated earlier in this chapter, block size greatly impacts an application's overall performance. However, there are limits that must be understood concerning who has control over the I/O boundary. Every application has the capability to set its own I/O block request size, but the key is to understand the limits and locations. In Linux, excluding applications and filesystems, the sd driver blocks all I/O on the largest block depending on medium (such as SCSI LVD or FCP). An I/O operation on the SCSI bus with any typical SCSI RAID controller (not passing any other port drivers, such as Qlogic, or Emulex FCP HBA) holds around 128KB. However, in our case, through FCP, the largest block size is set to 512KB, as shown in the previous example when doing a raw sequential read access through dd. However, it goes without saying that other factors have influence, as shown later in this chapter when additional middle layer drivers are installed for I/O manipulation.

To determine the maximum blocking factor, or max I/O size, of a request at the SD/FCP layer through a raw sequential read access, we must focus on the following items captured by the previous dd request in iostat examples.

The following example explains how to calculate block size.

```
Device:              tps   Blk_read/s   Blk_wrtn/s   Blk_read   Blk_wrtn

sdj              303.00    311296.00         0.00     311296          0
```

As the output shows, the number of blocks read per second is 311296.00, and the number of transactions per second is 303.00.

$$(\text{sectors read/sec})/(\text{read/sec}) =\sim 1024 \text{ sectors}$$

note

=~ means approximation.

Recall that a sector has 512 bytes.

$$(1024 \text{ sectors}) \times (512 \text{ bytes/sector}) = 524288 \text{ bytes}$$

Now convert the value to KB.

$$(524288 \text{ bytes}) / (1024 \text{ bytes/KB}) = 512KB$$

Another way to calculate the block size of an I/O request is to simply look at the avgrq-sz data from iostat. This field depicts the average number of sectors requested in a given I/O request, which in turn only needs to be multiplied by 512 bytes to yield the block I/O request size in bytes.

Now that we have demonstrated how to calculate the in-route block size on any given I/O request, we need to return to our previous discussion about round-trip time and follow up with queue length.

Importance of a Queue

Service time only includes the amount of time required for a device to complete the request given to it. It is important to keep an eye on svctm so that any latency with respect to the end device can be noted quickly and separated from the average wait time. The average wait time (await) is not only the amount of time required to service the I/O at the device but also the amount of wait time spent in the dispatch queue and the round-trip time. It is important to keep track of both times because the difference between the two can help identify problems with the local host.

To wrap things up with I/O time and queues, we need to touch on queue length.. If you are familiar with C programming, you may find it useful to look at how these values are calculated. The following depicts the calculation for average queue length and wait time found in iostat source code.

```
nr_ios = sdev.rd_ios + sdev.wr_ios;
tput   = ((double) nr_ios) * HZ / itv;
util   = ((double) sdev.tot_ticks) / itv * HZ;
svctm  = tput ? util / tput : 0.0;
/*
 * kernel gives ticks already in milliseconds for all platforms
 * => no need for further scaling.
 */
await  = nr_ios ?
   (sdev.rd_ticks + sdev.wr_ticks) / nr_ios : 0.0;
arqsz  = nr_ios ?
   (sdev.rd_sectors + sdev.wr_sectors) / nr_ios : 0.0;

printf("%-10s", st_hdr_iodev_i->name);
if (strlen(st_hdr_iodev_i->name) > 10)
   printf("\n            ");
/*       rrq/s wrq/s   r/s   w/s  rsec  wsec   rkB   wkB \
         rqsz  qusz await svctm %util */
printf(" %6.2f %6.2f %5.2f %5.2f %7.2f %7.2f %8.2f %8.2f \
         %8.2f %8.2f %7.2f %6.2f %6.2f\n",
      ((double) sdev.rd_merges) / itv * HZ,
      ((double) sdev.wr_merges) / itv * HZ,
      ((double) sdev.rd_ios) / itv * HZ,
      ((double) sdev.wr_ios) / itv * HZ,
      ((double) sdev.rd_sectors) / itv * HZ,
```

```
((double) sdev.wr_sectors) / itv * HZ,
((double) sdev.rd_sectors) / itv * HZ / 2,
((double) sdev.wr_sectors) / itv * HZ / 2,
arqsz,
((double) sdev.rq_ticks) / itv * HZ / 1000.0,
await,
/* The ticks output is biased to output 1000 ticks per second */
svctm,
/* Again: ticks in milliseconds */
util / 10.0);
```

Though it is nice to understand the calculations behind every value provided in performance tools, the most important thing to recall is that a large number of outstanding I/O requests on any given bus is not desirable when faced with performance concerns.

In the following iostat example, we use an I/O request size of 2K, which results in low service time and queue length but high disk utilization.

```
atlorca2:~ # dd if=/dev/raw/raw8 of=/dev/null bs=2k &

atlorca2:~ # iostat -t -d -x 1 100

Device:    rrqm/s wrqm/s   r/s   w/s rsec/s  wsec/s   rkB/s     \
wkB/s avgrq-sz avgqu-sz   await  svctm  %util

sdj           0.00   0.00 5492.00  0.00 21968.00   0.00 10984.00    \
0.00    4.00     0.97    0.18   0.18  96.70
sdj           0.00   0.00 5467.00  0.00 21868.00   0.00 10934.00    \
0.00    4.00     0.95    0.17   0.17  94.80
sdj           0.00   0.00 5413.00  0.00 21652.00   0.00 10826.00    \
0.00    4.00     0.96    0.18   0.18  96.40
sdj           0.00   0.00 5453.00  0.00 21812.00   0.00 10906.00    \
0.00    4.00     0.98    0.18   0.18  97.80
sdj           0.00   0.00 5440.00  0.00 21760.00   0.00 10880.00    \
0.00    4.00     0.97    0.18   0.18  96.60
```

Notice how the %util remains high, while the request size falls to 4 sectors/(I/O), which equals our 2048-byte block size. In addition, the average queue size remains small, and wait time is negligible along with service time. Recall that wait time includes round-trip time, as discussed previously. Now that we have low values for avgrq-sz, avgqu-sz, await, and svctm, we must decide whether we have a performance problem. In this example, the answer is both yes and no. Yes, the device is at its peak performance for a single thread data query, and no, the results for the fields typically focused on to find performance concerns are not high.

Multiple Threads (Processes) of I/O to a Disk

Now that we have covered the basics, let us address a multiple read request to a device.

In the following example, we proceed with the same block size, 2K, as discussed previously; however, we spawn a total of six read threads to the given device to illustrate how service time, queue length, and wait time differ. Let's run six dd commands at the same time.

```
atlorca2:~ # dd if=/dev/raw/raw8 of=/dev/null bs=2k &
atlorca2:~ # dd if=/dev/raw/raw8 of=/dev/null bs=2k &
atlorca2:~ # dd if=/dev/raw/raw8 of=/dev/null bs=2k &
atlorca2:~ # dd if=/dev/raw/raw8 of=/dev/null bs=2k &
atlorca2:~ # dd if=/dev/raw/raw8 of=/dev/null bs=2k &
atlorca2:~ # dd if=/dev/raw/raw8 of=/dev/null bs=2k &
```

Note that the previous code can be performed in a simple for loop:

```
for I in 1 2 3 4 5 6
do
dd if=/dev/raw/raw8 of=/dev/null bs=2k &
done
```

Let's use iostat again to look at the dd performance.

```
atlorca2:~ # iostat -t -d -x 1 100
```

```
Device:    rrqm/s wrqm/s    r/s    w/s rsec/s  wsec/s     rkB/s      \
wkB/s avgrq-sz avgqu-sz   await  svctm  %util

sdj          0.00   0.00 5070.00  0.00 20280.00    0.00 10140.00      \
0.00    4.00    4.96    0.98  0.20 100.00
sdj          0.00   0.00 5097.00  0.00 20388.00    0.00 10194.00      \
0.00    4.00    4.97    0.98  0.20 100.00
sdj          0.00   0.00 5103.00  0.00 20412.00    0.00 10206.00      \
0.00    4.00    4.97    0.97  0.20 100.00
```

The queue length (avgqu-sz) is 4.97, while the max block request size holds constant.
The service time for the device to act on the request remains at 0.20ms. Furthermore, the
average wait time has increased to 0.98ms due to the device's response to multiple simul-
taneous I/O requests requiring a longer round-trip time. It is useful to keep the following
example handy when working with a large multithreaded performance problem because
the device may be strained, and striping at a volume manager level across multiple
devices would help relieve this type of strain.

Using a Striped lvol to Reduce Disk I/O Strain

To illustrate the reduction of strain, let us create a VG and 4000MB lvol striped across
two disks with a 16k stripe size.

```
atlorca2:/home/greg/sysstat-5.0.6 # pvcreate /dev/sdi
  No physical volume label read from /dev/sdi
  Physical volume "/dev/sdi" successfully created

atlorca2:/home/greg/sysstat-5.0.6 # pvcreate /dev/sdj
  No physical volume label read from /dev/sdj
  Physical volume "/dev/sdj" successfully created

atlorca2:/home/greg/sysstat-5.0.6 # vgcreate vg00 /dev/sdi /dev/sdj
  Volume group "vg00" successfully created
```

```
atlorca2:/home/greg/sysstat-5.0.6 # lvcreate -L 4000m -i 2 -I 16 -n \
lvol1 vg00
  Logical volume "lvol1" created


atlorca2:/home/greg/sysstat-5.0.6 # lvdisplay -v /dev/vg00/lvol1
    Using logical volume(s) on command line
    ------ Logical volume ------
  LV Name              /dev/vg00/lvol1
  VG Name              vg00
  LV UUID              UQB5AO-dp8Z-N0ce-Dbd9-9ZEs-ccB5-zG7fsF
  LV Write Access      read/write
  LV Status            available
  # open               0
  LV Size              3.91 GB
  Current LE           1000
  Segments             1
  Allocation           next free (default)
  Read ahead sectors   0
  Block device         253:0
```

We again use sequential 2k reads with dd to measure the performance of the disks.

```
atlorca2:/home/greg/sysstat-5.0.6 # raw /dev/raw/raw9 /dev/vg00/lvol1 \
/dev/raw/raw9: bound to major 253, minor 0
atlorca2:/home/greg/sysstat-5.0.6 # dd if=/dev/raw/raw9 of=/dev/null \
bs=2k &
atlorca2:/home/greg/sysstat-5.0.6 # dd if=/dev/raw/raw9 of=/dev/null \
bs=2k &
atlorca2:/home/greg/sysstat-5.0.6 # dd if=/dev/raw/raw9 of=/dev/null \
bs=2k &
atlorca2:/home/greg/sysstat-5.0.6 # dd if=/dev/raw/raw9 of=/dev/null \
bs=2k &
atlorca2:/home/greg/sysstat-5.0.6 # dd if=/dev/raw/raw9 of=/dev/null \
bs=2k &
atlorca2:/home/greg/sysstat-5.0.6 # dd if=/dev/raw/raw9 of=/dev/null \
bs=2k &
```

Note that the previous command can be performed in a simple `for` loop, as previously illustrated. Again we use `iostat` to measure disk throughput.

```
atlorca2:/home/greg # iostat -x 1 1000

avg-cpu:   %user    %nice    %sys %iowait   %idle
           0.01     0.01     0.03    0.11   99.84
Device:    rrqm/s wrqm/s    r/s   w/s rsec/s  wsec/s    rkB/s    \
wkB/s avgrq-sz avgqu-sz   await  svctm  %util

sdi          0.00   0.00 2387.00  0.00 9532.00    0.00  4766.00    \
0.00     3.99     3.04    1.28   0.42 100.00
sdj          0.00   0.00 2380.00  0.00 9536.00    0.00  4768.00    \
0.00     4.01     2.92    1.22   0.42 100.00
sdi          0.00   0.00 2318.00  0.00 9288.00    0.00  4644.00    \
0.00     4.01     3.14    1.35   0.43  99.70
sdj          0.00   0.00 2330.00  0.00 9304.00    0.00  4652.00    \
0.00     3.99     2.82    1.21   0.43  99.50
```

Notice that the average wait time per I/O and the service time have increased slightly in this example. However, the average queue has been cut almost in half, as well as the physical I/O demand on the device `sdj`. The result is similar to a seesaw effect: As one attribute drops, another rises. In the previous scenario, the LUN (`sdj`) is physically composed of multiple physical mechanisms in the array called (array group), which remains a hidden attribute to the OS. By using the LVM strategy, we reduce some of the contingency for one LUN or array group to handle the entire load needed by the device (`lvol`). With the previous demonstration, you can see the advantages of striping, as well as its weaknesses. It seems true here that, for every action, there is an equal and opposite reaction.

Striped lvol Versus Single Disk Performance

In the following example, we compare a striped raw `lvol` to a raw single disk. Our objective is to watch the wait time remain almost constant, while the queue size is cut almost in half when using a `lvol` stripe instead of a single disk.

First let's look at performance using the lvol. In this example, we start six dd commands that perform sequential reads with block size set to 512k. The dd commands run at the same time and read a raw device bound to the lvol (as illustrated previously) with a 16k stripe size. Remember, iostat shows two disk devices for our lvol test because the lvol is striped across two disks. At 512KB, iostat yields values as follows:

```
Device:     rrqm/s wrqm/s    r/s  w/s  rsec/s wsec/s     rkB/s    \
wkB/s avgrq-sz avgqu-sz    await  svctm  %util

sdi           0.00   0.00 152.00  0.00 156672.00    0.00 78336.00   \
0.00  1030.74     3.00    19.60   6.58 100.00
sdj           0.00   0.00 153.00  0.00 155648.00    0.00 77824.00   \
0.00  1017.31     2.99    19.69   6.54 100.00


sdi           0.00   0.00 154.00  0.00 157696.00    0.00 78848.00   \
0.00  1024.00     2.98    19.43   6.49 100.00
sdj           0.00   0.00 154.00  0.00 157696.00    0.00 78848.00   \
0.00  1024.00     3.01    19.42   6.49 100.00
```

Notice that the I/O queue length when reading lvol1 is much shorter than the following identical dd sequential read test on a raw disk sdj as shown next. Though the identical blocking size of 512k is used, the service time decreases. Here are the results of the test with a raw disk.

```
Device:     rrqm/s wrqm/s    r/s  w/s  rsec/s wsec/s     rkB/s    \
wkB/s avgrq-sz avgqu-sz    await  svctm  %util

sdj           0.00   0.00 311.00  0.00 318464.00    0.00 159232.00  \

0.00  1024.00     5.99    19.30   3.22 100.00
sdj           0.00   0.00 310.00  0.00 317440.00    0.00 158720.00  \
0.00  1024.00     5.99    19.31   3.23 100.00
sdj           0.00   0.00 311.00  0.00 318464.00    0.00 159232.00  \
0.00  1024.00     5.99    19.26   3.22 100.00
```

The raw device, sdj in the test using lvol1, reflects that the read requests per second (r/s) remain constant (152 on disk device sdi and 153 on disk device sdj), yielding a net result of 305 read requests per second. The lvol test also shows an improvement in the average wait time; however, we hurt the service time. The service time for the lvol test is about 6.5ms, whereas it is 3.2ms for the raw disk. Upon closer inspection, we notice that the service time is higher due to the I/O issued to the device. In the lvol example, we have in fact submitted 512KB every other time (because we are striping and blocking our I/O both on 512k) so that each total I/O submitted to the device is in a smaller queue, thereby reducing the wait time to be serviced. However, in the single device example, the queue wait time is high because we are waiting on the device to finish on the given I/O request, so with no overhead, the return is faster for the service. This example illustrates the seesaw effect discussed previously, in which a device (single LUN or lvol) is slammed, in which case the end user would need to address the application's need to perform such heavy I/O with a single device. In the previous example, tweaking the device or lvol buys no performance gain; it just moves the time wait status to another field.

note

> With a wider stripe, some performance would be gained in the previous sequential I/O example, but it is unrealistic in the real world. In addition to adding more disks for a wider stripe, you could add more paths to the storage for multipath I/O. However, multipath I/O comes with its own list of constraints.

Multipath I/O

Many administrators have heard about load balance drivers, which allow disk access through multiple paths. However, very few multipath I/O drivers provide load balance behavior to I/Os across multiple HBA paths as found in enterprise UNIX environments. For example, device drivers such as MD, Autopath, Secure Path (spmgr), and Qlogic's secure path are dedicated primarily to providing an alternate path for a given disk. Though HP's Secpath does offer a true load balance policy for EVA HSG storage on Linux, all the other drivers mentioned only offer failover at this time.

The one true load balancing driver for Linux (HP's Secure Path) provides a round robin (RR) load balance scheduling policy for storage devices on EVA and HSG arrays. Unfortunately, just because a driver that provides load balancing, such as the HP Secure

Path driver, exists does not mean support is available for your system. Support for array types is limited. Review your vendor's storage requirements and device driver's hardware support list before making any decisions about which driver to purchase. Keeping in mind that restrictions *always* exist, let's review a typical RR policy and its advantages and disadvantages.

Though we want to discuss load balancing, the vast majority of Linux enterprise environments today use static (also known as "manual") load balancing or preferred path. With this in mind, we keep the discussion of RR to a minimum.

In the next example, we proceed with a new host and new array that will allow the RR scheduling policy.

The following example illustrates RR through Secure Path on Linux connected through Qlogic HBAs to an EVA storage array. Due to configuration layout, we use a different host for this example.

```
[root@linny5 swsp]# uname -a
Linux linny5.cxo.hp.com 2.4.21-27.ELsmp #1 SMP Wed Dec 1 21:59:02 EST \
2004 i686 i686 i386 GNU/Linux
```

Our host has two HBAs, /proc/scsi/qla2300/0 and /proc/scsi/qla2300/1, with Secure Path version 3.0cFullUpdate-4.0.SP, shown next.

```
[root@linny5 /]# cat /proc/scsi/qla2300/0
QLogic PCI to Fibre Channel Host Adapter for QLA2340:
        Firmware version:  3.03.01, Driver version 7.01.01
Entry address = f88dc060
HBA: QLA2312 , Serial# G8762
```

```
[root@linny5 swsp]# cat /etc/redhat-release
Red Hat Enterprise Linux AS release 3 (Taroon Update 3)
```

Continuing with our raw device testing, we must bind the block device to the character device.

```
[root@linny5 swsp]# raw /dev/raw/raw8 /dev/spdev/spd
```

Use the Secure Path command spmgr to display the product's configuration.

```
[root@linny5 swsp]# spmgr display
  Server:  linny5.cxo.hp.com    Report Created: Tue, May 10 19:10:04 2005
  Command: spmgr display
= = = = = = = = = = = = = = = = = = = = = = = = = = = = = = = = = = = =
  Storage:  5000-1FE1-5003-1280
  Load Balance: Off  Auto-restore: Off
  Path Verify: On    Verify Interval: 30
  HBAs: 2300-0  2300-1
  Controller:  P66C5E1AAQ20AL, Operational
               P66C5E1AAQ20AD, Operational
  Devices:  spa  spb  spc  spd
```

To reduce space needed for this example, a large part of the spmgr display has been truncated, and we focus only on device spd, as per the following:

```
TGT/LUN   Device       WWLUN_ID                                   #_Paths
  0/  3   spd          6005-08B4-0010-056A-0000-9000-0025-0000       4


      Controller  Path_Instance    HBA        Preferred?  Path_Status
        P66C5E1AAQ20AL                              YES
            hsx_mod-0-0-0-4    2300-0      no          Available
            hsx_mod-1-0-2-4    2300-1      no          Active


      Controller  Path_Instance    HBA        Preferred?  Path_Status
        P66C5E1AAQ20AD                              no
            hsx_mod-0-0-1-4    2300-0      no          Standby
            hsx_mod-1-0-1-4    2300-1      no          Standby
```

Notice that two HBAs and two controllers are displayed. In this case, the EVA storage controller P66C5E1AAQ20AL has been set to preferred active on this particular LUN, in which both of the fabric N_ports enable connection to the fabric. In this configuration, each N_Port connects to different fabrics, A and B, which are seen by Qlogic 0 and 1. In addition, each HBA also sees the alternate controller in case a failure occurs on the selected preferred controller.

We should also to mention that not all arrays are Active/Active on all paths for any LUN at any given time. In this case, the EVA storage array is an Active/Active array because both N_Ports on any given controller have the capability to service an I/O. However, any one LUN can only access a single N_Port at any moment, while another LUN can access the alternate port or alternate controller. Now that we have a background in EVA storage, we need to discuss how the worldwide name (WWN) of a given target device can be found. In the following illustration, we simply read the content of the device instance for the filter driver swsp.

```
[root@linny5 swsp]# cat /proc/scsi/swsp/2
swsp LUN information:


Array WWID:    50001FE150031280
```

Next, we initiate load balancing and start our raw device test, which is identical to the test performed earlier in this chapter.

```
[root@linny5 swsp]# spmgr set -b on 50001FE150031280


[root@linny5 swsp]# dd if=/dev/raw/raw8 of=/dev/null bs=512k
```

While this simple test runs, we collect iostat-x-d1 100 measurements, and we collect a few time captures.

```
Device:    rrqm/s wrqm/s   r/s   w/s rsec/s  wsec/s    rkB/s    \
wkB/s avgrq-sz avgqu-sz   await svctm %util

sdd         0.00   0.00 5008.00  0.00 319488.00   0.00 159744.00   \
0.00   63.80    9.81    1.96  0.19 93.00
sdd         0.00   0.00 4992.00  0.00 320512.00   0.00 160256.00   \
0.00   64.21    9.96    1.96  0.18 91.00
sdd         0.00   0.00 4992.00  0.00 318464.00   0.00 159232.00   \
0.00   63.79    9.80    2.00  0.18 92.00
sdd         0.00   0.00 4992.00  0.00 319488.00   0.00 159744.00   \
0.00   64.00    9.89    1.98  0.19 95.00
```

Notice that the blocking factor for a given I/O has changed to 64 sectors per I/O, which equals 32k block size from the swsp module. To get a good comparison between a sequential read test with RR enabled and one with RR disabled, we must disable load balance and rerun the same test. We disable load balancing in the following example.

```
[root@linny5 swsp]# spmgr set -b off 50001FE150031280


[root@linny5 swsp]# dd if=/dev/raw/raw8 of=/dev/null bs=512k


[root@linny5 swsp]# iostat -x 1 100

Device:    rrqm/s wrqm/s   r/s   w/s  rsec/s  wsec/s    rkB/s   \
wkB/s avgrq-sz avgqu-sz   await  svctm  %util

sdd          0.00   0.00 4718.00  0.00 302080.00   0.00 151040.00   \
0.00    64.03     9.48    2.01   0.21  98.00
sdd          0.00   0.00 4710.00  0.00 302080.00   0.00 151040.00   \
0.00    64.14     9.61    2.02   0.20  94.00
sdd          0.00   0.00 4716.00  0.00 302080.00   0.00 151040.00   \
0.00    64.05     9.03    1.91   0.20  95.00
sdd          0.00   0.00 4710.00  0.00 301056.00   0.00 150528.00   \
0.00    63.92     8.23    1.76   0.20  96.00
```

Iostat reports that the block size remains constant and that the average wait time for a given I/O round trip is slightly higher. This makes sense now that all I/O is on a single path. Because more I/O is loaded on a single path, average wait time increases, as do service times. Now that we have drawn a quick comparison between spmgr being enabled and disabled on a sequential read, we need to recap the advantages seen thus far.

In the previous example, no performance gain was seen by enabling load balancing with regard to spmgr. As we can see, no obvious performance increase was seen when RR was enabled through the host measurements. However, though the host's overall benefit from enabling load balancing was insignificant, the SAN load was cut in half. Keep in mind that a simple modification can impact the entire environment, even outside the host. Something as minor as having a static load balance with a volume manager strip across multiple paths or having a filter driver automate the loading of paths can have a large impact on the overall scheme.

Finally, with respect to load balance drivers, it is important to watch for the max block size for any given transfer. As seen in the previous `iostat` examples, the Secure Path product reduces the block size to 32k, and if LVM were to be added on top of that, the block would go to 16K. This small block transfer is great for running small, block-heavy I/O traffic, but for large data pulls, it can become a bottleneck.

Filesystems

Application data access through a filesystem is much more common than access through raw storage. Filesystem meta structures are maintained by the filesystem's driver, removing the overhead from the application. For this reason, very few applications are written to perform raw I/O, except for a few database systems whose creators believe they can maintain the integrity or performance better than a standardized filesystem. This section addresses performance characteristics with regards to multiple filesystems and draws a comparison to the previous section on raw device access.

The configuration for this section is identical to the previous section. We use the IA64 host `atlorca2`. Filesystem types used for comparisons are `xfs` and `ext3`. To begin, we define a filesystem using the same disks from previous examples. By creating a filesystem, we simply add an additional layer to the data management overhead.

Journaling to a Separate Disk

The following `fdisk` output shows device `sdj` with one primary partition of type `83` known as Linux native. The objective is to compare performance of a large sequential read. We compare performance with raw to performance with XFS, illustrating performance overhead.

The first step in comparing performance between raw and filesystem is to set a baseline. Here we set a performance baseline for a single threaded read on a raw device named `/dev/sdj`.

```
atlorca2:~ # fdisk -l /dev/sdj

Disk /dev/sdj: 250.2 GB, 250219069440 bytes
255 heads, 63 sectors/track, 30420 cylinders
```

```
Units = cylinders of 16065 * 512 = 8225280 bytes
```

```
   Device Boot      Start        End     Blocks  Id  System
/dev/sdj1               1      30420  244348618+  83  Linux
```

The fdisk output shows that partition 1 is active, with 250GB of capacity.

The XFS filesystem type offers the performance feature of creating a journal log on a disk separate from the filesystem data. Next we demonstrate this feature and test it. In this example, device sdk is the journal log device, and sdj is used for the metadata device.

```
atlorca2:~ # mkfs.xfs -f -l logdev=/dev/sdk1,size=10000b /dev/sdj1
```

```
meta-data=/dev/sdj1                  isize=256    agcount=16, \
agsize=3817947 blks
         =                           sectsz=512
data     =                           bsize=4096   blocks=61087152, \
imaxpct=25
         =                           sunit=0      swidth=0 blks, \
unwritten=1
naming   =version 2                  bsize=4096
log      =/dev/sdk1                  bsize=4096   blocks=10000, version=1
         =                           sectsz=512   sunit=0 blks
realtime =none                       extsz=65536  blocks=0, rtextents=0
```

The following demonstrates a large block write and the performance boost that an external logger offers.

```
atlorca2:/xfs.test # dd if=/dev/zero of=/xfs.test/zero.out bs=512k
```

```
atlorca2:~ # iostat -x 1 100| egrep "sdj|sdk"
```

```
Device:    rrqm/s wrqm/s  r/s  w/s rsec/s wsec/s    rkB/s    \
wkB/s avgrq-sz avgqu-sz   await  svctm  %util

sdj         0.00 32512.00  0.00 281.00   0.00 262144.00     0.00 \
131072.00   932.90   141.99  394.24   3.56 100.00
```

```
sdk          0.00    0.00   0.00   0.00      0.00    0.00      0.00     0.00   \
0.00      0.00    0.00    0.00    0.00
sdj          0.00 36576.00  0.00 277.00      0.00 294929.00      0.00 \
147464.50  1064.73   142.75  511.21    3.61 100.00
sdk          0.00    0.00   0.00   1.00      0.00    5.00      0.00     2.50   \
5.00      0.10  105.00 105.00   10.50
sdj          0.00 35560.00  0.00 279.00      0.00 286736.00      0.00 \
143368.00  1027.73   141.26  380.54    3.58 100.00
sdk          0.00    0.00   0.00   0.00      0.00    0.00      0.00     0.00   \
0.00      0.00    0.00    0.00    0.00
sdj          0.00 36576.00  0.00 277.00      0.00 294912.00      0.00 \
147456.00  1064.66   142.35  204.65    3.61 100.00
sdk          0.00    0.00   0.00   0.00      0.00    0.00      0.00     0.00   \
0.00      0.00    0.00    0.00    0.00
```

The journal log device provides little to no added performance. There is almost no I/O to disk sdk, which contains the log. Putting the log on a separate disk won't help performance because we are not diverting a meaningful amount of I/O. The journal log device provides no added benefit because the intent to modify/write is established at the beginning of the file access. From this point forward, the I/O is completed on the meta device, as depicted in the previous iostat.

Determining I/O Size for Filesystem Requests

As shown previously, the dd command bs option sets the block size to 512k for each I/O transaction. We can see this in iostat. To calculate this value, find the average request size (avgrq-sz) column from iostat. In this example, we find that avgrq-sz has a value of 1024 sectors. To calculate the block size, multiply avgrq-sz by the sector size (512 bytes). In this example:

$$1024 \text{ (sectors)} \times 512 \text{ (bytes/sector)} = 524288 \text{ (bytes)} / 1024 \text{ (KB/bytes)} = 512\text{KB}$$

However, the same dd command using the XFS filesystem reveals that the largest avgrq-sz value set forth by a sequential read is equal to 256 (sectors) regardless of block size set by dd. Following the same calculations, we determine that an XFS sequential read has a block size set to 128KB. The block size of any I/O is an important item to understand because not all programs control the block size. A program can request a given block size; however, a lower-layer driver can require that the I/O request be broken into smaller requests as illustrated in the previous iostat output.

Thus we have demonstrated that using a remote journal provides no performance improvements for large data access on sequential reads and writes. However, when writing to our XFS filesystem with a large number of small files, the opposite becomes true: The remote journal does in fact help.

Loading a Filesystem with Small Block I/O Transfers

In the next test, we write 512KB files as fast as the system allows while watching the load on the journal device and the filesystem meta device. To run this test, we must write a short, simple program to control the number of files to create during our test phase. The program is as follows:

```
#!/bin/sh
count=1
total=0
while [ $total -ne $* ]
do
total='expr $total + $count'
  touch $total
        dd if=/xfs.test/zero.out of=/xfs.test/$total bs=512k > \
        /dev/null 2>&1  #Using dd to control the BS.
        done
```

This program uses the same dd command used throughout our testing. It is important to always keep the control in any test constant. By running the previous program, thousands of 512KB files are created, causing an increased load on the journal log device (sdk), as depicted in the following listing:

```
atlorca2:/xfs.test # ./count_greg.sh 10000
atlorca2:~ # iostat -x 1 100| egrep "sdj|sdk"


Device:     rrqm/s wrqm/s   r/s    w/s  rsec/s   wsec/s     rkB/s     \
wkB/s avgrq-sz avgqu-sz    await  svctm  %util

sdj          0.00 16219.00  0.00 181.00    0.00 131169.00      0.00 \
65584.50   724.69     9.31   54.90    2.77   50.20
sdk          0.00    0.00  0.00 53.00     0.00  3200.00      0.00  \
1600.00     60.38     1.43   28.96    9.40   49.80
sdj          0.00 20274.00  0.00 201.00    0.00 163936.00         \
0.00 81968.00   815.60    11.90   54.74    2.83   56.90
sdk          0.00    0.00  0.00 39.00     0.00  2752.00      0.00  \
1376.00     70.56     1.19   26.26   14.00   54.60
sdj          0.00 20273.00  0.00 198.00    0.00 163936.00         \
0.00 81968.00   827.96    10.96   54.34    2.77   54.80
sdk          0.00    0.00  0.00 50.00     0.00  3072.00      0.00  \
1536.00     61.44     1.43   30.48   10.90   54.50
sdj          0.00 16217.00  0.00 200.00    0.00 131138.00         \
0.00 65569.00   655.69    10.22   56.56    2.71   54.10
sdk          0.00    0.00  0.00 50.00     0.00  2982.00      0.00  \
1491.00     59.64     1.37   28.78   10.92   54.60
```

By creating thousands of files or modifying the same file thousands of times a minute, we can see the added load on the journal device sdk as well as the filesystem device sdj. By understanding the end goal, we can make better decisions about how to size and lay out a filesystem.

In addition, notice the block size of the I/O request submitted to the filesystem and how the filesystem responded. In the previous example on a sequential read, the block size is restricted to 128K. However, on a sequential write, the blocking structure on the XFS filesystem is that which is set forth by the command calling the SCSI write, setting the average request size to 512k as shown in the previous iostat illustration. However, will the same results be found using a completely different filesystem?

Let's repeat our test on ext3, also known as ext2 with journaling, to depict I/O latency and blocking factors.

```
atlorca2:/ext3.test # dd if=/ext3.test/usr.tar of=/dev/null bs=512k
atlorca2:/ # iostat -x 1 100¦ grep sdj


Device:    rrqm/s wrqm/s   r/s   w/s rsec/s  wsec/s     rkB/s    \
wkB/s avgrq-sz avgqu-sz   await  svctm  %util

sdj         60.00   0.00 898.00  0.00 229856.00    0.00 114928.00    \
0.00   255.96    0.98    1.10   1.09  98.20
sdj         58.00   0.00 939.00  0.00 240360.00    0.00 120180.00    \
0.00   255.97    0.98    1.04   1.04  97.50
sdj         62.00   1.00 918.00  3.00 234984.00   32.00 117492.00    \
16.00   255.17    0.97    1.06   1.05  97.00
sdj         62.00   0.00 913.00  0.00 233704.00    0.00 116852.00    \
0.00   255.97    0.98    1.07   1.07  97.80
sdj         58.00   0.00 948.00  0.00 242664.00    0.00 121332.00    \
0.00   255.97    0.96    1.01   1.01  96.20
sdj         62.00   0.00 933.00  0.00 238824.00    0.00 119412.00    \
0.00   255.97    0.97    1.04   1.04  97.30
```

The sequential read test holds the same blocking factor as previously seen on XFS, with a little savings on overhead with respect to average wait time and service time. To continue our example, let's proceed with the file create script discussed previously.

```
#!/bin/sh
count=1
total=0
while [ $total -ne $* ]
do
total='expr $total + $count'
  touch $total
        dd if=/ext3.test/zero.out of=/ext3.test/$total bs=512k > \
        /dev/null 2>&1   #Using dd to control the BS.
done
```

```
atlorca2:/ext3.test # ./count_greg.sh 10000


atlorca2:/ # iostat -x 1 100| grep sdj

Device:    rrqm/s wrqm/s   r/s   w/s rsec/s  wsec/s    rkB/s    \
wkB/s avgrq-sz avgqu-sz   await  svctm  %util


sdj          0.00 51687.00  0.00 268.00    0.00 416864.00     0.00 \
208432.00  1555.46    128.62   346.74   3.45  92.40
sdj          0.00 27164.00  1.00 264.00    8.00 219040.00     4.00 \
109520.00   826.60    139.42   521.48   3.77 100.00
sdj          0.00 656.00  1.00 113.00    8.00 5312.00    4.00 2656.00 \
46.67    21.95   516.42   3.85  43.90
sdj          0.00    0.00  1.00  0.00    8.00    0.00    4.00    0.00 \
8.00     0.00     1.00    1.00   0.10
sdj          0.00    0.00  0.00  0.00    0.00    0.00    0.00    0.00 \
0.00     0.00     0.00    0.00   0.00
sdj          0.00 52070.00  1.00 268.00    8.00 419936.00     4.00 \
209968.00  1561.13    128.44   346.09   3.43  92.30
sdj          0.00 27800.00  0.00 271.00    0.00 224160.00     0.00 \
112080.00   827.16    139.27   513.93   3.69 100.00
sdj          0.00 662.00  2.00 112.00   16.00 5368.00    8.00 2684.00 \
47.23    20.45   489.31   3.91  44.60
sdj          0.00    0.00  0.00  0.00    0.00    0.00    0.00    0.00 \
0.00     0.00     0.00    0.00   0.00
sdj          0.00    0.00  1.00  0.00    8.00    0.00    4.00    0.00
8.00     0.00     0.00    0.00   0.00
sdj          0.00 51176.00  0.00 273.00    0.00 412792.00     0.00 \
206396.00  1512.06    128.12   336.55   3.37  92.00
sdj          0.00 27927.00  0.00 274.00    0.00 225184.00     0.00 \
112592.00   021.84    138.00   510.66   3.65 100.00
sdj          0.00 658.00  0.00 105.00    0.00 5328.00    0.00 2664.00 \
50.74    17.44   492.92   3.57  37.50
sdj          0.00    0.00  1.00 128.00    8.00 1024.00    4.00  512.00 \
8.00     2.88    22.32    0.35   4.50
```

Notice how the filesystem buffers the outbound I/O, submitting them to the SCSI layer in a burst pattern. Though nothing is wrong with this I/O pattern, you must understand that the larger the burst, the larger the strain on the storage array. For example, exchange servers save up and de-stage out a burst of I/O operations, which can flood an array's write pending cache, so you should monitor for excessive write burst. However, the write block size maintains a 512k average block, which is similar to the XFS on writes with large block requests.

Utilizing Key Benefits of a Filesystem

As we've seen, I/O block sizes, stripe size, and filesystem layouts have unique benefits that aid I/O performance. In addition to these items, most filesystems have unique characteristics that are designed to guess the next request, trying to save resources by anticipating requests. This is accomplished by read-ahead algorithms. Ext2, Ext3, JFS, and XFS all have the capability to perform read-ahead, as shown with XFS in the following XFS source code for mounting `/usr/src/linux/fs/xfs/xfs_mount.c`:

```
/*
 * Set the number of readahead buffers to use based on
 * physical memory size.
 */
if (xfs_physmem <= 4096)                    /* <= 16MB */
        mp->m_nreadaheads = XFS_RW_NREADAHEAD_16MB;
else if (xfs_physmem <= 8192)    /* <= 32MB */
        mp->m_nreadaheads = XFS_RW_NREADAHEAD_32MB;
else
        mp->m_nreadaheads = XFS_RW_NREADAHEAD_K32;
if (sbp->sb_blocklog > readio_log) {
        mp->m_readio_log = sbp->sb_blocklog;
} else {
        mp->m_readio_log = readio_log;
}
mp->m_readio_blocks = 1 << (mp->m_readio_log - sbp->sb_blocklog);
if (sbp->sb_blocklog > writeio_log) {
        mp->m_writeio_log = sbp->sb_blocklog;
```

```
    } else {
          mp->m_writeio_log = writeio_log;
    }
    mp->m_writeio_blocks = 1 << (mp->m_writeio_log - sbp->sb_blocklog);
```

Although read-ahead is a powerful attribute, a concern exists. It is not fair to say that read-ahead causes these drawbacks, as a true increase in read performance can be seen on any filesystem that uses read-ahead functionality. When using read-ahead, filesystem block size is an important factor. For example, if filesystem block size is 8k and sequential read pattern exist where an application is reading 1K sequential blocks (index), read-ahead kicks in and pulls an extra predefined number of blocks, where each block is equal to the filesystem block size. To sum up the concern with read-ahead, one must be careful not to read in more data than is needed. Another performance boost can be found by utilizing buffer cache.

Filesystems such as XFS, Reiser, Ext2, and Ext3 use the buffer cache and reduce the amount of memory for an application to process data in the buffer cache, forcing more physical I/O (PIO). Later in this chapter we discuss the difference between raw, Oracle Cluster File System (OCFS), and XFS in an example with buffer cache and read-ahead. Before we jump too far ahead, though, we need to cover one last topic with respect to disk performance.

Linux and Windows Performance and Tuning Sector Alignments

We have covered some in-depth I/O troubleshooting tactics for character and block devices. Now we need to address the rumor mill about disk geometry alignment. Geometry alignment, also known as sector alignment, is the new craze in Windows performance tweaking. Cylinders lie in a small band, like a ring on a platter. The cylinders are then divided into tracks (wedges), which contain sectors, which are described in great detail in Chapter 6, "Disk Partitions and File Systems." However, to discuss performance concerns with sector alignment, we would like to first depict sector locations (see Figure 4-1).

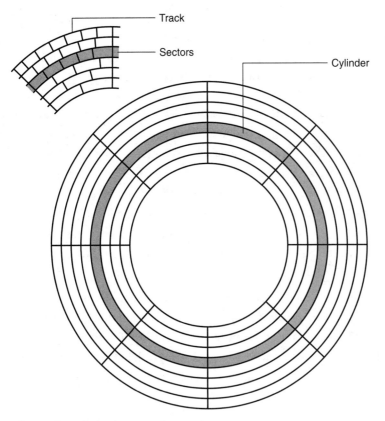

Figure 4-1 Cylinders, tracks, and sectors

Sector alignment provides little to no performance boost in Linux. To date, no issues exist with regards to how partitions and filesystems interact with sectors alignment for a given platter, regardless of whether the platter is logical or physical within Linux. However, for those who are interested, a performance boost has been documented with respect to DOS 6.X, Windows 2000, and greater. See http://www.microsoft.com/ resources/documentation/Windows/2000/server/reskit/en-us/Default.asp?url=/ resources/documentation/Windows/2000/server/reskit/en-us/prork/pree_exa_oori.asp

and http://www.microsoft.com/resources/documentation/windows/2000/professional/
reskit/en-us/part6/proch30.mspx for more information.

Performance Tuning and Benchmarking Using bonnie++

Now that we have covered some basics guidelines about I/O performance metrics, we
need to revisit our primary goal. As already mentioned, our primary goal is to deliver
methods for finding performance problems. In all circumstances, a good performance
snapshot should be taken at every data center before and after changes to firmware roles,
fabric changes, host changes, and so on.

The following is generalized performance data from a single LUN RAID 5 7d+1p, and
it is provided to demonstrate the performance benchmark tool called bonnie. The following test does not depict the limit of the array used for this test. However, the following example enables a brief demonstration of a single LUN performance characteristic
between three filesystems. The following bonnie++ benchmark reflects the results of the
equipment used throughout this chapter with XFS and Ext3 filesystems.

```
atlorca2:/ext3.test # bonnie++ -u root:root -d \
/ext3.test/bonnie.scratch/ -s 8064m -n 16:262144:8:128



Version  1.03 ------Sequential Output------ --Sequential Input- --Random-
               -Per Chr- --Block-- -Rewrite- -Per Chr- --Block-- --Seeks--
Machine  Size K/sec %CP K/sec %CP K/sec %CP K/sec %CP K/sec %CP  /sec %CP
atlorca2 8064M 15029  99 144685  44 52197   8 14819  99 124046    7 893.3  1
               ------Sequential Create------ --------Random Create--------
               -Create-- --Read--- -Delete-- -Create-- --Read--- -
Delete--
```

```
files:max:min       /sec %CP  /sec %CP  /sec %CP  /sec %CP  /sec %CP \
/sec %CP
  16:262144:8/128    721  27 14745  99 4572  37   765  28  3885  28 \
6288  58
```

Testing with XFS and journal on the same device yields the following:

```
atlorca2:/ # mkfs.xfs -f -l size=10000b /dev/sdj1
meta-data=/dev/sdj1              isize=256    agcount=16, \
agsize=3817947 blks
         =                       sectsz=512
data     =                       bsize=4096   blocks=61087152, \
imaxpct=25
         =                       sunit=0      swidth=0 blks, \
unwritten=1
naming   =version 2             bsize=4096
log      =internal log          bsize=4096   blocks=10000, version=1
         =                       sectsz=512   sunit=0 blks
realtime =none                   extsz=65536  blocks=0, rtextents=0


atlorca2:/ # mount -t xfs -o logbufs=8,logbsize=32768 /dev/sdj1 \
/xfs.test
atlorca2:/ # mkdir /xfs.test/bonnie.scratch/
atlorca2:/ # mount -t xfs -o logbufs=8,logbsize=32768 /dev/sdj1 \
/xfs.test


atlorca2:/xfs.test # bonnie++ -u root:root -d /xfs.test/bonnie.scratch/ \
-s 8064m -n 16:262144:8:128


Version  1.03   ------Sequential Output------ --Sequential Input- --
Random-
               -Per Chr- --Block-- -Rewrite- -Per Chr- --Block-- --Seeks--
Machine  Size K/sec %CP K/sec %CP K/sec %CP K/sec %CP K/sec %CP  /sec %CP
```

```
atlorca2       8064M 15474  99 161153  21 56513    8 14836  99 125513    9 \
938.8    1
                        ------Sequential Create------ --------Random Create--
------
                        -Create-- --Read--- -Delete-- -Create-- --Read--- -
Delete--
files:max:min          /sec %CP  /sec %CP  /sec %CP  /sec %CP  /sec %CP \
/sec %CP
    16:262144:8/128  1151   24 12654 100  9705   89  1093   22 12327   99 \
6018   71
```

Testing with XFS without remote journal provides these results:

```
atlorca2:~ # mount -t xfs -o logbufs=8,logbsize=32768,logdev=/dev \
/sdk1/dev/sdj1 /xfs.test

atlorca2:/xfs.test # mkdir bonnie.scratch/
atlorca2:/xfs.test # bonnie++ -u root:root -d /xfs.test/bonnie.scratch/ \
-s 8064m -n 16:262144:8:128
```

```
Version  1.03        ------Sequential Output------ --Sequential Input- --
Random-
                     -Per Chr- --Block-- -Rewrite- -Per Chr- --Block-- --
Seeks--
Machine      Size K/sec %CP K/sec %CP K/sec %CP K/sec %CP K/sec %CP \
/sec %CP
atlorca2     8064M 15385  99 146197  20 58263    8 14833  99 126001    9 \
924.6    1
                     ------Sequential Create------ --------Random Create--------
                     -Create-- --Read--- -Delete-- -Create-- --Read--- -
Delete--
files:max:min          /sec %CP  /sec %CP  /sec %CP  /sec %CP  /sec %CP \
/sec %CP
    16:262144:8/128  1175   24 12785 100 10236   95  1097   22 12280   99 \
6060   72
```

Just by changing the filesystem and journal log location, we pick up some nice performance on sequential I/O access with respect to XFS. The point of the previous demonstration is to identify factors other than hardware that increase performance. As we have seen, simply changing the filesystem layout or type can increase performance greatly. One other performance tool we enjoy using for SCSI measurements is IOzone, found at www.iozone.org.

Assessing Application CPU Utilization Issues

As with any performance problem, usually more than one factor exists. Our troubleshooting performance journey continues with coverage of application CPU usage and how to monitor it. In this section, CPU usage and application-specific topics are covered, focusing on process threads.

Determining What Processes Are Causing High CPU Utilization

To begin, we want to demonstrate how a few lines of code can load a CPU to a 100% busy state. The C code "using SLES 9 with long integer" illustrates a simple count program, which stresses the CPU in user space. It is important to understand that our application is not in system space, also called kernel mode, because we are not focusing on any I/O as previously discussed in this chapter.

Example 1 goes like this:

```
#include <stdio.h>
#include <sched.h>
#include <pthread.h>  /* POSIX threads */
#include <stdlib.h>

#define num_threads  1

void *print_func(void *);

int main ()
```

```
{
        int x;
        printf("main() process has PID= %d PPID= %d\n", getpid(),
        getppid());

        pthread_t tid[num_threads];
        /* Now to create pthreads */
        for (x=0; x <= num_threads;x++)
        pthread_create(tid + x, NULL, print_func, NULL );

        /*wait for termination of threads before main continues*/
        for (x=0; x < num_threads;x++)
        {
        pthread_join(tid[x], NULL);
        printf("Main() PID %d joined with thread %d\n", getpid(),
        tid[x]);
        }
}


void *print_func (void *arg)
{
        long int y;
        printf("PID %d  PPID = %d  TID = %d\n",getpid(), getppid(),
        pthread_self());
        /* creating a very large loop for the CPU to chew on  :) */
/* Note, the following line may be changed to: for (y=1;y>0;y++) */
        for (y=1; y<10000000000000;y++)
        printf ("%d\n", y);
        return 0;
}
```

Note that instead of just counting to a large integer, you may want to create an infinite loop. The C code in Example 2 (also shown in Chapter 8, "Linux Processes: Structures, Hangs, and Core Dumps") generates an infinite loop with a signal handler used to kill the threads.

```
#include <pthread.h> /* POSIX threads */
#include <signal.h>
#include <stdlib.h>
#include <linux/unistd.h>
#include <errno.h>

#define num_threads  8

void *print_func(void *);
void threadid(int);
void stop_thread(int sig);
_syscall0(pid_t,gettid)

int main ()
{
        int x;
        pid_t tid;
        pthread_t threadid[num_threads];

        (void) signal(SIGALRM,stop_thread); /*signal handler */

        printf("Main process has PID= %d PPID= %d and TID= %d\n",
        getpid(), getppid(), gettid());

        /* Now to create pthreads */
        for (x=1; x <= num_threads;++x)
        pthread_create(&threadid[x], NULL, print_func, NULL );

        sleep(60); /* Let the threads warm the cpus up!!! :) */
        for (x=1; x < num_threads;++x)
                pthread_kill(threadid[x], SIGALRM);

        /*wait for termination of threads before main continues*/
        for (x=1; x < num_threads;++x)
        {
```

```
        printf("%d\n",x);
        pthread_join(threadid[x], NULL);
        printf("Main() PID %d joined with thread %d\n", getpid(),
        threadid[x]);
        }
}


void *print_func (void *arg)
{
        printf("PID %d  PPID = %d  Thread value of pthread_self = %d and
        TID= %d\n",getpid(), getppid(), pthread_self(),gettid());
        while(1);  /* nothing but spinning */
}


void stop_thread(int sig) {
pthread_exit(NULL);
}
```

To continue with Example 1, compile the code and run the application as follows:

```
atlorca2:/home/greg # cc -o CPU_load_count CPU_Load_count.c -lpthread
atlorca2:/home/greg # ./CPU_load_count | grep -i pid
main() process has PID= 5970 PPID= 3791
PID 5970  PPID = 3791  TID = 36354240
PID 5970  PPID = 3791  TID = 69908672
```

When running top, shown next, we find that our CPUs have a load, yet the PID reports zero percent usage for the CPU_load_count program. So where is the load coming from? To answer this question, we must look at the threads spawned by the parent process.

```
atlorca2:~ # top
top - 20:27:15 up 36 min, 3 users, load average: 1.24, 1.22, 1.14
Tasks: 79 total,  1 running, 78 sleeping,  0 stopped,  0 zombie
 Cpu0 :  0.1% us,  0.6% sy,  0.0% ni, 99.1% id,  0.2% wa,  0.0% hi, \
0.0% si
```

```
 Cpu1 :  1.7% us,  1.6% sy,  0.0% ni, 96.7% id,  0.0% wa,  0.0% hi, \
0.0% si
 Cpu2 : 44.1% us, 19.0% sy,  0.0% ni, 36.9% id,  0.0% wa,  0.0% hi, \
0.0% si
 Cpu3 : 43.3% us, 21.0% sy,  0.0% ni, 35.7% id,  0.0% wa,  0.0% hi, \
0.0% si
Mem:   4142992k total,   792624k used,  3350368k free,   176352k buffers
Swap:  1049568k total,        0k used,  1049568k free,   308864k cached

  PID USER       PR  NI  VIRT  RES  SHR S %CPU %MEM    TIME+   \
PPID RUSER      UID WCHAN       COMMAND
 5974 root       16   0  3632 2112 3184 R  0.7  0.1   0:00.13  3874 \
root        0 -          top
 5971 root       15   0  3168 1648 2848 S  3.3  0.0   0:02.16  3791 \
root        0 pipe_wait grep
 5970 root       17   0 68448 1168 2560 S  0.0  0.0   0:00.00  3791 \
root        0 schedule_ CPU_load_count
 5966 root       16   0  7376 4624 6128 S  0.0  0.1   0:00.01  5601 \
root        0 schedule_ vi
 5601 root       15   0  5744 3920 4912 S  0.0  0.1   0:00.11  5598 \
root        0 wait4     bash
 5598 root       16   0 15264 6288  13m S  0.0  0.2   0:00.04  3746 \
root        0 schedule_ sshd
```

You can see top shows that the CPU_Load_count program is running, yet it reflects zero load on the CPU. This is because top is not thread-aware in SLES 9 by default.

A simple way to determine a thread's impact on a CPU is by using ps with certain flags, as demonstrated in the following. This is because in Linux, threads are separate processes (tasks).

```
atlorca2:/proc # ps -elfm >/tmp/ps.elfm.out
```

vi the file, find the PID, and focus on the threads in running (R) state.

```
F S UID        PID  PPID  C PRI  NI ADDR SZ WCHAN  STIME TTY      \
TIME CMD
4 - root      5970  3791  0   -   - - 4276 -       20:26 pts/0  \
00:00:00 ./CPU_load_count
4 S root         -     -  0  77   0 -       - schedu 20:26 - \
00:00:00 -
1 R root         -     - 64  77   0 -       - schedu 20:26 - \
00:02:41 -
1 S root         -     - 64  79   0 -       - schedu 20:26 - \
00:02:40 -
```

Though top provides a great cursory view of your system, other performance tools are sometimes required to find the smoking gun, such as the ps command in the preceding example. Other times, performance trends are required to isolate a problem area, and products such as HP Insight Manager with performance plug-ins may be more suited.

Using Oracle statspak

In the following example, we use Oracle's statistics package, called statspak, to focus on an Oracle performance concern.

```
DB Name      DB Id  Instance  Inst Num  Release      Cluster Host
----------- ----------- ---------- -------- --------- ------- ----------
DB_NAME     1797322438 DB_NAME       3 9.2.0.4.0     YES     Server_name


             Snap Id     Snap Time      Sessions Curs/Sess Comment
           ------- ------------------ -------- --------- ------------------
Begin Snap:                          23942 Date 11:39:12    144      3.0

  End Snap:                          23958 Date 11:49:17    148      3.1

  Elapsed:                               10.08 (mins)


Cache Sizes (end)
~~~~~~~~~~~~~~~~~
             Buffer Cache:   6,144M     Std Block Size:     8K
         Shared Pool Size:   1,024M        Log Buffer: 10,240K
```

```
Load Profile
~~~~~~~~~~~~                 Per Second  Per Transaction
                            ---------------  ---------------
              Redo size:    6,535,063.00        6,362.58
          Logical reads:       30,501.36           29.70 <-Cache Reads LIO
          Block changes:       15,479.36           15.07
         Physical reads:        2,878.69            2.80 <-Disk reads PIO
        Physical writes:        3,674.53            3.58 <-Disk Writes PIO
             User calls:        5,760.67            5.61
                Parses:            1.51            0.00
           Hard parses:            0.01            0.00
                 Sorts:          492.41            0.48
                Logons:            0.09            0.00
              Executes:        2,680.27            2.61
          Transactions:        1,027.11
```

```
     % Blocks changed per Read:  50.75   Recursive Call %:      15.27
    Rollback per transaction %:   0.01   Rows per Sort:          2.29
```

Instance Efficiency Percentages (Target 100%)
~~~~~~
```
              Buffer Nowait %:  99.98      Redo NoWait %:     100.00
              Buffer  Hit   %:  90.57   In-memory Sort %:     100.00
             Library Hit   %: 100.00       Soft Parse %:      99.45
          Execute to Parse %:  99.94       Latch Hit %:       98.37
   Parse CPU to Parse Elapsed %:  96.00     % Non-Parse CPU:     99.99
```

```
    Shared Pool Statistics      Begin    End
                                ------   ------
              Memory Usage %:    28.16   28.17
        % SQL with executions>1:  82.91   81.88
       % Memory for SQL w/exec>1:  90.94   90.49
```

```
Top 5 Timed Events

~~~~~~~~~~~~~~~~~~                                      % Total
Event                              Waits    Time (s)   Ela Time
----------------------------    -----------  -----------  --------

db file sequential read        1,735,573      17,690      51.88
log file sync                    664,956       8,315      24.38
CPU time                                       3,172       9.32
global cache open x            1,556,450       1,136       3.36
log file sequential read           3,652         811       2.35


-> s  - second
-> cs - centisecond -     100th of a second
-> ms - millisecond -    1000th of a second
-> us - microsecond - 1000000th of a second

                                                   Avg
                                        Total Wait  Wait    Waits
Event                   Waits  Timeouts  Time (s)   (ms)    /txn
-------------------- ----------- ---------- ---------- ------ --------

db file sequential read  1,738,577        0    17,690     10     2.8
```

This statspak output is truncated to conserve space. Some of the key points of interest are highlighted in bold: Logical reads (LIO), Physical reads/writes (PIO), Latches, Buffered I/O, and db file sequential read. Please understand that many hundred parameters exist, and Oracle has published many performance documents and created many classes that we recommend reading and taking. However, this chapter's main goal is performance troubleshooting from a wide view, or in other words, a quick reference guide to performance troubleshooting. The bold areas in the previous listing are some critical places to focus, especially with LIO and PIO.

To elaborate on the bold elements in the previous listing, we begin with LIO and PIO. LIO is the access of a memory register, residing in the database buffer cache, and PIO is an I/O operation request from Oracle to the system for a data block fetch from spindle. In short, LIO is faster than PIO, but PIO is not always the bottleneck. A critical piece of the puzzle with regards to performance problems on any database connected to any storage device is understanding that a small percentage of PIOs (from Oracle's viewpoint) are actually a read from the host cache, storage cache, or both. Thus, a PIO from the database's perspective may in fact still be a read from cache, so having a high number of PIOs is not always a bad omen. In the previous example, the PIO reads were around 1.7 million with an average latency of 10ms, which, by the way, is not bad. However, although the I/O is fine, a memory control performance problem may still linger in the background.

Thus, while I/O may in fact be fine, memory lock control also must be addressed for smooth, fast database operation. Note that in this example, the Latch hit percentage is around 98%, which raises a red flag. A latch is basically a protection agent for access control with regards to shared memory within the system's global area (SGA). In short, the goal is to keep memory available so that the latch-free count remains high, keeping the percentage of Latch hit percentage around 99.5%. Latch info can be viewed by reviewing both the willing-to-wait and not-willing-to-wait latches found in the `immediate_gets` and `immediate_misses` columns by using `V$LATCH` or by looking at Oracle's `statspack`. In addition to waiting on free memory segments with regards to latches, we need to touch on buffer waits.

When a database starts to show an increase in buffer waits, the objective is to focus on the two main issues. The first issue is that memory is running low, which is impacting the second issue, that of physical I/O read/writes. A buffer wait is logged when the database must flush a write to spindle to clear up some available cache for data processing. The quick solution to this problem is to run raw (or other proprietary filesystem such as OCFS) to bypass host buffer cache so that buffer cache is used for data processing only. However, the huge drawback to using a non-buffer cache filesystem is the loss of performance with respect to read-ahead as discussed earlier in this chapter.

Now that we have covered some I/O basics, both physical and logical, and memory control with respect to latches, we present an example of an application failing to initialize due to lack of shared memory space. We demonstrate a lack of shared memory without going into detail about system V message queues, semaphores, or shared memory. As with all applications, more memory equals faster performance, and without enough memory, system failure is imminent.

Troubleshooting "No Space Left on Device" Errors When Allocating Shared Memory

Our example shows a common error 28 example using a 64-bit kernel, with a 64-bit application failing to initialize due to a memory address problem. Our focus is on interprocess communication (IPCS), as with any large application that spawns multiple threads/processes. Using our 64-bit machine, we bring a 64-bit Oracle 10g instance online, which fails with the following error to demonstrate a failed IPCS.

```
ORA-27102: out of memory
Linux-x86_64 Error: 28: No space left on device
```

System parameters are as follows:

```
# ipcs
------ Shared Memory Segments --------
key shmid owner perms bytes nattch status
0x00000000 1245184 gdm 600 393216 2 dest
0x852af124 127926273 oracle 640 8558477312 15
------- Semaphore Arrays --------
key semid owner perms nsems
0x3fbfeb1c 1933312 oracle 640 154

==== kernel parameters ======
# sysctl -a
kernel.sem = 250 32000 100 128
kernel.msgmnb = 16384
kernel.msgmni = 16
kernel.msgmax = 8192
kernel.shmmni = 4096
kernel.shmall = 2097152
kernel.shmmax = 34359738368
==== process ulimits (bash shell)
$ ulimit -a
core file size (blocks, -c) 0
data seg size (kbytes, -d) unlimited
file size (blocks, -f) unlimited
max locked memory (kbytes, -l) 4
max memory size (kbytes, -m) unlimited
open files (-n) 65536
pipe size (512 bytes, -p) 8
```

```
stack size (kbytes, -s) 10240
cpu time (seconds, -t) unlimited
max user processes (-u) 16384
virtual memory (kbytes, -v) unlimited
```

This failure is a result of the kernel not being able to fulfill the shared memory request. Not enough space is a condition explained in /usr/src/linux/ipc/shm.c, which reads:

```
if (shm_tot + numpages >= shm_ctlall)
        return -ENOSPC;
```

The program we tried to start previously required more shared memory than we had allocated, which in turn caused the Oracle application to fail on initialization. The solution is to increase shared memory by the kernel parameter. In this example, we simply increase it to shmall=8388608.

Additional Performance Tools

As we conclude this chapter, we cover some uncommon tools that can be used to monitor performance characteristics and build charts in most cases. isag, RRDtool, Ganglia (which uses RRDtool to monitor grid computing and clustering), and Nagios are great performance tools. More monitoring tools exist, but for the most part, they are common tools used every day such as sar, iostat, top, and netstat. Due to space limitations, we only cover isag in this chapter. However, the other tools are easy to find and configure if one so desires. isag, found at http://www.volny.cz/linux_monitor/isag/index.html, provides a nice graphical front end to sar. After systat tools have been loaded, isag should be included, as depicted here:

```
atlorca2:/tmp # rpm -qf /usr/bin/isag
sysstat-5.0.1-35.1
```

isag

Most engineers who work with sar, iostat, and other performance tools will enjoy using isag, the GUI front end to sar. To give a quick demonstration of how the tool works, we must enable sar to collect some data. To achieve a real-world demonstration, we repeat our previous bonnie++ test while running sar -A to collect as much detail as possible and display it through isag.

To demonstrate, we mount an XFS filesystem with a local journal and use an NFS mount point to a HPUX server to demonstrate both disk and network load through bonnie++ while monitoring through sar and isag.

```
atlorca2:/var/log/sa # mount -t xfs -o logbufs=8,logbsize=32768 \
/dev/sdj1 /xfs.test

atlorca2:/var/log/sa # df
Filesystem            1K-blocks        Used Available Use% Mounted on

hpuxos.atl.hp.com:/scratch/customers
                      284470272   50955984 218940848  19% \
/scratch/customers
/dev/sdj1             244308608        4608 244304000   1% /xfs.test

atlorca2:/var/log/sa #  sar -A -o 1 100 #This will build a fine in \
/var/log/sa that isag will use.

atlorca2:/var/log/sa # isag
```

The resulting screenshots provide information on CPU utilization (see Figure 4-2) and swap utilization (see Figure 4-3).

Remember, if you are swapping, you need more memory.

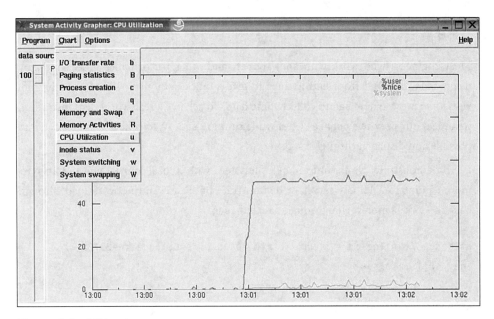

Figure 4-2 CPU utilization

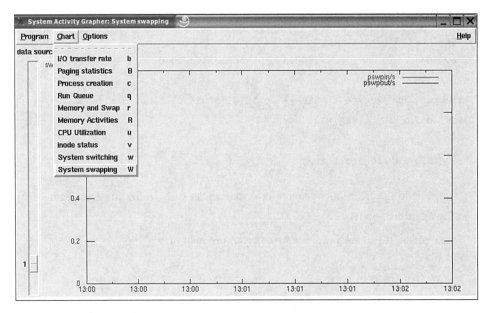

Figure 4-3 Swap utilization

Summary

Performance troubleshooting relies upon comparison. To know that performance is bad, you must have a preexisting benchmark from when performance was good. Though we can continue giving hundreds of examples of performance-related issues, a better approach is to understand the tools and know what to focus on.

To solve storage-related performance problems, you must be familiar with common tools such as `sar` and `iostat`. For threaded applications, make sure your version of `top` shows threads. Otherwise, focus on the `ps` command with the `m` flag. Other performance monitoring tools exist, such as Oprofile, Prospect, q-tools (q-syscollect, q-view, and q-dot), Perfmon, and Caliper.

5

Adding New Storage via SAN with Reference to PCMCIA and USB

"Nothing has changed on my system" is a common statement made by people calling an IT helpline for assistance. It is a well-known fact that no system remains stagnant forever, so for those who try to achieve life eternal for their systems, ultimate failure awaits. Take racing as an apt analogy. If a racer never upgrades to a newer engine (CPU) or chassis (model), then the racer will have a hard time staying competitive. Thus, in this chapter, we discuss how to add more to our "racer."

The term storage area network (SAN) will become, if it is not already, a common one among system administrators. The capability to consolidate all storage in a data center into large frames containing many drives is indeed the direction companies will, and need to, take. Large enterprise operating systems such as HPUX, AIX, Solaris, SGI, MVS, and others have made very impressive leaps in that direction. Therefore, Linux must "Lead, follow, or get out of the way." With vendor support from Emulex, QLogic, and others, Fibre Channel storage has become commonplace for Linux, and now system administrators must learn the tricks of the trade to become power players.

In this chapter, we discuss adding disk storage (the most commonly added item) through SAN and touch on PCMCIA/USB. We begin by defining the configuration used to demonstrate our examples and by discussing some highlights. We then discuss the addition of a PCI device to connect additional storage. Next, we move to a discussion of adding storage to a defined PCI device. Due to its complex nature, we conclude this chapter by covering a few topics with respect to adding storage through PCMCIA/USB.

Configuration

With any SAN, consideration for the balance between performance and capacity always must be paramount. If too much emphasis is placed on capacity, performance will surely suffer, so heed the word of your storage vendor about storage layout. In this chapter, we focus only on how to increase storage with a simple storage layout, and not on performance.

We use the following two servers to illustrate our concepts.

The particulars on Machine 1 are as follows:

```
[root@cyclops root]# uname -a
Linux cyclops 2.4.9-e.10custom-gt #4 SMP Mon Nov 1 14:17:36 EST 2004 \
i686 unknown
[root@cyclops root]# cat /etc/redhat-release
Red Hat Linux Advanced Server release 2.1AS (Pensacola)
```

Machine 2 looks like this:

```
atlorca4:~ # uname -a
Linux atlorca4 2.6.5-7.97-default #1 SMP Fri Jul 2 14:21:59 UTC 2004 \
ia64 ia64 ia64 GNU/Linux
atlorca4:~ # cat /etc/SuSE-release
SUSE LINUX Enterprise Server 9 (ia64)
VERSION = 9
```

The following representations outline the two servers within the SAN.

First, Machine 1 (Cyclops):

```
(Cyclops) Has two Emulex LP8000 HBAs
 |-LP8000-|-WWN 10000000c9241327 ----> FCID 0x7b0f00 on Brocade 28000

Storage location for Brocade 28000 Domain 0x7b

Brocade 28000 Domain 0x7b port 0 -->--ISL --> Domain 0x78 Brocade 2800 \
Port 1
```

```
Domain 0x78 Brocade 2800  port 5 connects to >--- Storage array



|-LP8000-|-WWN 10000000c9286bda --> FCID 0x7f0d00 on Brocade 28000

Storage location for Brocade 28000 Domain 0x7f

Two ISL hopes:

Brocade 28000 Domain 0x7f port 0 -->--ISL --> Domain 0x7b Brocade 28000 \
  port 1, then port 0 -->--ISL --> Domain 0x78 Brocade 2800 Port 1

Domain 0x78 Brocade 2800  port 5 connects to >--- Storage array
```

This design is nothing more than an example of fault-tolerant Host Bus Adapter (HBA). If we lose the storage port, our host loses access to the storage.

Then we have Machine 2 (`atlorca4`):

```
|-LP9802-|-WWN 10000000c93d3fc5 --> FCID 0x652d13 on Mcdata 6064 director \
port 41 (2d hex = 45 dec subtract 4 = 41)
```

note

This calculation works on any McDATA switch, calculating the port number from the `FCID` area field. Many tricks exist for different switches, but they are beyond the scope of this chapter.

As you can see in the previous example, the storage array plugs into port 41 on FCID 0x652b13 of McDATA 6064, yielding 100% locality for this host.

Kernel Module

After successful configuration is achieved, you can move on to making the device function under Linux. This is done at the driver module level. First determine whether the system can support the new hardware.

The simplest way to begin is by examining the system to determine whether another similar device is attached. See the following example of how to make this determination in a Linux environment.

Scenario 5-1: Determine Whether a Similar Device Exists

In our example, we begin by adding "another" PCI Emulex HBA LP9802 to our existing SUSE Linux Enterprise Server 9 (ia64) - Kernel 2.6.5-7.97-default machine. Again, our first step must be to confirm whether the kernel can control the newly added device.

First, determine whether a similar device exists. Begin by confirming the running OS distribution, as demonstrated next.

```
atlorca4:~ # cat /etc/SuSE-release
SUSE LINUX Enterprise Server 9 (ia64)
VERSION = 9
atlorca4:~ # cat /etc/lsb-release
LSB_VERSION="1.3"
```

Note that these files exist on almost all distributions of Linux. In Red Hat, the filename would be /etc/redhat-release. You should always check the file to confirm which operating system version is in use.

Understanding the exact OS with regards to library versions is the next step. In the next example, we depict the PCI devices with different commands to illustrate different ways to determine which PCI adapters we have installed. In the following examples, we are looking for Emulex HBAs.

```
atlorca4:~ # lspci
0000:00:00.0 Communication controller: Hewlett-Packard Company Auxiliary
Diva Serial Port (rev 01)
0000:00:00.1 Serial controller: Hewlett-Packard Company Diva Serial [GSP]
Multiport UART (rev 03)
0000:00:03.0 SCSI storage controller: LSI Logic / Symbios Logic 53c1010
66MHz  Ultra3 SCSI Adapter (rev 01)
0000:00:03.1 SCSI storage controller: LSI Logic / Symbios Logic 53c1010
66MHz  Ultra3 SCSI Adapter (rev 01)
0000:30:01.0 SCSI storage controller: LSI Logic / Symbios Logic 53c1010
66MHz  Ultra3 SCSI Adapter (rev 01)
```

```
0000:40:01.0 PCI bridge: IBM PCI-X to PCI-X Bridge (rev 02)

0000:41:01.0 SCSI storage controller: LSI Logic / Symbios Logic 53c1010
66MHz  Ultra3 SCSI Adapter (rev 01)

0000:41:01.1 SCSI storage controller: LSI Logic / Symbios Logic 53c1010
66MHz  Ultra3 SCSI Adapter (rev 01)

0000:41:04.0 Ethernet controller: Broadcom Corporation NetXtreme BCM5701
Gigabit Ethernet (rev 15)
```

**0000:50:01.0 Fibre Channel: Emulex Corporation LP9802 Fibre Channel
Adapter (rev 01)**

```
0000:60:01.0 PCI bridge: Intel Corp. 21154 PCI-to-PCI Bridge

0000:61:04.0 USB Controller: NEC Corporation USB (rev 41)

0000:61:04.1 USB Controller: NEC Corporation USB (rev 41)

0000:61:04.2 USB Controller: NEC Corporation USB 2.0 (rev 02)

0000:61:05.0 VGA compatible controller: ATI Technologies Inc Radeon RV100
QY [Radeon 7000/VE]
```

**0000:70:01.0 Fibre Channel: Emulex Corporation LP9802 Fibre Channel
Adapter (rev 01)**

Scenario 5-2: Mapping with /proc/ioports

Now that we have confirmed that existing devices match what we are trying to add, the next logical step is checking the installed driver version. In addition, we need to confirm that a driver exists for the device that is on the PCI bus. Yes, logic dictates that if the device is present, so is the driver, but that is not always the case. The easiest way to match a hardware device to the driver is by using /proc/ioports on IA64 or by using an open source tool called lshw found at http://ezix.sourceforge.net/software/lshw.html for IA64- or IA32-based machines. Scenario 5-2 shows examples of how to make the correlation through /proc/ioports to a given device.

```
atlorca4:~ # cat /proc/ioports
00000000-00000fff : PCI Bus 0000:00
  00000060-0000006f : i8042
  00000500-000005ff : 0000:00:03.0
    00000500-000005ff : sym53c8xx
  00000600-000006ff : 0000:00:03.1
    00000600-000006ff : sym53c8xx
```

```
00001000-00001fff : PCI Bus 0000:08
00002000-00003fff : PCI Bus 0000:10
00004000-00005fff : PCI Bus 0000:20
00006000-00007fff : PCI Bus 0000:30
    00006000-000060ff : 0000:30:01.0
        00006000-000060ff : sym53c8xx
00008000-00009fff : PCI Bus 0000:40
    00008000-000080ff : 0000:41:01.0
        00008000-000080ff : sym53c8xx
    00008100-000081ff : 0000:41:01.1
        00008100-000081ff : sym53c8xx
0000a000-0000bfff : PCI Bus 0000:50 ***<-Hardware address
    0000a000-0000a0ff : 0000:50:01.0 ***<-Hardware address
        0000a000-0000a0ff : lpfc *******<-LP9802 driver
0000c000-0000dfff : PCI Bus 0000:60
    0000c000-0000c0ff : 0000:61:05.0
0000e000-0000ffff : PCI Bus 0000:70 ***<-Hardware address
    0000e000-0000e0ff : 0000:70:01.0 ***<-Hardware address
        0000e000-0000e0ff : lpfc *******<-LP9802 driver
```

Note that determining the HBA is difficult because of the lack of detailed information. However, looking at the same data through `lshw` yields valuable information about the HBA, as well as other features of the server. In the following example of `lshw`, we only present the computer description, CPU, and Emulex HBAs to save space.

```
atlorca4:~/lshw-B.02.03 # lshw
atlorca4
    description: Computer
    product: server rx7620
    vendor: hp
    serial: USE4415CHJ
    capabilities: smbios-2.3 dmi-2.3
    configuration: uuid=8785E28C-17A4-D811-964E-E240B01E4A4B
  *-core
      description: Motherboard
      physical id: 0
```

```
*-firmware
        description: BIOS
        vendor: HP
        physical id: 0
        version: 000.018
        size: 1MB
        capacity: 11MB
*-memory
        description: System memory
        physical id: 2
        size: 2016MB
*-cpu:0
        product: Itanium 2
        vendor: Intel Corp.
        physical id: 4
        bus info: cpu@0
        version: 5
        size: 1300MHz
*-cpu:1
        product: Itanium 2
        vendor: Intel Corp.
        physical id: 5
        bus info: cpu@1
        version: 5
        size: 1300MHz
        capabilities: emulated hyperthreading
...
```

We skip a great deal to focus on the Fibre HBAs.

```
...
*-fiber:0
        description: Fibre Channel
        product: LP9802 Fibre Channel Adapter
        vendor: Emulex Corporation
        physical id: 8
```

```
                bus info: pci@50:01.0
                logical name: scsi5
                version: 01
                width: 64 bits
                clock: 66MHz
                capabilities: bus_master cap_list scsi-host
                configuration: driver=lpfc
                resources: iomemory:10040000-10040fff \
                iomemory:10041000-100410ff irq:75


   *-fiber:1
                description: Fibre Channel
                product: LP9802 Fibre Channel Adapter
                vendor: Emulex Corporation
                physical id: 1
                bus info: pci@70:01.0
                version: 01
                width: 64 bits
                clock: 66MHz
                capabilities: bus_master cap_list
                configuration: driver=lpfc
                resources: iomemory:30040000-30040fff \
                iomemory:30041000-300410ff irq:83
```

Though the previous lshw and /proc/ioports examples indicate that we have identical hardware and a driver capable of running such hardware, we have two outstanding issues. The first issue concerns the driver version, and the second concerns adding hardware when a driver or the existing hardware does not match the new hardware.

Scenario 5-3: Determine Driver Version

To address the first issue, we need to discuss methods of finding a driver for a given device. Many methods exist, but due to their speed, the following two are our favorites. The fastest way to determine the driver version is to use the cat command on the driver instance, found in /proc filesystem. In Scenario 5-2, we know that the driver is lpfc, and that it falls under the SCSI layer. In the /proc/scsi/ directory, we find that the lpfc directory contains multiple instances (HBAs), as indicated in this scenario.

```
atlorca4:/proc/scsi/lpfc # cat 5
Emulex LightPulse FC SCSI 2.10f
HBA: Emulex LightPulse LP9802 (2 Gigabit) on PCI bus 50 device 08 irq 75
SerialNum: P6C640BTEPZPLU
Firmware Version: 1.01A2 (H2D1.01A2)
Hdw: 2003806d
VendorId: 0xf98010df
Portname: 10:00:00:00:c9:3d:3f:c5   Nodename: 20:00:00:00:c9:3d:3f:c5


Link Up - Ready:
   PortID 0x652d13
   Fabric
   Current speed 2G


lpfc0t00 DID 652b13 WWPN 50:06:0e:80:03:4e:46:11 WWNN \
\50:06:0e:80:03:4e:46:11
```

Note that depending on the applicable driver, manufacturer, or both, the information contained in these files can vary greatly. In the following illustration, we moved to a different host running Red Hat Linux and QLogic HBAs.

The first step to checking driver and HBA types is to determine the OS generation, as in the following example:

```
[root@cmtlinp3 qla2300]# cat /etc/lsb-release
LSB_VERSION="1.3"


[root@cmtlinp3 qla2300]# cat /etc/redhat-release
Red Hat Enterprise Linux ES release 3 (Taroon Update 4)
Linux cmtlinp3.atl.hp.com 2.4.21-27.ELsmp #1 SMP Wed Dec 1 21:59:02 EST \
2004 i686 i686 i386 GNU/Linux
```

The second step is to check the driver for the QLogic cards. Note that lshw is used to find the QLogic cards. Then we go to the /proc/scsi/qla2300 directory.

```
[root@cmtlinp3 qla2300]# pwd
/proc/scsi/qla2300
[root@cmtlinp3 qla2300]# ll
total 0
-rw-r--r--   1 root     root            0 Apr  1 13:33 1
crw-------   1 root     root     254,   0 Apr  1 13:33 HbaApiNode


[root@cmtlinp3 qla2300]# cat 0
QLogic PCI to Fibre Channel Host Adapter for QLA2340            :
        Firmware version:  3.03.01, Driver version 7.01.01
Entry address = e0834060
HBA: QLA2312 , Serial# S95189
Request Queue = 0x1f8f0000, Response Queue = 0x1f8e0000
Request Queue count= 512, Response Queue count= 512
Total number of active commands = 0
Total number of interrupts = 977
Total number of IOCBs (used/max) = (0/600)
Total number of queued commands = 0
    Device queue depth = 0x20
Number of free request entries = 19
Number of mailbox timeouts = 0
Number of ISP aborts = 0
Number of loop resyncs = 0
Number of retries for empty slots = 0
Number of reqs in pending_q= 0, retry_q= 0, done_q= 0, scsi_retry_q= 0
Host adapter:loop state= <READY>, flags= 0x860a13
Dpc flags = 0x1000000
MBX flags = 0x0
SRB Free Count = 4096
Link down Timeout = 008
Port down retry = 030
Login retry count = 030
Commands retried with dropped frame(s) = 0
Configured characteristic impedence: 50 ohms
Configured data rate: 1-2 Gb/sec auto-negotiate
```

```
SCSI Device Information:
scsi-qla0-adapter-node=200000e08b1c15eb;
scsi-qla0-adapter-port=210000e08b1c15eb;
scsi-qla0-target-0=50060b00001a0b12;


SCSI LUN Information:
(Id:Lun)  * - indicates lun is not registered with the OS.
( 0: 0): Total reqs 298, Pending reqs 0, flags 0x0, 0:0:6c,
( 0: 1): Total reqs 97, Pending reqs 0, flags 0x0, 0:0:6c,
( 0: 2): Total reqs 97, Pending reqs 0, flags 0x0, 0:0:6c,
( 0: 3): Total reqs 97, Pending reqs 0, flags 0x0, 0:0:6c,
( 0: 4): Total reqs 97, Pending reqs 0, flags 0x0, 0:0:6c,
( 0: 5): Total reqs 97, Pending reqs 0, flags 0x0, 0:0:6c,
( 0: 6): Total reqs 97, Pending reqs 0, flags 0x0, 0:0:6c,
( 0: 7): Total reqs 97, Pending reqs 0, flags 0x0, 0:0:6c,
```

As you can see, a great deal of information can be provided, and the amount depends on the driver author. If the driver exists, as shown previously, adding the new hardware can be an easy step without taking the server offline. However, the phrase "adding hardware online" needs to be clearly defined.

As used throughout the remainder of this chapter (and as in the phrase, "adding hardware online"), "online" means not having to reboot the OS. Although this can be a great thing, note that it currently is not possible in most (if any) PCI-based machines with the Linux OS. However, adding storage to an existing PCI controller is fully allowed by almost all vendors.

To add PCI devices on the fly, first, the Processor Dependent Code (PDC) must initiate a scan to address any PCI slots that have been filled, which is done on initial power up. After the scan is complete, a wake-up command must be sent to the BIOS/PDC to reinitialize the scan procedure and power up a PCI slot. This step is followed by a rescan of the OS's PCI bus. To reverse this process, the OS must be able to suspend any driver instance (not the entire module, which would halt all instances of the driver), allowing a PCI slot to be powered down. The capability to power down a PCI slot exists in most enterprise servers such as HPUX, Solaris, and AIX among others, but this feature has not been perfected in the same hardware platforms running Linux. Hopefully, it is just a matter of time before the systems running Linux have this capability. However, in the meantime, a reboot is needed to add a PCI device, as long as the driver exists or is noted in the `/etc/sysconfig/kernel` under the variable `INITRD_MODULES` or `/etc/modules.conf`.

When installing a new PCI device, it does not matter whether the driver is installed before or after the device is inserted into the PCI slot. But again, at the current time in Linux, most PCI buses do not detect a newly added PCI device without a reboot.

In the next examples, we discuss adding LUNs through the PCI bus over the HBAs. In one example, we demonstrate adding LUNs online, whereas in another example, we discuss adding LUNs when there is no existing device driver.

Adding LUNs via PCI

Many different methods of adding devices are discussed throughout this book. However, the most important method is one in which the operating system and application can stay online. In this section, we discuss ways to add LUNs to a PCI bus device on the fly (online) and offline.

In the following discussion, we shed some light on limitations with the Linux kernel SCSI source code from older kernels. The SCSI source code responsible for scanning SCSI devices is located at `/usr/src/linux/drivers/scsi/scsi_scan.c` and contains the code and parameters for spawning the scan on a given bus.

With older kernels such as 2.4.9-e.10, the definitions for the `BLIST_` parameters were listed as follows:

```
#define BLIST_NOLUN       0x001   /* Don't scan for LUNs */
#define BLIST_FORCELUN    0x002   /* Known to have LUNs, force scanning */
#define BLIST_BORKEN      0x004   /* Flag for broken handshaking */
#define BLIST_KEY         0x008   /* Needs to be unlocked by special
                                     command */
#define BLIST_SINGLELUN   0x010   /* LUNs should better not be used in
                                     parallel */
#define BLIST_NOTQ        0x020   /* Buggy Tagged Command Queuing */
#define BLIST_SPARSELUN   0x040   /* Non consecutive LUN numbering */
#define BLIST_MAX5LUN     0x080   /* Avoid LUNS >= 5 */
#define BLIST_ISDISK      0x100   /* Treat as (removable) disk */
#define BLIST_ISROM       0x200   /* Treat as (removable) CD-ROM */
```

Today, with the 2.6.X kernels, the following items have been added or changed:

```
#define BLIST_NOLUN              0x001  /* Only scan LUN 0 */
#define BLIST_LARGELUN           0x200  /* LUNs past 7 on a SCSI-2
                                           device */
#define BLIST_INQUIRY_36         0x400  /* override additional length
                                           field */
#define BLIST_INQUIRY_58         0x800  /* ... for broken inquiry
                                           responses */
#define BLIST_NOSTARTONADD       0x1000 /* do not do automatic start on
                                           add */
#define BLIST_MS_SKIP_PAGE_08    0x2000 /* do not send ms page 0x08 */
#define BLIST_MS_SKIP_PAGE_3F    0x4000 /* do not send ms page 0x3f */
#define BLIST_USE_10_BYTE_MS     0x8000 /* use 10 byte ms before 6 byte
                                           ms */
#define BLIST_MS_192_BYTES_FOR_3F        0x10000 /*  192 byte ms page 0x3f
                                           request */
#define BLIST_REPORTLUN2         0x20000 /* try REPORT_LUNS even for SCSI-
                                           2 devs
#define BLIST_NOREPORTLUN        0x40000 /* don't try REPORT_LUNS scan
                                           (SCSI-3 devs) */
```

Within the previous fields, the most important thing to do if you are having issues with scanning storage is to confirm that the dev_info fields have been defined with the appropriate functions.

In the 2.4.X kernels, the dev_info was contained within the scsi_scan.c file; however, in the later kernels, the list of supported devices has become very lengthy and deserving of its own file, scsi_devinfo.c. Either way, the following example holds true for depicting device definitions according to the limits of scsi_scan.c with respect to kernel version.

Throughout the remainder of this chapter, we use an HP XP1024 or XP128 storage array, in which devices are defined as open-X, where X is a value according to the defined array group. Within the scsi_scan.c or scsi_devinfo.c file, you should find a field containing the following:

```
{"HP", "OPEN-", "*", BLIST_SPARSELUN},                    /* HP XP Arrays */
```

We now know the reason why we only find LUNs 0–7 (no greater than LUN 8). It is due to the missing `BLIST_LARGELUN` function. To correct the problem, correct the line as follows:

```
{"HP", "OPEN-", "*", BLIST_SPARSELUN | BLIST_LARGELUN}, /* HP XP Arrays */
```

If only it were that simple. . . . Well, yes, it is that simple if the kernel source or SCSI source in the working kernel source is up to date. Unfortunately, the older Red Hat AS 2.1 server, defined in this chapter as Machine 1, is running an outdated SCSI source tree. Remember, each time that a change is made in the source, you must recompile and boot the new kernel.

Now that we have discussed some brief limitations of the `scsi_scan` source with respect to the device information section, let us discuss another scenario. In the following example, we refer to Machine 1, which is attached to the storage array previously mentioned. The array has only two LUNs presented through one storage port into a fabric. The host has two HBAs logging into the fabric, so it has twice the opportunity to see the devices. For simplicity, in the following example, assume that the zoning and LUN assignments are correct on the array.

In the example, we have added two LUNs with hex values 7 and 8 to the storage and proceeded to remove and add the Emulex driver to call the `scsi_scan` code manually. Note that this is an offline procedure because all storage, if any existed, would go offline after the driver is removed.

```
[root@cyclops scsi]# dmesg
```

The kernel reports no information.

```
[root@cyclops scsi]# insmod lpfcdd
Using /lib/modules/2.4.9-e.10custom-gt/kernel/drivers/scsi/lpfcdd.o
Warning: loading /lib/modules/2.4.9-e.10custom-gt/kernel/drivers/
scsi/lpfcdd.o will taint the kernel: no license
```

You should ignore the taint message because it is just a notification that the driver or module does not adhere to the open source guidelines.

```
[root@cyclops scsi]# dmesg
Emulex LightPulse FC SCSI/IP 4.20p
PCI: Enabling device 01:03.0 (0156 -> 0157)
!lpfc0:045:Vital Product Data  Data: 82 23 0 36
!lpfc0:031:Link Up Event received  Data: 1 1 0 0
PCI: Enabling device 01:04.0 (0156 -> 0157)
!lpfc1:031:Link Up Event received  Data: 1 1 0 0
scsi2 : Emulex LPFC (LP8000) SCSI on PCI bus 01 device 18 irq 17
scsi3 : Emulex LPFC (LP8000) SCSI on PCI bus 01 device 20 irq 27
```

As depicted previously, no LUNs were found. Next, we could proceed to determine whether this is a fabric zoning issue or an array LUN assignment problem. Note that in the previous test, however, we are trying to depict a true code limitation.

With Machine 1, we can depict the limitation in the scsi_scan.c source code by reviewing the definitions set forth in the code. An example of this limitation follows:

```
#define BLIST_NOLUN        0x001   /* Don't scan for LUNs */
#define BLIST_FORCELUN     0x002   /* Known to have LUNs, force
                                      scanning */
#define BLIST_BORKEN       0x004   /* Flag for broken handshaking */
#define BLIST_KEY          0x008   /* Needs to be unlocked by special
                                      command */
#define BLIST_SINGLELUN    0x010   /* LUNs should better not be used
                                      in parallel */
#define BLIST_NOTQ         0x020   /* Buggy Tagged Command Queuing */
#define BLIST_SPARSELUN    0x040   /* Non consecutive LUN numbering */
#define BLIST_MAX5LUN      0x080   /* Avoid LUNS >= 5 */
#define BLIST_ISDISK       0x100   /* Treat as (removable) disk */
#define BLIST_ISROM        0x200   /* Treat as (removable) CD-ROM */
```

Note that BLIST_LARGELUN does not exist because it was added some time around the 2.4-21 kernel. BLIST_LARGELUN allows for device scanning over seven LUNs. However, the BLIST_SPARSELUN exists but did not help us find our sparse LUNs because LUN 0 must exist to start scanning the bus. Some drivers build a pseudo LUN 0 so that this condition never exists; however, most system administrators argue that skipping LUN 0 is not helpful. Nevertheless, LUN 0 does not have to exist if different scanning software is implemented.

By using `scsidev-2.35 scsidev -l`, we can bypass this limitation and find our disk on the fly. At this point in the process, keeping track of the devices becomes substantially more difficult.

In the following example, only Hex LUN value 8 exists on the array. Because LUN 0 is not defined, the `BLIST_SPARSELUN` is not called, so dmesg reports no new disk.

After you issue the `insmod lpfcdd` commands, the following results are found in dmesg.

```
Emulex LightPulse FC SCSI/IP 4.20p
PCI: Enabling device 01:03.0 (0156 -> 0157)
!lpfc0:045:Vital Product Data  Data: 82 23 0 36
!lpfc0:031:Link Up Event received  Data: 1 1 0 0
PCI: Enabling device 01:04.0 (0156 -> 0157)
!lpfc1:031:Link Up Event received  Data: 1 1 0 0
scsi2 : Emulex LPFC (LP8000) SCSI on PCI bus 01 device 18 irq 17
scsi3 : Emulex LPFC (LP8000) SCSI on PCI bus 01 device 20 irq 27
```

Again, no LUNs were found. Even by running the following command, we cannot get around this issue because it uses the same `scsi_scan.c` code.

```
[root@cyclops scsi]# /tmp/scsidev-2.35/scsidev

/proc/scsi/scsi extensions not found. Fall back to scanning.
```

After the full scan starts, `scsidev` creates a symbolic device pointer that points to the internal SCSI disk /dev/sda. Note, however, that we do not need or use this device link in our servers. We have truncated a lot just to show the external SCSI disk.

```
Found /dev/scsi/sgh0-2800c0i0l0 (Type 00)    on sym53c8xx-1.7.3c-20010512
Found /dev/scsi/sgh0-2800c0i1l0 (Type 00)    on sym53c8xx-1.7.3c-20010512
Found /dev/scsi/sgh0-2800c0i2l0 (Type 00)    on sym53c8xx-1.7.3c-20010512
Found /dev/scsi/sgh0-2800c0i3l0 (Type 00)    on sym53c8xx-1.7.3c-20010512
Found /dev/scsi/sgh0-2800c0i4l0 (Type 00)    on sym53c8xx-1.7.3c-20010512
Found /dev/scsi/sgh0-2800c0i5l0 (Type 00)    on sym53c8xx-1.7.3c-20010512
Found /dev/scsi/sgh0-2800c0i11l0 (Type 03)   on sym53c8xx-1.7.3c-20010512
Found /dev/scsi/sgh0-2800c0i15l0 (Type 03)   on sym53c8xx-1.7.3c-20010512
```

However, note that by adding a LUN 0 to the array, we can get around this problem, as indicated next.

```
[root@cyclops scsi]# rmmod lpfcdd
[root@cyclops scsi]# insmod lpfcdd
[root@cyclops scsi]# dmesg
...
Emulex LightPulse FC SCSI/IP 4.20p
PCI: Enabling device 01:03.0 (0156 -> 0157)
!lpfc0:045:Vital Product Data  Data: 82 23 0 36
!lpfc0:031:Link Up Event received  Data: 1 1 0 0
PCI: Enabling device 01:04.0 (0156 -> 0157)
!lpfc1:031:Link Up Event received  Data: 1 1 0 0
scsi2 : Emulex LPFC (LP8000) SCSI on PCI bus 01 device 18 irq 17
scsi3 : Emulex LPFC (LP8000) SCSI on PCI bus 01 device 20 irq 27
  Vendor: HP        Model: OPEN-9-CVS      Rev: 2111
  Type:   Direct-Access                   ANSI SCSI revision: 02
  Vendor: HP        Model: OPEN-9-CVS      Rev: 2111
  Type:   Direct-Access                   ANSI SCSI revision: 02
  Vendor: HP        Model: OPEN-9-CVS      Rev: 2111
  Type:   Direct-Access                   ANSI SCSI revision: 02
  Vendor: HP        Model: OPEN-9-CVS      Rev: 2111
  Type:   Direct-Access                   ANSI SCSI revision: 02
  Vendor: HP        Model: OPEN-9-CVS      Rev: 2111
  Type:   Direct-Access                   ANSI SCSI revision: 02
  Vendor: HP        Model: OPEN-9-CVS      Rev: 2111
  Type:   Direct-Access                   ANSI SCSI revision: 02
Attached scsi disk sdg at scsi2, channel 0, id 0, lun 0
Attached scsi disk sdh at scsi2, channel 0, id 0, lun 1
Attached scsi disk sdi at scsi2, channel 0, id 0, lun 10
Attached scsi disk sdj at scsi3, channel 0, id 0, lun 0
Attached scsi disk sdk at scsi3, channel 0, id 0, lun 1
Attached scsi disk sdl at scsi3, channel 0, id 0, lun 10
SCSI device sdg: 103680 512-byte hdwr sectors (53 MB)
 sdg: unknown partition table
SCSI device sdh: 103680 512-byte hdwr sectors (53 MB)
```

```
sdh: unknown partition table
SCSI device sdi: 103680 512-byte hdwr sectors (53 MB)
 sdi: unknown partition table
SCSI device sdj: 103680 512-byte hdwr sectors (53 MB)
 sdj: unknown partition table
SCSI device sdk: 103680 512-byte hdwr sectors (53 MB)
 sdk: unknown partition table
SCSI device sdl: 103680 512-byte hdwr sectors (53 MB)
 sdl: unknown partition table
```

Having a LUN 0 or sparse LUNs is dependent on the driver and the parameters set forth in the scsi_scan.c file. Though each setting has a large impact, no impact is as great as when a single LUN is added to the PCI bus, which causes applications to crash. The next example demonstrates how a single LUN can have such an enormous impact.

We first must cover some basics. Again in this example, we use a few LUNs from a storage array. The LUN values are 0, 1, 2, 3, 10, and 11. There is no particular reason for the LUN values to be scattered as such, but any system administrator will run into this configuration at some point. With this setup, the user needs to be made aware of several issues that must be handled appropriately. For example, one issue is to determine how many targets an HBA sees.

```
[root@cyclops tmp]# cat /proc/scsi/lpfc/2
Emulex LightPulse LPFC Driver Version: 2.01g
HBA: Emulex LightPulse LP8000 1 Gigabit PCI Fibre Channel Adapter
SerialNum: 2R04714316
Firmware Version: 3.82A1 (D2D3.82A1)
Hdw: 2002506d
VendorId: 0xf80010df
Portname: 10:00:00:00:c9:24:13:27   Nodename: 20:00:00:00:c9:24:13:27

Link Up - Ready:
   PortID 0x7b0f00
   Fabric
   Current speed 1G
```

```
lpfc0t00 DID 770d00 WWPN 50:00:60:e8:02:ea:81:00 WWNN
50:00:60:e8:02:ea:81:00 <---Target is an XP48 port CL1-A
lpfc0t01 DID 780500 WWPN 50:06:0e:80:03:4e:46:05 WWNN
50:06:0e:80:03:4e:46:05 <---Target is an XP128 port CL1-F
```

Do not forget to look at all targets presented by every HBA, as continued next:

```
[root@cyclops tmp]# cat /proc/scsi/lpfc/3
Emulex LightPulse LPFC Driver Version: 2.01g
HBA: Emulex LightPulse LP8000 1 Gigabit PCI Fibre Channel Adapter
SerialNum: 0000c9286bda
Firmware Version: 3.90A7 (D2D3.90A7)
Hdw: 2002506d
VendorId: 0xf80010df
Portname: 10:00:00:00:c9:28:6b:da    Nodename: 20:00:00:00:c9:28:6b:da

Link Up - Ready:
   PortID 0x7f0d00
   Fabric
   Current speed 1G

lpfc1t00 DID 770d00 WWPN 50:00:60:e8:02:ea:81:00 WWNN
50:00:60:e8:02:ea:81:00 <---Target is an XP48 port CL1-A
lpfc1t01 DID 780500 WWPN 50:06:0e:80:03:4e:46:05 WWNN
50:06:0e:80:03:4e:46:05 <---Target is an XP128 port CL1-F
```

Though this is not a true dual-path configuration (because it has only a single storage path), it still is a good illustration of the following fault. As shown previously, the HBA in question must be connected to a fabric because of 24-bit FCID 0x7b0f00. However, the dmesg and /var/log/ messages only show LUNs from a single target.

```
Attached scsi disk sdg at scsi2, channel 0, id 1, lun 0
Attached scsi disk sdh at scsi2, channel 0, id 1, lun 1
Attached scsi disk sdi at scsi2, channel 0, id 1, lun 2
Attached scsi disk sdj at scsi2, channel 0, id 1, lun 3
Attached scsi disk sdk at scsi2, channel 0, id 1, lun 10
```

```
Attached scsi disk sdl at scsi2, channel 0, id 1, lun 11
Attached scsi disk sdm at scsi3, channel 0, id 1, lun 0
Attached scsi disk sdn at scsi3, channel 0, id 1, lun 1
Attached scsi disk sdo at scsi3, channel 0, id 1, lun 2
Attached scsi disk sdp at scsi3, channel 0, id 1, lun 3
Attached scsi disk sdq at scsi3, channel 0, id 1, lun 10
Attached scsi disk sdr at scsi3, channel 0, id 1, lun 11
```

All the previous LUNs are on target 1 rather than target 0. After adding a few LUNs on target 0, we simply need to run the following command:

```
echo "scsi add-single-device 2 0 00 01" >/proc/scsi/scsi
```

Upon reviewing dmesg, we find that the device was added and bound to /dev/sds.

```
scsi singledevice 2 0 0 1
blk: queue dfb84a1c, I/O limit 4095Mb (mask 0xffffffff)
  Vendor: HP        Model: OPEN-E-CM       Rev: 0119
  Type:   Direct-Access                   ANSI SCSI revision: 03
blk: queue dfb8461c, I/O limit 4095Mb (mask 0xffffffff)
Attached scsi disk sds at scsi2, channel 0, id 0, lun 1
SCSI device sds: 28452960 512-byte hdwr sectors (14568 MB)
 sds:
```

After careful review, we add two other disks, LUNs 6 and 2, in that order:

```
echo "scsi add-single-device 2 0 00 06" >/proc/scsi/scsi
```

dmesg prints the following for LUN 6:

```
scsi singledevice 2 0 0 6
blk: queue e5c65c1c, I/O limit 4095Mb (mask 0xffffffff)
  Vendor: HP        Model: OPEN-3*2        Rev: 0119
  Type:   Direct-Access                   ANSI SCSI revision: 03
blk: queue e5c65e1c, I/O limit 4095Mb (mask 0xffffffff)
Attached scsi disk sdt at scsi2, channel 0, id 0, lun 6
```

```
SCSI device sdt: 9613440 512-byte hdwr sectors (4922 MB)
 sdt: unknown partition table


echo "scsi add-single-device 2 0 00 02" >/proc/scsi/scsi
```

dmesg prints the following for LUN 2:

```
scsi singledevice 2 0 0 2
blk: queue e5c6501c, I/O limit 4095Mb (mask 0xffffffff)
  Vendor: HP          Model: OPEN-E          Rev: 0119
  Type:   Direct-Access                  ANSI SCSI revision: 03
blk: queue e5c6521c, I/O limit 4095Mb (mask 0xffffffff)
Attached scsi disk sdu at scsi2, channel 0, id 0, lun 2
SCSI device sdu: 28452960 512-byte hdwr sectors (14568 MB)
 sdu: unknown partition table
```

The new list of devices is as follows:

```
Attached scsi disk sdt at scsi3, channel 0, id 0, lun 1
Attached scsi disk sdg at scsi2, channel 0, id 1, lun 0
Attached scsi disk sdh at scsi2, channel 0, id 1, lun 1
Attached scsi disk sdi at scsi2, channel 0, id 1, lun 2
Attached scsi disk sdj at scsi2, channel 0, id 1, lun 3
Attached scsi disk sdk at scsi2, channel 0, id 1, lun 10
Attached scsi disk sdl at scsi2, channel 0, id 1, lun 11
Attached scsi disk sdm at scsi3, channel 0, id 1, lun 0
Attached scsi disk sdn at scsi3, channel 0, id 1, lun 1
Attached scsi disk sdo at scsi3, channel 0, id 1, lun 2
Attached scsi disk sdp at scsi3, channel 0, id 1, lun 3
Attached scsi disk sdq at scsi3, channel 0, id 1, lun 10
Attached scsi disk sdr at scsi3, channel 0, id 1, lun 11
Attached scsi disk sds at scsi2, channel 0, id 0, lun 1
Attached scsi disk sdt at scsi2, channel 0, id 0, lun 6
Attached scsi disk sdu at scsi2, channel 0, id 0, lun 2
```

The biggest problem is with LUNs 6 and 2 at the bottom of the list. The next time that the host is rebooted, the LUNs swap `sdt` and `sdu` values to the hard disk map point. This type of problem is why Linux developers created the `scsidev` project.

After running `scsidev`, `/dev/scsi` block devices are built and listed by the SCSI interface, channel, ID, and LUN value as follows:

```
brw-rw----    1 root      disk       65,  32 Apr 10 20:13 sdh2-0c0i0l1
brw-rw----    1 root      disk       65,  64 Apr 10 20:13 sdh2-0c0i0l2
brw-rw----    1 root      disk       65,  48 Apr 10 20:13 sdh2-0c0i0l6
brw-rw----    1 root      disk        8,  96 Apr 10 20:16 sdh2-0c0i1l0
brw-rw----    1 root      disk        8, 112 Apr 10 20:16 sdh2-0c0i1l1
brw-rw----    1 root      disk        8, 160 Apr 10 20:16 sdh2-0c0i1l10
brw-rw----    1 root      disk        8, 176 Apr 10 20:16 sdh2-0c0i1l11
brw-rw----    1 root      disk        8, 128 Apr 10 20:16 sdh2-0c0i1l2
brw-rw----    1 root      disk        8, 144 Apr 10 20:16 sdh2-0c0i1l3
brw-rw----    1 root      disk        8, 192 Apr 10 20:16 sdh3-1c0i1l0
brw-rw----    1 root      disk        8, 208 Apr 10 20:16 sdh3-1c0i1l1
brw-rw----    1 root      disk       65,   0 Apr 10 20:16 sdh3-1c0i1l10
brw-rw----    1 root      disk       65,  16 Apr 10 20:13 sdh3-1c0i1l11
brw-rw----    1 root      disk        8, 224 Apr 10 20:16 sdh3-1c0i1l2
brw-rw----    1 root      disk        8, 240 Apr 10 20:16 sdh3-1c0i1l3
```

Of course, modify the `/etc/fstab` accordingly so that if the `/dev/sdX` changes after a reboot, the `/dev/scsi/sdhX-XcXiXlX` does not.

The new LUN has been found at `/dev/scsi/sgh2-0c0i0l0`, and a symbolic link has been made at `/dev/sdq` with the alternate path on `/dev/sdj` for block control. The nice feature of using `scsidev` to find new devices is that you don't have to worry about the LUN order.

Think of it this way. A deck of cards has been stacked neatly on a table. If you remove the card on the bottom of the stack, the entire deck shifts down. In normal circumstances, this is of no concern. However, let's assume that a number has been written upon each card. The cards are numbered in order from 0 to 52, starting from the bottom. If you remove the number two card, does the number three card become number two? No, the value written on the card stays the same. That is the function that `scsidev` provides. Using the standard device addressing in Linux, the number three card becomes number two when the number two card is removed, which causes a great mess in `/etc/fstab` and any user application hardbound to a SCSI device file.

Adding Storage via PCMCIA/USB

Other methods of adding storage include USB, FireWire, and PCMCIA devices, and similar troubleshooting techniques are used for each. The unique aspect of PCMCIA storage is how the drivers are called with regard to sharing a single interrupt for multiple function devices. Among PCMCIA devices, the most common device type is a modem or Ethernet combo card (storage type PCMCIA cards are very rare). Note that combo cards share a single interrupt. In the following example, a single-function PCMCIA card illustrates the drivers that are loaded after the PCMCIA core finds the newly added device.

1. Collect `lsmod` so that a pre-driver list can be collected.
2. Insert PCMCIA storage device with IDE interface connecting a 5200-RPM laptop drive.
3. Run `lsmod` so that a post-driver list can be collected.
4. Run `dmesg` to view the actions taken by the kernel.

When you run `dmesg`, it reports:

```
cs: memory probe 0xa0000000-0xa0ffffff: excluding 0xa0000000-0xa01fffff
Probing IDE interface ide2...
hde: HITACHI_DK239A-65B, ATA DISK drive
ide2 at 0x180-0x187,0x386 on irq 3
hde: max request size: 128KiB
hde: 12594960 sectors (6448 MB) w/512KiB Cache, CHS=13328/15/63
hde: cache flushes not supported
 hde: hde1 hde2 < hde5 hde6 > hde3 hde4
ide-cs: hde: Vcc = 5.0, Vpp = 0.0
```

The `lsmod` output reflects that the kernel module `ide_cs` was installed, which bound to modules `ds`, `yenta_socket`, and `pcmcia_core`.

This is what you see before the driver installation:

```
ds                      17796  6
yenta_socket            19840  0
pcmcia_core             66100  2 ds,yenta_socket
```

This is what you see after the driver installation:

```
ide_cs                   7556  1
ds                      17796  7 ide_cs
yenta_socket            19840  1
pcmcia_core             66100  3 ide_cs,ds,yenta_socket
```

But how does the correct driver become installed? To answer this question, we look at the PCMCIA core definitions located in directory /etc/pcmcia/. In this directory, a configuration file exists called config.

Within this file, sections exist such as the following:

```
card "ATA/IDE Fixed Disk"
function fixed_disk
bind "ide-cs"
```

The sections define how the newly attached device should be handled with respect to the driver. Within this same directory, another file exists that allows certain parameters always to be in play when a newly added PCMCIA device is attached using only IDE. The file is called ide.opts and contains options such as the following:

```
#INFO="Sample IDE setup"
#DO_FSTAB="y" ; DO_FSCK="y" ; DO_MOUNT="y"
#FSTYPE="msdos"
#OPTS=""
#MOUNTPT="/mnt/ide"
```

Some of the ATA/IDE fixed-disk device parameters follow:

* DO_FSTAB—A boolean (y/n) setting that specifies whether an entry should be added to /etc/fstab for this device.

- DO_FSCK—A boolean (y/n) setting that specifies whether the filesystem should be checked before being mounted with `fsck -Ta'`.

- DO_MOUNT—A boolean (y/n) setting that specifies whether this device should be automatically mounted at card insertion time.

- FSTYPE OPTS MOUNTPT—The filesystem type mount options and mount point to be used for the `fstab` entry and/or mounting the device.

The following example of an `ide.opts` entry demonstrates the first partition of any ATA/IDE card with an XFS filesystem to be mounted on `/mnt`.

```
case "$ADDRESS" in
*,*,*,1)
    #INFO="Sample IDE setup"
    DO_FSTAB="y" ; DO_FSCK="n" ; DO_MOUNT="y"
    #FSTYPE="xfs"
    #OPTS=""
    #MOUNTPT="/mnt"
    ;;
*,*,*)
    #PARTS="1"
    # Card eject policy options
    NO_CHECK=n
    NO_FUSER=n
    ;;
esac
```

With any new Linux machine, adding PCMCIA storage is second nature; however; on the special occasion in which we find ourselves with an older IDE device and kernel, we must remember that spin-up times vary. Longer spin-up times can surpass the maximum allowed card setup time. A simple workaround for this feature, "a positive spin on a bad issue," was developed starting around release 3.0.6 of the `ide_cs` driver to automatically retry the device probe. This workaround provides any device with ample time to initialize. However, if you find yourself with an even older version of `ide_cs`, load the `pcmcia_core` module with the following:

```
CORE_OPTS="unreset_delay=400"
```

For those who are trying to use a PCMCIA ATA/IDE CD-ROM device, your kernel must be compiled with `CONFIG_BLK_DEV_IDECD` enabled. Again, this is the default for almost all newer kernels; however, it is something to remember when developing a new custom kernel.

Summary

Though we can add storage through many methods, the particular methods discussed in this chapter can be characterized as both "common" and "troublesome." They are "common" because SANs have become common in enterprise environments. They are "troublesome" because with the capability to handle multiple interrupts, some PCMCIA hardware vendors make device support difficult. We hope the troubleshooting steps discussed in this chapter shed a little light on both SAN and PCMCIA storage devices.

6

Disk Partitions and Filesystems

Cylinders, sectors, tracks, and heads are the building blocks of spindle storage. Understanding the millions of bytes confined to a space that is half an inch thick, two inches wide, and three inches in length is critical to data recovery.

Consider the smallest form of storage that every person, at one time or another, has held in the palm of his or her hand. Most of us over the age of 25 recollect ravaging our desk, digging for the all-important, "critical-to-life" 1.44 MB floppy. This critical piece of plastic never fails to be found under the heaviest object on the desk. It is amazing that any data survives on the floppy after removing the seven-pound differential equations bible that was covering it. However, today's storage needs require much larger devices and more advanced methods to protect and recover the data they hold.

The following key topics are discussed in this chapter:

* SCSI and IDE data storage concepts
* The Ext2/3 filesystem
* The concepts of Cylinder, Head, and Sector (CHS)
* Global unique identification
* Partition tables

Throughout the chapter, we present scenarios that deliver real-world examples of the topic discussed in each section.

Background

Let's examine the following key filesystems and disk partitions concepts before getting into details: Intelligent/Integrated Drive Electronics (IDE), SCSI, and bit functions. Simply saying that data resides on a platter in the form of magnetic polarization of the surface greatly oversimplifies the nature of the beast.

IDE and SCSI

IDE is perhaps the most common drive type used by Linux, although it is slowly losing ground to SCSI in the Linux market because of the increasing popularity of large storage arrays. SCSI has not been around much longer than IDE; it was renamed around 1981/1982 from Shugart Associates System Interface (SASI) to Small Computer Systems Interface (SCSI). The IBM Mainframe 360 had the capability to speak to several devices simultaneously on any given I/O bus as early as 1960, so it could be said that SCSI started then. No matter the case, with more and more companies using storage consolidation, SCSI disk arrays are truly becoming commonplace.

Bit Calculation

Another key concept is bit calculation. Regardless of SCSI, IDE, or other storage medium you choose, you should always start with the basics: the calculation of bits and bytes. The best way to depict the combinations is through a chart, as shown in Table 6-1.

Table 6-1   Bit and Byte Calculations

8 bits	**1 byte**
1024 byte	1 Kilobyte (KB)
1024 Kilobytes	1 Megabyte (MB)
1024 Megabytes	1 Gigabyte (GB)
1024 Gigabytes	1 Terabyte (TB)
1024 Terabytes	1 Pentabyte (PB)
1024 Pentabytes	1 Exabyte (EB)

Eight bits written as 00000000 or 0000 0000 defines an eight-bit address with 256 possible combinations, as listed in Table 6-2.

Table 6-2 Bit Combinations

Bit	1	1	1	1	1	1	1	1
Base^{exponent}	2^7	2^6	2^5	2^4	2^3	2^2	2^1	2^0
Value	128	64	32	16	8	4	2	1

Each bit has a value of either "0" for off or "1" for on, instructing a virtual gate/door to allow 5 volts DC (power-conservative machines and newer technologies use 3.2 volts DC) to pass. Given that a bit only has two states (on or off) rather simplifies the importance of a single entity.

The following is a list of key terms and their definitions to help you understand the data on a platter discussed later in this chapter.

- sBit—Single binary element defined as on or off (1 or 0, respectively).
- Nibble—Four bits.
- Byte—Two nibbles, eight bits, or a character.
- Word—Sixteen bits, or two bytes. # on most hardware implementations.

Other terms, such as "binary," "octal hex/decimal," and "ASCI," are just other ways to represent the same value under different systems. Table 6-3 lists binary value "bits" converted to decimal and hexadecimal values.

Each bit has a mathematical value defined as 2^X, whereby we define the base value of every bit equal to numeric value 2 multiplied by an exponent X. The combined value of the eight bits depends on the order in which they are interpreted, "left to right" or "right to left."

The values of bits are calculated utilizing the Endian order, which is the direction the bits are read. Binary data is written and calculated by the majority of humans in most significant bit (MSB), LEFT, to least significant bit (LSB), RIGHT, order. Starting right to left, the bit values have exponential values beginning with zero and incrementing to seven. Although the exponent values change, the base value always remains at two. Note that the

Table 6-3   Converted Binary Values

Binary (4 bits)	Decimal	Hexadecimal	Octal
0000	0	0	0
0001	1	1	1
0010	2	2	2
0011	3	3	3
0100	4	4	4
0101	5	5	5
0110	6	6	6
0111	7	7	7
1000	8	8	10
1001	9	9	11
1010	10	A	12
1011	11	B	13
1100	12	C	14
1101	13	D	15
1110	14	E	16
1111	15	F	17
0001 0000 (8 bits)	16	10	20
0010 0000 (8 bits)	17	11	21
0011 0000 (8 bits)	18	12	22
0100 0000 (8 bits)	19	13	23

hardware platform determines the default bit order, which is referred to as "Little Endian or Big Endian." The following shows the MSB and LSB difference through od and bvi:

```
"od -h /dev/disk_device_file | head"
"dd if=/dev/disk_device of=/tmp/disk_device.out bs=512 count=1" utilize
"bvi /tmp/disk_device.out".
```

. . .

```
"0001 0e83 143f 003f 0000 4d46 0000 0000"  By od -h
"0100 830E 3F14 3F00 0000 464D 0000 8000" By bvi
...
```

When reviewing binary data in Hex, we use the nibbles to perform calculations at great speed. Each nibble has a decimal value of 0 to 15 or Hex 0 to F.

The following is an example of a binary value being converted into a Hex value:

$$1010 \quad 1001 = A9$$

This conversion is a two-step process. First, we need to address the left nibble. Break down the left nibble, "MSB," by doing the following:

$$2^3 \quad 2^2 \quad 2^1 \quad 2^0$$

on, off, on, off

8, 0, 2, 0, = decimal 10, or Hex A

Then do the same for the right nibble, "LSB," to achieve a value of 9 in Hex, as listed in Table 6-3.

Partition Table/Master Boot Record: Location

This section explores how to locate the Master Boot Record (MBR) and partition table for any disk.

We start with the location of the MBR on a standard Linux core drive. Core drive implies the root, or primary drive, that the operating system resides on in this example. cfdisk, fdisk with expert mode, dd, and many other tools enable us to collect the partition data. For an IDE or SCSI drive, just type cfdisk -P rst /dev/device_file where r equals RAW, s equals SECTORS, and t equals TABLE. This tool provides a look at a clean drive, as shown in the following example:

```
[root@localhost root]# cfdisk -P rst /dev/hde
Disk Drive: /dev/hde
```

```
Sector 0:
0x000: 00 00 00 00 00 00 00 00 00 00 00 00 00 00 00 00
0x010: 00 00 00 00 00 00 00 00 00 00 00 00 00 00 00 00
0x020: 00 00 00 00 00 00 00 00 00 00 00 00 00 00 00 00
0x030: 00 00 00 00 00 00 00 00 00 00 00 00 00 00 00 00
0x040: 00 00 00 00 00 00 00 00 00 00 00 00 00 00 00 00
0x050: 00 00 00 00 00 00 00 00 00 00 00 00 00 00 00 00
0x060: 00 00 00 00 00 00 00 00 00 00 00 00 00 00 00 00
0x070: 00 00 00 00 00 00 00 00 00 00 00 00 00 00 00 00
0x080: 00 00 00 00 00 00 00 00 00 00 00 00 00 00 00 00
0x090: 00 00 00 00 00 00 00 00 00 00 00 00 00 00 00 00
0x0A0: 00 00 00 00 00 00 00 00 00 00 00 00 00 00 00 00
0x0B0: 00 00 00 00 00 00 00 00 00 00 00 00 00 00 00 00
0x0C0: 00 00 00 00 00 00 00 00 00 00 00 00 00 00 00 00
0x0D0: 00 00 00 00 00 00 00 00 00 00 00 00 00 00 00 00
0x0E0: 00 00 00 00 00 00 00 00 00 00 00 00 00 00 00 00
0x0F0: 00 00 00 00 00 00 00 00 00 00 00 00 00 00 00 00
0x100: 00 00 00 00 00 00 00 00 00 00 00 00 00 00 00 00
0x110: 00 00 00 00 00 00 00 00 00 00 00 00 00 00 00 00
0x120: 00 00 00 00 00 00 00 00 00 00 00 00 00 00 00 00
0x130: 00 00 00 00 00 00 00 00 00 00 00 00 00 00 00 00
0x140: 00 00 00 00 00 00 00 00 00 00 00 00 00 00 00 00
0x150: 00 00 00 00 00 00 00 00 00 00 00 00 00 00 00 00
0x160: 00 00 00 00 00 00 00 00 00 00 00 00 00 00 00 00
0x170: 00 00 00 00 00 00 00 00 00 00 00 00 00 00 00 00
0x180: 00 00 00 00 00 00 00 00 00 00 00 00 00 00 00 00
0x190: 00 00 00 00 00 00 00 00 00 00 00 00 00 00 00 00
0x1A0: 00 00 00 00 00 00 00 00 00 00 00 00 00 00 00 00
0x1B0: 00 00 00 00 00 00 00 00 00 00 00 00 00 00 00 00
0x1C0: 00 00 00 00 00 00 00 00 00 00 00 00 00 00 00 00
0x1D0: 00 00 00 00 00 00 00 00 00 00 00 00 00 00 00 00
0x1E0: 00 00 00 00 00 00 00 00 00 00 00 00 00 00 00 00
0x1F0: 00 00 00 00 00 00 00 00 00 00 00 00 00 00 55 AA
```

```
Partition Table for /dev/hde


              First    Last
  # Type      Sector   Sector   Offset  Length   Filesystem Type (ID)
Flags

-- -------  --------  ---------  ------  --------  -------------------- -------

    Pri/Log       0  12594959         0#12594960  Free Space
None (00)
Partition Table for /dev/hde


             ---Starting---    ----Ending----   Start Number of
  # Flags Head Sect Cyl    ID  Head Sect Cyl    Sector   Sectors

-- ----- ---- ---- ----  ----  ---- ---- ----  -------- ---------

  1  0x00    0    0    0  0x00    0    0    0        0         0
  2  0x00    0    0    0  0x00    0    0    0        0         0
  3  0x00    0    0    0  0x00    0    0    0        0         0
  4  0x00    0    0    0  0x00    0    0    0        0         0
```

Determining the start and end addresses of the partition table on the last example is rather easy because the drive is totally zeroed out. Bytes 1FE and 1FF with value "55 AA" are defined as the signature bytes (also known as the magic cookie) or standard word. These values define the end of the partition table and MBR. In this example, we cannot determine the exact starting point of the partition table without first determining the location of the signature bytes and counting backward.

The MBR contains two critical pieces of information: bootloader and partition table. Byte 01BE defines the start point of a partition table, though byte 0 defines the starting point of the MBR. In both cases, everything ends at byte 1FF.

In addition, cfdisk, fdisk, or any other tool will fail to control the drive without the signature word, as described previously with the value of "55 AA." When new disks are discovered, cfdisk or fdisk requests a label if the magic cookie is null. After the magic cookie is established, any of the previous tools will enable a user to define partitions of any type. Note that raw data access does not follow this restriction and is not part of this chapter.

Partition Table/Master Boot Record: CHS Addressing

After the partition table has been identified, the user can proceed with Cylinder, Head, Sector (CHS) partition layout. The CHS model was the first defining structure that was developed for partitions, but due to size limits, it was replaced by Logical Block Addressing (LBA), which controls almost all disk partitions today. We begin with CHS to build a foundation for absolute addressing (CHS), thus limiting the total size, and then we discuss relative addressing (LBA).

With CHS, the start, end, and total sectors are defined within the constraints of a 6-bit sector, 10-bit cylinder, and 8-bit head, thus limiting this model to a max capacity of 8.4GB. In the following sections, examples and scenarios are included to help illustrate this concept.

Defining a Primary Partition

Pick your favorite tool and define a 100MB primary partition with type Linux, flagged as a bootable partition on a newly added disk starting at sector 0.

When complete, view your work by using `dd if=/dev/disk_device_file of=/tmp/disk_device_file.out bs=512 count=1` where `disk_device_file` is equal to `/dev/sdX` or `/dev/hdX` depending on IDE or SCSI devices. Then, after using `bvi`, the partition info under the MBR should look similar to the following:

```
"bvi /tmp/disk_device_file.out"
```

```
****    0  1  2  3  4  5  6  7  8  9 0A 0B 0C 0D 0E 0F
0x1B0: 00 00 00 00 00 00 00 00 00 00 00 00 00 00 80 01
0x1C0: 01 00 83 0E 3F 14 3F 00 00 00 46 4D 00 00 00 00
0x1D0: 00 00 00 00 00 00 00 00 00 00 00 00 00 00 00 00
0x1E0: 00 00 00 00 00 00 00 00 00 00 00 00 00 00 00 00
0x1F0: 00 00 00 00 00 00 00 00 00 00 00 00 00 00 55 AA
```

Note that the bold row beginning with **** does not actually exist; however, it is included here for illustrative purposes to identify the column.

Ending in "55 AA," focus on byte 1BE with value 80, which is a boot flag mark. With byte 1BE set to 80, the BIOS loads the bootloader into memory. In the previous example, byte location 1BF–1C1 equals "01 01, 00," which defines the CHS for the starting address space. Later, we discuss how to calculate C:H:S, but for now, these bytes are read (C)ylinders (H)eads (S)ectors, and these values are common on almost all first partition bootable drives.

note

CHS does not align on the byte boundary; CHS is covered in more detail later in this chapter.

Byte 1C2 defines the partition type. In this example, byte 1C2 has value 83, which implies Linux native. Some of the possible values for byte 1C2 are:

```
4   FAT16 <32M    3c   PartitionMagic   82   Linux swap   c6   DRDOS/sec (FAT-
5   Extended      40   Venix 80286      83   Linux        c7
```

A complete list can be found using fdisk, but beware that some of these values are not common and sometimes have multiple meanings. For example, what if byte 1C2 from sector 0 had a value of 42? By only considering the partition types defined by fdisk or cfdisk, we would most likely conclude that the partition type holds a secure filesystem (SFS). However, it's much more probable that the partition is a Windows dynamic disk.

note

For the remainder of this chapter, we denote Hex with *value*(H), Binary with *value*(B), Octal with *value*(O), and Decimal with *value*(D).

Byte 01C3 has value "0E," which defines the ending head value in the current partition. 0E (H) = 14(D) heads exist in partition 1.

Bytes 01C4 and 01C5 have a value of "3F 14," which defines the last sector and cylinder count for the partition. Because we are playing with a partition smaller than 8.4GB, we use absolute addressing for the CHS count. This changes when a partition is over 8.4GB to LBA, which we discuss later.

Using absolute addressing, only 6 bits are needed to define the last sector, and 10 bits are required to define the last cylinder, both of which are difficult to depict. Taking the values from locations 01C4 and 01C5 from the previous example and using Table 6-3, we can depict the sector and cylinder counts as follows:

```
    Sector      Cylinder

  0011 1111   0001 0100

   "3" "F"     "1"  "4"
```

Again, note that the sector only needs 6 bits, and 10 bits are required for the cylinder count. To meet this requirement, the bit order must be reestablished. Move the high-value bits from the first byte and extend the high-value bits on the last byte.

```
0011 11{11   0001 0100} <---Placing brackets around 6 and 10 bits.
```

The following shows the move:

```
1111 11  {00 0001 0100}


  3  F    {0   1   4}
```

The cylinder count leaves us with 014(H) = 20 cylinders.

The sector count leaves us with 3F(H) = 63 sectors.

(Cylinder) × (Heads) × (Sectors) = (21) × (15) × (63) = 19845 sectors. However, do not forget about the offset. Offset is determined by byte 01C6–01C9.

Bytes 01C6–01C9 have the value "3F 00 00 00."

Offset value 3F(H) = 63(D) sectors. The total size of our partition is 19845–63 = 19782 sectors.

To demonstrate the same value described previously through a faster, automated procedure, we can use cfdisk.

```
# > cfdisk -P t /dev/hde
Partition Table for /dev/hde
```

		---Starting---				----Ending----			Start	Number of
#	Flags	Head	Sect	Cyl	ID	Head	Sect	Cyl	Sector	Sectors
1	0x80	1	1	0	0x83	14	63	20	63	19782
2	0x00	0	0	0	0x00	0	0	0	0	0
3	0x00	0	0	0	0x00	0	0	0	0	0
4	0x00	0	0	0	0x00	0	0	0	0	0

In this example, the primary partition "1" is fully described. The remaining possible primary partitions are listed, but they are defined with zero placeholders. This is just a characteristic of cfdisk, which always reports all possible primary partitions but only represents values for the logical partitions that are defined.

To continue with our example, bytes 01CA–01CD have the value "46 4D 00 00," which defines the total sectors for the partition. In this example, 4D46(H) = 19782 sectors. These bits will be critical later when we stop using absolute addressing and move to LBA addressing (or relative addressing).

Determining Whether Additional Partitions Can Be Created

Now that we have discussed the location of the bits that define the capacity of a partition, let us move to the common question of whether additional partitions can be created. With this next example, we show limitations of primary partitions. Only four primary partitions can exist within a partition table. To illustrate the limitation of primary partitions, we have created four primary partitions, each of which is 10MB in size.

```
[root@localhost root]# cfdisk -P rst /dev/hde

Disk Drive: /dev/hde
Sector 0:
0x000: 00 00 00 00 00 00 00 00 00 00 00 00 00 00 00 00
0x010: 00 00 00 00 00 00 00 00 00 00 00 00 00 00 00 00

~~~~~~
```

```
0x1A0:  00 00 00 00 00 00 00 00 00 00 00 00 00 00 00 00
0x1B0:  00 00 00 00 00 00 00 00 00 00 00 00 00 00 80 01
0x1C0:  01 00 83 0E 3F 14 3F 00 00 00 46 4D 00 00 80 00
0x1D0:  01 15 83 0E 3F 29 85 4D 00 00 85 4D 00 00 80 00
0x1E0:  01 2A 8E 0E 3F 3E 0A 9B 00 00 85 4D 00 00 80 00
0x1F0:  01 3F 82 0E 3F 53 8F E8 00 00 85 4D 00 00 55 AA
```

Partition Table for /dev/hde

# Type Flags	First Sector	Last Sector	Offset	Length	Filesystem Type (ID)	
1 Primary	0	19844	63	19845	Linux (83)	Boot (80)
2 Primary	19845	39689	0	19845	Linux (83)	Boot (80)
3 Primary	39690	59534	0	19845	Linux LVM (8E)	Boot (80)
4 Primary	59535	79379	0	19845	Linux swap (82)	Boot (80)
None	79380	12594959	0	12515580	Unusable	None (00)

Partition Table for /dev/hde

#	Flags	---Starting--- Head	Sect	Cyl	ID	----Ending---- Head	Sect	Cyl	Start Sector	Number of Sectors
1	0x80	1	1	0	0x83	14	63	20	63	19782
2	0x80	0	1	21	0x83	14	63	41	19845	19845
3	0x80	0	1	42	0x8E	14	63	62	39690	19845
4	0x80	0	1	63	0x82	14	63	83	59535	19845

The Number of Sectors on the second, third, and fourth partitions equals 19845 because the 63 sector offset is not present. Therefore, we lost 63 sectors on the first partition.

Bytes 1CF–1D1 define the starting sector in absolute partitions, which is the same calculation previously shown on bytes 01C3–01C5.

For primary partition 2, 01CF–01D1 equals "00 01 15." The starting CHS address for the partition is byte 01CF, which has a value of 00. This implies a head value of 0.

Bytes 01D0–01D1 have a value of "01 15," which equals 0000 00 {01 0001 0101}. Recall that you must have 10 bits for the cylinder count. Move the high-value bits from the first byte and extend the high-value bits on the last byte.

The following shows the bit move:

```
01 0001 {00 0001 0101}
```

The decoded values look like this:

```
01 {001} = 1 sector {21 cylinders}
```

Byte 01D3 has value "0E" and has the same meaning as 01C3, which defines the last head of the partition. To prevent partitions from overlapping, the start of the next consecutive partition sector count is equal to the end of the previous partition plus one. Therefore, 01D4–01D5, 01E4–01E5, and 01F4–01F5 differ. Refer to 01C3–01C5 at the beginning of the chapter for calculation rules.

Byte 01DA–01DD define the total sectors in the partition that differ between partition 1, 2, 3, and 4 due to the first 63 sector offset for the primary partition. The 63 sector offset is due to BIOS software called dynamic drive overlay (DDO). DDO enables BIOSs that do not support LBA addressing to address drives larger than 528MB. In short, it is an old fix that became a standard.

Scenario 6-1: Error Message While Adding Partitions

The plan is to add a new 72GB disk to a server and then to create several partitions. The customer's machine in this example uses a Compaq Smartarray Controller utilizing the cciss driver. In this case study, the customer adds many partitions until an error message, "Value out of range," displays while adding partitions. The following example is from the Linux server's console.

```
ml350linux-> fdisk /dev/cciss/c0d0


Command (m for help): p
Disk /dev/cciss/c0d0: 72.8 GB, 72833679360 bytes
255 heads, 32 sectors/track, 17433 cylinders
Units = cylinders of 8160 * 512 = 4177920 bytes
Device Boot Start End Blocks Id System
/dev/cciss/c0d0p1 * 1 50 203984 83 Linux
/dev/cciss/c0d0p2 51 1078 4194240 83 Linux
```

```
/dev/cciss/c0d0p3 1079 1592 2097120 83 Linux
/dev/cciss/c0d0p4 1593 8716 29065920 f Win95 Ext'd (LBA)
/dev/cciss/c0d0p5 1593 3134 6291344 83 Linux
/dev/cciss/c0d0p6 3135 4668 6258704 83 Linux
/dev/cciss/c0d0p7 4669 5696 4194224 83 Linux
/dev/cciss/c0d0p8 5697 6724 4194224 83 Linux
/dev/cciss/c0d0p9 6725 7238 2097104 83 Linux
/dev/cciss/c0d0p10 7239 7752 2097104 82 Linux swap
/dev/cciss/c0d0p11 7753 8266 2097104 83 Linux
/dev/cciss/c0d0p12 8267 8645 1546304 83 Linux
Command (m for help):
Command (m for help): n
First cylinder (8646-8716, default 8646):
Using default value 8646
Last cylinder or +size or +sizeM or +sizeK (8646-8716, default 8716): \
+1000M
Value out of range.
Last cylinder or +size or +sizeM or +sizeK (8646-8716, default 8716): \
Using default value 8716
```

Solution 6-1

fdisk uses blocks rather than sectors. One block is equal to 1024 bytes, so the block count is always half the sector count. The problem in this example is that the primary partitions 1–4 are defined, and the last primary partition, 4, was defined too small.

Notice that partition 4 is marked with the extended partition flag, which means logical partitions reside within it. If fdisk, cfdisk, or a GUI tool such as diskdrak, disk druid, or yast2-partitioner were used to delete primary partition 4 and redefine it with all cylinders, the customer would have been able to define his new volume.

warning

By deleting partition 4 in this example, all *logical* volumes under the extended partition would be deleted.

```
/dev/cciss/c0d0p4 1593 8716 29065920 f Win95 Ext'd (LBA)  <--- largest
# of sectors is set to low...
/dev/cciss/c0d0p5 1593 3134 6291344 83 Linux
/dev/cciss/c0d0p6 3135 4668 6258704 83 Linux
/dev/cciss/c0d0p7 4669 5696 4194224 83 Linux
/dev/cciss/c0d0p8 5697 6724 4194224 83 Linux
/dev/cciss/c0d0p9 6725 7238 2097104 83 Linux
/dev/cciss/c0d0p10 7239 7752 2097104 82 Linux swap
/dev/cciss/c0d0p11 7753 8266 2097104 83 Linux
/dev/cciss/c0d0p12 8267 8645 1546304 83 Linux
```

Partition Table/Master Boot Record: Logical/Extended

Continuing with the CHS model, we can achieve more than four partitions by utilizing extended partitions within a primary partition. Extended partitions are also known as logical partitions, and they can only exist within a primary partition with an extended flag, also known as a partition type (05) set.

In the following example, partition 1 is defined as "extended," as depicted by the fact that byte 1C2's value is equal to "05." We then define partition 1 to occupy 39690 sectors and contain two logical partitions.

```
[root@localhost root]# cfdisk -P rst /dev/hde

Disk Drive: /dev/hde
Sector 0:
0x000: 00 00 00 00 00 00 00 00 00 00 00 00 00 00 00 00
~~~~~
0x190: 00 00 00 00 00 00 00 00 00 00 00 00 00 00 00 00
0x1A0: 00 00 00 00 00 00 00 00 00 00 00 00 00 00 00 00
0x1B0: 00 00 00 00 00 00 00 00 00 00 00 00 00 00 00 01
0x1C0: 01 00 05 0E 3F 29 3F 00 00 00 CB 9A 00 00 00 00
0x1D0: 00 00 00 00 00 00 00 00 00 00 00 00 00 00 00 00
0x1E0: 00 00 00 00 00 00 00 00 00 00 00 00 00 00 00 00
0x1F0: 00 00 00 00 00 00 00 00 00 00 00 00 00 00 55 AA
```

```
Sector 63:
0x000: 00 00 00 00 00 00 00 00 00 00 00 00 00 00 00 00
~~~~~~
0x1A0: 00 00 00 00 00 00 00 00 00 00 00 00 00 00 00 00
0x1B0: 00 00 00 00 00 00 00 00 00 00 00 00 00 00 80 02
0x1C0: 01 00 83 0E 3F 14 3F 00 00 00 07 4D 00 00 00 00
0x1D0: 01 15 05 0E 3F 29 46 4D 00 00 85 4D 00 00 00 00
0x1E0: 00 00 00 00 00 00 00 00 00 00 00 00 00 00 00 00
0x1F0: 00 00 00 00 00 00 00 00 00 00 00 00 00 00 55 AA


Sector 19845:
0x000: 00 00 00 00 00 00 00 00 00 00 00 00 00 00 00 00
~~~~~~
0x1A0: 00 00 00 00 00 00 00 00 00 00 00 00 00 00 00 00
0x1B0: 00 00 00 00 00 00 00 00 00 00 00 00 00 00 00 01
0x1C0: 01 15 83 0E 3F 29 3F 00 00 00 46 4D 00 00 00 00
0x1D0: 00 00 00 00 00 00 00 00 00 00 00 00 00 00 00 00
0x1E0: 00 00 00 00 00 00 00 00 00 00 00 00 00 00 00 00
0x1F0: 00 00 00 00 00 00 00 00 00 00 00 00 00 00 55 AA


Partition Table for /dev/hde
```

#	Type	First Sector	Last Sector	Offset	Length	Filesystem Type (ID)	Flags
1	Primary	0	39689	63	39690	Extended (05)	None (00)
2	0x00	0	0	0 0x00	0 0	0	0
3	0x00	0	0	0 0x00	0 0	0	0
4	0x00	0	0	0 0x00	0 0	0	0
5	Logical	63*	19844	63	19782*	Linux (83)	Boot (80)
6	Logical	19845	39689	63	19845	Linux (83)	None (00)
	Pri/Log	39690	12594959	0	12555270	Free Space	None (00)

```
Partition Table for /dev/hde
```

```
            ---Starting---      ----Ending----    Start Number of
   # Flags Head Sect Cyl    ID Head Sect Cyl     Sector  Sectors
   -- ----- ---- ---- ---- ----- ---- ---- ---- -------- ---------

   1  0x00    1    1    0 0x05   14   63   41       63    39627

   5  0x80    2    1    0 0x83   14   63   20       63    19719

   6  0x00    1    1   21 0x83   14   63   41       63    19782
```

A few items about logical partitions need to be noted. Notice how primary partitions are represented with numeric values 1, 2, 3, and 4, whereas logical partitions are represented with numeric values 5 and greater. In addition, notice the location of the bootable partition. We set the logical partition number to 5 for the boot device. When using LILO, this boot configuration will fail with old versions of LILO due to the 1024 sector limit. This limitation on LILO has been removed and never existed on GRUB.

Scenario 6-2: Multiple Partitions Exist, but fdisk Only Reports a Single Partition

As previously discussed, primary and extended partitions can be displayed through cfdisk, fdisk -l, or another tool. However, with Linux on IA64, fdisk reports only a primary partition. In the following example, we depict multiple partitions with extensible firmware interface (EFI), and fdisk reports only a single partition.

```
[root@atlorca2 root]# df
Filesystem              1K-blocks      Used Available Use% Mounted on
/dev/sda2               32891620   6077808  25143012  20% /
/dev/sda1                 102182      4598     97584   5% /boot/efi
none                     2067344         0   2067344   0% /dev/shm
[root@atlorca2 root]# fdisk -l /dev/sda

Disk /dev/sda: 36.4 GB, 36420075520 bytes
255 heads, 63 sectors/track, 4427 cylinders
Units = cylinders of 16065 * 512 = 8225280 bytes

   Device Boot    Start       End    Blocks   Id  System
/dev/sda1             1      4428  35566479+   ee  EFI GPT
```

fdisk reports only a single partition because the Global Unique Identification (GUID) Partition Table (or GPT) is used with the extensible firmware interface (EFI) on IA64. Before we go into detail about the solution, let's discuss EFI for a moment.

EFI is nothing more than a firmware interface for the system's firmware (BIOS) that has the capability to call an OS's bootloader. A complete history can be found at http://developer.intel.com/technology/efi/efi.htm. Now let's proceed to the solution.

Solution 6-2

You can use other tools to review the partition table, such as partx,

```
partx /dev/sda
# 1:        34-   204833 (   204800 sectors,    104 MB)
# 2:    204834- 67036926 ( 66832093 sectors,  34218 MB)
# 3:  67036927- 71132926 (  4096000 sectors,   2097 MB)
```

or parted, as shown in the following example:

```
parted
GNU Parted 1.6.3
Copyright (C) 1998, 1999, 2000, 2001, 2002 Free Software Foundation, Inc.
This program is free software, covered by the GNU General Public License.


This program is distributed in the hope that it will be useful, but
WITHOUT ANY WARRANTY; without even the implied warranty of MERCHANTABILITY
or FITNESS FOR A PARTICULAR PURPOSE. See the GNU General Public License
for more details.


Using /dev/sda
(parted) p
Disk geometry for /dev/sda: 0.000-34732.890 megabytes
Disk label type: gpt
Minor    Start      End      Filesystem  Name               Flags
1          0.017    100.016  fat16                           boot
2        100.017  32732.874  ext3
3      32732.875  34732.874  linux-swap
```

```
(parted) ?
  check MINOR                    do a simple check on the filesystem
  cp [FROM-DEVICE] FROM-MINOR TO-MINOR    copy filesystem to another \
                                            partition
  help [COMMAND]                 prints general help, or help on COMMAND
  mklabel LABEL-TYPE             create a new disklabel (partition table)
  mkfs MINOR FS-TYPE             make a filesystem FS-TYPE on partition
MINOR
  mkpart PART-TYPE [FS-TYPE] START END      make a partition
  mkpartfs PART-TYPE FS-TYPE START END      make a partition with a \
                                              filesystem
  move MINOR START END           move partition MINOR
  name MINOR NAME                name partition MINOR NAME
  print [MINOR]                  display the partition table, or a \
                                   partition
  quit                           exit program
  rescue START END               rescue a lost partition near START and \
                                   END
  resize MINOR START END         resize filesystem on partition MINOR
  rm MINOR                       delete partition MINOR
  select DEVICE                  choose the device to edit
  set MINOR FLAG STATE           change a flag on partition MINOR
```

Partition Table/Master Boot Record: Logical Block Addressing (LBA)

As mentioned earlier, LBA is the other method for addressing large-capacity drives. Despite being armed with primary partitions, logical partitions, and optional flag sets for partitions, we still cannot adequately address large-capacity drives using the CHS scheme. Using the LBA model addresses this limitation and allows for very large drives to be defined. In the following example, note that the values defined for the ending CHS do not have the capability to mark the end of the partition.

```
nc6000:/burn # cfdisk -P rst /dev/sda
Disk Drive: /dev/sda
Sector 0:
0x000: 33 C0 8E D0 BC 00 7C FB 50 07 50 1F FC BE 1B 7C
~~~~Skipped to save space~~~~
0x1B0: 00 00 00 00 00 00 00 00 2C 88 3E 6F CF C9 00 01
0x1C0: 01 00 0C FE FF FF 3F 00 00 00 82 91 A8 04 00 00
0x1D0: 00 00 00 00 00 00 00 00 00 00 00 00 00 00 00 00
0x1E0: 00 00 00 00 00 00 00 00 00 00 00 00 00 00 00 00
0x1F0: 00 00 00 00 00 00 00 00 00 00 00 00 00 00 55 AA


Partition Table for /dev/sda
```

# Type (ID) Flag	First Sector	Last Sector	Offset	Length	Filesystem Type	
1 Primary	0	78156224	63	78156225	W95 FAT32 (LBA) (0C)	None
Pri/Log	78156225	80292869	0	2136645	Free Space	None

```
Partition Table for /dev/sda
```

# Flags	---Starting--- Head Sect Cyl	ID	----Ending---- Head Sect Cyl	Start Sector	Number of Sectors
1 0x00	1 1 0	0x0C	254 63 1023	63	78156162

Calculating the ending sector should be achieved by multiplying the CHS counts. However, the factor of these values from the previous example ($254 \times 63 \times 1023 = 16370046$ sectors) should mark the ending sector, noting the 63 sector offset. In this case, it does. The CHS addressing scheme would fall short approximately 33GB. To elaborate, remember that each sector has a value of 512 bytes, 16370046×512 bytes = 8381463552 bytes; divide by 1024 bytes/KB = 8185023KB / 1024KB/MB = 7993.18MB. A new method is required to address the growing capacity of today's drives: LBA.

As we have established, the CHS cannot mark the boundaries of the previous example. However, bytes 01CA–01CD have the value "82 91 A8 04" and state the value of total sectors for the partition. LBA utilizes the total sector count to determine the end of one partition and the start of the next. Reversing the Endian order on bytes 01CA–01CD, 4A89182(H) = 78156162 sectors. Applying 512 bytes per sector, we get 78156162 × 512 bytes = 40015954944, 40015954944 bytes / 1024 bytes/KB = 39078081KB / 1024KB/MB = 38162.188MB or a 38GB drive.

A key point about the LBA method is that partition locations are now relative rather than absolute. Another way to describe this behavior is that the end of a partition marks the beginning of the next.

Partition Table/Master Boot Record: Bootloader

Now that we have an understanding of partition address models, we can locate the boot-loader. With the exact location of the boot code identified, we can determine whether this area has been modified in the event of a boot failure.

LILO is a well-known bootloader for Linux, although GRUB is quickly growing in popularity. After installing LILO or any other bootloader, the assembler code is written between byte 0 and 1BD(H) of the MBR. To modify or view any such bootloader code or partition table, we must use tools such as Binary Editor And Viewer (beav), Linux Disk Editor (lde), Binary vi (bvi), or any other Linux binary editor.

In the following example, we demonstrate the exact LILO bootloader code. Before writing the bootloader, the partition is cleaned using the following command: dd if=/dev/zero of=/dev/disk_device_file bs=512 count=1. After the partition table is wiped, we use cfdisk to generate a simple partition. Next, we issue lilo -M /dev/disk_device_file to write the assembler code to the bytes already defined.

To review the bootloader, we use dd if=/dev/hde of=/tmp/mbr_out count=1 bs=512 and bvi to open the file.

```
dd if=/dev/hde of=/tmp/mbr_out count-1 bs-512
bvi /tmp/mbr_out (Same data as seen above from od -h).
```

```
00000000   FA EB 31 12 00 00 4C 49 4C 4F 16 05 10 00 01 00   ..1...LILO......
00000010   00 7C 00 00 00 00 00 00 00 00 00 00 5E AC 08 C0   .|..........^...
00000020   74 09 B4 0E BB 07 00 CD 10 EB F2 B9 13 00 B4 86   t...............
00000030   CD 15 CD 18 31 C0 8E D0 BC 00 7C FB 89 E1 06 53   ....1.....|....S
00000040   56 52 89 CE FC 8E D8 8E C0 BF 00 06 B9 00 01 F3   VR..............
00000050   A5 EA 56 06 00 00 60 B8 00 12 B3 36 CD 10 61 66   ..V...`....6..af
00000060   8B 3E B8 07 66 09 FF 74 1B B4 08 B2 80 CD 13 0F   .>..f..t........
00000070   B6 CA 92 BA 80 00 E8 9A 00 66 3B 3E B8 7D 74 04   .........f;>.}t.
00000080   42 E2 F3 92 BE BE 07 B9 04 00 F6 04 80 89 F5 78   B..............x
00000090   33 83 C6 10 E2 F4 E8 83 FF 4E 6F 20 70 61 72 74   3........No part
000000A0   69 74 69 6F 6E 20 61 63 74 69 76 65 0D 0A 00 F6   ition active....
000000B0   04 80 79 10 E8 65 FF 49 6E 76 61 6C 69 64 20 50   ..y..e.Invalid P
000000C0   54 0D 0A 00 83 C6 10 E2 E6 89 EE 66 8B 44 08 66   T..........f.D.f
000000D0   A3 14 06 E8 3D 00 81 3E FE 7D 55 AA 75 11 31 C0   ....=..>.}U.u.1.
000000E0   58 3C FE 75 06 88 D4 5E 5B 07 92 FF 2E 10 06 E8   X<.u...^[.......
000000F0   2A FF 4E 6F 20 62 6F 6F 74 20 73 69 67 6E 61 74   *.No boot signat
00000100   75 72 65 20 69 6E 20 70 61 72 74 69 74 69 6F 6E   ure in partition
00000110   0D 0A 00 60 BD 0C 00 BE 0C 06 BB AA 55 B4 41 CD   ...`........U.A.
00000120   13 72 0F 81 FB 55 AA 75 09 F6 C1 01 74 04 B4 42   .r...U.u....t..B
00000130   EB 3F 52 B4 08 CD 13 72 43 51 C0 E9 06 86 E9 89   .?R....rCQ......
00000140   CF 59 C1 EA 08 92 40 83 E1 3F F7 E1 93 A1 14 06   .Y....@..?......
00000150   8B 16 16 06 39 DA 73 22 F7 F3 39 F8 77 1C C0 E4   ....9.s"..9.w...
00000160   06 86 E0 92 F6 F1 08 E2 89 D1 41 5A 88 C6 B8 01   ..........AZ....
00000170   02 C4 5C 04 CD 13 72 05 61 C3 B4 40 5A 4D 74 06   ..\...r.a..@ZMt.
00000180   30 E4 CD 13 EB 91 E8 93 FE 44 69 73 6B 20 72 65   0........Disk re
00000190   61 64 20 65 72 72 6F 72 0D 0A 00 00 00 00 00 00   ad error........
000001A0   00 00 00 00 00 00 00 00 00 00 00 00 00 00 00 00   ................
000001B0   00 00 00 00 00 00 00 00 42 5C 48 62 CF C9 80 01   ........B\Hb....
000001C0   01 00 83 0E 3F CE 3F 00 00 00 E0 FB 02 00 00 00   ....?.?.........
000001D0   00 00 00 00 00 00 00 00 00 00 00 00 00 00 00 00   ................
000001E0   00 00 00 00 00 00 00 00 00 00 00 00 00 00 00 00   ................
000001F0   00 00 00 00 00 00 00 00 00 00 00 00 00 00 55 AA   ..............U.
```

Another way to view the raw data from the drive is to use od. Reading MBR through od -h is difficult due to the 16-bit address MSB/LSB, which appears in reverse order, as discussed earlier. An example of an octal dump hex read from the same drive as mentioned previously follows:

```
dd if=/dev/hde count=1 bs=512 | od -h
1+0 records in
1+0 records out

0000000 ebfa 1231 0000 494c 4f4c 0516 0010 0001
0000020 7c00 0000 0000 0000 0000 0000 ac5e c008
0000040 0974 0eb4 07bb cd00 eb10 b9f2 0013 86b4
0000060 15cd 18cd c031 d08e 00bc fb7c e189 5306
0000100 5256 ce89 8efc 8ed8 bfc0 0600 00b9 f301
0000120 eaa5 0656 0000 b860 1200 36b3 10cd 6661
0000140 3e8b 07b8 0966 74ff b41b b208 cd80 0f13
0000160 cab6 ba92 0080 9ae8 6600 3e3b 7db8 0474
0000200 e242 92f3 bebe b907 0004 04f6 8980 78f5
0000220 8333 10c6 f4e2 83e8 4eff 206f 6170 7472
0000240 7469 6f69 206e 6361 6974 6576 0a0d f600
0000260 8004 1079 65e8 49ff 766e 6c61 6469 5020
0000300 0d54 000a c683 e210 89e6 66ee 448b 6608
0000320 14a3 e806 003d 3e81 7dfe aa55 1175 c031
0000340 3c58 75fe 8806 5ed4 075b ff92 102e e806
0000360 ff2a 6f4e 6220 6f6f 2074 6973 6e67 7461
0000400 7275 2065 6e69 7020 7261 6974 6974 6e6f
0000420 0a0d 6000 0cbd be00 060c aabb b455 cd41
0000440 7213 810f 55fb 75aa f609 01c1 0474 42b4
0000460 3feb b452 cd08 7213 5143 e9c0 8606 89e9
0000500 59cf eac1 9208 8340 3fe1 e1f7 a193 0614
0000520 168b 0616 da39 2273 f3f7 f839 1c77 e4c0
0000540 8606 92e0 f1f6 e208 d189 5a41 c688 01b8
0000560 c102 045c 13cd 0572 c361 40b4 4dba 0674
0000600 e430 13cd 91eb 93e8 44fe 7369 206b 6572
0000620 6461 6520 7272 726f 0a0d 0000 0000 0000
0000640 0000 0000 0000 0000 0000 0000 0000 0000
0000660 0000 0000 0000 0000 5c42 6248 c9cf 0180
```

```
0000700 0001 0e83 ce3f 003f 0000 fbe0 0002 0000
0000720 0000 0000 0000 0000 0000 0000 0000 0000
*
0000760 0000 0000 0000 0000 0000 0000 0000 aa55
```

Byte Review on a Used Drive

Before we continue our bootloader discussion, we must address one common difficulty in byte review. Most administrators never clean a drive before installing an OS. When installing an OS such as Linux on a partition in which an OS previously existed, byte review can be misleading and challenging, as shown in the following example. Using cfdisk, we depict the LILO boot code as loaded in a way almost identical to that just shown; however, in the following example, bytes 19A–1B7 have data from a previous load that is not utilized by LILO. The key point here is that byte 1BE has a value equal to "80." As mentioned, this byte signifies the boot device, and as you can see in the following example, even a Windows hibernation partition can be marked bootable for Linux.

```
"cfdisk -P rts"
Disk Drive: /dev/hda
Sector 0:
0x000: FA EB 20 01 B5 01 4C 49 4C 4F 16 05 A1 9D 32 41
0x010: 00 00 00 00 74 9C 6B 40 AC C8 AC C8 81 80 60 CD
0x020: C0 11 00 B8 C0 07 8E D0 BC 00 08 FB 52 53 06 56
0x030: FC 8E D8 31 ED 60 B8 00 12 B3 36 CD 10 61 B0 0D
0x040: E8 68 01 B0 0A E8 63 01 B0 4C E8 5E 01 60 1E 07
0x050: 80 FA FE 75 02 88 F2 BB 00 02 8A 76 1D 89 D0 80
0x060: E4 80 30 E0 78 0A 3C 10 73 06 F6 46 1C 40 75 2C
0x070: 88 F2 66 8B 7E 18 66 09 FF 74 21 52 B4 08 B2 80
0x080: CD 13 72 55 92 98 91 BA 7F 00 42 66 31 C0 40 E8
0x090: 71 00 66 3B BF B8 01 74 03 E2 EF 5A 53 8A 76 1E
0x0A0: BE 1F 00 E8 4B 00 B4 99 66 81 7F FC 4C 49 4C 4F
0x0B0: 75 27 5E 68 80 08 07 31 DB E8 35 00 75 FB BE 06
0x0C0: 00 89 F7 B9 0A 00 F3 A6 75 0D B0 02 AE 75 08 06
0x0D0: 55 B0 49 E8 D5 00 CB B4 9A B0 20 E8 CD 00 E8 BA
0x0E0: 00 FE 4E 00 74 08 BC E8 07 61 60 E9 60 FF F4 EB
0x0F0: FD 66 AD 66 09 C0 74 0A 66 03 46 10 E8 04 00 80
```

```
0x100: C7 02 C3 60 55 55 66 50 06 53 6A 01 6A 10 89 E6
0x110: 53 F6 C6 60 74 58 F6 C6 20 74 14 BB AA 55 B4 41
0x120: CD 13 72 0B 81 FB 55 AA 75 05 F6 C1 01 75 4A 52
0x130: 06 B4 08 CD 13 07 72 58 51 C0 E9 06 86 E9 89 CF
0x140: 59 C1 EA 08 92 40 83 E1 3F F7 E1 93 8B 44 08 8B
0x150: 54 0A 39 DA 73 38 F7 F3 39 F8 77 32 C0 E4 06 86
0x160: E0 92 F6 F1 08 E2 89 D1 41 5A 88 C6 EB 06 66 50
0x170: 59 58 88 E6 B8 01 02 EB 02 B4 42 5B BD 05 00 60
0x180: CD 13 73 0F 4D 74 09 31 C0 CD 13 61 EB F1 B4 40
0x190: E9 46 FF 88 64 1F 8D 64 10 61 C3 C1 C0 04 E8 03
0x1A0: 00 C1 C0 04 24 0F 27 04 F0 14 40 60 BB 07 00 B4
0x1B0: 0E CD 10 61 C3 00 44 63 AC C8 AC C8 00 00 80 01
0x1C0: 01 00 A0 EF 3F 02 3F 00 00 00 F1 B0 00 00 00 00
0x1D0: 01 03 05 EF FF FF 30 B1 00 00 50 78 53 02 00 00
0x1E0: 00 00 00 00 00 00 00 00 00 00 00 00 00 00 00 00
0x1F0: 00 00 00 00 00 00 00 00 00 00 00 00 00 00 55 AA


Sector 45360:
0x000: EB 52 90 4E 54 46 53 20 20 20 20 00 02 08 00 00
~~~~~~~ Skip to save space~~~~
0x1A0: 0D 0A 4E 54 4C 44 52 20 69 73 20 6D 69 73 73 69
0x1B0: 6E 67 00 0D 0A 4E 54 4C 44 52 20 69 73 20 00 01
0x1C0: 01 03 83 EF 3F 60 3F 00 00 00 A1 AF 15 00 00 00
0x1D0: 01 61 05 EF 3F CC E0 AF 15 00 C0 EA 18 00 00 00
0x1E0: 00 00 00 00 00 00 00 00 00 00 00 00 00 00 00 00
0x1F0: 00 00 00 00 00 00 00 00 00 00 00 00 00 00 55 AA


Sector 1466640:
0x000: 2B 38 04 C8 86 4A 47 E0 EB 54 E3 EA 00 CC 53 CC
~~~~~~~ Skip to save space~~~~
0x1B0: 43 54 7C D2 10 5D D1 43 2F 86 90 31 04 94 00 01
0x1C0: 01 61 82 EF 3F CC 3F 00 00 00 81 EA 18 00 00 00
0x1D0: 01 CD 05 EF FF FF A0 9A 2E 00 B0 DD 24 02 00 00
0x1E0: 00 00 00 00 00 00 00 00 00 00 00 00 00 00 00 00
0x1F0: 00 00 00 00 00 00 00 00 00 00 00 00 00 00 55 AA
```

```
Sector 3099600:
0x000: 4D 5F 47 75 69 64 50 6F 6F 6C 01 00 0D 43 4F 4D
~~~~~~~ Skip to save space~~~~
0x1B0: 44 53 33 64 42 75 66 66 65 72 3B 49 29 56 00 01
0x1C0: 01 CD 8E EF FF FF 3F 00 00 00 71 DD 24 02 00 00
0x1D0: 00 00 00 00 00 00 00 00 00 00 00 00 00 00 00 00
0x1E0: 00 00 00 00 00 00 00 00 00 00 00 00 00 00 00 00
0x1F0: 00 00 00 00 00 00 00 00 00 00 00 00 00 00 55 AA
```

```
Partition Table for /dev/hda
```

#	Type	First Sector	Last Sector	Offset	Length	Filesystem Type (ID)	Flags
1	**Primary**	**0**	**45359**	**63**	**45360**	**IBM Thinkpad hibe (A0)**	
	Boot (80)						
2	Primary	45360	39070079	0	39024720	Extended (05)	None (00)
5	Logical	45360	1466639	63	1421280	Linux (83)	None (00)
6	Logical	1466640	3099599	63	1632960	Linux swap (82)	None (00)
7	Logical	3099600	39070079	63	35970480	Linux LVM (8E)	None (00)

```
Partition Table for /dev/hda
```

#	Flags	---Starting--- Head	Sect	Cyl	ID	----Ending---- Head	Sect	Cyl	Start Sector	Number of Sectors
1	0x80	1	1	0	0xA0	239	63	2	63	45297
2	0x00	0	1	3	0x05	239	63	1023	45360	39024720
5	0x00	1	1	3	0x83	239	63	96	63	1421217
6	0x00	1	1	97	0x82	239	63	204	63	1632897
7	0x00	1	1	205	0x8E	239	63	1023	63	35970417

BIOS Initializing the Bootloader

Now that we have covered the bootloader location and difficulties of byte review, we need to cover how the BIOS calls the bootloader and how the bootloader responds. You would think that the first byte of a drive would be the primary thing to focus on.

However, the first course of action taken by the BIOS is to search for a partition with the boot flag set. It is important that only one partition be marked as a bootable partition, even though every partition can contain bootable code. If more than one partition contains a boot flag, most BIOSs fail to boot, and some partition tools, such as fdisk, can fail.

Using lilo -M to write the boot code to a disk partition fails if a bootable partition is not flagged or if more than one is flagged. The first byte "0" of a partition that contains LILO boot code has a value of FA(H) on the first sector, first track, and first cylinder of the partition represented by 1111 1010 (B). LILO defines this byte as a Clear Interrupt (CLI), documented in "first.S." The second byte defines the location of the bootloader code, and LILO defines this as EB "jump short" or E9 "jump near." But, jump to what? The jump condition starts the location of the bootloader code (LILO, in this case) defined in probe.c. Complete details on LILO's boot code can be reviewed as needed because LILO is open source. The topic of decoding a bootloader is beyond the scope of this chapter. However, covering the boot stage is critical to troubleshooting OS initialization.

When booting LILO, for example, the bootloader displays the letters L I L O one at a time, each of which has meaning. Beginning with the display of L, the first stage of the LILO bootloader has completed. Next, I appears, signifying the start of the second stage bootloader and floppy check. Lastly, LO appears, completing the second stage of the bootloader confirming kernel images. Based on the LILO configuration, a kernel is booted.

Partition Table/Master Boot Record: Backup

Now that we have defined the location of the master bootloader and some of its functions and limits, we need to discuss how this region is backed up. As would be expected, the partition table is the most important disk region because it defines the location of data. Although boot code and the master partition table reside in the MBR, boot code is much easier than the MBR to repair.

Recovering data from a failing boot drive does not require a successful restore of the bootloader. The boot code can be bypassed by booting from a repair CD or simply by booting from a different drive. Successful data recovery in this scenario requires only that the partition table be intact. Losing the partition table renders the data inaccessible.

To recover a partition table, we need an MBR backup. Loaders, such as LILO, write a backup MBR by default. This backup is usually found in /boot in a file called /boot/boot.XXXX. File boot.XXXX is a raw copy of the primary bootable partition. Another way to create this backup is by running the following command as root: dd if=/dev/disk_device_file of=/boot/boot.XXXX bs=512 count=1. Restoration of the MBR can be achieved in either method by issuing the following command: dd if= boot/boot.XXXX of=/dev/disk_device_file bs=512 count=1. However, in the event of a partition loss, recovering the raw MBR file from /boot filesystem becomes a daunting task. This task is further compounded by the fact that we can only recover the primary partition table, not the logical tables throughout the drive.

Partition Recovery Walkthrough

After backup is obtained, restoration can begin. We need to be aware of the expected results when an MBR is destroyed and the steps necessary for recovery. In the following section, we discuss the destruction and restoration of the MBR with detailed examples.

First, we must confirm that the partition table is correct. In our example, a simple partition table has been defined and depicted using cfdisk. Note that in the next listing, highlighted in bold are four partitions, all marked primary, and the first is bootable.

```
[root@localhost root]# cfdisk -P rst /dev/hde
Disk Drive: /dev/hde
Sector 0:
0x000: 00 00 00 00 00 00 00 00 00 00 00 00 00 00 00 00
~~~~~~~ Skip to save space~~~~
0x1A0: 00 00 00 00 00 00 00 00 00 00 00 00 00 00 00 00
0x1B0: 00 00 00 00 00 00 00 00 00 00 00 00 00 00 (80 01 <—Boot
0x1C0: 01 00 83 FE 3F 00 3F 00 00 00 82 3E 00 00) (00 00 <-pri 2
0x1D0: 01 01 83 FE 3F 01 C1 3E 00 00 C1 3E 00 00) (00 00 <-pri 3
0x1E0: 01 02 83 FE 3F 02 82 7D 00 00 C1 3E 00 00) (00 00 <-pri 4
0x1F0: 01 03 83 FE 3F 0E 43 BC 00 00 0C F1 02 00) [55 AA] END
```

```
Partition Table for /dev/hde


            First   Last
  # Type    Sector  Sector  Offset  Length  Filesystem Type (ID)
Flags
-- -------  ------- -------- ------- ------- ----------------- --------
  1 Primary       0   16064      63   16065  Linux (83)
Boot (80)
  2 Primary   16065   32129       0   16065  Linux (83)
None (00)
  3 Primary   32130   48194       0   16065  Linux (83)
None (00)
  4 Primary   48195  240974       0  192780  Linux (83)
None (00)
    None    240975 12594959      0 12353985 Unusable
None (00)
Partition Table for /dev/hde


              ---Starting---        ----Ending----    Start Number of
  # Flags Head Sect Cyl    ID  Head Sect Cyl   Sector   Sectors
-- ----- ---- ---- ----  ---- ---- ---- ---- -------- ---------
  1 0x80    1    1    0 0x83  254   63    0       63    16002
  2 0x00    0    1    1 0x83  254   63    1    16065    16065
  3 0x00    0    1    2 0x83  254   63    2    32130    16065
  4 0x00    0    1    3 0x83  254   63   14    48195   192780
```

Next, we create a filesystem on the first partition and mount the partition's filesystem to demonstrate its availability to the end user.

```
[root@localhost root]# mke2fs -j /dev/hde1
mke2fs 1.34 (25-Jul-2003)
Filesystem label=
OS type: Linux
Block size=1024 (log=0)
Fragment size=1024 (log=0)
2000 inodes, 8000 blocks
400 blocks (5.00%) reserved for the super user
```

```
First data block=1
1 block group
8192 blocks per group, 8192 fragments per group
2000 inodes per group

Writing inode tables: done
Creating journal (1024 blocks): done
Writing superblocks and filesystem accounting information: done

This filesystem will be automatically checked every 30 mounts or
180 days, whichever comes first.  Use tune2fs -c or -i to override.
```

```
[root@localhost root]# mount /dev/hde1 /hde-test/
[root@localhost root]# df
Filesystem          Size  Used Avail Use% Mounted on
/dev/ide/host2/bus0/target0/lun0/part1
                    7.6M  1.1M  6.2M  15% /hde-test   <----Confirmation
that our filesystem and partition are avail.
```

Demonstrating a Failure

Now that we have a valid partition table with a filesystem on partition 1, we need to
demonstrate a failure. Next, we unmount the filesystem, create an MBR backup, and
destroy the MBR. We then confirm that the MBR is flawed with cfdisk, viewing the
partition.

```
[root@localhost root]# umount /hde-test
[root@localhost root]# dd if=/dev/hde of=/tmp/hde.mbr.primary.part
bs=512 count=1
1+0 records in
1+0 records out
[root@localhost root]# dd if=/dev/zero of=/dev/hde bs=512 count=1
1+0 records in
1+0 records out
```

```
[root@localhost root]# cfdisk -P rst /dev/hde

[root@localhost root]# echo $?
3
```

cfdisk returns an error code of 3. Error codes for cfdisk include the following:

* 0—No errors.
* 1—Invocation error.
* 2—I/O error.
* 3—Cannot get geometry <---It is very important to understand that "55 AA at block 0x1FF" is missing.
* 4—Bad partition table on disk.

Though we have proven that the MBR/partition table has been destroyed, we have neither rebooted the OS nor updated the kernel resident memory for the device structure. Because the kernel has not been updated with the MBR info cleared, we can still mount the drive. For example:

```
[root@localhost root]# mount /dev/hde1 /hde-test/
[root@localhost root]# df
Filesystem              Size  Used Avail Use% Mounted on
/dev/ide/host2/bus0/target0/lun0/part1
                        7.6M  1.1M  6.2M  15% /hde-test  <---Filesystem/
partition mounted even though no table exists to instruct
the kernel of a partition location.
[root@localhost root]# umount /hde-test
```

To understand this example, we just need to remember that the running kernel memory still contains all the partition information for the filesystem. Until we rescan the partition table, this data structure remains constant. In our example, we just disconnect the running drive, removing the driver from the kernel (rmmod). After a few seconds, we reactivate the driver (insmod), and a rescan of the drive is initiated. The kernel is unable to find a usable partition table on the first 512 bytes of the drive or any other LBA location, so mounting the filesystem fails. It is important to understand that the filesystem is still intact, but it is lying on a disk with no boundaries.

Mounting a Partition

Next, we demonstrate the mounting of partition 1 after the drive has been removed and added back to the running kernel.

```
[root@localhost root]# mount /dev/hde1 /hde-test/
/dev/hde1: Invalid argument
mount: you must specify the filesystem type
```

Note that /dev/hde1 is an invalid argument to the mount command because no partitions are defined.

```
[root@localhost root]# cfdisk -P rst /dev/hde

[root@localhost root]# echo $?
3  <---Review previous notes to determine this error return code.
```

The next step is to recover the partition table.

```
[root@localhost root]# dd if=/tmp/hde.mbr.primary.part of=/dev/hde
bs=512 count=1
1+0 records in
1+0 records out
[root@localhost root]# cfdisk -P rst /dev/hde
Disk Drive: /dev/hde
Sector 0:
0x000: 00 00 00 00 00 00 00 00 00 00 00 00 00 00 00 00
~~~~~~~ Skip to save space~~~~
0x1A0: 00 00 00 00 00 00 00 00 00 00 00 00 00 00 00 00
0x1B0: 00 00 00 00 00 00 00 00 00 00 00 00 00 00 80 01
0x1C0: 01 00 83 FE 3F 00 3F 00 00 00 82 3E 00 00 00 00
0x1D0: 01 01 83 FE 3F 01 C1 3E 00 00 C1 3E 00 00 00 00
0x1E0: 01 02 83 FE 3F 02 82 7D 00 00 C1 3E 00 00 00 00
0x1F0: 01 03 83 FE 3F 0E 43 BC 00 00 0C F1 02 00 55 AA
```

Now we mount the filesystem located at the first partition. Remember that the running kernel is not aware of the new partition table. The mount should fail.

```
[root@localhost root]# mount /dev/hde1 /hde-test/
/dev/hde1: Invalid argument
mount: you must specify the filesystem type
```

In fact, the mount did fail. To work around this issue, a scan must be initiated to update the kernel memory. Perform the same steps as before: rmmod the driver controlling the external or internal device and insmod after a few seconds.

```
[root@localhost root]# mount /dev/hde1 /hde-test/
[root@localhost root]# df
Filesystem              Size  Used Avail Use% Mounted on
/
/dev/hde1               7.6M  1.1M  6.2M  15% /hde-test
```

The same procedure can be used for logical partitions. However, you must know the locations because they are relative to the last partition, as mentioned earlier in this chapter.

Recovering Superblock and Inode Table on ext Filesystems

Filesystem superblock recovery is very similar to partition table recovery. Without the superblock on an extent-based filesystem and many other filesystems, locating the data within the filesystem becomes a daunting challenge.

In the following exercise, we depict a simple partition table and filesystem, and we demonstrate steps to find, back up, and destroy a superblock table.

To begin, choose a tool to create a small partition. Results should look something like this:

```
[root@localhost root]# cfdisk -P rst /dev/hde
Disk Drive: /dev/hde
Sector 0:
0x000: 00 00 00 00 00 00 00 00 00 00 00 00 00 00 00 00
~~~~~~~ Skip to save space~~~~
0x1B0: 00 00 00 00 00 00 00 00 00 00 00 00 00 00 80 01
```

```
0x1C0: 01 00 83 0E 3F CE 3F 00 00 00 E0 FB 02 00 00 00
0x1D0: 00 00 00 00 00 00 00 00 00 00 00 00 00 00 00 00
0x1E0: 00 00 00 00 00 00 00 00 00 00 00 00 00 00 00 00
0x1F0: 00 00 00 00 00 00 00 00 00 00 00 00 00 00 55 AA


Partition Table for /dev/hde


             First    Last
 # Type      Sector   Sector   Offset  Length    Filesystem Type (ID)
Flags
 -- ------- -------- --------- ------ --------- ---------------- --------

 1 Primary        0   195614       63   195615  Linux (83)  Boot (80)
   Pri/Log   195615 12594959        0 12399345  Free Space None (00)
Partition Table for /dev/hde


        ---Starting---      ----Ending----    Start Number of
 # Flags Head Sect Cyl   ID Head Sect Cyl    Sector  Sectors
 -- ----- ---- ---- ---- ---- ---- ---- ---- -------- ---------

 1 0x80    1    1    0 0x83  14   63  206       63    195552
 2 0x00    0    0    0 0x00   0    0    0        0         0
 3 0x00    0    0    0 0x00   0    0    0        0         0
 4 0x00    0    0    0 0x00   0    0    0        0         0
```

Build a filesystem on the created partition.

```
mkfs.ext3 /dev/hde1
mke2fs 1.34 (25-Jul-2003)
Filesystem label=
OS type: Linux
Block size=1024 (log=0)
Fragment size=1024 (log=0)
24480 inodes, 97776 blocks
4888 blocks (5.00%) reserved for the super user
First data block=1
12 block groups
```

```
8192 blocks per group, 8192 fragments per group
2040 inodes per group
Superblock backups stored on blocks:    <--- Note the superblock
locations...
        8193, 24577, 40961, 57345, 73729

Writing inode tables: done
Creating journal (4096 blocks): done
Writing superblocks and filesystem accounting information: done
```

Note that the block size can differ depending on the size of the actual filesystem. In this example, the first superblock (SB) resides at:

```
dd if=/dev/hde of=/tmp/hde_sb.out bs=512 count=8 skip=65

8+0 records in
8+0 records out
```

Remember to skip the first 63 sectors to reach the location of partition one—the SB block resides at block 1 or at 1024 bytes, which is the size of the filesystem block. SB is two bytes in size.

```
[root@localhost root]# dd if=/dev/zero of=/dev/hde count=8 bs=512 seek=65
8+0 records in
8+0 records out
[root@localhost root]# df
Filesystem          Size  Used Avail Use% Mounted on
/dev/vg01/home      2.0G  1.7G  290M  86% /home
```

Confirm that /hde-test is not mounted.

```
[root@localhost root]# mount /dev/hde1 /hde-test/
mount: you must specify the filesystem type

[root@localhost root]# tune2fs -l /dev/hde1
tune2fs 1.34 (25-Jul-2003)
tune2fs: Bad magic number in super-block while trying to open /dev/hde1
Couldn't find valid filesystem superblock.
```

We have successfully destroyed the superblock. The next step is to recover it by using the alternate superblock.

```
[root@localhost root]# e2fsck -b 8193 /dev/hde1
e2fsck 1.34 (25-Jul-2003)
/dev/hde1 was not cleanly unmounted, check forced.
Pass 1: Checking inodes, blocks, and sizes
Pass 2: Checking directory structure
Pass 3: Checking directory connectivity
Pass 4: Checking reference counts
Pass 5: Checking group summary information
Block bitmap differences:  +(1--4387)
Fix<y>? yes

Free blocks count wrong for group #0 (3806, counted=3805).
Fix<y>? yes

Free blocks count wrong (90552, counted=90551).
Fix<y>? yes

Inode bitmap differences:  +(1--12)
Fix<y>? yes

Free inodes count wrong for group #0 (2029, counted=2028).
Fix<y>? yes

Free inodes count wrong (24469, counted=24468).
Fix<y>? yes

/dev/hde1: ***** FILE SYSTEM WAS MODIFIED *****
/dev/hde1: 12/24480 files (0.0% non-contiguous), 7225/97776 blocks
```

Now the true test . . . Is the filesystem available to be mounted? Next, we prove that the filesystem is restored and that data is available.

```
[root@localhost root]# mount /dev/hde1 /hde-test/    <--- mount successful
[root@localhost root]# ll /hde-test/
total 13
-rw-r--r--   1 root     root              65 Sep  8 19:17
greg_greg_greg_.txt  <--- File exists...
drwx------   2 root     root           12288 Sep  8 19:11 lost+found/
```

These steps show how to restore a superblock and confirm the availability of the data.

Other methods exist for making backups for superblocks. Confirming the location of the superblocks is only half the battle. The other half is knowing how to back it up. If an alternate superblock resides at block 8193 of the filesystem on a 1024-byte block with a 63-byte offset, the following command can be used to grab the superblock:

```
dd if=/dev/hde of=/tmp/hde_sb.out2 bs=512 count=8 skip=16449
```

After a backup has been made of the MBR, including the filesystem's superblock and data within filesystem, we should cover one last hurdle. Filesystem capacity is restricted in more ways than just raw capacity. The superblock controls two basic limits, which include raw capacity and inodes.

When troubleshooting filesystem capacity errors, partition tables and superblocks are usually the last resort. Many Linux users encounter the simple inode limit when millions of small files reside in a filesystem. As shown next, a while loop creates thousands of files, each taking up an available inode, which exceeds the filesystem's capacity with regards to inode count, not raw capacity.

```
#!/bin/sh
count=1
total=0
while [ $total -ne $* ]
do
total=`expr $total + $count`
  echo "$total"> /hde-test/$total
done

./count_greg.sh 50000
./count_greg.sh: line 7: /hde-test/24437: No space left on device
```

This program creates thousands of files, which occupy all available inodes yet leave plenty of capacity for the filesystem.

```
[greg@localhost tmp]$ df
Filesystem           Size  Used Avail Use% Mounted on
/dev/hde1            93M   29M   60M  33% /hde-test
```

```
tune2fs -l /dev/hde1
tune2fs 1.34 (25-Jul-2003)
Filesystem volume name:   <none>
Last mounted on:          <not available>
Filesystem UUID:          19826da5-0597-47e2-955b-b5aa81fcca55
Filesystem magic number:  0xEF53
Filesystem revision #:    1 (dynamic)
Filesystem features:      has_journal filetype needs_recovery sparse_super
Default mount options:    (none)
Filesystem state:         clean with errors
Errors behavior:          Continue
Filesystem OS type:       Linux
Inode count:              24480
Block count:              97776
Reserved block count:     4888
Free blocks:              65737
Free inodes:              0    <--- Zero inodes left so filesystem has
no available pointers though space remains.
First block:              1
Block size:               1024
Fragment size:            1024
Blocks per group:         8192
Fragments per group:      8192
Inodes per group:         2040
Inode blocks per group:   255
Filesystem created:       Wed Sep  8 19:11:15 2004
Last mount time:          Wed Sep  8 22:21:40 2004
```

```
Last write time:          Wed Sep  8 22:30:57 2004
Mount count:              2
Maximum mount count:      21
Last checked:             Wed Sep  8 21:36:09 2004
Check interval:           15552000 (6 months)
Next check after:         Mon Mar  7 20:36:09 2005
Reserved blocks uid:      0 (user root)
Reserved blocks gid:      0 (group root)
First inode:              11
Inode size:               128
Journal inode:            8
Default directory hash:   tea
Directory Hash Seed:      64a819b6-d567-49d7-bd11-f50c35d961fb
```

It's important to back up superblocks, especially for those extremely large filesystems over 2TB. If an application fails, and the superblock is overwritten or left in an unstable state, the data may be valid, but with no pointers to the data, recovery becomes time consuming.

Further Scenarios

The following scenarios describe real-world failures with tactical solutions. Use the scenarios to develop troubleshooting skills and broaden the foundation of your knowledge.

Scenario 6-3: Drives Scan in the Wrong Order

After adding the driver to scan external storage, the drives scan in the wrong order on boot. The boot drive was once at the beginning of the line—that is, /dev/sda or hda. However, now the boot drive fails inline after all other disks are found.

Solution 6-3

There are several ways to work around the issue. The simplest way is to modify /etc/modules.conf.

```
alias eth0 tulip
alias scsi_hostadapter sym53c8xx
alias scsi_hostadapter1 cciss
alias scsi_hostadapter2 lpfcdd
```

In this example, `lpfcdd` is the last driver loaded. Any devices found on the `lpfcdd` driver must follow any device found on the `cciss` and `sym53c8xx` drivers.

Scenario 6-4: vgcreate Fails

In this scenario, `vgcreate` fails when using a 1TB LUN.

```
# vgcreate /dev/vg01 /dev/sdb1
vgcreate -- INFO: using default physical extent size 4 MB
vgcreate -- INFO: maximum logical volume size is 255.99 Gigabyte
vgcreate -- doing automatic backup of volume group "main"
vgcreate -- volume group "main" successfully created and activated
```

The command completed but only used 256GB of a 1TB disk. How do we correct this issue?

Solution 6-4

The default PE size for LVM in Linux equals 4MB. To resolve the issue, use the `-s` option under LVM to choose larger PE size.

Extend the PE size to 32MB, and then you can create the maximum 2TB VG.

```
# vgcreate -s 32M /dev/vg01 /dev/sdb1
```

Scenario 6-5: Not Possible to Put /boot under LVM Control with Linux

With Linux, it's not possible to put `/boot` under LVM control due to bootloader constraints. However, `/` can be managed by LVM. For this to be successful, we must separate `/boot` from `/`.

Solution 6-5

Bind /boot to a physical partition with the ext2 filesystem to enable the bootloader(s) to find the kernel in /boot. Afterward, / can be placed within LVM control.

An example follows:

```
/boot /dev/sda1
/     /dev/vg00/lvol1
```

note

Make sure you have created an lvol (this example uses lvol1). Don't forget to copy / data to your new lvol. /boot is not needed, but for simplicity, use it in the copy command.

Generic steps to achieve this solution follow this example:

```
lvcreate -n lvol1 -L 200m /dev/vg00
mke2fs /dev/vg00/lvol1
mount /dev/vg00/lvol1 /lvol1fs
find / -xdev | cpio -pdumv /lvol1fs
```

Now for the procedure:

1. Boot from a Linux rescue CD.

2. Activate LVM and mount filesystems.

    ```
    /sbin/vgscan
    /sbin/vgchange -a y
    mount /dev/vg00/lvol1 /lvol1fs
    mount /dev/sda1 /boot
    ```

3. Create your own initrd.

    ```
    dd if=/dev/zero of=/lvol1fs/tmp/initrd.uncompressed bs=1024 \
    count=8192
    mke2fs -m 0 /lvol1fs/tmp/initrd.uncompressed
    ```

4. Mount the `initrd` filesystem.

    ```
    mkdir /new_initrd
    mount -o loop /lvol1fs/tmp/initrd.uncompressed /new_initrd
    ```

5. Use an existing `initrd`.

    Create an `initrd` using the command `mkinitrd` if you do not have an image.

    ```
    export INITRD_MODULES=" ";mk_initrd /new_initrd
    ```

    However, because we copied / to `lvol1`, the original `initrd` image is now located under both `/lvol1fs/boot/initrd` and `/boot`.

    ```
    gzip -cd /lvol1fs/boot/initrd >
    /lvol1fs/tmp/orig_initrd.uncompressed
    mkdir /orig_initrd
    mount -o /lvol1fs/tmp/orig_initrd.uncompressed /orig_initrd
    ```

6. Copy all files from this image to our new `initrd` image.

    ```
    cp -a /orig_initrd/* /new_initrd
    ```

7. Add files necessary for LVM (if you have static binaries, use them; otherwise, make sure to copy all needed shared libraries, too).

    ```
    cp /sbin/vg* /new_initrd/bin
    ```

    Confirm that all dynamic libraries are included. For example:

    ```
    nc6000:/tmp/init # ldd /sbin/lvm
    linux-gate.so.1 =>  (0xffffe000)
    libdevmapper.so.1.00 => /lib/libdevmapper.so.1.00 (0x4003c000)
    libdl.so.2 => /lib/libdl.so.2 (0x40043000)
    libc.so.6 => /lib/tls/libc.so.6 (0x40047000)
    /lib/ld-linux.so.2 => /lib/ld-linux.so.2 (0x40000000)
    ```

    Next, copy them to `/new_initrd/lib`.

8. Create LVM device files.

    ```
    cp /dev/sda* /new_initrd/dev (remember sda = scsi, hda = ide)
    ```

9. We also must provide for the proc filesystem:

```
mkdir /new_initrd/proc
mkdir /new_initrd/etc
cp -a /bin/mount /bin/umount /bin/rm /new_initrd/bin
```

10. Modify the linuxrc script so that all modules are loaded to recognize the discs.

```
echo "Mounting /proc"
/bin/mount -t proc proc /proc
echo "Activating lvm"
/bin/vgscan
/bin/vgchange -a y
echo "Unmounting /proc"
/bin/umount /proc
```

11. Clean up the files.

```
umount /new_initrd
umount /orig_initrd
rm -rf /new_initrd /orig_initrd
```

12. Put the new initrd image into place.

```
gzip -c /lvol1fs/tmp/initrd.uncompressed > /boot/initrd.lvm
```

Change /lvol1fs/etc/lilo.conf.
initrd=/boot/boot/initrd.lvm

Update the bootloader.
lilo -C /lvol1fs/etc/lilo.conf

note

/dev/sda1 will be mounted to the /boot directory, but all the kernel's images and initrd images reside in a directory called boot because this was the original / filesystem. We need to clean up this issue at a later date, but it works for now.

Reboot and enjoy our LVM as root-filesystem.

Scenario 6-6: LUN Limitation

We want to have over 140 LUNs visible from our storage array. Each LUN has an alternate path, which equals more than 280 LUNs visible. The problem is that a default Linux kernel only allows 128 LUNs.

Solution 6-6

One solution is to increase the size of the LUNs to reduce the count and then to create a large number of logical volumes under LVM. However, another solution is to modify the kernel to expand the total number of allowed LUNs.

By default, the maximum number of SCSI LUNs that can be loaded as modules is 128, which depends on the vendor kernel build.

Under "SCSI Support," you could modify `CONFIG_SD_EXTRA_DEVS` to a number greater than 128 and recompile the kernel.

Summary

By discussing the simple nature of a bit at the beginning of this chapter, we demonstrated how and where a system places a table for slicing up a storage device. We continued our journey by discussing how a BIOS of any modern computer finds a bootloader and the partition in which the bootloader must activate the running OS. We concluded the chapter with LVM and filesystem maintenance, including several scenarios to cover some of the most basic partition troubleshooting tactics.

7

Device Failure and Replacement

Whether the red LED is flashing or the `syslog` is filling up with cryptic messages, a hardware failure is never a day at the beach. The goal of this chapter is to provide a guide for identifying and remedying device failures. We begin with a discussion of supported devices before proceeding with a discussion of how to look for errors. We then discuss how to identify a failed device. Finally, we consider replacements and alternative options to remedy the problem.

Supported Devices

Before spending hours determining why a device has failed, we must first confirm that the device is supported by the running kernel. Next, we must confirm that the device meets the hardware requirements set forth by the vendor. Of course, most of us never check to see whether a device we are about to play with is supported; instead, we just plug it in, and if the lights come on, we think we have struck gold. Though this approach might work most of the time, to reduce a system's downtime, troubleshooting a failed component should start with the fundamentals.

Each OS distribution provides a supported hardware list, so it is best to check with your applicable distribution to determine whether the device in question is supported. A good example is Red Hat's complete hardware support matrix, which is located at http://hardware.redhat.com/hcl/?pagename=hcl&view=allhardware#form. Another example is Mandriva's supported hardware database, which is found at http://wwwnew .mandriva.com/en/hardware/. For our last example, the SUSE Linux hardware support list can be found at http://hardwaredb.suse.de/index.php?LANG=en_UK.

It is not sufficient merely to determine that the device is supported. As previously noted, it also is crucial to confirm that the device meets the hardware requirements set forth by the vendor. Each driver for any given device is designed with certain hardware restrictions. For example, Emulex Corporation writes a driver that enables its Host Bus Adapters (HBAs) to function with the Linux kernel, yet restrictions do apply. Emulex has a vast number of HBAs to choose from, so determining which adapter, as well as which driver, is supported on any given kernel is critical. Determining these boundaries makes remedying the problem more manageable. Of course, recall that when a new hardware device such as an HBA is acquired, it is important to check its supportability with the distribution's hardware support matrix. Finally, the driver code for a device also contains information regarding the supported hardware types. This is demonstrated in the following example. Upon reviewing the source code for the Emulex HBA in file `fcLINUXfcp.c`, which is used to build the driver module `lpfcdd.o`, we find the following:

```
if(pdev != NULL) {
    switch(pdev->device){
    case PCI_DEVICE_ID_CENTAUR:
      sprintf(buf,
        "Emulex %s (LP9000) SCSI on PCI bus %02x device %02x irq %d",
        multip, p_dev_ctl->pcidev->bus->number, p_dev_ctl->pcidev->devfn,
        p_dev_ctl->pcidev->irq);
      break;
```

Although the previous example provides us with the information needed to determine the supported HBA types for Emulex, a faster method of extracting the same data exists. As with any hardware vendor, common characteristics exist with naming conventions. For example, Emulex starts all its HBAs with "LP." By using this shortcut, we can extract the supported HBA types at a greater speed than with the previous command. The following command demonstrates this faster method:

```
[root@cyclops lpfc]# cat fcLINUXfcp.c | grep "Emulex %s (LP"

"Emulex %s (LP9000) SCSI on PCI bus %02x device %02x irq %d",
          "Emulex %s (LP8000) SCSI on PCI bus %02x device %02x irq %d",
          "Emulex %s (LP7000) SCSI on PCI bus %02x device %02x irq %d",
          "Emulex %s (LP950) SCSI on PCI bus %02x device %02x irq %d",
          "Emulex %s (LP850) SCSI on PCI bus %02x device %02x irq %d",
```

We also can identify the version of the kernel for which the source is designed and confirm that the driver source works with the applicable kernel we are using. As shown in the following example, we can distinguish that the source code for our Emulex HBAs, contained in fcLINUXfcp.c, has notes pertaining to which kernels are supported.

```
/*
* LINUX specific code for lpfcdd driver
 * This driver is written to work with 2.2 and 2.4 LINUX kernel threads.
 *
 */
```

Next, we need to determine the driver version for the source code we are reviewing. To find the driver version, simply search for "version" and "driver" simultaneously. The driver developers usually make it easy to find out which source code version is being used. See the next example:

```
root@cyclops lpfc]# cat fcLINUXfcp.c| grep -i version | grep -i driver
#define LPFC_DRIVER_VERSION "4.20p
...
```

Note that we also can determine other needed information about the device from the manufacturer or Linux distribution. Data requirements with respect to drivers, kernels, hardware, and so on always can be found at the OS distribution's Web site, from the hardware vendor, or in the driver code. The README files provided with almost all drivers contain specifications to adhere to as well. Always check the previous data points before continuing down a broken path.

Where to Look for Errors

The second step to remedying a device failure is to locate the error. Many tools are available to assist a user in looking for an error. Determining the problem for a device requires the utilization of these tools. They include dmesg, lspci, lsmod, syslog/messages, and the /proc filesystem, among others. This section covers dmesg and syslog/messages in detail. The remaining tools are discussed in more detail later in this chapter.

dmesg is often helpful; therefore, it is a good place to begin. dmesg is a command that reads the kernel ring buffer, which holds the latest kernel messages. dmesg reports the current errors detected by the kernel with respect to the hardware or application. This tool provides a fast and easy way to capture the latest errors from the kernel. We provide the man page here for dmesg for quick reference:

DMESG(8)   DMESG(8)

NAME
        dmesg - print or control the kernel ring buffer

SYNOPSIS
        dmesg [-c] [-n level] [-s bufsize]

DESCRIPTION
        dmesg is used to examine or control the kernel ring buffer.

        The program helps users to print out their bootup messages.
        Instead of copying the messages by hand, the user need only:
            dmesg > boot.messages
        and mail the boot.messages file to whoever can debug their problem.

Although the dmesg command is simple to use, its extensive reports are critical to finding errors promptly. To assist in your understanding of dmesg, we now walk you through an example of a standard dmesg from a booted Linux machine.

```
greg@nc6000:/tmp> dmesg
Linux version 2.6.8-24.11-default (geeko@buildhost) (gcc version 3.3.4
(pre 3.3.5 20040809)) #1 Fri Jan 14 13:01:26 UTC 2005
BIOS-provided physical RAM map:
 BIOS-e820: 0000000000000000 - 000000000009fc00 (usable)
 BIOS-e820: 000000000009fc00 - 00000000000a0000 (reserved)
 BIOS-e820: 00000000000e0000 - 0000000000100000 (reserved)
 BIOS-e820: 0000000000100000 - 000000001ffd0000 (usable)
 BIOS-e820: 000000001ffd0000 - 000000001fff0c00 (reserved)
 BIOS-e820: 000000001fff0c00 - 000000001fffc000 (ACPI NVS)
 BIOS-e820: 000000001fffc000 - 0000000020000000 (reserved)
```

As shown in this example, the first line of the `dmesg` output provides information about the running kernel version, including who built the kernel, what compiler was used, and when the kernel was compiled. Therefore, if you are compiling source and have a GCC failure, this is a place to start looking. Next, we see the following:

```
502MB vmalloc/ioremap area available.
```

`vmalloc` is defined in `arch/i386/kernel/setup.c` for IA32 machines. Similarly, `vmalloc` for IA64 machines is defined in `arch/ia64/kernel/perfmon.c`. Complete details on memory structure are outside the scope of this chapter, but knowing where to look for details and documentation is a critical starting point. Also note that `ioremap.c` defines the space for kernel access. In the following code, we see basic boundaries of High and Low memory limits detected on boot by the communication between the BIOS and kernel.

```
0MB HIGHMEM available.
511MB LOWMEM available.
On node 0 totalpages: 131024
  DMA zone: 4096 pages, LIFO batch:1
  Normal zone: 126928 pages, LIFO batch:16
  HighMem zone: 0 pages, LIFO batch:1
DMI 2.3 present.
ACPI: RSDP (v000 COMPAQ                                    ) @ 0x000f6f80
ACPI: RSDT (v001 HP      HP0890   0x23070420 CPQ  0x00000001) @ 0x1fff0c84
ACPI: FADT (v002 HP      HP0890   0x00000002 CPQ  0x00000001) @ 0x1fff0c00
ACPI: DSDT (v001 HP       nc6000 0x00010000 MSFT 0x0100000e) @ 0x00000000
ACPI: PM-Timer IO Port: 0x1008
ACPI: local apic disabled
Built 1 zonelists
```

The following is the bootloader command for calling the kernel. Whether using GRUB or LILO, the bootloader is called similarly to the line shown next.

```
Kernel command line: root=/dev/hda1 vga=0x317 selinux=0
resume=/dev/hda5 desktop elevator=as splash=silent PROFILE=Home
bootsplash: silent mode.
```

If a user forgets the boot options provided at boot time, dmesg or syslog will have the values recorded. Note that Chapter 6, "Disk Partitions and Filesystems," discusses Master Boot Record (MBR) in great detail, offering information about how the BIOS uses a bootloader such as GRUB or LILO. Continuing with dmesg output, we see in the following that the processor and video console are detected:

```
Initializing CPU#0
PID hash table entries: 2048 (order: 11, 32768 bytes)
Detected 1694.763 MHz processor.
Using pmtmr for high-res timesource
Console: colour dummy device 80x25
```

The next entries report directory entry and inode cache allocation.

```
Dentry cache hash table entries: 131072 (order: 7, 524288 bytes)
Inode-cache hash table entries: 65536 (order: 6, 262144 bytes)
```

The document located in kernel source at /usr/src/linux/Documentation/ filesystems/vfs.txt describes dentry and inode cache in great detail. Following dentry and inode cache, the amount of system memory is detected and displayed:

```
Memory: 513740k/524096k available (2076k kernel code, 9744k reserved,
780k data, 212k init, 0k highmem)
Checking if this processor honours the WP bit even in supervisor
mode... Ok.
```

Now, let us wrap up this short demonstration of dmesg with some information about BogoMIPS. In linux/arch/i386/kdb/kdba_io.c, the "Kernel Debugger Architecture Dependent Console I/O handler" defines the BogoMIPS. In simplest terms, BogoMIPS is merely a benchmark tool for comparing similar CPUs. However, this tool is never used, which is the reason for its name ("bogus"). Please note that certain structures use the output of BogoMIPS within the kernel, but the end user will find no large benefit in it. More details on BogoMIPS can be found at http://www.tldp.org/HOWTO/BogoMips/.

```
Calibrating delay loop... 3358.72 BogoMIPS (lpj=1679360)
```

In addition to dmesg, there are other places to look for hardware errors. As we have shown, dmesg reports everything to the syslog daemon, which in turn records to log file

/var/log/messages by default. Although other tools exist for reporting hardware errors, dmesg and syslog are the most prominent. Other tools such as lspci are used in conjunction with dmesg/syslog later in this chapter to locate a failed hardware component.

Identifying Failed Devices

After an error is located, the failed device can be identified. The goal is to determine the root cause. As previously mentioned, dmesg and /var/log/messages are commonly used with lspci and the /proc filesystem. These combined tools are used to troubleshoot and locate hardware faults.

The lspci command presents a user with the hardware layout on a machine. In the following example, we use a small Linux IA32 server with dual processors and Fibre Channel attached storage to demonstrate what an lspci would look like. First, we display the kernel we are using with the uname command.

```
[root@cyclops lpfc]# uname -a
Linux cyclops 2.4.9-e.10custom-gt #4 SMP Mon Nov 1 14:17:36 EST 2004
i686 unknown
```

We continue with dmesg to list the PCI bus. Note that because we use the Emulex HBAs often in this chapter's examples, they are shown in bold.

```
[root@cyclops lpfc]# dmesg ¦ grep PCI
PCI: PCI BIOS revision 2.10 entry at 0xfda11, last bus=1
PCI: Using configuration type 1
PCI: Probing PCI hardware
PCI: Discovered primary peer bus 01 [IRQ]
PCI->APIC IRQ transform: (B0,I2,P0) -> 22
PCI->APIC IRQ transform: (B0,I8,P0) -> 23
PCI->APIC IRQ transform: (B0,I15,P0) -> 33
PCI->APIC IRQ transform: (B1,I3,P0) -> 17 <-Bus 1, interface/slot 3,
function/port 0 (Emulex HBA), lspci will help identify this HBA in a
future example.
PCI->APIC IRQ transform: (B1,I4,P0) -> 27 <-Bus 1, interface/slot 4,
function/port 0 (Emulex HBA), lspci will help identify this HBA in a
future example.
```

```
PCI->APIC IRQ transform: (B1,I5,P0) -> 24
PCI->APIC IRQ transform: (B1,I5,P1) -> 25
Serial driver version 5.05c (2001-07-08) with MANY_PORTS MULTIPORT
SHARE_IRQ SERIAL_PCI ISAPNP enabled
ide: Assuming 33MHz PCI bus speed for PIO modes; override with idebus=xx
ServerWorks OSB4: IDE controller on PCI bus 00 dev 79
pci_hotplug: PCI Hot Plug PCI Core version: 0.3
sym53c8xx: at PCI bus 1, device 5, function 0
sym53c8xx: at PCI bus 1, device 5, function 1
```

We conclude by using lspci to depict the PCI bus devices.

```
[root@cyclops lpfc]# lspci
00:00.0 Host bridge: ServerWorks CNB20LE Host Bridge (rev 06)
00:00.1 Host bridge: ServerWorks CNB20LE Host Bridge (rev 06)
00:02.0 Ethernet controller: Intel Corporation 82557 [Ethernet Pro 100]
(rev 08)
00:07.0 VGA compatible controller: ATI Technologies Inc Rage XL (rev 27)
00:08.0 Ethernet controller: Intel Corporation 82557 [Ethernet Pro 100]
(rev 08)
00:0f.0 ISA bridge: ServerWorks OSB4 South Bridge (rev 50)
00:0f.1 IDE interface: ServerWorks OSB4 IDE Controller
00:0f.2 USB Controller: ServerWorks OSB4/CSB5 OHCI USB Controller (rev 04)
01:03.0 Fibre Channel: Emulex Corporation: Unknown device f800 (rev 02)
01:04.0 Fibre Channel: Emulex Corporation: Unknown device f800 (rev 02)
01:05.0 SCSI storage controller: LSI Logic / Symbios Logic (formerly NCR)
53c1010 Ultra3 SCSI Adapter (rev 01)
01:05.1 SCSI storage controller: LSI Logic / Symbios Logic (formerly NCR)
53c1010 Ultra3 SCSI Adapter (rev 01)
```

Note that lspci uses /proc/bus/pci to build its device tree. All devices have a descriptor commonly referred to as the Virtual Page Descriptor (VPD), in which lspci uses the source decode list at /usr/share/pci.ids to determine the devices' characteristics (note that the latest PCI IDs are maintained at http://pciids.sf.net/). By using lspci with the -v flag, a user can obtain complete details of PCI devices including subsystem, flags, memory, I/O ports, and expansion ROM locations. However, using the -t flag with the -v flag yields only the basic description. Although the -v output is missing great detail when used in conjunction with the -t flag, the -t flag remains a very nice option because it delivers a table view of the devices seen from the master bus.

For example, the following lspci -t -v output is from the same machine as the dmesg and lspci discussed previously. In addition, notice how the Emulex HBAs are denoted by the lspci as unknown under the function code f800. This is due to the fact that we are using a 2001 pci.ids update on our test server. Our latest production lab machine has a mid-August 2004 version loaded. With the pci.ids file dated 2004-08-24, f800 is decoded to be "LP8000 Fibre Channel Host Adapter," as shown in the following example. Note there is no penalty for having an older pci.ids file. However, be prepared for lots of "unknown" devices to appear in lspci's output. In addition, the pci.ids file is updated for each distribution, but it also can be researched manually by going to http://pciids.sourceforge.net/.

```
[root@cyclops root]# lspci -t -v


-+-[01]-+-03.0  Emulex Corporation: Unknown device f800
 |       +-04.0  Emulex Corporation: Unknown device f800
 |       +-05.0  LSI Logic / Symbios Logic (formerly NCR) 53c1010 Ultra3
 |                SCSI Adapter
 |       \-05.1  LSI Logic / Symbios Logic (formerly NCR) 53c1010 Ultra3
 |                SCSI Adapter
 \-[00]-+-00.0  ServerWorks CNB20LE Host Bridge
        +-00.1  ServerWorks CNB20LE Host Bridge
        +-02.0  Intel Corporation 82557 [Ethernet Pro 100]
        +-07.0  ATI Technologies Inc Rage XL
        +-08.0  Intel Corporation 82557 [Ethernet Pro 100]
        +-0f.0  ServerWorks OSB4 South Bridge
        +-0f.1  ServerWorks OSB4 IDE Controller
        \-0f.2  ServerWorks OSB4/CSB5 OHCI USB Controller
```

Having a good understanding of the bus structure is critical to finding the device that is failing. In the next example, we find that the SCSI disk errors are being reported by syslogd, which by default writes to /var/log/messages (we can confirm where syslogd writes by viewing /etc/syslogd.conf or by using the logger command), and we can view the same errors through the dmesg buffer. The error code looks like the following:

```
SCSI disk error : host 2 channel 0 id 0 lun 2 return code = 70022
 I/O error: dev 08:80, sector 5439488
SCSI disk error : host 2 channel 0 id 0 lun 2 return code = 70022
 I/O error: dev 08:80, sector 5439552
```

Viewing the same data in /var/log/messages, note that a timestamp is included.

```
Feb  4 14:04:37 cyclops kernel: SCSI disk error : host 2 channel 0 id 0
lun 2 return code = 70022
Feb  4 14:04:37 cyclops kernel:  I/O error: dev 08:80, sector 5439488
Feb  4 14:04:37 cyclops kernel: SCSI disk error : host 2 channel 0 id 0
lun 2 return code = 70022
Feb  4 14:04:37 cyclops kernel:  I/O error: dev 08:80, sector 5439552
```

The previous error log reports a disk I/O error on host 2, channel 0, id 0, lun 2, with a return code of 70022. The next task is to decipher the return code. The following is an example of deciphering the return code. In the example, we break down an I/O error from a different host in our lab, which received a return code of 2603007f. Note that the return code is always 4 bytes (8 digits) long, so in our previous example, 70022 is actually 00070022.

Next, we have broken down a SCSI I/O error from a syslog entry. In this example, the error code is 2603007f, and we complete the example by breaking down every component of the syslog entry for the I/O error.

```
Month Day Hour:Min:Sec localhost kernel: SCSI disk error :
     host 0 channel 0 id 0 lun 0  return code = 2603007f
Month Day Hour:Min:Sec localhost kernel: scsidisk I/O error:
     dev 08:01, sector 10
Month Day Hour:Min:Sec localhost kernel: raid1: Disk failure on
     sda1, disabling device.
```

As shown here, the first entry in the syslog with respect to the SCSI error contains the device that is failing. The next challenge is breaking down the return code. In this case, we have a SCSI disk error on host 0, channel 0, id 0, lun 0, which breaks down as follows:

Host	=	Host Bus Adapter
Channel	=	SCSI Adapter Channel
ID	=	SCSI ID
LUN	=	Logical Unit

It is important to break down the return code to determine root cause. The first entry in the previous example not only determines the location of the error but also provides the return code. Breaking down the return code of 2603007f is not very difficult, as long as bit order is maintained. Bit order is explained in greater detail in Chapter 6.

To break down the return code, we must look at scsi_lib.c from the SCSI source included in a current Linux kernel release. Reviewing the source, we see that the breakdown of the SCSI hardware address is as follows:

```
printk("SCSI error : <%d %d %d %d> return code = 0x%x\n",
                   cmd->device->host->host_no,
                   cmd->device->channel,
                   cmd->device->id,
                   cmd->device->lun, result);
```

Upon reviewing the scsi_ioctl.c code, we find the following:

```
*       If the SCSI command succeeds then 0 is returned.
*       Positive numbers returned are the compacted SCSI error codes
(4 bytes in one int) where the lowest byte is the SCSI status.
See the drivers/scsi/scsi.h file for more information on this.
```

While reviewing drivers/scsi/scsi.h, we determine that the driver design for SCSI is changing and that the file provides a reference point for many SCSI subsets. However, the scope of this chapter excludes building drivers and focuses on device failure and status return codes.

Now that we have a general understanding of the device location of the PCI bus, we need to understand the order of the return code bytes. The return code is made up of four bytes, appearing in the order of 3, 2, 1, 0 and breaking down as follows:

```
lsb |    ...    |    ...    | msb
======|==========|==========|============
status | sense key | host code | driver byte
```

```
(far left)    Byte 3:    SCSI driver status byte
              Byte 2:    Host adapter driver status byte
              Byte 1:    Message following the status byte returned by the
drive
(far right)   Byte 0:    Status byte returned by the drive (bits 5-1)
```

Now that we have defined the byte locations, we need to define the possible values to be able to decode the return code. Again, upon reviewing include/scsi/scsi.h, the user finds that the previous bytes are defined as follows:

```
...
/*
 *  SCSI Architecture Model (SAM) Status codes. Taken from SAM-3 draft
 *  T10/1561-D Revision 4 Draft dated 7th November 2002.
 */
#define SAM_STAT_GOOD              0x00
#define SAM_STAT_CHECK_CONDITION 0x02
#define SAM_STAT_CONDITION_MET     0x04
#define SAM_STAT_BUSY              0x08
#define SAM_STAT_INTERMEDIATE      0x10
#define SAM_STAT_INTERMEDIATE_CONDITION_MET 0x14
#define SAM_STAT_RESERVATION_CONFLICT 0x18
#define SAM_STAT_COMMAND_TERMINATED 0x22 /* obsolete in SAM-3 */
#define SAM_STAT_TASK_SET_FULL     0x28
#define SAM_STAT_ACA_ACTIVE        0x30
#define SAM_STAT_TASK_ABORTED      0x40
```

```
/** scsi_status_is_good - check the status return.
 *
 * @status: the status passed up from the driver (including host and
 *          driver components)
 *
 * This returns true for known good conditions that may be treated as
 * command completed normally
 */
static inline int scsi_status_is_good(int status)
{
        /*
         * FIXME: bit0 is listed as reserved in SCSI-2, but is
         * significant in SCSI-3.  For now, we follow the SCSI-2
         * behaviour and ignore reserved bits.
         */
        status &= 0xfe;
        return ((status == SAM_STAT_GOOD) ||
                (status == SAM_STAT_INTERMEDIATE) ||
                (status == SAM_STAT_INTERMEDIATE_CONDITION_MET) ||
                /* FIXME: this is obsolete in SAM-3 */
                (status == SAM_STAT_COMMAND_TERMINATED));
}


/*
 *   Status codes. These are deprecated as they are shifted 1 bit right
 *   from those found in the SCSI standards. This causes confusion for
 *   applications that are ported to several OSes. Prefer SAM Status codes
 *   above.
 */



#define GOOD                 0x00
#define CHECK_CONDITION      0x01
#define CONDITION_GOOD       0x02
#define BUSY                 0x04
#define INTERMEDIATE_GOOD    0x08
```

```
#define INTERMEDIATE_C_GOOD  0x0a
#define RESERVATION_CONFLICT 0x0c
#define COMMAND_TERMINATED   0x11
#define QUEUE_FULL           0x14


#define STATUS_MASK          0x3e


/*
 *  SENSE KEYS
 */


#define NO_SENSE             0x00
#define RECOVERED_ERROR      0x01
#define NOT_READY            0x02
#define MEDIUM_ERROR         0x03
#define HARDWARE_ERROR       0x04
#define ILLEGAL_REQUEST      0x05
#define UNIT_ATTENTION       0x06
#define DATA_PROTECT         0x07
#define BLANK_CHECK          0x08
#define COPY_ABORTED         0x0a
#define ABORTED_COMMAND      0x0b
#define VOLUME_OVERFLOW      0x0d
#define MISCOMPARE           0x0e


/*
 * Host byte codes
 */


#define DID_OK         0x00   /* NO error                             */
#define DID_NO_CONNECT 0x01   /* Couldn't connect before timeout period */
#define DID_BUS_BUSY   0x02   /* BUS stayed busy through time out period */
#define DID_TIME_OUT   0x03   /* TIMED OUT for other reason           */
#define DID_BAD_TARGET 0x04   /* BAD target.                          */
#define DID_ABORT      0x05   /* Told to abort for some other reason  */
```

```
#define DID_PARITY      0x06    /* Parity error                         */
#define DID_ERROR       0x07    /* Internal error                       */
#define DID_RESET       0x08    /* Reset by somebody                    */
#define DID_BAD_INTR    0x09    /* Got an interrupt we weren't expecting */
#define DID_PASSTHROUGH 0x0a    /* Force command past mid-layer         */
#define DID_SOFT_ERROR  0x0b    /* The low level driver just wish a retry */
#define DID_IMM_RETRY   0x0c    /* Retry without decrementing retry count */
#define DRIVER_OK       0x00    /* Driver status                        */


/*
 * These indicate the error that occurred, and what is available.
 */

#define DRIVER_BUSY          0x01
#define DRIVER_SOFT          0x02
#define DRIVER_MEDIA         0x03
#define DRIVER_ERROR         0x04

#define DRIVER_INVALID       0x05
#define DRIVER_TIMEOUT       0x06
#define DRIVER_HARD          0x07
#define DRIVER_SENSE         0x08

#define SUGGEST_RETRY        0x10
#define SUGGEST_ABORT        0x20
#define SUGGEST_REMAP        0x30
#define SUGGEST_DIE          0x40
#define SUGGEST_SENSE        0x80
#define SUGGEST_IS_OK        0xff

#define DRIVER_MASK          0x0f
#define SUGGEST_MASK         0xf0
    ...
```

The return code from our previously mentioned example had a value of `2603007f`, and it breaks down as follows:

```
26 = SCSI driver byte = 0010 0110 = RR10011R = Reserved code.
03 = Host adapter driver byte    (DID_TIME_OUT - TIMED OUT
                                  for other reason)
00 = Message byte                (COMMAND_COMPLETE)
7f = Status byte                 (bogus value), bits 5-1 = 1f
```

Additional information to help break down SCSI error detection can be found for the following topics at http://tldp.org/HOWTO/SCSI-Generic-HOWTO/index.html (search for scsi—the documents will change over time):

- SCSI programming HOWTO
- Decoding SCSI error status
- Sense codes and sense code qualifiers

Now that we have discussed where to find status codes and how to decode return codes for SCSI errors, we can decipher our lab error code of `00070022`.

- `00 =` define `GOOD: 0x00`, Driver status code is Good. We can now tell that it is not a driver issue.
- `07 =` define `DATA_PROTECT: 0x07`, Sense key data points us in the right direction. It has informed us that the suspect drive has set a read/write exclusive lock; however, we need to know why this has occurred.
- `00 =` define `DID_OK: 0x00` NO error. No error with respect to Host.
- `22 =` Breakdown of two nibbles:
    - `0x02 =` define `DRIVER_SOFT`.
    - `0x20 =` define `SUGGEST_ABORT`.

Note that in our previous lab case, the return code indicated a driver problem with the final byte; however, the indication of a driver issue is a little misleading. The actual cause is a *drive* issue. The sense key was the critical piece of data that helped to determine the source of the problem. Although the drive appeared to be visible, based upon the sense key data, we can conclude that the drive was locked. In fact, we did lock all the read and write I/Os to a drive while the LUN remained visible to the host, thus causing the error return codes to be misleading.

Replacement of a Failed Device

After we determine the applicable error and decoding information, we are ready to determine whether replacement is necessary and possible. Replacement might not be necessary if a good workaround is applicable. Furthermore, it might be impossible to replace a device for a number of reasons—most importantly, the need for keeping the system online.

To determine whether a device can be replaced online or offline, we must first define these terms. Within the computer industry, the terms online and offline simply refer to the application's status. In short, the primary goal should always be to keep the application online. When a disk-type failure occurs, unless you are using a large type storage array, such as an HP XP storage array, EMC, or IBM shark, then you must be able to handle a disk failure through other means, such as a hardware RAID controller or a software RAID, such as logical volume manager mirroring.

If errors are being logged for disk I/O failures, as shown previously, the easiest thing to do is find the device driver that controls the device and determine the impact of removing it.

In the previous example, we saw an I/O error on a LUN within a storage array connected to an Emulex HBA. Installing the `lpfcdd.o` driver in a 2.4.9-e.10 kernel allowed access to many LUNs for the HP storage array through the Emulex HBA. It is critical to understand how to map the LUNs back to the driver that allows access. As with any SCSI LUN, the SCSI I/O driver allows read and write I/O; however, the `lpfcdd` driver allows the path to be available for all the LUNs down the HBA path.

By using `dmesg`, after running the command `insmod lpfcdd`, we can see the newly found disk, as depicted in the following example.

```
[root@cyclops root]# insmod lpfcdd
Using /lib/modules/2.4.9-e.10custom-gt/kernel/drivers/scsi/lpfcdd.o
Warning: loading /lib/modules/2.4.9-e.10custom-
gt/kernel/drivers/scsi/lpfcdd.o will taint the kernel: no license
(Note: Tainting of kernel is discussed in Chapter 2)
```

```
[root@cyclops log]# dmesg
Emulex LightPulse FC SCSI/IP 4.20p
PCI: Enabling device 01:03.0 (0156 -> 0157)
!lpfc0:045:Vital Product Data  Data: 82 23 0 36
!lpfc0:031:Link Up Event received  Data: 1 1 0 0
PCI: Enabling device 01:04.0 (0156 -> 0157)
scsi2 : Emulex LPFC (LP8000) SCSI on PCI bus 01 device 18 irq 17
scsi3 : Emulex LPFC (LP8000) SCSI on PCI bus 01 device 20 irq 27
  Vendor: HP        Model: OPEN-9-CVS-CM    Rev: 2110   <---
Scsi_scan.c code scanning PCI bus to find devices...
  Type:   Direct-Access                 ANSI SCSI revision: 02
  Vendor: HP        Model: OPEN-9-CVS-CM    Rev: 2110
  Type:   Direct-Access                 ANSI SCSI revision: 02
  Vendor: HP        Model: OPEN-8*13        Rev: 2110
  Type:   Direct-Access                 ANSI SCSI revision: 02
Attached scsi disk sdg at scsi2, channel 0, id 0, lun 0
Attached scsi disk sdh at scsi2, channel 0, id 0, lun 1
Attached scsi disk sdi at scsi2, channel 0, id 0, lun 2
SCSI device sdg: 1638720 512-byte hdwr sectors (839 MB)
 sdg: sdg1
SCSI device sdh: 1638720 512-byte hdwr sectors (839 MB)
 sdh: sdh1
SCSI device sdi: 186563520 512-byte hdwr sectors (95521 MB)
 sdi: unknown partition table  <---VERY Important... MBR is discussed
in great detail in chapter 6.
```

We can force I/O on a drive by using the dd command. For example, dd if=/dev/sdi of=/dev/null bs=1024k easily creates 55+ MBps of read on a quality array device. The following depicts the I/O load discussed previously. For a complete picture, a general background must first be established.

The HBA used on our Linux server connects to a brocade switch on port 15, with port 2 going to an upstream ISL for its storage allocation. By using the switchshow command, we can see the WWN of the HBA connected to port 15, and by using the portperfshow command, we can determine the exact performance of our previous dd command. Again, the following demonstrates a heavy I/O performance during a total I/O failure. First, switchshow illustrates the HBA, followed by portperfshow, which illustrates the performance.

```
roadrunner:admin> switchshow
switchName:      roadrunner
switchType:      5.4
switchState:     Online
switchMode:      Interop
switchRole:      Subordinate
switchDomain:    123
switchId:        fffc7b
switchWwn:       10:00:00:60:69:10:6b:0e
switchBeacon:    OFF
Zoning:          ON (STC-zoneset-1)
port  0: sw  Online       E-Port  10:00:00:60:69:10:64:7e "coyote"\
                          (downstream)
port  1: sw  Online       E-Port  10:00:00:60:69:10:2b:37 "pepe"\
                          (upstream) < - Upstream ISL to Storage Switch.
port  2: --  No_Module
port  3: sw  Online       F-Port  20:00:00:05:9b:a6:65:40
port  4: sw  Online       F-Port  50:06:0b:00:00:0a:b8:9e
port  5: sw  Online       F-Port  50:00:0e:10:00:00:96:e4
port  6: sw  Online       F-Port  50:00:0e:10:00:00:96:ff
port  7: sw  Online       F-Port  50:00:0e:10:00:00:96:e5
port  8: sw  Online       F-Port  50:00:0e:10:00:00:96:fe
port  9: sw  Online       F-Port  20:00:00:e0:69:c0:81:b3
port 10: sw  Online       L-Port  1 private, 1 phantom
port 11: sw  No_Sync
port 12: sw  Online       L-Port  1 private, 1 phantom
port 13: sw  No_Sync
port 14: sw  No_Light
port 15: sw  Online       F-Port  10:00:00:00:c9:24:13:27  <--- HBA on \
                          Linux host
```

```
roadrunner:admin> portperfshow
    0   1   2   3   4   5   6   7   8   9  10  11  12  13  14  15
   ----------------------------------------------------------------
    0  57m  0   0   0   0   0   0   0   0   0   0   0   0   0  57m
    0  55m  0   0   0   0   0   0   0   0   0   0   0   0   0  55m
```

To create a complete hardware failure, we disable port 15, thus halting all I/O. By using dmesg, we can capture what the kernel is logging about the failure.

After disabling the port 15, dmesg logs the following:

```
!lpfc0:031:Link Down Event received  Data: 2 2 0 20
```

After waiting 60 seconds for the I/O acknowledgement, the Emulex driver abandons the bus, forcing the SCSI layer to recognize the I/O failure. The dmesg command shows the following:

```
[root@cyclops log]# dmesg
!lpfc0:120:Device disappeared, nodev timeout:   Data: 780500 0 0 1e
 I/O error: dev 08:80, sector 5140160
 I/O error: dev 08:80, sector 5140224
 I/O error: dev 08:80, sector 5140160
 I/O error: dev 08:80, sector 5140224
```

The user shell prompt looks similar to the following:

```
[root@cyclops proc]# dd if=/dev/sdi of=/dev/null bs=1024k

dd: reading '/dev/sdi': Input/output error
12067+1 records in
12067+1 records out
[root@cyclops proc]#
```

In the previous case, the Emulex driver detected a Fibre Channel Protocol (FCP) failure and deallocated the storage. After the path was restored, the link and I/O access return to normal. To demonstrate I/O returning, we simply issue the portenable command on the brocade port 15, thus enabling the HBA FCP connection. The following dd command demonstrates the I/O returning with the host not going offline. Note that in this case, the application would have lost access to the device, resulting in an offline condition to the application.

```
[root@cyclops proc]# dd if=/dev/sdi of=/dev/null bs=1024k
57+0 records in
57+0 records out
[root@cyclops proc]#
```

In the meantime, while the `portenable` and `dd` commands are being issued, `dmesg` reports the following:

```
[root@cyclops proc]# dmesg
!lpfc0:031:Link Up Event received  Data: 3 3 0 20
!lpfc0:031:Link Up Event received  Data: 5 5 0 74
!lpfc1:031:Link Up Event received  Data: 1 1 0 0
!lpfc1:031:Link Up Event received  Data: 3 3 0 74
[root@cyclops proc]#
```

In the previous condition, the entire device was offline. Although recovery was simple, applications would have failed. Depending on application parameters, such as buffer cache, remaining I/O operations could cause a system-like hang. Hangs of this nature are discussed in Chapter 2, "System Hangs and Panics." Having a complete hardware device failure on an entire bus, in a SAN, or on some other type of storage network is usually quick to isolate and recover with the tactics described in this chapter; however, data integrity is another matter. Data integrity is beyond the scope of this chapter.

As mentioned earlier, logical path failures are easier to manage than the failure of a given device on a logical path. In the following example, we block the I/O to a given LUN on a bus, as done previously in this chapter to illustrate return code 70022. However, now the goal is to determine the best course of corrective action.

Repeating the same LUN I/O block as before, the `dd` read test results in the following errors:

```
[root@cyclops root]# dd if=/dev/sdi of=/dev/null bs=1024k
dd: reading '/dev/sdi': Input/output error
6584+1 records in
6584+1 records out
```

Notice how the prompt did not return; instead, this process is hung in kernel space (discussed in Chapter 8, "Linux Processes: Structure, Hangs, and Core Dumps"). This behavior results because the kernel knows the size of the disk and because we set the block size so large; the remaining I/O's should fail, and the process will die.

```
[root@cyclops root]# dmesg
SCSI disk error : host 2 channel 0 id 0 lun 2 return code = 70022
 I/O error: dev 08:80, sector 13485760
SCSI disk error : host 2 channel 0 id 0 lun 2 return code = 70022
 I/O error: dev 08:80, sector 13485824
SCSI disk error : host 2 channel 0 id 0 lun 2 return code = 70022
 I/O error: dev 08:80, sector 13485762
SCSI disk error : host 2 channel 0 id 0 lun 2 return code = 70022
 I/O error: dev 08:80, sector 13485826
SCSI disk error : host 2 channel 0 id 0 lun 2 return code = 70022
 I/O error: dev 08:80, sector 13485760
~~~Errors continue
```

While the read I/O errors continue, we have already decoded the return code. This informed us that the disk is read/write protected; thus, we must find a way to restore I/O or move the data to a new location. To get all the information with regards to the PID accessing the device, we run the command ps -ef | grep dd. This command enables us to confirm the PID of 8070. After the PID is established, we go to the PID directory found under the /proc filesystem and check the status of the process using the following method:

```
root@cyclops / ]# cd /proc/8070
root@cyclops 8070]# cat status
Name:    dd
State:   D (disk sleep)   <--- Note the state.  The state should be in R
(running) condition.
Pid:     8070
PPid:    8023
TracerPid:       0
Uid:     0       0       0       0
Gid:     0       0       0       0
TGid:    8070
FDSize: 256
```

```
Groups: 0 1 2 3 4 6 10
VmSize:     1660 kB
VmLck:         0 kB
VmRSS:       580 kB
VmData:       28 kB
VmStk:        24 kB
VmExe:        28 kB
VmLib:      1316 kB
SigPnd: 0000000000000000
SigBlk: 0000000000000000
SigIgn: 0000000000000000
SigCgt: 0000000000001206
CapInh: 0000000000000000
CapPrm: 00000000fffffeff
CapEff: 00000000fffffeff


[root@cyclops 8070]# cat cpu
cpu   8 8534
cpu0 8 8527
cpu1 0 7


[root@cyclops 8070]# cat cmdline
ddif/dev/sdiof/dev/nullbs1024k
```

The status of the process on the device is disk sleep, meaning that the process is waiting on the device to return the outstanding request before processing the next one. In this condition, I/O errors will not continue forever; they will stop after the read I/O block has expired or timed out at the SCSI layer. However, if an application continues to queue multiple I/O threads to the device, removing any device driver from the kernel will be impossible.

```
~~~~Errors continue~~~~~
SCSI disk error : host 2 channel 0 id 0 lun 2 return code = 70022
 I/O error: dev 08:80, sector 13485822
SCSI disk error : host 2 channel 0 id 0 lun 2 return code = 70022
 I/O error: dev 08:80, sector 13485886
```

Notice the last sector that failed; the difference between the last sector and the previous failed sector is 64,512 bytes or 126 sectors at 512 bytes each. No matter the drive size, if a user issues a dd command on a failed drive, the duration of the I/O hang depends on the size of the outstanding block request. Setting the block size to 64K or less hangs the I/O at the SCSI layer on a buffer wait on each outstanding 2048-byte read request. To see the wait channel, issue `ps -ef | grep dd`, and then using the PID, issue `ps -eo comm,pid,wchan | grep PID` to find something such as dd   ##### wait_on_buffer. Refer to Chapter 8 to acquire a better understanding of process structure because a discussion of system calls is beyond the scope of this chapter. The point of this general discussion is to demonstrate that the I/O will eventually time out or abort.

Again, the most important thing to understand with a failed device on a given bus is that we cannot remove the driver that controls the bus access path, such as `lpfcdd.o`, and of course we cannot remove the protocol driver, such as SCSI in this case. This is due to the fact that all remaining devices on the bus are online and in production transmitting I/Os. Issuing a command, such as `rmmod lpfcdd`, simply yields the result "device busy." The only recovery method for this particular example is to restore access to the given device. If this involves replacing the device, such as installing a new LUN, the running kernel will have the incorrect device tree characteristics for the data construct. This is discussed in great detail in Chapter 8. In this particular case, device access must be restored. Otherwise, a new device will have to be put online and the server rebooted with the data restored from backup.

Summary

Whether a user decides to replace, repair, or remove old hardware, isolating and understanding the error return codes is critical to determining how to conduct the repair. We hope that this chapter provided you with insight into troubleshooting SCSI devices and the necessary tools to make the replacement decision easier, and possibly faster, the next time around.

8

Linux Processes: Structure, Hangs, and Core Dumps

Troubleshooting a Linux process follows the same general methodology as that used with traditional UNIX systems. In both systems, for process hangs, we identify the system resources being used by the process and attempt to identify the cause for the process to stop responding. With application core dumps, we must identify the signal for which the process terminated and proceed with acquiring a stack trace to identify system calls made by the process at the time it died. There exists neither a "golden" troubleshooting path nor a set of instructions that can be applied for all cases. Some conditions are much easier to solve than others, but with a good understanding of the fundamentals, a solution is not far from reach.

This chapter explains various facets of Linux processes. We begin by examining the structure of a process and its life cycle from creation to termination. This is followed by a discussion of Linux threads. The aforementioned establish a basis for proceeding with a discussion of process hangs and core dumps.

Process Structure and Life Cycle

This section begins with an overview of process concepts and terms, noting the similarities and differences between UNIX and Linux. We then move on to discuss process relationships, process creation, and process termination.

Process/Task Overview

It is helpful to begin with a general comparison of processes in UNIX and in Linux. Both operating systems use processes; however, the terminology employed by each differs slightly. Both use the term "process" to refer to process structure. Linux also uses the term "task" to refer to its processes. Therefore, in Linux, the terms "process" and "task" are used interchangeably, and this chapter also so uses them. Note that UNIX does not use the term "task."

The process structures of the two operating systems differ more dramatically, which is easily recognized when observing a multithreaded program in action. The thread is the actual workhorse of the process and is sometimes referred to as a lightweight process (LWP). In Linux, every thread is a task or process; however, this is not the case with UNIX.

As described previously, the UNIX process model places its threads within the process structure. This structure contains the process's state, process ID (PID), parent process ID (PPID), file table, signal table, thread(s), scheduling, and other information. Thus, there is only one PID for a process that can have many threads. However, when a process calls the pthread_create() subroutine in Linux, it creates another task/PID, which just happens to share the same address space. Figure 8-1 depicts this fundamental difference.

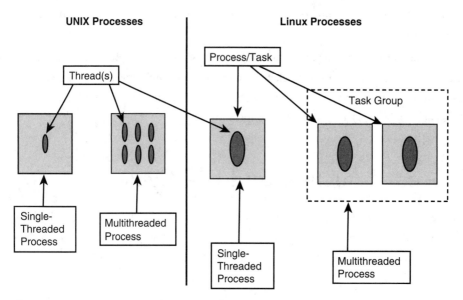

Figure 8-1 Comparison of UNIX and Linux processes

Unlike UNIX, Linux does not have a kernel object that represents the process structure; instead, it uses a task structure. Each task has a unique ID just like a UNIX PID. However, the Linux task model only represents a single thread of execution. In this way, a task can be thought of as a single UNIX thread. Just like the UNIX process structure, the Linux task structure contains the task's state, PID, PPID, file table, address space, signals, scheduling, and so on. In addition, it contains the Task Group ID (tgid), which we elaborate on later in this chapter.

Process Relationships

When troubleshooting a process, it is crucial to identify all related tasks/processes, and there are several approaches to doing so. A task could hang or dump core because a resource it requires is in use by another process, or a parent could mask a signal that the child needs to execute properly. When it comes to identifying a process's relationship to others, you could use the /proc/<pid>/ directory to manually search out a process's information and its relationship to others. Relationships can also be determined by the use of commands such as ps, pstree, and top, among others, which make use of this pseudo filesystem. These tools make short work of obtaining a picture of a process's state and its relationship to others.

Linux Process Creation

An understanding of process creation is necessary for troubleshooting a process. Processes are created in Linux in much the same way as they are created in UNIX. When executing a new command, the fork() system call sets up the child's context to reference the parent's context and creates a new stack. This referencing of the parent's context (essentially a pointer to the parent's task_struct() structure) increases overall OS performance. The child's context references the parent's context until modification is required, at which point the parent's address space is copied and modified. This is achieved by the copy-on-write (COW) design.

Shortly after fork() has set up the new task for execution, the exec system call is made. This is where the copy-on-write does its magic. The parent's structure is no longer just referenced; rather, it is copied into a new virtual location. Next, the object file (command) is copied into this location, overwriting the copied pages. Now the new task's context is set up, and the new process is running.

There are some differences between how processes are created in UNIX and how they are created in Linux. For example, some flavors of UNIX perform a copy-on-access, for which the fork() copies the context of the parent to a new virtual memory address with no references pointing back to the parent's context. One is no better than the other because in a majority of instances, the referenced pages must be modified, causing the COW method to copy the pages anyway.

An Example of Linux Process Creation

In this section, we demonstrate the fork() system call by tracing the parent process. In this example, we use the ls command to list a file. Because the ls program is the child of its local shell, we need to trace the shell from which the ll (ls -al alias) command is executed. Two shell windows are required to perform this test.

1. **Window one**: Determine the pseudo terminal and PID of shell.

    ```
    # echo $$
    16935
    ```

    The parent shell's PID is 16935. Now we must start the trace in a second window.

2. **Window two:** Start trace of shell process.

    ```
    # strace -o /tmp/ll.strace -f -p 16935
    ```

    Now that the trace is running in window two, we need to issue the ll command in window one.

3. **Window one:** Issue the ll command.

    ```
    # ll test
    -rw-r--r--    1 chris    chris       46759 Sep  7 21:53 test
    ```

note

Check the stdout in window two and stop the trace by sending an interrupt (type Ctrl+c).

4. **Window two:** Here are the results of the stdout and stopping the trace.

```
# strace -o /tmp/ll.strace -f -p 16935
Process 16935 attached <-- Trace running on 16935
Process 17424 attached  <-- forked child process
Process 17424 detached <-- child ending returning to parent
Process 16935 detached <-- ctrl +c ending trace
```

The trace shows the fork() and execve() calls. Note that we are not showing the entire trace because so many system calls take place for each seemingly simple command.

```
...
16935 fork()                            = 17424  <-- NEW task's PID
17424 --- SIGSTOP (Stopped (signal)) @ 0 (0) ---
17424 getpid()                          = 17424
17424 rt_sigprocmask(SIG_SETMASK, [RTMIN], NULL, 8) = 0
17424 rt_sigaction(SIGTSTP, {SIG_DFL}, {SIG_IGN}, 8) = 0
17424 rt_sigaction(SIGTTIN, {SIG_DFL}, {SIG_IGN}, 8) = 0
17424 rt_sigaction(SIGTTOU, {SIG_DFL}, {SIG_IGN}, 8) = 0
17424 setpgid(17424, 17424)             = 0
17424 rt_sigprocmask(SIG_BLOCK, [CHLD TSTP TTIN TTOU], [RTMIN], 8) = 0
17424 ioctl(255, TIOCSPGRP, [17424])    = 0
17424 rt_sigprocmask(SIG_SETMASK, [RTMIN], NULL, 8) = 0
17424 rt_sigaction(SIGINT, {SIG_DFL}, {0x8087030, [], SA_RESTORER, \
0x4005aca8}, 8) = 0
17424 rt_sigaction(SIGQUIT, {SIG_DFL}, {SIG_IGN}, 8) = 0
17424 rt_sigaction(SIGTERM, {SIG_DFL}, {SIG_IGN}, 8) = 0
17424 rt_sigaction(SIGCHLD, {SIG_DFL}, {0x80776a0, [], SA_RESTORER, \
0x4005aca8}, 8) = 0
17424 execve("/bin/ls", ["ls", "-F", "--color=auto", "-l", "test"], \
[/* 56 vars */]) = 0
```

Summary of Process Creation

The fork() call creates a new task and assigns a PID, and this step is soon followed by the execve() call, executing the command along with its arguments. In this case, we see that the ll test command is actually ls -F --color=auto -l test.

Linux Process Termination

An understanding of process termination is useful for troubleshooting a process. As with process creation, the termination or exiting of a process is like that of any other UNIX flavor. If signal handling is implemented, the parent can be notified when its children terminate irregularly. Additionally, the parent process can also wait for the child to exit with some variation of `wait()`. When a process terminates or calls `exit()`, it returns its exit code to the caller (parent). At this point, the process is in a zombie or defunct state, waiting for the parent to reap the process. In some cases, the parent has long since died before the child. In these cases, the child has become orphaned, at which point `init` becomes the parent, and the return codes of the process are passed to `init`.

Linux Threads

No discussion of process fundamentals is complete without an explanation of Linux threads because an understanding of threads is crucial for troubleshooting processes. As mentioned earlier, the implementation of threads in Linux differs from that of UNIX because Linux threads are not contained within the `proc` structure. However, Linux does support multithreaded applications. "Multithreading" just means two or more threads working in parallel with each other while sharing the same address space. Multithreaded applications in Linux just use more than one task. Following this logic in the source, `include/linux/sched.h` shows that the `task_struct` structure maintains a one-to-one relationship with the task's thread through the use of a pointer to the `thread_info` structure, and this structure just points back to the task structure.

Excerpts from the source illustrate the one-to-one relationship between a Linux task and thread.

```
include/linux/sched.h


...
struct task_struct {
    volatile long state;    /* -1 unrunnable, 0 runnable, >0 stopped */
    struct thread_info *thread_info;

...
```

To see the `thread_info` structure point back to the task, we review `include/asm-i386/thread_info.h`.

```
...

    struct thread_info {
        struct task_struct      *task;            /* main task structure */
...
```

Using multithreaded processes has its advantages. Threading allows for better processor loading and memory utilization. A drawback is that it also significantly increases the program's complexity. On a single-CPU machine, a multithreaded program for the most part performs no better than a single-threaded program. However, well-designed multithreaded applications executed on a Symmetric Multi-Processor (SMP) machine can have each thread executing in parallel, thereby significantly increasing application performance.

Threaded application performance is enhanced by the fact that threads share resources. Different types of processes share resources in different ways. The initial process is referred to as the heavyweight process (HWP), which is a prerequisite for lightweight processes. Traditionally, a thread of a process is referred to as a lightweight process (LWP), as mentioned earlier. The main difference between these two is how they share their resources. Simply stated, when an HWP forks a new process, the only thing that is shared is the parent's text. If an HWP must share information with another HWP, it uses techniques such as pipes, PF_UNIX (UNIX sockets), signals, or interprocess communication's (IPCS) shared memory, message queues, and semaphores. On the other hand, when an HWP creates an LWP, these processes share the same address space (except the LWP's private stack), thus making utilization of system resources more efficient.

Note that although several forms of threads exists, such as user space GNU Portable Threads (PTH) and DCE threads, in this chapter, we only cover the concept of POSIX threads because they are the most commonly used threads in the industry. POSIX threads are implemented by the `pthread` library. The use of POSIX threads ensures that programs will be compatible with other distributions, platforms, and OSs that support POSIX threads. These threads are initiated by the `pthread_create()` system call; however, the Linux kernel uses the `clone()` call to create the threads. As implied by its name, it clones the task. Just as `fork()` creates a separate process structure, `clone()` creates a new task/thread structure by cloning the parent; however, unlike `fork()`, flags are set that determine what structures are cloned. Only a select few flags of the many flags available are required to make the thread POSIX compliant.

The Linux kernel treats each thread as an individual task that can be displayed with the ps command. At first, this approach might seem like a large waste of system resources, given that a process could have a great number of threads, each of which would be a clone of the parent. However, it's quite trivial because most task structures are kernel objects, which enables the individual threads to just reference the address space. An example is the HWP's file descriptor table. With clone(), all threads just reference the kernel structure by using the flag CLONE_FILES.

With help from developers from around the world, the Linux kernel is developing at an extraordinary rate. A prime example is the fork() call. With the IA-64 Linux kernel, the fork() call actually calls clone2(). In addition, pthread_create() also calls clone2(). The clone2() system call adds a third argument, ustack_size. Otherwise, it is the same as clone(). With the IA-32 2.6 kernel release, the fork() call has been replaced with the clone() call. The kernel clone() call mimics fork() by adjusting clone() flags.

Detailed next are examples of tasks and threads being created on different versions and distributions of Linux:

* IA-32 (2.4.19) Fork call

```
2970  fork()                          = 3057  <-- The PID for the new HWP
```

* IA-32 (2.4.19) Thread creation

```
3188  clone(child_stack=0x804b8e8,
flags=CLONE_VM|CLONE_FS|CLONE_FILES|CLONE_SIGHAND) = 3189 <-- LWP
```

* IA-32 (2.6.3) Fork call

```
12383 clone(child_stack=0,
flags=CLONE_CHILD_CLEARTID|CLONE_CHILD_SETTID|SIGCHLD,
child_tidptr=0x4002cba8) = 12499 <-- HWP
```

* IA-32 (2.6.3) Thread creation

```
12440 <... clone resumed> child_stack=0x42184b08,
flags=CLONE_VM|CLONE_FS|CLONE_FILES|CLONE_SIGHAND|CLONE_THREAD|CLONE_SYS
VSEM|CLONE_SETTLS
```

```
|CLONE_PARENT_SETTID|CLONE_CHILD_CLEARTID|CLONE_DETACHED,
parent_tidptr=0x42184bf8, {entry_number:6, base_addr:0x42184bb0,
limit:1048575, s
eg_32bit:1, contents:0, read_exec_only:0, limit_in_pages:1,
seg_not_present:0, useable:1}, child_tidptr=0x42184bf8) = 12444  <--LWP
```

  * IA-64 (2.4.21) Fork call

```
24195 clone2(child_stack=0, stack_size=0,
flags=CLONE_CHILD_CLEARTID|CLONE_CHILD_SETTID|SIGCHLD,
child_tidptr=0x200000000002cdc0) = 24324 <--HWP
```

  * IA-64 (2.4.21) Thread creation

```
24359 clone2(child_stack=0x20000000034f4000, stack_size=0x9ff240,
flags=CLONE_VM|CLONE_FS|CLONE_FILES|CLONE_SIGHAND|CLONE_THREAD|CLONE_SYSV
SEM|CLONE_SETTLS|CLONE_PARENT_SETTID|CLONE_CHILD_CLEARTID|CLONE_DETACHED,
parent_tidptr=0x2000000003ef3960, tls=0x2000000003ef3f60,
child_tidptr=0x2000000003ef3960) = 24365 <--LWP
```

As the previous examples show, the kernel `clone()` call creates threads, whereas `clone2()` creates threads, new processes, or both. In addition, the previous traces reveal the creation of threads and the flags needed to make them POSIX compliant, as defined in the next listing.

```
clone(child_stack=0x804b8e8,
flags=CLONE_VM|CLONE_FS|CLONE_FILES|CLONE_SIGHAND)
child_stack:      Unique process stack
CLONE_VM :        Parent and child run in the same address space
CLONE_FS:         Parent and child share file system info
CLONE_FILES:      Parent and child share open file table
CLONE_SIGHAND:    Parent and child share signal handlers
```

Identifying Threads

As previously discussed, the `ps` command lists all tasks in Linux, preventing the user from distinguishing the HWP from the LWP. At approximately the 2.4.9 kernel release, the Task Group ID (tgid) was added to `fs/proc/array.c`. This placed a task's tgid in the `/proc/<pid>/status` file. A key point is that the tgid is equal to the HWP's PID. This new feature enables users to identify threads of a multithreaded process with ease.

Reviewing the source, we see:

```
# ./fs/proc/array.c
...
static inline char * task_state(struct task_struct *p, char *buffer)
{
        int g;
        read_lock(&tasklist_lock);
        buffer += sprintf(buffer,
                "State:\t%s\n"
                "Tgid:\t%d\n"
                "Pid:\t%d\n"
                "PPid:\t%d\n"
                "TracerPid:\t%d\n"
                "Uid:\t%d\t%d\t%d\t%d\n"
                "Gid:\t%d\t%d\t%d\t%d\n",
                get_task_state(p), p->tgid,

...
```

Linux commands, such as ps, were modified to make use of this new value, enabling them to display only the parent HWP task (tgid), or all threads of a task by passing the -m or -eLf flag.

In Listing 8-1, we have included a small example of a threaded program that demonstrates how threads appear in Linux. Note that this code makes no attempt either to lock threads with mutex locks or semaphores or to perform any special signal masking. This code just creates threads that perform sequential counts to exercise the CPU(s).

Listing 8-1

Example of a Threaded Program

```
#include <pthread.h> /* POSIX threads */
#include <signal.h>
#include <stdlib.h>
#include <linux/unistd.h>
#include <errno.h>
```

```
#define num_threads  8


void *print_func(void *);
void threadid(int);
void stop_thread(int sig);
/* gettid() is not portable.. if compiling on other Operating Systems, \
remove reference to it */
_syscall0(pid_t,gettid)


int main ()
{
        int x;
        pid_t tid;
        pthread_t threadid[num_threads];


        (void) signal(SIGALRM,stop_thread); /*signal handler */


        printf("Main process has PID= %d PPID= %d and TID= %d\n", \
        getpid(), getppid(), gettid());


        /* Now to create pthreads */
        for (x=1; x <= num_threads;++x)
        pthread_create(&threadid[x], NULL, print_func, NULL );


        sleep(60); /* Let the threads warm the cpus up!!! :) */
        for (x=1; x < num_threads;++x)
                pthread_kill(threadid[x], SIGALRM);


        /*wait for termination of threads before main continues*/
        for (x=1; x < num_threads;++x)
        {
        printf("%d\n",x);
        pthread_join(threadid[x], NULL);
        printf("Main() PID %d joined with thread %d\n", getpid(), \
        threadid[x]);
        }
}
```

```
void *print_func (void *arg)
{
        printf("PID %d  PPID = %d  Thread value of pthread_self = %d and \
        TID= %d\n",getpid(), getppid(), pthread_self(),gettid());
        while(1);  /* nothing but spinning */
}


void stop_thread(int sig) {
pthread_exit(NULL);
}
```

Using Listing 8-1, create a binary by compiling on any UNIX/Linux system that supports POSIX threads. Reference the following demonstration:

1. Compile the source.

    ```
    # gcc -o thread_test thread_test.c -pthread
    ```

    Next, execute thread_test and observe the tasks with pstree. Note that we have trimmed the output of pstree to save space.

2. Execute the object.

    ```
    #./thread_test
    ```

3. In a different shell, execute:

    ```
    # pstree -p

    init(1)-+-apmd(1177)


    ~~~~~~Saving space~~~~~


              |-kdeinit(1904)-


    ~~~~~~Saving space~~~~~
    ```

```
        |                    |-kdeinit(2872)-+-bash(2874)---thread_test
                             (3194)-+-thread_test(3195)

        |                    |               |
|-thread_test(3196)

        |                    |               |
|-thread_test(3197)

        |                    |               |
|-thread_test(3198)

        |                    |               |
|-thread_test(3199)

        |                    |               |
|-thread_test(3200)

        |                    |               |
|-thread_test(3201)

        |                    |               |
`-thread_test(3202)


~~~~~~Saving space~~~~~


        |                    |                       `-bash(3204)---
pstree(3250)


~~~~~~Saving space~~~~~
```

4. We can display more details with the ps command. (Note that the PIDs
    would have matched if we had run these examples at the same time.)

    ```
    # ps -eo pid,ppid,state,comm,time,pri,size,wchan | grep test
    28807 28275 S thread_test      00:00:12  18 82272 \
    schedule_timeout
    ```

    Display threads with -m.

    ```
    # ps -emo pid,ppid,state,comm,time,pri,size,wchan | grep test
    28807 28275 S thread_test      00:00:00  18 82272 \
    schedule_timeout
    28808 28807 R thread_test      00:00:03  14 82272 -
    28809 28807 R thread_test      00:00:03  14 82272 \
    ia64_leave_kernel
    ```

```
28810 28807 R thread_test      00:00:03  14 82272 \
ia64_leave_kernel
28811 28807 R thread_test      00:00:03  14 82272 \
ia64_leave_kernel
28812 28807 R thread_test      00:00:03  14 82272 -
28813 28807 R thread_test      00:00:02  14 82272 \
ia64_leave_kernel
28814 28807 R thread_test      00:00:02  14 82272 \
ia64_leave_kernel
28815 28807 R thread_test      00:00:03  14 82272 -
```

Even though some UNIX distributions have modified commands such as ps or top to display a process with all its threads by including special options such as -m or -L, HPUX has not. Therefore, the HPUX ps command only shows the HWP process and not the underlying threads that build the process. On the other hand, Solaris can display the LWP of a process by using the -L option with its ps command.

Other vendors have created their own tools for displaying threads of a process. HPUX's glance is a good example. Using the same procedures as earlier, we demonstrate multithreads in HPUX to show the main difference between UNIX threads and Linux's implementation of threads.

```
HPUX 11.11:
# cc -o thread_test thread_test.c -lpthread


hpux_11.11 #glance
Process Name   PID   PPID Pri Name   ( 700% max)   CPU   IO Rate   RSS \
Cnt
-------------------------------------------------------------------------
thread_test          14689  14579 233 root       698/ 588   57.3  0.0/ 0.2 \
560kb     9
```

Thus, using HPUX's glance, we can see that the thread count is nine, with one thread representing the main HWP and eight additional threads that were created by the program as shown in the source. Each thread does not have its own PID as with Linux threads. In addition, Linux tools such as top do not show the threads of a process consuming CPU cycles. This can be tested by executing the thread_test program in one tty and the top program in another tty.

Identifying Process Hangs

Now that we have covered the building blocks of processes and threads, it is time to address process hangs and their potential causes. There is little hope that killing an offending process with -9 (sigkill) will lead to discovering the root cause of a process hang. Neither will rebooting the OS unless you are dealing with a stale file handle. Furthermore, these steps will not prevent these anomalies from reoccurring. However, by applying the knowledge of how processes are created and how resources are used, the root cause can be identified.

When a process appears hung, the first step toward a solution is determining certain critical information about the task. Using the ps command, start by determining the task's state, threads, priority, parent, and wait channel. In addition, identify the cumulative CPU time and the initial start time of the task. A holistic approach is needed because although a single ps command is a good start, it will not deliver all the needed information.

Let us first determine whether the process is hung because sometimes a process appears to be blocked when it actually is in the middle of a computation or non-blocking I/O. If cumulative CPU time constantly grows, the task's state will most likely be R. In this state, the process is on the run queue and does not have a wait channel. Monitor its cumulative CPU time. If the process remains in the run queue, it might be performing some calculation that takes a while. Even the fastest computers in the world take a while to calculate an infinite loop! Nevertheless, note that a process in the run state could be the normal operation of that program, an application "feature," or a driver problem.

If an offending process is consuming system resources at an extraordinary rate and starving production applications, killing the offending process is justified *if the process can be killed.* However, sometimes a process cannot be killed. When a process has exhausted its timeslice, it is put to sleep() with a given priority. When the priority of the process falls below PZERO, it is in an uninterruptible state and cannot be signaled; however, signals can be queued, and for some operations, this is normal. For others, where the program has hung and never returns, the cause is usually located in the driver or hardware. If the process has a state of D (blocked on I/O), it is uninterruptible and cannot be killed. For example, a process accessing a file over a failed hard NFS mount would be in a state of D while attempting to stat() a file or directory.

Uninterruptible processes usually take place when entering I/O calls, at which point the process has called into the kernel, which is in driver code, during which the process cannot receive signals from user space. In this state, a command cannot be signaled even by a SIGKILL (kill -9). It is important to note that signals are queued if not ignored by a sigmask and executed after the code returns from kernel space. Some signals cannot be masked; see the signal man page for more details.

Here is an excerpt from the signal man page:

```
...
Using  a  signal  handler function for a signal is called "catching the
signal".  The signals SIGKILL and SIGSTOP cannot be caught or ignored.
...
```

A zombie process is another process that a user cannot kill. These processes, however, should not be consuming any CPU cycles or memory resources other than the overhead of having the task structure in the kernel's Virtual Address Space (VAS). The main goal of troubleshooting a zombie process is determining why the parent died without reaping its children. In short, you should focus on why and how the parent dies.

Listed next are process state codes pulled right out of the source code.

```
./linux/fs/proc/array.c
/*
 * The task state array is a strange "bitmap" of
 * reasons to sleep. Thus "running" is zero, and
 * you can test for combinations of others with
 * simple bit tests.
 */
static const char *task_state_array[] = {
        "R (running)",          /*  0 */
        "S (sleeping)",         /*  1 */
        "D (disk sleep)",       /*  2 */
        "Z (zombie)",           /*  4 */
        "T (stopped)",          /*  8 */
        "W (paging)"            /* 16 */
};
...
```

In Scenario 8-1, we demonstrate an instance in which a process cannot be killed.

Scenario 8-1: Troubleshooting a Process That Does Not Respond to kill

A user begins rewinding a tape but realizes that the wrong tape is in the drive. The user tries to kill the job but must wait for the process to finish.

Why?

The mt command has made an ioctl call to the SCSI tape driver (st) and must wait for the driver to release the process back to user space so that use signals will be handled.

```
# mt -f /dev/st0 rewind
# ps -emo state,pid,ppid,pri,size,stime,time,comm,wchan | grep mt
D  9225  8916  24 112 20:46 00:00:00 mt              wait_for_completion


[root@atlorca2 root]# kill -9 9225
[root@atlorca2 root]# echo $?   # This produces the return code for the
previous command.  0 = success
0
[root@atlorca2 root]# ps -elf | grep 9225
0 D root     9225 8916  0  24  0   -   112 wait_f 20:46 pts/1
00:00:00 mt -f /dev/st0
```

The mt command has entered a wait channel, and after the code returns from the driver, the signal will be processed.

Let's check the pending signals:

```
cat ../9225/status
Name:   mt
State:  D (disk sleep)
Tgid:   9225
Pid:    9225
PPid:   8916
TracerPid:      0
Uid:    0       0       0       0
Gid:    0       0       0       0
FDSize: 256
Groups: 0 1 2 3 4 6 10
```

```
VmSize:    2800 kB

VmLck:        0 kB

VmRSS:      640 kB

VmData:      96 kB

VmStk:       16 kB

VmExe:       32 kB

VmLib:     2560 kB
```

SigPnd: 0000000000000100 <-- **SigPnd is a bit mask which indicates the value of the pending signal. Each byte accounts for 4 bits. In this case, the pending signal has a value of 9, so the first bit on the 3rd byte is set. This algorithm is detailed in linux/fs/proc/array.c under the render_sigset_t() function. The following table illustrates this function.**

Signal   : 1 2 3 4 . 5 6 7 8 . 9 10 11 12 . 13 14 15 16
bit value : 1 2 4 8 . 1 2 4 8 . 1 2 4 8 . 1 2 4 8

kill -3 yields bit mask 0000000000000004
kill -9 yields bit mask 0000000000000100


```
ShdPnd: 0000000000000100
SigBlk: 0000000000000000
SigIgn: 0000000000000000
SigCgt: 0000000000000000
CapInh: 0000000000000000
CapPrm: 00000000fffffeff
CapEff: 00000000fffffeff
```

Troubleshooting the hung process involves these steps:

1. Identify all the tasks (threads) for the program.

2. Assess the hanging process. Is it easily reproducible?

3. Assess the other things going on. What else is the machine doing? Check load and other applications' response time.

The following scenario demonstrates a way of troubleshooting a process that periodically hangs and then continues.

Scenario 8-2: Troubleshooting a Hanging Web Browser

A user complains that her machine is working great except for her Web browsing application. When accessing Web sites, the browser hangs for a few minutes every so often. The user has installed several different versions and tried other browsers to no avail.

You ask her the following question: Has it ever worked? The reply is "Yes . . . several days ago it was fine."

For the sake of simplicity, we attempt to find the problem with a light Web browser with little overhead.

```
# strace -f -F -r -T -o /tmp/lynx.strace_2 lynx http://www.hp.com
```

Using the vi editor and greping for network calls, such as poll(), we can identify what seems to be a problem right away:

```
:g/poll/p
3660        0.000085 poll([{fd=0, events=POLLIN}], 1, 0) = 0 <0.000020>
3660        0.000186 poll([{fd=0, events=POLLIN}], 1, 0) = 0 <0.000008>
3660        0.000049 poll([{fd=3, events=POLLIN}], 1, 5000) = 0 <5.005154>
3660        0.000043 poll([{fd=3, events=POLLIN}], 1, 5000) = 0 <5.009763>
3660        0.000042 poll([{fd=3, events=POLLIN}], 1, 5000) = 0 <5.008875>
3660        0.000043 poll([{fd=3, events=POLLIN}], 1, 5000) = 0 <5.009264>
3660        0.000042 poll([{fd=3, events=POLLIN}], 1, 5000) = 0 <5.009216>
3660        0.000043 poll([{fd=3, events=POLLIN, revents=POLLIN}], 1, \
            5000) = 1 <0.001146>
3660        0.000081 poll([{fd=0, events=POLLIN}], 1, 0) = 0 <0.000017>
3660        0.000088 poll([{fd=0, events=POLLIN}], 1, 0) = 0 <0.000008>
3660        0.000088 poll([{fd=0, events=POLLIN}], 1, 0) = 0 <0.000022>
```

We see that some poll() calls took over five seconds each. That would explain the Web browser hanging and taking a long time to browse sites.

Focusing on the trace, we see the following:

```
3660        0.000254 socket(PF_INET, SOCK_DGRAM, IPPROTO_IP) = 3 <0.000044>
3660        0.000095 connect(3, {sa_family=AF_INET, sin_port=htons(53), \
            sin_addr=inet_addr("15.50.74.40")}, 28) = 0 <0.000017>
3660        0.000108 send(3, "\245`\1\0\0\1\0\0\0\0\0\0\3www\2hp\3com\0\0\
            34\0\1", 28, 0) = 28    <0.000404>
```

```
3660      0.000476 gettimeofday({1097369839, 928119}, NULL) = 0 <0.000005>
3660      0.000049 poll([{fd=3, events=POLLIN}], 1, 5000) = 0 <5.005154>
3660      5.005262 send(3, "\245`\1\0\0\1\0\0\0\0\0\0\3www\2hp\3com\0\0\
          34\0\1", 28, 0) = 28 <0.000426>
```

Checking the man page on `poll`, we see that it is waiting for an event to take place on a file descriptor.

```
# ls -al /proc/3660/fd/3 -> socket:[52013]
```

This confirms a network issue. After reviewing the `/etc/resolv.conf` file, we see that 15.50.64.40 is the nameserver.

The user contacted her IT department and found that the nameserver configuration for her network had changed. Switching to a different nameserver in the `resolv.conf` file alleviated the five-second `poll()` call and resolved the problem.

Commands commonly used to troubleshoot a hung process include the following:

* `ps`—Concentrate on `pid`, `ppid`, `state`, `comm`, `time`, `pri`, `size`, and `wchan` flags.
* `lsof`—Determine the open files on the system.
* `pstree`—Focus on processes and how they relate to each other.
* `strace`—Flags most commonly used: `-f -F -r -T -o <outfile>`.
* `man pages`—Believe it or not, the manual helps.
* source code—Use it to determine what the application is doing.
* `/proc filesystem`—It offers a wealth of information.

In Scenario 8-3, we show a process that appears to be hung but is not.

Scenario 8-3: Troubleshooting an Apparent Process Hang

In this scenario, a user's goal is to create a file that takes data, automatically compresses it, and sends it to a new file. To perform this task, the user creates a named pipe and issues `gzip`, redirecting input from the pipe to a new file. The odd part is that the `gzip` process seems to hang, and the user cannot find the `gzip` process when searching `ps -ef`.

So you devise an action plan: Re-create the event and trace the process involved.

1. Create a named pipe.

```
$ mknod /tmp/named_pipe p
$ ll /tmp/named_pipe
prw-r--r--   1 chris    chris          0 Oct  9 16:53
/tmp/named_pipe|
```

2. Acquire the current process ID.

```
$ echo $$   # note that the current PID = the shell
5032
```

3. From the same shell window, start the gzip process on the named pipe.

```
$ gzip < /tmp/named_pipe > /tmp/pipe.out.gz
```

4. Find the process with a parent of 5032.

```
$ ps -emo pid,ppid,state,comm,time,pri,size,wchan | grep 5032
5236  5032 S bash                00:00:00  30 1040 pipe_wait
```

Notice that the command name is bash, and it is in the sleep state, sleeping on wait channel pipe_wait. Yet gzip was the command executed.

5. In another shell window, start a trace on the parent before executing the gzip command.

```
$ strace -o /tmp/pipe.strace -f -F -r -T -v -p 5032
Process 5032 attached - interrupt to quit ........Parent shell \
process
Process 5236 attached ...................................The gzip \
process being forked
Process 5032 suspended
```

As mentioned earlier, fork() essentially creates a process structure by copying the parent. Until execve() executes the binary, the new executable is not loaded into memory, so ps -ef | grep gzip does not show the process. In this case, the gzip process waits for something to be sent to the pipe before executing gzip.

6. A review of the trace explains why the ps -ef | grep gzip command does not show the process.

```
PID        Time                call()
...
5032        0.000079 fork()    = 5236 <0.000252>........."GZIP was
executed at command line"
5032        0.000678 setpgid(5236, 5236) = 0 <0.000008>
5032        0.000130 rt_sigprocmask(SIG_SETMASK, [RTMIN], NULL, 8)
= 0 <0.000007>
...
5032        0.000074 waitpid(-1,  <unfinished ...>..........."man
waitpid: -1 means wait on child"
5236        0.000322 --- SIGSTOP (Stopped (signal)) @ 0 (0) ---
5236        0.000078 getpid() = 5236 <0.000006>
5236        0.000050 rt_sigprocmask(SIG_SETMASK, [RTMIN], NULL, 8)
= 0 <0.000007>
5236        0.000067 rt_sigaction(SIGTSTP, {SIG_DFL}, {SIG_IGN},
8) = 0 <0.000009>
5236        0.000060 rt_sigaction(SIGTTIN, {SIG_DFL}, {SIG_IGN},
8) = 0 <0.000007>
5236        0.000057 rt_sigaction(SIGTTOU, {SIG_DFL}, {SIG_IGN},
8) = 0 <0.000007>
5236        0.000055 setpgid(5236, 5236) = 0 <0.000008>
5236        0.000044 rt_sigprocmask(SIG_BLOCK, [CHLD TSTP TTIN
TTOU], [RTMIN], 8) = 0 <0.000007>
5236        0.000071 ioctl(255, TIOCSPGRP, [5236]) = 0 <0.000058>
5236        0.000102 rt_sigprocmask(SIG_SETMASK, [RTMIN], NULL, 8)
= 0 <0.000007>
5236        0.000060 rt_sigaction(SIGINT, {SIG_DFL}, {0x8087030,
[], SA_RESTORER, 0x4005aca8}, 8) = 0 <0.000007>
5236        0.000075 rt_sigaction(SIGQUIT, {SIG_DFL}, {SIG_IGN},
8) = 0 <0.000007>
5236        0.000057 rt_sigaction(SIGTERM, {SIG_DFL}, {SIG_IGN},
8) = 0 <0.000007>
5236        0.000058 rt_sigaction(SIGCHLD, {SIG_DFL}, {0x80776a0,
[], SA_RESTORER, 0x4005aca8}, 8) = 0 <0.000007>
5236        0.000262 open("/tmp/named_pipe", O_RDONLY|O_LARGEFILE)
= 3 <141.798572>
5236       141.798719 dup2(3, 0) = 0 <0.000008>
```

```
5236        0.000051 close(3) = 0 <0.000008>
5236        0.000167 open("/tmp/pipe.out.gz",
O_WRONLY|O_CREAT|O_TRUNC|O_LARGEFILE, 0666) = 3 <0.000329>
5236        0.000394 dup2(3, 1) = 1 <0.000007>
5236        0.000042 close(3) = 0 <0.000008>
5236        0.000127 execve("/usr//bin/gzip", ["gzip"]
```

So 141.79 seconds after opening, the named pipe data was received, evecve() executed gzip, and the data was compressed and redirected to the file /tmp/pipe.out.gz. Only at this point would the gzip process show up in the ps listing. So what was initially thought to be a hung process is simply a sleeping process waiting on data.

7. Now ps -ef | grep gzip works.

```
$ ps -ef | grep 5236
chris      5236  5032  0 17:01 pts/4    00:00:00 gzip
```

Process Cores

Now that we have sufficiently covered structure and hangs as they pertain to Linux processes, let us move on to process core dumps. A core dump enables the user to visually inspect a process's last steps. This section details how cores are created and how to best use them.

Signals

Process core dumps are initiated by the process receiving a signal. Signals are similar to hardware interrupts. As with interrupts, a signal causes a task to branch from its normal execution, handling a routine and returning to the point of interruption. Normal executing threads encounter signals throughout their life cycles. However, there are a finite number of signal types that result in a core dump, whereas other signal types result in process termination.

A process can receive a signal from three sources: the user, the process, or the kernel.

From the User

A user can send a signal in two ways: either using an external command such as `kill` or within a controlling `tty`, typing Ctrl+c to send a `sigint` as defined by `stty -a`. (Note that by definition, daemons do not have a controlling `tty` and therefore cannot be signaled in this manner.)

```
# stty -a
speed 9600 baud; rows 41; columns 110; line = 0;
intr = ^C; quit = ^\; erase = ^?; kill = ^U; eof = ^D; eol = <undef>;
eol2 = <undef>; start = ^Q; stop = ^S;
```

From the Program

From a program, you can perform the `raise()` or `alarm()` system call, allowing a program to signal itself. Consider this example: a ten-second sleep without using the `sleep` call.

```
main()
{
alarm(10);
pause()
}
```

From the Kernel

The kernel can send a `signal`, such as `SIGSEGV`, to a process when it attempts an illegal action, such as accessing memory that it does not own or that is outside of its address range.

Linux supports two types of signals: standard and real-time. A complete overview of signals is outside the scope of this chapter; however, there are a few key differences to note. Standard signals have predefined meanings, whereas real-time signals are defined by the programmer. Additionally, only one standard signal of each type can be queued per process, whereas real-time signals can build up. An example of this was shown earlier in this chapter when a process was blocked on I/O. A kill -9 sigkill was sent to the process and placed in SigPnd.

```
SigPnd: 0000000000000100  <- A signal waiting to be processed, in this
case sigkill
```

In troubleshooting a process, a user might want to force a process to dump core. As stated, this is accomplished by sending the appropriate signal to the process. Sometimes after this step is taken, the dump does not follow because the process has not returned from an interrupt due to some other issue. The result is a pending signal that needs to be processed. Because the signals that result in a core are standard signals, sending the same signal multiple times does not work because subsequent signals are ignored until the pending signal has been processed. The pending signals are processed after the program returns from the interrupt but before proceeding to user space. This fact is illustrated in the entry.S source file, as shown in the following:

```
arch/i386/kernel/entry.S
...
ret_from_intr()
...
_reschedule()
...
_signal_return()
...
        jsr     do_signal      ; arch/cris/kernel/signal.c
...
```

It is also possible to have difficulty achieving the dump because signals are being blocked (masked), caught, or ignored. An application might have signal handlers that catch the signal and perform their own actions. Signal blocking prevents the delivery of the signal to the process. Ignoring a signal just means that the process throws it away upon delivery. Additionally, the signal structure of a process is like any other structure in that the child inherits the parent's configuration. That being stated, if a signal is blocked for the parent, the child of that process has the same signals blocked or masked. However, some signals cannot be masked or ignored, as detailed in the man page on signal. Two such signals are sigkill and sigstop.

The user can obtain a list of signals from the `kill` command. This yields a list of signals that the user can send to a process. Possible signals include the following (note that this is not a complete list):

```
$ kill -l
 1) SIGHUP       2) SIGINT      3) SIGQUIT      4) SIGILL
 5) SIGTRAP      6) SIGABRT     7) SIGBUS       8) SIGFPE
 9) SIGKILL     10) SIGUSR1    11) SIGSEGV     12) SIGUSR2
13) SIGPIPE     14) SIGALRM    15) SIGTERM     17) SIGCHLD
...
```

As mentioned earlier and illustrated next, the man page on `signal` details the signals that produce a core file.

```
$ man 7 signal
...
Signal      Value    Action    Comment
----------------------------------------------------------------
    SIGHUP      1       Term     Hangup detected on controlling terminal
                                 or death of controlling process
    SIGINT      2       Term     Interrupt from keyboard
    SIGQUIT     3       Core     Quit from keyboard
    SIGILL      4       Core     Illegal Instruction
    SIGABRT     6       Core     Abort signal from abort(3)
    SIGFPE      8       Core     Floating point exception
...
```

The source code on `signal` also provides this list as illustrated next:

```
linux/kernel/signal.c
...
#define SIG_KERNEL_COREDUMP_MASK (\
        M(SIGQUIT)   | M(SIGILL)    | M(SIGTRAP)   | M(SIGABRT)   | \
        M(SIGFPE)    | M(SIGSEGV)   | M(SIGBUS)    | M(SIGSYS)    | \
        M(SIGXCPU)   | M(SIGXFSZ)   | M_SIGEMT                    )
...
```

Limits

By default, most Linux distributions disable the creation of process core dumps; however, the user can enable this capability. The capability to create or not create core dumps is accomplished by the use of resource limits and the setting of a *core file size*. Users can display and modify their resource limits by using the `ulimit` command.

In this listing, we depict core dumps being disabled by displaying the user soft limits:

```
$ ulimit -a
core file size          (blocks, -c) 0  <- COREs have been disabled
data seg size           (kbytes, -d) unlimited
file size               (blocks, -f) unlimited
max locked memory       (kbytes, -l) unlimited
max memory size         (kbytes, -m) unlimited
open files                      (-n) 1024
pipe size            (512 bytes, -p) 8
stack size              (kbytes, -s) 8192
cpu time              (seconds, -t) unlimited
max user processes              (-u) 4095
virtual memory          (kbytes, -v) unlimited
```

There are two limits for each resource: a soft limit (shown previously) and a hard limit. The two limits differ in how they can be modified. The hard limit can be thought of as a ceiling that defines the maximum value of a soft limit. Users can change their hard limit only once, whereas they can change their soft limits to any values at any time as long as they do not exceed the hard limit.

Rerunning the `ulimit` command with the `-Ha` option as shown below, we see the hard limits for each resource.

```
$ ulimit -Ha
core file size          (blocks, -c) unlimited
data seg size           (kbytes, -d) unlimited
file size               (blocks, -f) unlimited
max locked memory       (kbytes, -l) unlimited
max memory size         (kbytes, -m) unlimited
```

```
open files                    (-n) 1024
pipe size           (512 bytes, -p) 8
stack size            (kbytes, -s) unlimited
cpu time             (seconds, -t) unlimited
max user processes            (-u) 4095
virtual memory        (kbytes, -v) unlimited
```

A user can set a hard or soft limit to unlimited, as in the previous example. unlimited just means that the process does not have an artificial limit imposed by setrlimit. However, the kernel must represent "unlimited" with a value so that it has a manageable range. The program is limited by what the kernel can address or the physical limits of the machine, whichever comes first. Thus, even when set to unlimited, a limit exists. The 32-bit representation of unlimited (denoted "infinity") is defined in sys_ia32.c as indicated next:

```
...
#define RLIM_INFINITY32 0xffffffff   <-- Equals  4294967295 bytes ~ 4Gig
#define RESOURCE32(x) ((x > RLIM_INFINITY32) ? RLIM_INFINITY32 : x)

struct rlimit32 {
        unsigned        rlim_cur;    <-- soft limit
        unsigned        rlim_max;    <-- hard limit
};
...
```

Anytime a process dumps core and the resource limit core file size is anything other than zero, the kernel writes the core image. There are times, however, when user limits are set to low, resulting in a corrupt or unusable core image. If the core file resource limit is not adequate to accommodate the process's core image, the kernel either does not produce a dump, truncates the dump, or attempts to save only the stack portion of the process's context.

What occurs if the kernel is unable to create the dump depends on the type of executing process. Linux supports a multitude of executable formats. Originally, the a.out binary was used, which contains a magic number in its header. Traditionally, this magic number was used to characterize the binary type—for example, exec magic, demand magic, `shared_mem` magic, and so on. However, it was decided early on that the Executable and Linking Format (ELF) would be Linux's default binary format because of its flexibility. Although AT&T defined the original ELF-32 binary format, UNIX System Laboratories performed the original development of this format. Later HP and INTEL defined the ELF-64 binary format. Today's Linux systems contain very few, if any, `a.out` binaries, and support has been removed from the main kernel and placed into a module called `binfmt_aout.o`, which must be loaded before executing one of these binaries.

Referencing the `binfmt` source for each format details what action is taken in the event of a process attempting to produce a core file, as illustrated next.

The following snippet is from `fs/binfmt_aout.c`.

```
...
/* If the size of the dump file exceeds the rlimit, then see what would
happen
   if we wrote the stack, but not the data area.  */
...
```

The next snippet is from `fs/binfmt_elf.c`.

```
...
/*
 * Actual dumper
 *
 * This is a two-pass process; first we find the offsets of the bits,
 * and then they are actually written out.  If we run out of core limit
 * we just truncate.
 */
```

The Core File

After the core file is generated, we can use it to determine the reason for the core dump. First, we must identify the process that created the core and the signal that caused the process to die. The most common way of determining this information is through the `file` command. Next, we determine whether the program in question has had its symbols stripped. This information can be determined by executing the `file` command against the binary. As mentioned earlier, the core file is the process's context, which includes the magic number or type of executable that created the core file. The `file` command uses a data file to keep track of file types, which by default is located in /etc/magic.

In Scenario 8-4, we show an example of a program with an easily reproducible hang. We can use tools such as `gdb` and other GNU debuggers/wrappers such as `gstack` to solve the problem.

Scenario 8-4: Using GDB to Evaluate a Process That Hangs

We use `gdb` to evaluate a core file created when a program was terminated because it hangs.

```
$ ll gmoo*
-rwxr-xr-x    1 chris    chris      310460 Jan  2 20:25 gmoo.stripped*
-rwxr-xr-x    1 chris    chris      321486 Jan  2 22:25 gmoo.not.stripped*
```

The `file` command informs us of the type of executable (defined in /etc/magic). In the previous example, we have one binary that hangs when executing.

It is helpful to determine the type of binary, as in the following example:

```
$ file gmoo.*
gmoo.not.stripped: ELF 32-bit LSB executable, Intel 80386, version 1
(SYSV), for GNU/Linux 2.2.5, dynamically linked (uses shared libs), not
stripped
gmoo.stripped:     ELF 32-bit LSB executable, Intel 80386, version 1
(SYSV), for GNU/Linux 2.2.5, dynamically linked (uses shared libs),
stripped
```

When the command is hung, we send a `kill -11` (`SIGSEGV`) to the program, causing the program to exit and dump core. An example of such a resulting core file follows:

```
$ file core.6753
core.6753: ELF 32-bit LSB core file Intel 80386, version 1 (SYSV), SVR4-
style, SVR4-style, from 'gmoo.stripped'
```

Using the GNU Project Debugger (GDB), we get the following:

```
$ gdb -q ./gmoo.striped ./core.6753
...
Core was generated by './gmoo.striped'.
Program terminated with signal 11, Segmentation fault.
Reading symbols from /usr/lib/libgtk-1.2.so.0...(no debugging symbols
found)...done.
Loaded symbols for /usr/lib/libgtk-1.2.so.0
Reading symbols from /usr/lib/libgdk-1.2.so.0...(no debugging symbols
found)...done.
Loaded symbols for /usr/lib/libgdk-1.2.so.0
Reading symbols from /usr/lib/libgmodule-1.2.so.0...(no debugging symbols
found)...done.
Loaded symbols for /usr/lib/libgmodule-1.2.so.0
Reading symbols from /usr/lib/libglib-1.2.so.0...(no debugging symbols
found)...done.
...
(gdb) backtrace
#0  0x4046b8e6 in connect () from /lib/i686/libpthread.so.0
#1  0x0806bef1 in gm_net_connect ()
#2  0x080853e1 in gm_world_connect ()
#3  0x0806c7cf in gm_notebook_try_add_world ()
#4  0x0806cd8c in gm_notebook_try_restore_status ()
#5  0x08061eab in main ()
#6  0x404c5c57 in __libc_start_main () from /lib/i686/libc.so.6
(gdb) list
No symbol table is loaded.  Use the "file" command.
(gdb)
```

Without the source, we have gone about as far as we can. We must use other tools, such as strace, in combination with gdb. Other tool suites such as valgrind can also prove useful.

Now, let us look at an example of the same hang with a non-stripped version of the binary.

```
$ gdb -q ./gmoo.not.stripped ./core.6881
...
Core was generated by './gmoo.not.stripped'.
Program terminated with signal 11, Segmentation fault.
Reading symbols from /usr/lib/libgtk-1.2.so.0...done.
Loaded symbols for /usr/lib/libgtk-1.2.so.0
Reading symbols from /usr/lib/libgdk-1.2.so.0...done.
Loaded symbols for /usr/lib/libgdk-1.2.so.0
Reading symbols from /usr/lib/libgmodule-1.2.so.0...done.
...
(gdb) backtrace
#0  0x40582516 in poll () from /lib/i686/libc.so.6
(gdb)
```

Although the stack trace appears to be different, we have identified the root cause. The program is hung on a network poll call, which, according to the man page, is a structure made up of file descriptors. Using other tools, such as lsof, strace, and so on, we can determine exactly the network IP address upon which the process is hung.

Summary

As is apparent from the discussion in this chapter, the topic of process structure, hangs, and core files is a complex one. It is crucial to understand the process structure to troubleshoot hangs and most efficiently use core files. New troubleshooting tools are always being developed, so it is important to keep up with changes in this area. Although troubleshooting process hangs can be intimidating, as you can conclude from this chapter, it simply requires a step-by-step, methodical approach that, when mastered, leads to efficient and effective resolution practices.

9

Backup/Recovery

One of the key jobs of a system administrator is to back up and recover systems and data. It is also one of the more vexing areas. Nothing gets an administrator in trouble faster than lost data. In this chapter, we discuss the key categories of backup and recovery, and we look at some important areas of concern.

The first distinction between backup types is remote versus local backups. Local backups to media are typically faster, but the incremental cost of adding media storage to every system becomes expensive quickly. The second option is to use a remote system as a backup server. This approach slows the backups somewhat and increases network bandwidth usage, but the backups typically happen in the middle of the night when most systems are quiet. This distinction is not a major focus of the chapter, but it is a fact of backup and recovery life and must be mentioned.

The main issues addressed in the chapter include backup media and the types of backup devices available, backup strategies, the benefits and limitations of different utilities, and ways to troubleshoot failing tape backups.

Media

Even if the data from a computer is backed up across the network, it must at some point be stored on some form of media. The three basic media for archiving data from computer systems are magnetic tape, optical disk, and hard drive. We deal with magnetic tape in the most depth because it is the most common method for backup and recovery.

Magnetic Tape

Magnetic tape was originally used for audio recordings but was later adapted to computer data. It is typically a magnetizable medium that moves with a constant speed past a recording head. Most modern tape drives use multiple heads offset into different tracks. The heads can also be skewed at angles to decrease the space that separates the tracks. This space is needed so that the signal recorded in one track does not interfere with the signal in another track.

The early tape drives were usually open-spooled half-inch magnetic tape (also known as reel to reel; see Figure 9-1). The amount of data on a particular tape was determined by the length of the tape, the number of tracks, tape speed, and the density at which the data was written onto the tape. Half-inch tape length was from 50 to 2400 feet. It was wound on reels up to 10.5 inches in diameter. It originally had seven tracks (six for data and one for parity), and later versions had nine tracks (eight for data and one for parity). Aluminum strips were glued several feet from the ends of the tape to serve as logical beginning and end of tape markers. A removable plastic ring in the back of the tape reels would write-protect the tape. A gap between records allowed the mechanism time to stop the tape when it was originally running. Table 9-1 provides a summary of the characteristics of a typical half-inch 2400-foot tape.

Tape systems later migrated to a closed cartridge format. This format was easier to load and store. A new technology also emerged to rival linear track tapes. Sony invented helical scan tape technology originally for video recording, but it was adapted for computer data. It records data using tracks that are at an angle to the edge of the tape (see Figure 9-2). Helical scan tapes can typically record at a higher density and have a longer life due to lower tape tension, lower tape speeds, and less back and forth traversal wear on the tape and the drive.

Figure 9-1 A half-inch magnetic open reel tape

Table 9-1   Characteristics of Half-Inch 2400-Foot Tape

Capacity

Formatted Data Capacity (2400 ft. tape)	20–700MB

Tape Speed

Transfer Rate	200–769KB/sec.
Rewind	90 sec. to rewind 2400 ft.

Density

Standard	6250bpi (GCR); 1600bpi (PE)

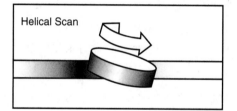
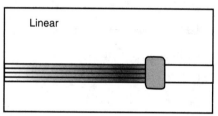

Figure 9-2 Helical scan and linear recording methods

Table 9-2 provides a comparison of the most common tape format types today.

How do you identify the tape drive originally you have? There are three places to start. You can look in /proc/scsi/, the syslog, or dmesg output. Looking in /proc/scsi/scsi is probably the best strategy.

```
# cat /proc/scsi/scsi
Attached devices:
Host: scsi1 Channel: 00 Id: 03 Lun: 00
  Vendor: HP        Model: Ultrium 2-SCSI    Rev: F48D
  Type:   Sequential-Access               ANSI SCSI revision: 03
```

If you look in /proc/scsi/scsi and you don't see the tape drive listed, there are several steps to take. The first is to confirm that the SCSI card shows up in lspci.

Table 9-2   Comparison of Tape Formats

Tape Format	Revision	Native Storage	Compressed Storage	Tape Cartridge	Native Data Transfer Rate	Compressed Data Transfer
DDS/DAT	DDS1	2GB	4GB	DDS1	250KB/s	500KB/s
	DDS2	4GB	8GB	DDS2	500KB/s	1MB/s
	DDS3	12GB	24GB	DDS3	1.5MB/s	3MB/s
	DDS4	20GB	40GB	DDS4	3MB/s	6MB/s
	DAT72	36GB	72GB	DDS72	3MB/s	6MB/s
DLT/SDLT	DLT4000	20GB	40GB	DLT IV	1.5MB/s	3MB/s
	DLT7000	35GB	70GB	DLT IV	5MB/s	10MB/s
	DLT8000	40GB	80GB	DLT IV	6MB/s	12MB/s
	SDLT220	110GB	220GB	SDLT I	11MB/s	22MB/s
	SDLT320	160GB	320GB	SDLT II	16MB/s	32MB/s
	SDLT600	300GB	600GB	SDLT II	36MB/s	72MB/s
	SDLT1200	600GB	1.2TB	SDLT II	Unknown	Unknown
LTO	Ultrium I	100GB	200GB	Ultrium I	15MB/s	30MB/s
	Ultrium II	200GB	400GB	Ultrium II	30MB/s	60MB/s
	Ultrium III	400GB	800GB	Ultrium III	68MB/s	136MB/s
	Ultrium IV	800GB	1.6TB	Ultrium IV	120MB/s	240MB/
Mammoth	Mammoth2	60GB	150GB	Mammoth	12MB/s	30MB/s
AIT/S-AIT	AIT1	35GB	90GB	AIT	4MB/s	10.4MB/s
	AIT2	50GB	130GB	AIT	6MB/s	15.6MB/s
	AIT3	100GB	260GB	AIT	12MB/s	31.2MB/s
	AIT4	200GB	520GB	AIT	24MB/s	62.4MB/s
	SAIT1	500GB	1.3TB	SAIT	30MB/s	78MB/s
	SAIT2	1TB	2.6TB	SAIT	60MB/s	156MB/s

```
# lspci
00:00.0 Host bridge: Broadcom CMIC-HE (rev 22)

00:00.1 Host bridge: Broadcom CMIC-HE

00:00.2 Host bridge: Broadcom CMIC-HE

00:00.3 Host bridge: Broadcom CMIC-HE

00:02.0 System peripheral: Compaq Computer Corporation Integrated Lights
Out Controller (rev 01)

00:02.2 System peripheral: Compaq Computer Corporation Integrated Lights
Out Processor (rev 01)

00:03.0 VGA compatible controller: ATI Technologies Inc Rage XL (rev 27)

00:0f.0 ISA bridge: Broadcom CSB5 South Bridge (rev 93)

00:0f.1 IDE interface: Broadcom CSB5 IDE Controller (rev 93)

00:0f.2 USB Controller: Broadcom OSB4/CSB5 OHCI USB Controller (rev 05)

00:0f.3 Host bridge: Broadcom CSB5 LPC bridge

00:10.0 Host bridge: Broadcom CIOB30 (rev 03)

00:10.2 Host bridge: Broadcom CIOB30 (rev 03)

00:11.0 Host bridge: Broadcom CIOB30 (rev 03)

00:11.2 Host bridge: Broadcom CIOB30 (rev 03)

01:01.0 RAID bus controller: Compaq Computer Corporation Smart Array
5i/532 (rev 01)

02:02.0 Ethernet controller: Intel Corporation 82546EB Gigabit Ethernet
Controller (Copper) (rev 01)

02:02.1 Ethernet controller: Intel Corporation 82546EB Gigabit Ethernet
Controller (Copper) (rev 01)

02:1e.0 PCI Hot-plug controller: Compaq Computer Corporation PCI
Hotplug Controller (rev 14)

06:01.0 Ethernet controller: Intel Corporation 82546EB Gigabit Ethernet
Controller (Copper) (rev 01)

06:01.1 Ethernet controller: Intel Corporation 82546EB Gigabit Ethernet
Controller (Copper) (rev 01)

06:02.0 SCSI storage controller: LSI Logic / Symbios Logic 53c1030 PCI-X
Fusion-MPT Dual Ultra320 SCSI (rev 07)

06:02.1 SCSI storage controller: LSI Logic / Symbios Logic 53c1030 PCI-X
Fusion-MPT Dual Ultra320 SCSI (rev 07)

06:1e.0 PCI Hot-plug controller: Compaq Computer Corporation PCI
Hotplug Controller (rev 14)

0a:01.0 RAID bus controller: Compaq Computer Corporation Smart Array
5300 Controller (rev 02)
```

```
0a:02.0 Ethernet controller: Broadcom Corporation NetXtreme BCM5701
Gigabit Ethernet (rev 15)
```

The dual-port SCSI controller is listed originally in the previous example at 06:02.0 and 06:02.1. If your SCSI card does not appear in the lspci output, you need to load the appropriate driver with modprobe.

After the SCSI card appears in the lspci output, you must confirm that the SCSI tape driver is loaded. You can do this by running lsmod.

```
# lsmod |grep st
# modprobe st
# lsmod |grep st
st                       31524   0
scsi_mod                115240   5  [sr_mod sg st cciss mptscsih sd_mod]
```

Autoloader/Tape Libraries

Backup software originally must perform two common tasks beyond the actual backup. These tasks are to move tapes around inside a tape library and to manage tapes when they are inside the tape drive. The mtx command moves tapes around within a tape library, and the mt command ejects, rewinds, and otherwise manages tapes inside the drive.

Autoloaders and tape libraries are mechanisms for managing larger backups that span multiple tapes. These devices typically are used only on central backup servers because of their cost. The devices range from a single tape drive unit that can switch up to six tapes to a huge tape silo with hundreds of tape drives and thousands of tapes. The common denominator is the concept of the drive, the slot, and the changer mechanism. The drive is obviously the tape drive. The slot is where a tape is stored in the unit when it is not being moved and is not in a drive. The changer is the robotic mechanism that moves the tapes. You can use any normal backup software to write to the drive when it has a tape in it, but most backup software doesn't have the capability to control the slots and the changer. The most common software that can control a changer under Linux is mtx, which is available from http://mtx.badtux.net. This Web page provides the following definition of mtx:

mtx is a set of low-level driver programs to control features of SCSI backup-related devices such as autoloaders, tape changers, media jukeboxes, and tape drives. It can also report much data, including serial numbers, maximum block sizes, and TapeAlert™ messages that most modern tape drives implement (to tell you the exact reason why a backup or restore failed), as well as do raw SCSI READ and WRITE commands to tape drives (not important on Linux, but important on Solaris due to the fact that the Solaris tape driver supports none of the additional features of tape drives invented after 1988). *mtx* is designed to be a low-level driver in a larger scripted backup solution, such as Amanda. *mtx* is not supposed to itself be a high-level interface to the SCSI devices that it controls.

The first mistake most people make when using mtx is trying to use it against the device driver for the tape drive rather than the device file for the changer mechanism. Issuing the command

```
mtx -f /dev/st2 inquiry
```

results in the following error message in the messages file:

```
st2: Write not multiple of tape block size.
```

The changer device file is typically of the /dev/sgX format. The /dev/sgX denotes a generic SCSI device. These are also sometimes known as passthrough devices because they pass through the SCSI command issued from software programs such as mtx to the hardware. The correct command is:

```
mtx -f /dev/sga inquiry
     Product Type: Tape Drive
     Vendor Id: HP
     Product ID: C1561A
```

One other common problem is that the changer mechanism never shows up. This sometimes indicates that the tape drive is stuck in "stacker mode." You must consult the drive's documentation on how to change it from "stacker mode" into a mode that enables you to control the changer. "Stacker mode" is also sometimes referred to as "sequential mode."

With mtx, if you want to set the default device file for the changer, you can run:

```
export CHANGER=/dev/sgc
```

This code can be prepended to a script or run from the command line, which saves the repetition of typing the option -f /dev/sgX for every command.

Another common problem is the lack of LUN support. You need to use or make a kernel with CONFIG_SCSI_MULTI_LUN=y in the CONFIG file. The kernel must probe for SCSI LUNs on boot.

An example of loading a tape from slot 1 to drive 2 is:

```
mtx load 1 2
```

An example of gathering an inventory of the drives and slots is:

```
mtx inventory
```

The following is more detail on the available commands from the man page:

```
COMMANDS
--version
Report the mtx version number (e.g. mtx 1.2.8) and exit.
inquiry
Report the product type (Medium Changer, Tape Drive, etc.), Vendor ID,
Product ID, Revision, and whether this uses the Attached Changer API
(some tape drives use this rather than reporting a Medium Changer on a
separate LUN or SCSI address).
noattach
Make further commands use the regular media changer API rather than the
_ATTACHED API, no matter what the "Attached" bit said in the Inquiry
info. Needed with some brain-dead changers that report Attached bit but
don't respond to _ATTACHED API.
inventory
Makes the robot arm go and check what elements are in the slots. This is
needed for a few libraries like the Breece Hill ones that do not
automatically check the tape inventory at system startup.
status
Reports how many drives and storage elements are contained in the device.
For each drive, reports whether it has media loaded in it, and if so,
from which storage slot the media originated. For each storage slot,
reports whether it is empty or full, and if the media changer has a bar
code, MIC reader, or some other way of uniquely identifying media without
loading it into a drive, this reports the volume tag and/or alternate
```

volume tag for each piece of media. For historical reasons drives are
numbered from 0 and storage slots are numbered from 1.

load <slotnum> [<drivenum>]

Load media from slot <slotnum> into drive <drivenum>. Drive 0 is assumed
if the drive number is omitted.

unload [<slotnum>] [<drivenum>]

Unloads media from drive <drivenum> into slot <slotnum>. If <drivenum>
is omitted, defaults to drive 0 (as do all commands). If <slotnum> is
omitted, defaults to the slot that the drive was loaded from. Note that
there's currently no way to say 'unload drive 1's media to the slot it
came from', other than to explicitly use that slot number as the
destination.

[eepos <operation>] transfer <slotnum> <slotnum>

Transfers media from one slot to another, assuming that your mechanism is
capable of doing so. Usually used to move media to/from an import/export
port. 'eepos' is used to extend/retract the import/export tray on certain
mid-range to high end tape libraries (if, e.g., the tray was slot 32, you
might say 'eepos 1 transfer 32 32' to extend the tray). Valid values for
eepos <operation> are 0 (do nothing to the import/export tray), 1, and 2
(what 1 and 2 do varies depending upon the library, consult your
library's SCSI-level documentation).

first [<drivenum>]

Loads drive <drivenum> from the first slot in the media changer. Unloads
the drive if there is already media in it. Note that this command may not
be what you want on large tape libraries -- e.g. on Exabyte 220, the
first slot is usually a cleaning tape. If <drivenum> is omitted, defaults
to first drive.

last [<drivenum>]

Loads drive <drivenum> from the last slot in the media changer. Unloads
the drive if there is already a tape in it.

next [<drivenum>]

Unloads the drive and loads the next tape in sequence. If the drive was
empty, loads the first tape into the drive.

SEE ALSO
 mt(1),tapeinfo(1),scsitape(1),loaderinfo(1)

   One other commonly scripted task is to eject the tape. This task can be accomplished
with the following command:

mt -f /dev/st0 offl

This command can be used with a standalone tape drive or a tape library that requires manual tape ejection before the changer can grab the tape.

Hardware Versus Software Compression

Backups are typically compressed to save space and sometimes to limit the bandwidth sent to the backup device. Two forms of compression are commonly used: hardware and software compression. Software compression is easier to troubleshoot and gauge than hardware compression.

You should use either hardware or software compression but not both. Using both methods creates a backup that is larger than the data when compressed only once.

Software compression typically comes from utilities such as `gzip`, `bzip`, and so on. It uses compression algorithms to compress a file.

For example, the following command uses `tar` to compress the `/etc` directory and write it to `/dev/st0` after passing the `tar` file through `gzip`.

```
tar cvzf /dev/st0 /etc
```

Another consideration is that binary data such as compiled binaries, audio, pictures, videos, and so on cannot be compressed as much as text.

Hardware compression uses a compression algorithm that is hard-coded into the chipset of the tape drive. Most modern tape drives support hardware compression. It is important to determine whether you are using hardware compression, and if so, you should stop using software compression. Hardware compression is typically enabled by default on most tape drives today. It can be disabled with a custom device file or on the tape device (either by dip switches or a front panel). If you back up a directory of already compressed files (such as gzipped files), you should expect little compression; in fact, the files could become bigger. You should also expect little or no compression when backing up a filesystem full of binary files.

Rewind Versus No-Rewind Devices

When backing up, you have the choice of backing up to a rewind or a no-rewind device. This is just as it sounds, but why would you want to back up to a no-rewind device? This is typically done with utilities such as `dump`, where you have only one filesystem per backup. You could then append each filesystem backup to the end of a tape through the

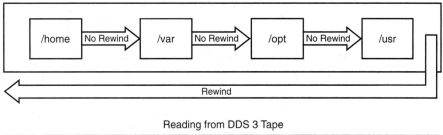

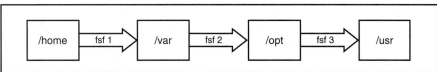

Figure 9-3 Multiple dumps on one tape

no-rewind device instead of having to use multiple tapes. This approach uses the tape space more efficiently. The device file specifies whether to rewind the tape. For example, /dev/nst0 is a no-rewind device, and /dev/st0 is a rewind device. A rewind device rewinds the tape to its beginning on close, whereas a no-rewind tape device does not rewind on close. The device files show a different minor number, which controls the device characteristics:

```
# file /dev/nst0
/dev/nst0: character special (9/128)
# file /dev/st0
/dev/st0: character special (9/0)
```

Using mt to Control the Tape Drive

As we stated earlier, controlling tapes is a task that backup software must perform. Tapes must be rewound and ejected before they can be moved to a slot with mtx. They also must be positioned at the correct archive if you are putting multiple archives on one tape using a no-rewind device.

Here is an excerpt from the mt man page that shows the options you can use to control the tape drive:

The available operations are listed below. Unique abbreviations are accepted. Not all operations are available on all systems, or work on all types of tape drives. Some operations optionally take a repeat count, which can be given after the operation name and defaults to 1.

eof, weof	Write count EOF marks at current position.
fsf	Forward space count files. The tape is positioned on the first block of the next file.
bsf	Backward space count files. The tape is positioned on the first block of the next file.
eom	Space to the end of the recorded media on the tape (for appending files onto tapes).
rewind	Rewind the tape.
offline, rewoffl	Rewind the tape and, if applicable, unload the tape.
status	Print status information about the tape unit.
retension	Rewind the tape, then wind it to the end of the reel, then rewind it again.
erase	Erase the tape.
eod, seod	Space to end of valid data. Used on streamer tape drives to append data to the logical end of tape.
setdensity	(SCSI tapes) Set the tape density code to count. The proper codes to use with each drive should be looked up from the drive documentation.
seek	(SCSI tapes) Seek to the count block on the tape. This operation is available on some Tandberg and Wangtek streamers and some SCSI-2 tape drives.
tell	(SCSI tapes) Tell the current block on tape. This operation is available on some Tandberg and Wangtek streamers and some SCSI-2 tape drives.
densities	(SCSI tapes) Write explanation of some common density codes to standard output.
Datcompression	(some SCSI-2 DAT tapes) Inquire or set the compression status (on/off). If the count is one the compression status is printed. If the count is zero, compression is disabled. Otherwise, compression is enabled. The command uses the SCSI ioctl to read and write the Data Compression Characteristics mode page (15). ONLY ROOT CAN USE THIS COMMAND.

If you want to position the tape to read the second archive on a tape, run:

```
# mt -t /dev/st1 rew; mt -t /dev/st1 fsf 1
```

If you want to rewind the tape drive to the beginning, run:

```
# mt -t /dev/st0 rew
```

If you want to eject the tape from the drive, run:

```
# mt -t /dev/st0 offline
```

Cleaning Tape Versus Built-in Cleaning

One of the most overlooked elements of good tape backups is a good cleaning routine. It is imperative that you purchase cleaning tapes and routinely run them through the tape drive. I even recommend this for "self-cleaning" drives such as the DLT. It is just too easy for magnetic tapes to put trash on the tape heads. I typically run a cleaning tape through four times in a row every few days to once a week. I know this might seem like overkill, but it is worth the time and expense. I would also keep a log of how many times each tape and each cleaning tape has been used and make sure to destroy and replace them at the recommended interval of the manufacturer.

Optical Disk

The second medium is optical disk. This term used to refer to WORM and optical disks, but now it more frequently refers to DVD or CD media. This method has recently become more cost effective for backing up smaller systems. The one downside of optical media when compared to tape is that some backup utilities write backup files to disk and then burn them to media instead of writing them directly to the optical disk. Backing up to CD can be handled by writing a backup to disk and then transferring that backup to CD using a utility such as cdrecord. The other alternative is to use a utility such as k3b to write files and directories to CD, but this method is uncommon except for one-off back-ups of particular files. Neither is well suited to whole-system backups. The only way to consistently write backups to CD is to use a utility such as mondo, which is discussed further in the "Bare Metal Recovery" section.

Hard Disk

The third medium is hard disk. This typically means one of three possibilities:

- Disk arrays with RAID or disk mirroring
- High-end disk arrays with business copy
- Removable USB disk storage

The first downside to this option is cost. The second (with the exception of USB disk storage) is the inability to have offsite backups. An offsite backup is vital. If a disaster destroys your datacenter, and you do not have offsite media storage, the disaster destroys all your backups. Offsite backups can be as simple as taking a briefcase of tapes home with you each day or as complex as shipping tapes daily to a hardened and secure third party. The one major exception to this limitation is mirroring data to a remote disk array. Most high-end disk array vendors offer this feature, but it is very expensive.

Backup Scope

Storage media has a cost, and the time available to perform a backup is finite. To minimize both factors, administrators have come up with strategies for limiting the scope of backups as much as possible. There are two common strategies: backing up only files that have changed since the last backup, and backing up only dynamic data files.

The first strategy is also called incremental backups. Assume that you have a directory with four files on day one (11/1):

```
File1        Last modified 10/1        size 1GB
File2        Last modified 10/1        size 10KB
File3        Last modified 10/4        size 1MB
File4        Last modified 9/22        size 2MB
```

On the first day, you complete a full backup, which backs up all the files on the system. In this example, it backs up all four files. The next day (11/2), you could complete a level one backup, which would back up all the files that had been modified since the last backup at the previous backup level. In this example, that would be the full backup completed on 11/1. A listing of the files at backup time on 11/2 shows:

```
File1       Last modified 10/1      size 1GB
File2       Last modified 11/2      size 10KB
File3       Last modified 10/4      size 1MB
File4       Last modified 11/2      size 2MB
```

This means that for the level one backup, only two files (File2 and File4) are backed up. This approach saves the time and space of backing up File1 and File3. It is not necessary because they haven't changed since the previous backup.

The downside to this method is that restoring data involves using as many tapes as you have backup levels. If you had to restore the directory from this example, you would need to recover the last full backup and the last level one backup to return to the most recently backed-up files.

You can also use the modified Towers of Hanoi method from http://en.wikipedia.org/wiki/Towers_of_Hanoi:

> The Tower of Hanoi (also called Towers of Hanoi) is a mathematical game or puzzle. It consists of three pegs, and a number of discs of different sizes which can slide onto any peg. The puzzle starts with the discs neatly stacked in order of size on one peg, smallest at the top, thus making a conical shape.

One recommended scheme is documented in the dump man page:

After a level 0, dumps of active file systems are taken on a daily basis, using a modified Tower of Hanoi algorithm, with this sequence of dump levels:

3 2 5 4 7 6 9 8 9 9...

For the daily dumps, it should be possible to use a fixed number of tapes for each day, used on a weekly basis. Each week, a level 1 dump is taken, and the daily Hanoi sequence repeats beginning with 3. For weekly dumps, another fixed set of tapes per dumped file system is used, also on a cyclical basis.

The second method is to do a full system backup and then to only back up directories that contain constantly changing data (such as application directories). This method also limits the time and size of backups, but it has two problems. The first is that even seemingly static directories have changes from time to time. It would be easy to miss backing up a change to a configuration file if it were not in a common directory. The second issue is that if you don't back up system logs, it would be possible to have them rotate off the system, leaving you without historic data to which to refer.

Basic Backup and Recovery Commands

An enormous number of open source and proprietary backup utilities is available. Each has its own positive and negative points. Table 9-3 highlights some of these areas. It is important to test each utility and pick the one that best suits your needs.

tar

tar is very easy to use and is the most common utility for moving and distributing files and directories to other computers. It is less useful as a system-level backup command, though. It can only create files of limited size, it has limited capability for incremental

Table 9-3   Positive and Negative Qualities of Backup Utilities

Method	Backup Levels Supported?	Ease of Use	Backup Across Network?	Appendable?
tar	Limited (only on mtime)	Simple	Using pipe	Yes
cpio	No	Moderate	Using pipe	No
dump	Yes	Simple	Yes	No
dd	No	Moderate	Using pipe	No
mkisofs	No	Difficult	No	Not easily
rsync	No*	Moderate	Yes	No

*rsync only synchronizes files that have changed.

backups (using mtime only), and it lacks integrated capability to use the find command in the way that cpio does. tar is also very unforgiving of media errors. tar must also search an entire volume to find a file to recover, so it is bad for very large archives. Examples of compressing, listing, and extracting a tar archive follow.

In the following example, we compress files into a tar archive. The cvzf switches denote create archive (c), verbose output (v), compress the output file (z), and specified device file (f):

```
# tar cvzf /dev/st0 /work
tar: Removing leading '/' from member names
/work/
/work/lost+found/
/work/vmware/
/work/vmware/state/
/work/vmware/installer.sh
/work/vmware/config
/work/vmware/locations
/work/vmware/vmnet1/
/work/vmware/vmnet1/dhcpd/
/work/vmware/vmnet1/dhcpd/dhcpd.conf
/work/vmware/vmnet1/dhcpd/dhcpd.leases~
/work/vmware/vmnet1/dhcpd/dhcpd.leases
/work/vmware/vmnet8/
/work/vmware/vmnet8/nat/
/work/vmware/vmnet8/nat/nat.conf
/work/vmware/vmnet8/dhcpd/
/work/vmware/vmnet8/dhcpd/dhcpd.conf
/work/vmware/vmnet8/dhcpd/dhcpd.leases~
/work/vmware/vmnet8/dhcpd/dhcpd.leases
```

In the following example, we list files in a tar archive. The tvzf switches denote list archive (t), verbose output (v), compress the output file (z), and specified device file (f):

```
# tar tvzf /dev/st0

drwxr-xr-x root/root        0 2005-11-19 14:36:23 work/
drwx------ root/root        0 2005-11-19 14:35:51 work/lost+found/
```

```
drwxr-xr-x root/root          0 2005-11-19 14:36:23 work/vmware/
drwxr-xr-x root/root          0 2005-11-19 14:36:23 work/vmware/state/
-r-xr-xr-x root/root      36011 2005-11-19 14:36:23 \
work/vmware/installer.sh
-rw-r--r-- root/root        264 2005-11-19 14:36:23 work/vmware/config
-rw-r--r-- root/root       4987 2005-11-19 14:36:23 work/vmware/locations
drwxr-xr-x root/root          0 2005-11-19 14:36:23 work/vmware/vmnet1/
drwxr-xr-x root/root          0 2005-11-19 14:36:23 \
work/vmware/vmnet1/dhcpd/
-r--r--r-- root/root        743 2005-11-19 14:36:23 \
work/vmware/vmnet1/dhcpd/dhcpd.conf
-rw-r--r-- root/root          0 2005-11-19 14:36:23 \
work/vmware/vmnet1/dhcpd/dhcpd.leases~
-rw-r--r-- root/root        417 2005-11-19 14:36:23 \
work/vmware/vmnet1/dhcpd/dhcpd.leases
drwxr-xr-x root/root          0 2005-11-19 14:36:23 work/vmware/vmnet8/
drwxr-xr-x root/root          0 2005-11-19 14:36:23 \
work/vmware/vmnet8/nat/
-r--r--r-- root/root       1251 2005-11-19 14:36:23 \
work/vmware/vmnet8/nat/nat.conf
drwxr-xr-x root/root          0 2005-11-19 14:36:23 \
work/vmware/vmnet8/dhcpd/
-r--r--r-- root/root        771 2005-11-19 14:36:23 \
work/vmware/vmnet8/dhcpd/dhcpd.conf
-rw-r--r-- root/root          0 2005-11-19 14:36:23 \
work/vmware/vmnet8/dhcpd/dhcpd.leases~
-rw-r--r-- root/root        417 2005-11-19 14:36:23 \
work/vmware/vmnet8/dhcpd/dhcpd.leases
```

In the following example, we extract files from a tar archive. The tvzf switches
denote extract archive (x), verbose output (v), compress the output file (z), and specified
device file (f):

```
# rm /work/vmware/installer.sh
# tar xvzf /dev/st0 work/vmware/installer.sh
work/vmware/installer.sh
# ll /work/vmware/installer.sh
-r-xr-xr-x  1 root root 36K 2005-11-20 10:53 /work/vmware/installer.sh
```

cpio

cpio is the most versatile backup command. cpio is more complicated to use, but it offers a high degree of flexibility. cpio does a great job of handling media errors and tries to skip bad spots on restore. cpio reads and writes files and directories to be backed up through stdin and stdout, which gives you incredible flexibility. Typically, you pipe find commands through cpio, but you can also run find with the -cpio option to direct the output to cpio. cpio also easily spans multiple tapes. You must use custom scripting to create incremental backups with cpio because the command doesn't have built-in support for backups. However, this scripting can be done without too much pain. cpio also forces the user to read the entire tape to find a file, so it might be less useful for larger backups.

An example of cpio in action follows:

```
# find find /work -print |cpio -ovH newc >/dev/st0
/work
/work/lost+found
/work/vmware
/work/vmware/state
/work/vmware/installer.sh
/work/vmware/config
/work/vmware/locations
/work/vmware/vmnet1
/work/vmware/vmnet1/dhcpd
/work/vmware/vmnet1/dhcpd/dhcpd.conf
/work/vmware/vmnet1/dhcpd/dhcpd.leases~
/work/vmware/vmnet1/dhcpd/dhcpd.leases
/work/vmware/vmnet8
/work/vmware/vmnet8/nat
/work/vmware/vmnet8/nat/nat.conf
/work/vmware/vmnet8/dhcpd
/work/vmware/vmnet8/dhcpd/dhcpd.conf
/work/vmware/vmnet8/dhcpd/dhcpd.leases~
/work/vmware/vmnet8/dhcpd/dhcpd.leases
```

```
# cpio -itv < /dev/st0
drwxr-xr-x  4 root     root             0 Nov 19 14:36 /work
drwx------  2 root     root             0 Nov 19 14:35 /work/lost+found
drwxr-xr-x  5 root     root             0 Nov 19 14:36 /work/vmware
drwxr-xr-x  2 root     root             0 Nov 19 14:36 /work/vmware/state
-r-xr-xr-x  1 root     root         36011 Nov 19 14:36 \
/work/vmware/installer.sh
-rw-r--r--  1 root     root           264 Nov 19 14:36 \
/work/vmware/config
-rw-r--r--  1 root     root          4987 Nov 19 14:36 \
/work/vmware/locations
drwxr-xr-x  3 root     root             0 Nov 19 14:36 \
/work/vmware/vmnet1
drwxr-xr-x  2 root     root             0 Nov 19 14:36 \
/work/vmware/vmnet1/dhcpd
-r--r--r--  1 root     root           743 Nov 19 14:36 \
/work/vmware/vmnet1/dhcpd/dhcpd.conf
-rw-r--r--  1 root     root             0 Nov 19 14:36 \
/work/vmware/vmnet1/dhcpd/dhcpd.leases~
-rw-r--r--  1 root     root           417 Nov 19 14:36 \
/work/vmware/vmnet1/dhcpd/dhcpd.leases
drwxr-xr-x  4 root     root             0 Nov 19 14:36 \
/work/vmware/vmnet8
drwxr-xr-x  2 root     root             0 Nov 19 14:36 \
/work/vmware/vmnet8/nat
-r--r--r--  1 root     root          1251 Nov 19 14:36 \
/work/vmware/vmnet8/nat/nat.conf
drwxr-xr-x  2 root     root             0 Nov 19 14:36 \
/work/vmware/vmnet8/dhcpd
-r--r--r--  1 root     root           771 Nov 19 14:36 \
/work/vmware/vmnet8/dhcpd/dhcpd.conf
-rw-r--r--  1 root     root             0 Nov 19 14:36 \
/work/vmware/vmnet8/dhcpd/dhcpd.leases~
-rw-r--r--  1 root     root           417 Nov 19 14:36 \
/work/vmware/vmnet8/dhcpd/dhcpd.leases
94 blocks
```

The following is an example of removing and restoring a file with cpio:

```
# rm /work/vmware/installer.sh
# cpio -i "*installer.sh" < /tmp/foo3.out
94 blocks
# ll /work/vmware/installer.sh
-r-xr-xr-x  1 root root 36K 2005-11-20 10:53 /work/vmware/installer.sh
```

A common mistake with cpio is illustrated next:

```
# find -print /etc/hosts |cpio –ov > /tmp/foo2.out
find: paths must precede expression
Usage: find [-H] [-L] [-P] [path...] [expression]
0 blocks
find /etc/hosts -print |cpio -ov >/tmp/foo2.out
/etc/hosts
2 blocks
```

```
# find /etc/hosts -print |cpio -ov /tmp/foo2.out
Usage: cpio {-o|--create} [-0acvABLV] [-C bytes] [-H format] [-M message]
[-O [[user@]host:]archive] [-F [[user@]host:]archive]
[--file=[[user@]host:]archive] [--format=format] [--message=message]
[--null] [--reset-access-time] [--verbose] [--dot] [--append][--block-
size=blocks] [--dereference] [--io-size=bytes] [--quiet][--force-local]
[--rsh-command=command] [--help] [--version] < name-list [> archive]
```

dump and Restore

dump only backs up a whole filesystem, so it is not a good choice for backing up just a few files or directories. dump supports up to nine levels of backups. It can restore files, directories, or the entire filesystem. dump does not produce a live index while backing up, but it has very easy interactive recovery capabilities. It is less easily recovered on other versions of UNIX than cpio and tar because it is more closely tied to the source filesystem type of an archive.

dump also has a much more complicated archive layout than cpio or tar. cpio and tar treat a backup not as a whole archive but rather as strings of file and directory records. dump writes a table of contents at the beginning of the archive, which is why recovery is faster with dump. This is also why you can use the interactive shell (including ls and cd) with dump.

```
# /sbin/dump -0uf /tmp/foo4.out /work
  DUMP: WARNING: no file '/etc/dumpdates', making an empty one
  DUMP: Date of this level 0 dump: Sat Nov 19 14:37:02 2005
  DUMP: Dumping /dev/mapper/vg00-test (/work) to /tmp/foo4.out
  DUMP: Label: none
  DUMP: Writing 10 Kilobyte records
  DUMP: mapping (Pass I) [regular files]
  DUMP: mapping (Pass II) [directories]
  DUMP: estimated 89 blocks.
  DUMP: Volume 1 started with block 1 at: Sat Nov 19 14:37:02 2005
  DUMP: dumping (Pass III) [directories]
  DUMP: dumping (Pass IV) [regular files]
  DUMP: Closing /tmp/foo4.out
  DUMP: Volume 1 completed at: Sat Nov 19 14:37:02 2005
  DUMP: Volume 1 90 blocks (0.09MB)
  DUMP: 90 blocks (0.09MB) on 1 volume(s)
  DUMP: finished in less than a second
  DUMP: Date of this level 0 dump: Sat Nov 19 14:37:02 2005
  DUMP: Date this dump completed:  Sat Nov 19 14:37:02 2005
  DUMP: Average transfer rate: 0 kB/s
  DUMP: DUMP IS DONE
```

dd

dd is not a backup command per se, but it can be used to copy a raw device to tape or to a file. It is not flexible at all, and the only way to restore is to perform a full restore. An example of backing up a device with dd is:

```
dd if=/dev/hda1 of=/dev/st0 bs=10k
```

To recover this data, you reverse the command and write from the tape drive to the disk device, which overwrites any contents.

```
dd if=/dev/st0 of=/dev/hda1 bs=10k
```

As you can see, dd is not the most flexible utility. It is commonly used either to back up raw data partitions for databases or to clone an entire disk.

mkisofs

mkisofs creates an ISO file, which is in CD/DVD format. This file can then be written to CD/DVD. mkisofs is usually paired with cdrecord to write the ISO file to CD/DVD. One option is to turn the files or directories directly into an ISO and burn it to CD/DVD.

```
# mkisofs -o home_backup.iso -JRVv /home/
# cdrecord -v -eject -multi speed=8 dev=0,1,0 home_backup.iso
```

Another possibility is to use tar to zip up the files or directories first and then make them into an ISO and burn them to CD/DVD.

```
# tar -cvzWf /tmp/home_backup.tar.gz /home/
# mkisofs -o home_backup.iso -JrVv /m_backup.tar.gz
# cdrecord -v -eject -multi speed=8 dev=0,1,0 home_backup.iso
```

rsync

rsync is an incredible command. It is typically used to synchronize two directories. The rsync man page states:

```
DESCRIPTION

rsync is a program that behaves in much the same way that rcp does, but
has many more options and uses the rsync remote-update protocol to
greatly speed up file transfers when the destination file already exists.
The rsync remote-update protocol allows rsync to transfer just the
differences between two sets of files across the network link, using an
efficient checksum-search algorithm described in the technical report
that accompanies this package.

Some of the additional features of rsync are:
    o      support for copying links, devices, owners, groups and
           permissions
```

o   exclude and exclude-from options similar to GNU tar

o   a CVS exclude mode for ignoring the same files that CVS
     would ignore

o   can use any transparent remote shell, including rsh or ssh

o   does not require root privileges

o   pipelining of file transfers to minimize latency costs

o   support for anonymous or authenticated rsync servers (ideal
     for mirroring)

rsync is typically used to mirror data between two servers. Here are two examples:

* rsync -e ssh -av
  raffi@BackupServer.your_domain.com::/home/Backup/xfer/*
  /destination/xfer

* rsync -avz --delete HomeServer::/home/* /Backup/destination

Bare Metal Recovery

A bare metal backup and recovery utility enables you to make bootable recovery media. Four common utilities are available for Linux:

* mondo / mindi
* partimage
* systemimager
* g4u (Ghost for UNIX)

These utilities are great for a base-level backup but are not good for a day-to-day backup utility. The most likely scenario would be to use a bare metal backup utility once a month and then do dump backups daily. If you lost the system, you could quickly restore the bare metal backup and then do a quicker restore from the dump tapes. This differs from "bootable recovery media" such as Knoppix, GRUB boot media, and so on. Those tools are used to boot a system and perform maintenance. Bare metal recovery utilities back up a system and then recover it by writing the image to the hard disk.

I Have a Tape, and I Don't Know What It Is . . .

From time to time, an administrator is asked to pull data from a tape by a user. Occasionally the user might not know how the tape was created. How do you satisfy this request? First, you can try to use dd to read the first four records of a tape and then try to use file to identify it.

```
# dd if=/dev/st0 of=/tmp/foo5.out bs=1k count=4
4+0 records in
4+0 records out
4096 bytes (4.1 kB) copied, 0.000115 seconds, 35.6MB/s
# file /tmp/foo5.out
/tmp/foo5.out: new-fs dump file (little endian), This dump Sat Nov 19
14:37:02 2005, Previous dump Wed Dec 31 19:00:00 1969, Volume 1, Level
zero, type: tape header, Label none, Filesystem /work, Device
/dev/mapper/vg00-test, Host linux, Flags 3
```

You can also use file on files of an unknown type in a filesystem.

```
# file starwatch
starwatch: Zip archive data, at least v1.0 to extract
# file *gz
cllinux: gzip compressed data, was "crossl.tar", from Unix
```

How Can I Tell Whether My Tape Problem Is Hardware or Software?

When you have backup or recovery issues, the first step is to identify whether it is a software or hardware problem. For recovery problems, you can use od -c to read the beginning of a tape or archive file and make sure it is still in a readable format. This approach does not work if software compression is used.

Table 9-4 describes the file record layout for tar.

Table 9-4   File Record Layout for `tar`

Field Size	Field Descriptor	Detail
100	name	Name of file
8	mode	File mode
8	uid	Owner user ID
8	gid	Owner group ID
12	size	Length of file in bytes
12	mtime	Modify time of file
8	chksum	Checksum for header
1	typeflag	Type of file
100	linkname	Name of linked file
6	magic	USTAR indicator
2	version	USTAR version
32	uname	Owner user name
32	gname	Owner group name
8	devmajor	Device major number
8	devminor	Device minor number
155	prefix	Prefix for filename

The following is the `tar` file header (USTAR format):

```
# od -c /dev/st0 |more


0000000   w   o   r   k   /  \0  \0  \0  \0  \0  \0  \0  \0  \0  \0  \0
0000020  \0  \0  \0  \0  \0  \0  \0  \0  \0  \0  \0  \0  \0  \0  \0  \0
*
0000140  \0  \0  \0  \0   0   0   0   0   7   5   5  \0   0   0   0   0
0000160   0   0   0  \0   0   0   0   0   0   0   0  \0   0   0   0   0
0000200   0   0   0   0   0   0   0  \0   1   0   3   3   7   6   7   7
0000220   2   6   7  \0   0   1   0   5   6   0  \0       5  \0  \0  \0
```

```
0000240  \0  \0  \0  \0  \0  \0  \0  \0  \0  \0  \0  \0  \0  \0  \0  \0
*
0000400  \0   u   s   t   a   r      \0   r   o   o   t  \0  \0  \0
0000420  \0  \0  \0  \0  \0  \0  \0  \0  \0  \0  \0  \0  \0  \0  \0  \0
0000440  \0  \0  \0  \0  \0  \0  \0  \0  \0   r   o   o   t  \0  \0  \0
0000460  \0  \0  \0  \0  \0  \0  \0  \0  \0  \0  \0  \0  \0  \0  \0  \0
*
0001000   w   o   r   k   /   v   m   w   a   r   e   /  \0  \0  \0  \0
0001020  \0  \0  \0  \0  \0  \0  \0  \0  \0  \0  \0  \0  \0  \0  \0  \0
*
0001140  \0  \0  \0  \0   0   0   0   0   7   5   5  \0   0   0   0   0
0001160   0   0   0  \0   0   0   0   0   0   0   0  \0   0   0   0   0
0001200   0   0   0   0   0   0   0  \0   1   0   3   4   0   1   1   6
0001220   0   2   5  \0   0   1   2   0   2   7  \0       5  \0  \0  \0
```

```
# dd if=/dev/st0 of=/tmp/foo.out bs=1k count=4; file /tmp/foo.out
/tmp/foo.out: POSIX tar archive
```

As you can see, the first field is the file or directory name, as you would expect. All the other fields including `magic` look intact.

The same can be done with `cpio`, as shown in Table 9-5.

The ASCII `cpio` file header looks like this:

```
# od -c /dev/st0
0000000   0   7   0   7   0   1   0   0   0   0   4   d   b   b   0   0
0000020   0   0   8   1   a   4   0   0   0   0   0   0   0   0   0   0
0000040   0   0   0   0   0   0   0   0   0   0   0   0   0   1   4   2
0000060   d   d   6   2   4   e   0   0   0   0   0   0   3   0   0   0
0000100   0   0   0   0   f   d   0   0   0   0   0   0   0   0   0   0
0000120   0   0   0   0   0   0   0   0   0   0   0   0   0   0   0   0
0000140   0   0   0   0   1   1   0   0   0   0   0   0   0   0   /   e
0000160   t   c   /   r   e   s   o   l   v   .   c   o   n   f  \0  \0
```

```
# dd if=/dev/st0 of=/tmp/foo.out bs=1k count=4; file /tmp/foo.out
/tmp/foo.out: ASCII cpio archive (SVR4 with no CRC)
```

Table 9-5 File Record Layout for `cpio`

Field Size	Field Descriptor	Detail
6	magic	Magic number "070707"
6	dev	Device where file resides
6	ino	I-number of file
6	mode	File mode
6	uid	Owner user ID
6	gid	Owner group ID
6	nlink	Number of links to file
6	rdev	Device major/minor for special file
11	mtime	Modify time of file
6	Namesize	Length of filename
11	filesize	Length of file to follow

That technique does not work as well with dump because the tape format is more complicated. You can still use dd to read the header and then run file against it, though.

```
# dd if=/dev/st0 of=/tmp/foo.out bs=1k count=4; file /tmp/foo4.out
/tmp/foo4.out: new-fs dump file (little endian), This dump Sat Nov 19
14:37:02 2005, Previous dump Wed Dec 31 19:00:00 1969, Volume 1, Level
zero, type: tape header, Label none, Filesystem /work, Device
/dev/mapper/vg00-test, Host linux, Flags 3
```

Another common problem is when you can read a tape on your system but not on others. This problem is usually caused by misalignment of the tape heads on the drive. The tracks are readable and writable on your drive because they align. When the tape is taken to another system, the heads are not aligned with the tracks, so the tape is unreadable. An additional problem results when you have the tape drive fixed. This makes the tapes unreadable to your drive.

Backup failures due to hardware issues are much easier to diagnose than software problems. If a `tar` to a device fails, you can try a `cpio`. If both fail, the problem is typically hardware. The one exception to this would be a problem with the device file.

If a problem is diagnosed as hardware, I usually follow these steps:

1. Try multiple tapes.

2. Run the cleaning tape through five times.

3. Try a new tape.

If the backups still fail, it is most likely a bad drive.

If you replace a tape drive, and it fails again after a short period of time, it can be maddening. What are the chances of two bad tape drives in a row? Oddly enough, it is most likely your tapes that have ruined the second drive. Tape drive failures are very commonly caused by damaged or fouled heads. These damaged drives can then damage or foul the tapes. If you replace the tape drive, and you still have dirty or damaged tapes, they can destroy the new tape drive. If you have a second drive failure in a row, then you should replace the drive and replace all the tapes.

Summary

This chapter addressed several facets of backup and recovery, including backup media and the types of backup devices available, backup strategies, the benefits and limitations of different utilities, and ways to troubleshoot failing tape backups. Of course, one of the primary duties of the system administrator is protecting data, and this chapter should help you do it successfully.

10

cron and at

The cron and at packages provide Linux users with a method for scheduling jobs. at is used to run a job once. cron is used to run jobs on a schedule. If a report should be run every Friday at 8 p.m., cron is perfect for the job. If a user wants to run a sweep of the system to find a misplaced file, the job can be scheduled to run that evening using the at command.

This chapter explains how cron and at work. You might not be familiar with the anacron and kcron packages, but they extend the features of cron. We also explain these tools in this chapter. We show how to use cron and the other utilities, but we also show how they work and provide examples of what can go wrong.

This chapter is organized into the following sections:

- cron—The basics of cron are explained. The crontab command is used to submit and edit jobs. The reader will see the various crontab syntaxes and the format of the cron configuration file. The other files cron uses are explained as well. The cron daemon runs the jobs submitted with crontab. This topic details how the daemon gets started, where it logs, and the differences between cron packages. We also discuss a graphical front end to crontab called kcron.

- anacron—anacron is a utility to run jobs cron missed due to system downtime. Learn how it works in this section.

- at—at is a utility similar to cron that runs jobs once. We show examples of submitting, removing, and monitoring jobs with at.

We conclude the chapter with a section on four troubleshooting scenarios that demonstrate good methodologies for fixing problems with cron.

cron

The crontab command is used to manage cron jobs. The -l option displays the current list of jobs for the user. The following example runs the report mentioned in this chapter's introduction:

```
[dave@sawnee dave]$ crontab -l
# DO NOT EDIT THIS FILE - edit the master and reinstall.
# (/tmp/crontab.9889 installed on Fri Oct 15 09:42:06 2004)
# (Cron version -- $Id: crontab.c,v 2.13 1994/01/17 03:20:37 vixie Exp $)
0 20 * * fri /home/dave/acct_prod_rpt.sh
```

The crontab command is the only user command that cron provides. There is a cron daemon to run jobs, but only crontab is run from the command line by users. It is used to create, edit, or display the crontab configuration file, which is called a crontab file for a user. Switches available for the crontab command are shown in Table 10-1.

Table 10-1   crontab Switches

Command and Switch	Description
crontab -l	Display the information for scheduled jobs
crontab -e	Edit the user's list of scheduled jobs
crontab -r	Remove the definition of scheduled jobs
crontab <filename>	Replace the current crontab file

We recommend using crontab -l rather than crontab -e to make crontab changes. For example:

```
$ crontab -l >crontab.out              # Saves the crontab file
$ cp crontab.out crontab.bkup          # Create backup
```

```
$ vi crontab.out            # Make desired changes
$ crontab crontab.out       # Activate the changes
$ crontab -l                # Verify changes
```

It took us five commands to modify the crontab file, but we do have a backup of the original as well as a copy of the new crontab. We could have just run crontab -e to edit the crontab file. When you run crontab -e for the first time, an editor starts with an empty document. Add the job command lines and save the file, and a crontab file is created for the user. If you would rather not use the default editor, set the EDITOR environment variable first. For example, run export EDITOR=vim;crontab -e to edit the crontab file with the vim editor.

The crontab entries can be set using monthly, weekly, daily, and hourly time definitions. The crontab(5) man page shows the format of the crontab lines. The time and date fields from the man page are shown in Table 10-2.

Table 10-2   Time and Date Fields and Allowable Values

Field	Allowed Values
Minute	0–59
Hour	0–23
Day of month	1–31
Month	1–12 (or names, see below)
Day of week	0–7 (0 or 7 is Sun, or use names)

Follow the scheduling fields with the command to be run. The following crontab entry runs a backup process every day at 11:00 p.m.:

```
00 23 * * * /prod_serv/scripts/prod_backup_2
```

This entry runs a report at 6:15 a.m. on the first of every month:

```
15 6 1 * * /prod_serv/scripts/monthly_reports
```

This one runs a report every weekday at 2 p.m.:

```
0 14 * * 1-5 /home/ted/daily_rpt.sh
```

The crontab command validates the formatting of the command lines. Look at the output from crontab -e when the minute and hour fields are reversed:

```
[ted@sawnee ted]$ crontab -e

9 50 * * * /home/ted/sweep.sh
~

~

~

~


no crontab for ted - using an empty one
crontab: installing new crontab
"/tmp/crontab.1279":0: bad hour
errors in crontab file, can't install.
Do you want to retry the same edit?
```

Consider inserting this snippet from the crontab(5) man page as a comment block in your crontab files so that it is easy to understand the format of the job command lines:

```
################################################################
#              field        allowed values
#              ------        --------------
#              minute        0-59
#              hour          0-23
#              day of month  1-31
#              month         1-12 (or names, see below)
#              day of week   0-7 (0 or 7 is Sun, or use names)
# min   hour   day   month   wkday
################################################################
```

crontab does not validate the paths of commands, however, as you can see here:

```
[ted@sawnee ted]$ crontab -l
# DO NOT EDIT THIS FILE - edit the master and reinstall.
# (/tmp/crontab.26370 installed on Mon Aug 30 08:57:28 2004)
# (Cron version -- $Id: crontab.c,v 2.13 1994/01/17 03:20:37 vixie Exp $)
```

```
DBHOME="/prod_serv"
03 09 * * * /home/ted/sweeper.sh
```

crontab accepted the file, but look at the email Ted receives when it is executed by cron:

```
From: root@sawnee.somecomp.com (Cron Daemon)
To: ted@sawnee.somecomp.com
Subject: Cron <ted@sawnee> /home/ted/sweeper.sh
X-Cron-Env: <DBHOME=/prod_serv>
X-Cron-Env: <SHELL=/bin/sh>
X-Cron-Env: <HOME=/home/ted>
X-Cron-Env: <PATH=/usr/bin:/bin>
X-Cron-Env: <LOGNAME=ted>


/bin/sh: line 1: /home/ted/sweeper.sh: No such file or directory
```

Environment variables can be added to the crontab file as well as comments. cron sets very few environment variables. The path is set to /usr/bin:/bin, and the shell is /bin/sh. If environment variables from the shell are needed, they must be set manually in the crontab file. For example, the following crontab sets DBHOME, DBINST, and the PATH variable:

```
# DO NOT EDIT THIS FILE - edit the master and reinstall.
# (/tmp/crontab.1828 installed on Mon Sep 13 17:26:58 2004)
# (Cron version -- $Id: crontab.c,v 2.13 1994/01/17 03:20:37 vixie Exp $)
DBHOME=/prod_serv/scripts
DBINST=prod
PATH=/home/susan/bin:/usr/local/bin:/usr/bin:/usr/X11R6/bin:/bin:/usr/gam
es:/opt/gnome/bin:/opt/kde3/bin:


30 17 * * * /prod_serv/scripts/prod_daily_report
```

Output from a cron job is mailed to the owner of the crontab. There is a cron environment variable MAILTO. If set, any cron email goes to the user specified by MAILTO. If MAILTO="", no email is sent by cron. For further information, see the crontab(5) man page.

cron and at are similar but not identical among Linux distributions. We show Red Hat and SUSE examples and provide techniques to understand the differences in other Linux distributions.

The crontab files are stored in the /var/spool/cron directory in Red Hat and /var/spool/cron/tabs in SUSE. The directory contains one file for every user with a cron schedule. The user name is the name of the crontab file. The crontab(1) man page has more detailed information.

The capability to use crontab can be restricted by the system administrator by creating an allow or deny file. In Red Hat, the files are /etc/cron.allow and /etc/cron.deny. In SUSE, the files are /var/spool/cron/allow and deny. The allow file is a list of users who can run the crontab command. The deny file is a list of users who cannot. Both files are just lists of user names. For example:

```
$ cat /etc/cron.allow
dave
root
```

If the allow file exists but does not contain dbuser, then the database administrator (DBA) sees the following message when trying to run crontab while logged in as dbuser:

```
$ crontab -e
You (dbuser) are not allowed to use this program (crontab)
See crontab(1) for more information
```

If the deny file exists and the allow file does not exist, all users can run crontab except those listed in the deny file. The allow file takes precedence. If both allow and deny exist, a user listed in both files can use crontab. To prevent any user from running crontab, including root, create an empty allow file. The at command uses /etc/at.allow and /etc/at.deny and follows the same rules as crontab.

The directory permissions on /var/spool/cron or /var/spool/cron/tabs limit access to only the root user to prevent users from manually creating or editing a crontab file. This forces users to use only the crontab command to change their crontab files. The system administrator should not manually edit these files either.

```
# ls -al /var/spool/cron
total 16
drwx------    2 root     root          4096 Aug 11 10:54 .
drwxr-xr-x   16 root     root          4096 Nov  6  2003 ..
-rw-------    1 root     dave           254 Jul 31 12:53 dave
-rw-------    1 root     dbadmin        280 Aug 11 10:51 dbadmin
```

The crontab command has the setuid bit set so that non-root users can edit their own crontab files:

```
# ls -l /usr/bin/crontab
-rwsr-xr-x    1 root     root        110114 Feb 19  2003
/usr/bin/crontab
```

Try to lock down the crontab command by changing the permissions to 555, and you receive the following error when running it as a non-root user:

```
[dave@sawnee dave]$ crontab -e
seteuid: Operation not permitted
```

Root has a special crontab file, /etc/crontab. The format is slightly different. The job command line has an additional field to specify what user cron should use to run the job. The default Red Hat /etc/crontab is:

```
SHELL=/bin/bash
PATH=/sbin:/bin:/usr/sbin:/usr/bin
MAILTO=root
HOME=/

# run-parts
01 * * * * root run-parts /etc/cron.hourly
02 4 * * * root run-parts /etc/cron.daily
22 4 * * 0 root run-parts /etc/cron.weekly
42 4 1 * * root run-parts /etc/cron.monthly
```

The /etc/crontab supplied with Red Hat Linux makes use of the run-parts script. On a Linux installation, there are probably several processes that should be run daily such as backups and reports. There can be weekly or monthly jobs such as reports, software updates, system scans, and so on. This is the beauty of the run-parts script. The /etc/crontab shown previously runs the daily jobs at 4:02 a.m., the weekly jobs at 4:22 a.m. on Sunday, and the monthly jobs at 4:42 a.m. on the first day of the month.

The /usr/bin/run-parts script expects to be supplied with a directory path as an argument. The run-parts script executes all the scripts contained in that directory except for those ending in rpmsave, rpmorig, rpmnew, and swp scripts. There is no man page for run-parts, but it is a simple script to read and understand.

The functionality provided by /usr/bin/run-parts is very important. A software package that includes a cron job can be written to place a file in the appropriate /etc/cron.hourly, cron.daily, cron.weekly, or cron.monthly directory rather than trying to manipulate root's crontab file. This capability makes creating packages containing cron jobs manageable. You can see which packages delivered cron jobs to a Linux system with the command rpm -qa --filesbypkg|grep '/etc/cron'.

The SUSE /etc/crontab file is similar to Red Hat's /etc/crontab:

```
SHELL=/bin/sh
PATH=/usr/bin:/usr/sbin:/sbin:/bin:/usr/lib/news/bin
MAILTO=root
#
# check scripts in cron.hourly, cron.daily, cron.weekly, and cron.monthly
#
-*/15 * * * *    root   test -x /usr/lib/cron/run-crons && /usr/lib/
cron/run-crons >/dev/null 2>&1
59 *   * * *     root   rm -f /var/spool/cron/lastrun/cron.hourly
14 4   * * *     root   rm -f /var/spool/cron/lastrun/cron.daily
29 4   * * 6     root   rm -f /var/spool/cron/lastrun/cron.weekly
44 4   1 * *     root   rm -f /var/spool/cron/lastrun/cron.monthly
```

SUSE Linux supplies the run-crons script. It runs the jobs in the /etc/cron.* directories like run-parts does on Red Hat. cron on SUSE is configured to use /var/spool/cron/lastrun to keep track of the last time that the /etc/cron.* scripts were run. cron does not log the run-crons job execution.

Make sure only root can write to the /etc/cron.hourly, /etc/cron.daily, /etc/cron.weekly, and /etc/cron.monthly directories. Otherwise, any user can save a script in one of these directories and use cron to run his or her process with root privileges. Notice that the command line indicates that root should run these scripts. Even if the script in /etc/cron.daily is owned by a user, it is executed with root privileges.

```
# ls -ld /etc/cron.*
drwxr-xr-x    2 root       root          4096 Feb 19  2003 /etc/cron.d
drwxr-xr-x    2 root       root          4096 Aug 10 04:08 /etc/cron.daily
drwxr-xr-x    2 root       root          4096 Nov  6  2003 /etc/cron.hourly
drwxr-xr-x    2 root       root          4096 Nov  6  2003 /etc/cron.monthly
drwxr-xr-x    2 root       root          4096 Nov  6  2003 /etc/cron.weekly
```

note

You can confirm that the permissions of a package are correct with the rpm -V cron_package_name command. You can confirm the permissions of a single file or directory with rpm -V -f filename. Troubleshooting using rpm is covered later in this chapter.

Here is a sample /etc/cron.daily:

```
# ll /etc/cron.daily
total 36
-rwxr-xr-x    1 root       root          135 Jan 25  2003 00webalizer
-rwxr-xr-x    1 root       root          276 Jan 24  2003 0anacron
-rwxr-xr-x    1 root       root          123 Jan 26  2003 inn-cron-expire
-rwxr-xr-x    1 root       root           51 Jan 24  2003 logrotate
-rwxr-xr-x    1 root       root          418 Feb 10  2003 makewhatis.cron
-rwxr-xr-x    1 root       root          135 May 14 15:59 rpm
-rwxr-xr-x    1 root       root          132 Jan 21  2004 slocate.cron
-rwxr-xr-x    1 root       root          164 May 17 09:18 sophos
-rwxr-xr-x    1 root       root          193 Feb 10  2003 tmpwatch
```

cron Daemon

The cron daemon (/usr/sbin/cron for SUSE and /usr/sbin/crond for Red Hat) is responsible for running the cron jobs. Every minute, the cron daemon looks at the crontabs, loads new or modified crontabs into memory, and checks whether any jobs are scheduled to execute during that minute. The cron daemon is started during the startup scripts at runlevels 2, 3, 4, and 5.

```
#chkconfig --list crond
crond            0:off   1:off   2:on    3:on    4:on    5:on    6:off
```

The startup script is /etc/init.d/crond in Red Hat and /etc/init.d/cron in SUSE. For more information on startup scripts, refer to Chapter 1, "System Boot, Startup, and Shutdown Issues."

A log entry is created when cron jobs are run, crontab commands are used, the cron daemon is started, and so on. cron uses the syslog daemon to log cron events. The syslog facility for cron messages is cron. See the syslogd(8) man page for an explanation of how syslog routes messages. The log file for cron is determined by /etc/syslog. conf. Red Hat has a log just for cron, /var/log/cron, to log cron messages. SUSE uses /var/log/messages. A Red Hat /etc/syslog.conf has the following entry to route cron messages to /var/log/cron:

```
# Log cron stuff
cron.*                                    /var/log/cron
```

With Red Hat, cron messages are not duplicated in /var/log/messages because of the cron.none on the following syslog.conf line:

```
*.info;mail.none;news.none;authpriv.none;cron.none /var/log/messages
```

It would be a simple matter to change SUSE systems to log cron messages to /var/log/cron. Here is a sample of the entries that are written to Red Hat's /var/log/cron file:

```
Aug 15 04:22:00 sawnee CROND[25198]: (root) CMD (run-parts
/etc/cron.weekly)
Aug 15 04:22:04 sawnee anacron[25202]: Updated timestamp for job
'cron.weekly' to 2004-08-15
```

```
Aug 15 05:01:00 sawnee CROND[2420]: (root) CMD (run-parts
/etc/cron.hourly)
Aug 15 06:01:00 sawnee CROND[2519]: (root) CMD (run-parts
/etc/cron.hourly)
Aug 15 07:01:00 sawnee CROND[2532]: (root) CMD (run-parts
/etc/cron.hourly)
Aug 15 08:01:00 sawnee CROND[2544]: (root) CMD (run-parts
/etc/cron.hourly)
Aug 15 09:01:00 sawnee CROND[2556]: (root) CMD (run-parts
/etc/cron.hourly)
Aug 15 10:01:00 sawnee CROND[2568]: (root) CMD (run-parts
/etc/cron.hourly)
Aug 15 11:01:00 sawnee CROND[2588]: (root) CMD (run-parts
/etc/cron.hourly)
Aug 15 12:01:00 sawnee CROND[2600]: (root) CMD (run-parts
/etc/cron.hourly)
Aug 15 13:01:00 sawnee CROND[2612]: (root) CMD (run-parts
/etc/cron.hourly)
Aug 15 14:01:00 sawnee CROND[2910]: (root) CMD (run-parts
/etc/cron.hourly)
Aug 15 14:35:46 sawnee crontab[3107]: (dave) LIST (dave)
Aug 15 14:36:56 sawnee crontab[3113]: (dave) BEGIN EDIT (dave)
Aug 15 14:37:03 sawnee crontab[3113]: (dave) REPLACE (dave)
Aug 15 14:37:03 sawnee crontab[3113]: (dave) END EDIT (dave)
Aug 15 14:37:09 sawnee crontab[3116]: (dave) BEGIN EDIT (dave)
Aug 15 14:37:13 sawnee crontab[3116]: (dave) REPLACE (dave)
Aug 15 14:37:13 sawnee crontab[3116]: (dave) END EDIT (dave)
Aug 15 14:38:00 sawnee crond[1792]: (dave) RELOAD (cron/dave)
Aug 15 14:38:00 sawnee CROND[3166]: (dave) CMD (/home/dave/daily_rpt)
```

The sample cron log shows cron activity on host sawnee. cron events are broken out by crond, crontab, and CROND (which shows jobs being started). The number between the [ ] is the process ID. Everything that crontab performs is logged. Note that run-parts is listed as one job and is not broken down by each job in /etc/cron.hourly.

As we noted earlier, cron and at are similar but not identical across Linux distributions. To understand the differences, look closely at the man pages, see which packages are installed, and look for additional documentation supplied with the packages. Run rpm -qa to see what packages are installed. This list is from a Red Hat 9.0 system:

```
# rpm -qa|grep cron
crontabs-1.10-5
vixie-cron-3.0.1-74
anacron-2.3-25
```

A typical SUSE 9.0 system might show:

```
# rpm -qa|grep cron
cron-3.0.1-824
```

The package name doesn't indicate it, but this is vixie-cron too, which can be verified in the README supplied with the package.

Look at the files delivered with the packages by running rpm -q --filesbypkg. Take note of man pages, READMEs, and other documentation provided with each package. You can see what commands are available with the package as well as what documentation you can review. Here are the files delivered with Red Hat 9.0:

```
# rpm -q --filesbypkg vixie-cron-3.0.1-74
vixie-cron              /etc/cron.d
vixie-cron              /etc/rc.d/init.d/crond
vixie-cron              /usr/bin/crontab
vixie-cron              /usr/sbin/crond
vixie-cron              /usr/share/man/man1/crontab.1.gz
vixie-cron              /usr/share/man/man5/crontab.5.gz
vixie-cron              /usr/share/man/man8/cron.8.gz
vixie-cron              /usr/share/man/man8/crond.8.gz
vixie-cron              /var/spool/cron

# rpm -q --filesbypkg crontabs-1.10-5
crontabs                /etc/cron.daily
crontabs                /etc/cron.hourly
crontabs                /etc/cron.monthly
crontabs                /etc/cron.weekly
crontabs                /etc/crontab
crontabs                /usr/bin/run-parts
```

SUSE 9.0 delivers the following files with the cron package:

```
# rpm -q --filesbypkg cron-3.0.1-824
cron                   /etc/crontab
cron                   /etc/init.d/cron
cron                   /usr/bin/crontab
cron                   /usr/lib/cron
cron                   /usr/lib/cron/run-crons
cron                   /usr/sbin/cron
cron                   /usr/sbin/rccron
cron                   /usr/share/doc/packages/cron
cron                   /usr/share/doc/packages/cron/CHANGES
cron                   /usr/share/doc/packages/cron/CONVERSION
cron                   /usr/share/doc/packages/cron/FEATURES
cron                   /usr/share/doc/packages/cron/MAIL
cron                   /usr/share/doc/packages/cron/MANIFEST
cron                   /usr/share/doc/packages/cron/README
cron                   /usr/share/doc/packages/cron/THANKS
cron                   /usr/share/man/man1/crontab.1.gz
cron                   /usr/share/man/man5/crontab.5.gz
cron                   /usr/share/man/man8/cron.8.gz
cron                   /var/spool/cron
cron                   /var/spool/cron/deny
cron                   /var/spool/cron/lastrun
cron                   /var/spool/cron/tabs
```

Listing the files delivered in the package makes it easy to see the differences between distributions.

kcron

A nice graphical front-end utility is available for the crontab command. The kcron utility is part of KDE and is supplied with the optional kdeadmin package. The kcron utility is a simple, intuitive method for users to manage their cron jobs. The English version of the kcron handbook is available at http://docs.kde.org/en/3.1/kdeadmin/kcron/

index.html. To start kcron, choose System Tools, Task Scheduler from the main KDE menu, and you will see the interface shown in Figure 10-1.

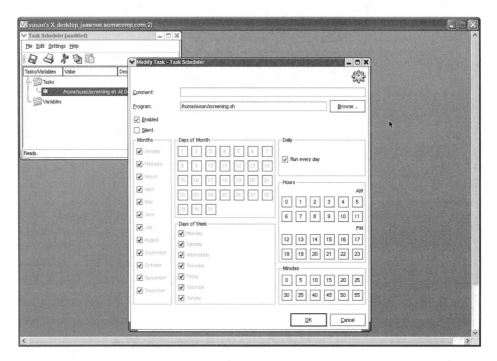

Figure 10-1 The kcron interface

No crontab knowledge is needed to schedule jobs when kcron is used. Users don't have to learn vi just to schedule a job. kcron inserts a header and a footer in the crontab file, so the system administrator knows it was saved from kcron. Here is an example:

```
$ crontab -l
# DO NOT EDIT THIS FILE - edit the master and reinstall.
# (/tmp/kde-susan/kcronzMmGJa.tmp installed on Tue Sep  7 09:47:40 2004)
# (Cron version -- $Id: crontab.c,v 2.13 1994/01/17 03:20:37 vixie Exp $)
#
5 4 * * *       /home/susan/screening.sh
# This file was written by KCron. Copyright (c) 1999, Gary Meyer
# Although KCron supports most crontab formats, use care when editing.
# Note: Lines beginning with "#\" indicates a disabled task.
```

There are a couple of wrinkles with kcron. kcron does not seem to be aware of the crontab allow and deny files, meaning users who are restricted from using the crontab command can still create cron tasks.

If kcron is run as root, the save function saves crontab files for every user on the system even if only root's jobs were modified. If the user already has a crontab file, kcron inserts its header and footer. If the user doesn't have a crontab file, kcron creates one with the normal crontab header plus the kcron header line. We don't recommend using kcron as root, but it is fine for other users.

To see the list of known bugs in kcron, visit http://bugs.kde.org/. We submitted new bug reports for those we mentioned here:

> Bug 89488: kcron doesn't prohibit crontab changes based on cron's allow and deny files.

> Bug 89491: kcron creates crontab files for all users when the root crontab is created.

More information about KDE is available at http://www.kde.org/.

anacron

anacron is similar to cron, and it works much the same way. anacron is intended to run jobs in /etc/crontab that cron missed due to system downtime. If a Linux box is left on continuously, anacron won't run any jobs because cron will run them. anacron has its own crontab file, /etc/anacrontab. Changes made to /etc/crontab need to be made in /etc/anacrontab as well. anacron is a utility for root only. There is no anacrontab command to edit the file for users. The system administrator should edit the file manually. Here is the anacrontab supplied with anacron on Red Hat systems:

```
# /etc/anacrontab: configuration file for anacron

# See anacron(8) and anacrontab(5) for details.

SHELL=/bin/sh
PATH=/usr/local/sbin:/usr/local/bin:/sbin:/bin:/usr/sbin:/usr/bin
```

```
1       65       cron.daily        run-parts /etc/cron.daily
7       70       cron.weekly       run-parts /etc/cron.weekly
30      75       cron.monthly      run-parts /etc/cron.monthly
```

The format is similar to the crontab files, but there are some differences. The first few lines set the shell and path. The remaining lines contain the scripts to execute; anacron calls these job description lines.

The first field of the job description line indicates how many days should occur between runs of the process. The second field indicates how many minutes to wait before starting the process. The third field is the job identifier. The last field and remainder of the line is the shell command to execute.

See the anacrontab(8) man page for further details.

The anacrontab file doesn't execute run-parts /etc/cron.hourly because the smallest time unit for anacron is one day.

There is a potential problem with the previous anacrontab file. The full path to the run-parts script is not given. The run-parts script is in /usr/bin. The /usr/local/ sbin and /usr/local/bin directories are searched before /usr/bin according to the PATH variable. If users have write permission to /usr/local/sbin or /usr/local/bin, a script called run-parts could be placed in those directories and would run instead of the intended /usr/bin/run-parts. This issue can be prevented by always using the full path for scripts in anacrontab. For example:

```
# /etc/anacrontab: configuration file for anacron

# See anacron(8) and anacrontab(5) for details.

SHELL=/bin/sh
PATH=/usr/local/sbin:/usr/local/bin:/sbin:/bin:/usr/sbin:/usr/bin

1       65       cron.daily        /usr/bin/run-parts /etc/cron.daily
7       70       cron.weekly       /usr/bin/run-parts /etc/cron.weekly
30      75       cron.monthly      /usr/bin/run-parts /etc/cron.monthly
```

anacron is started by a startup script.

```
#chkconfig --list anacron
anacron          0:off    1:off    2:on    3:on    4:on    5:on    6:off
```

anacron checks the timestamp files in /var/spool/anacron and runs any jobs that were missed.

```
# ls -al /var/spool/anacron
total 20
drwxr-xr-x    2 root     root         4096 Nov  6  2003 .
drwxr-xr-x   16 root     root         4096 Nov  6  2003 ..
-rw-------    1 root     root            9 Aug 14 12:53 cron.daily
-rw-------    1 root     root            9 Aug  1 04:42 cron.monthly
-rw-------    1 root     root            9 Aug  8 04:22 cron.weekly
```

anacron records whether cron is running normally so that jobs are not run twice. This is done with an anacron script in /etc/cron.daily, /etc/cron.weekly, and /etc/cron.monthly, which is executed by cron. The anacron -u command is run by this anacron script to update the timestamps and indicate that all jobs were run for that day by cron.

anacron messages route to the same log file as cron messages. anacron logs messages using syslogd with the facility value set to cron. Here are some sample anacron log entries:

```
Aug 18 10:43:58 sawnee anacron[2489]: Job 'cron.daily' started
Aug 18 10:43:58 sawnee anacron[2687]: Updated timestamp for job
'cron.daily' to 2004-08-18
```

The following files are delivered with anacron:

```
# rpm -q --filesbypkg anacron 2.3 25
anacron                  /etc/anacrontab
anacron                  /etc/cron.daily/0anacron
anacron                  /etc/cron.monthly/0anacron
```

anacron	/etc/cron.weekly/0anacron
anacron	/etc/rc.d/init.d/anacron
anacron	/usr/sbin/anacron
anacron	/usr/share/doc/anacron-2.3
anacron	/usr/share/doc/anacron-2.3/COPYING
anacron	/usr/share/doc/anacron-2.3/README
anacron	/usr/share/man/man5/anacrontab.5.gz
anacron	/usr/share/man/man8/anacron.8.gz
anacron	/var/spool/anacron

at

The /usr/bin/at command is used to submit jobs for later execution. Jobs submitted with at are run once at the specified time.

Specify the script or binary to run along with the time specification. Here are a few examples showing how a database administrator could submit a job to run a daily report:

```
at -f /prod_serv/scripts/prod_daily_report now + 1 minute
at -f /prod_serv/scripts/prod_daily_report now + 1 hour
at -f /prod_serv/scripts/prod_daily_report 13:55
at -f /prod_serv/scripts/prod_daily_report 4am + 3 days
```

The time specification format is very flexible. See the at(1) man page and /usr/share/doc/at-3.1.8/timespec for more details. Jobs submitted with at inherit the environment variables of the shell from which they were submitted.

Several more commands are provided with the at package. See the man page for a complete list and description. Here are a few useful examples.

To list jobs that are queued, use this command:

```
# atq
5        2004-08-18 04:00 a root
4        2004-08-15 14:54 a root
```

To remove a job with an ID number of 4, use this command:

```
# atrm 4
# atq
5        2004-08-18 04:00 a root
```

Linux provides a `batch` command that works similarly to `at`, except that the command runs when the load average of the system is less than .8 or the value specified with the `atrun` command. See the next topic for details on `atrun`. An execution time is not specified when submitting a job with the `batch` command. For example:

```
# batch -f /prod_serv/scripts/prod_daily_report
```

The `/etc/at.allow` and `/etc/at.deny` files can be used to control which users can run at and batch. Their format and use are the same as `cron`'s allow and deny files.

at jobs are queued as files in `/var/spool/at` in Red Hat and `/var/spool/atjobs` in SUSE. The job files are plain text files.

at Daemon and atrun

Jobs submitted using `at` are started either by a daemon `atd` process or by the `atrun` script. The newer method is to have `atd` run as a daemon. You can determine whether `atd` is started as a daemon by using `chkconfig`:

```
#chkconfig --list atd
atd             0:off   1:off   2:off   3:on    4:on    5:on    6:off
```

Here we see `atd` is started at runlevels 3, 4, and 5. If `atd` is not started as a daemon at startup, the `atrun` script should be started by `cron` periodically to run the at jobs. `atrun` is just a simple script to run `atd`:

```
#! /bin/ch
prefix=/usr
exec_prefix=/usr
exec /usr/sbin/atd -s "$@"
```

The at README (/usr/share/doc/at-3.1.8/README) suggests adding a line to root's crontab file to start atrun every five minutes:

```
* * * * 0,5,10,15,20,25,30,35,40,45,50,55 /usr/sbin/atrun
```

If atd runs as a daemon, the at jobs run instantly. The cost is one additional process as overhead, but that is a small price to pay. If atrun is started with the previous crontab entry, the at jobs are checked only every five minutes. The atrun command can be executed with the -l *load average* parameter to specify the load average at which jobs submitted with batch will run.

Here are the files delivered with the Red Hat 9.0 at package:

```
#  rpm -q --filesbypkg at
at                       /etc/at.deny
at                       /etc/rc.d/init.d/atd
at                       /usr/bin/at
at                       /usr/bin/atq
at                       /usr/bin/atrm
at                       /usr/bin/batch
at                       /usr/sbin/atd
at                       /usr/sbin/atrun
at                       /usr/share/doc/at-3.1.8
at                       /usr/share/doc/at-3.1.8/ChangeLog
at                       /usr/share/doc/at-3.1.8/Copyright
at                       /usr/share/doc/at-3.1.8/Problems
at                       /usr/share/doc/at-3.1.8/README
at                       /usr/share/doc/at-3.1.8/timespec
at                       /usr/share/man/man1/at.1.gz
at                       /usr/share/man/man1/atq.1.gz
at                       /usr/share/man/man1/atrm.1.gz
at                       /usr/share/man/man1/batch.1.gz
at                       /usr/share/man/man5/at.allow.5.gz
at                       /usr/share/man/man5/at.deny.5.gz
at                       /usr/share/man/man8/atd.8.gz
at                       /usr/share/man/man8/atrun.8.gz
at                       /var/spool/at
at                       /var/spool/at/.SEQ
at                       /var/spool/at/spool
```

Troubleshooting cron

We present four troubleshooting scenarios to demonstrate different strategies for resolving some common problems with cron. The examples are limited to cron because cron is by far the most popular of the utilities in this chapter. Also, these examples should provide the information needed to troubleshoot problems in the other utilities covered.

The first scenario shows how to use the information cron provides. Many issues can be resolved just by understanding what the emails from cron and cron's syslog messages mean. The second scenario shows that cron can start a process only to have it hang. The third scenario shows a problem with the cron daemon. Finally, we cover a problem common to many log files.

Scenario 10-1: Using cron Output for Debugging

The database administrator complains that his report doesn't run. Not that our DBA would mislead us intentionally, but let's check the crontab to verify the job entry.

We can confirm the job entry with the crontab command. We use the -u dbprod option to look at another user's crontab. Only root can do this.

```
# crontab -u dbprod -l
# DO NOT EDIT THIS FILE - edit the master and reinstall.
# (/tmp/crontab.3389 installed on Sun Aug 15 15:04:14 2004)
# (Cron version -- $Id: crontab.c,v 2.13 1994/01/17 03:20:37 vixie Exp $)
06 15 * * * /prod_serv/scripts/prod_daily_reports
```

We could just cat the crontab file as well:

```
# cat /var/spool/cron/dbprod
# DO NOT EDIT THIS FILE - edit the master and reinstall.
# (/tmp/crontab.3389 installed on Sun Aug 15 15:04:14 2004)
# (Cron version -- $Id: crontab.c,v 2.13 1994/01/17 03:20:37 vixie Exp $)
06 15 * * * /prod_serv/scripts/prod_daily_reports
```

The crontab entry looks good. The next step is to check the cron log to see if we can determine whether cron started the job. There should be a line in /var/log/cron similar to the following:

```
Aug 15 15:06:00 sawnee CROND[3400]: (dbprod) CMD
(/prod_serv/scripts/prod_daily_reports)
```

The cron log shows that cron did start the job at 15:06, and the process ID is 3400. We know the job ran. But did it finish? The crontab command line doesn't redirect standard output (stdout) or standard error (stderr), so any output should go to dbprod's mail.

```
From dbprod@sawnee.somecomp.com  Sun Aug 15 15:06:00 2004
Date: Sun, 15 Aug 2004 15:06:00 -0400
From: root@sawnee.somecomp.com (Cron Daemon)
To: dbprod@sawnee.somecomp.com
Subject: Cron <dbprod@sawnee> /prod_serv/scripts/prod_daily_reports
X-Cron-Env: <SHELL=/bin/sh>
X-Cron-Env: <HOME=/home/dbprod>
X-Cron-Env: <PATH=/usr/bin:/bin>
X-Cron-Env: <LOGNAME=dbprod>


/bin/sh: line 1: /prod_serv/scripts/prod_daily_reports: No such file or
directory
```

We can see from the message that the DBA probably made a typo. We should confirm this idea:

```
# ll /prod_serv/scripts/
total 12
-rwx------   1 dbprod   root           73 Aug  5 17:32 prod_backup_1
-rwx------   1 dbprod   root           42 Jul 27 18:15 prod_backup_2
-rwx------   1 dbprod   root           79 Aug 15 13:51 prod_daily_report
```

Looks like the DBA meant to run prod_daily_report rather than prod_daily_reports.

If dbprod's crontab redirects stdout (standard out) and stderr (standard error) to /dev/null, the output is thrown away. 1 is always the file number of stdout, and 2 is the file number for stderr. The >/dev/null 2>&1 on the following crontab entry means make stdout /dev/null and make stderr the same file as stdout, which throws away the script output and any error messages:

```
06 15 * * * /prod_serv/scripts/prod_daily_reports >/dev/null 2>&1
```

The /dev/null file is not a real file. The device file throws away anything written to it:

```
# ls -l /dev/null
crw-rw-rw-    1 root      root        1,   3 Oct  2 2003 /dev/null
```

cron jobs often redirect output to /dev/null to avoid having to trim a log file or delete lots of emails from cron. If the cron job stops working, the crontab line should be modified to send stdout and stderr to a log file so that any output from the script can be examined:

```
06 15 * * * /prod_serv/scripts/prod_daily_reports >/tmp/dbprod.out 2>&1
```

The crontab could be changed to email the user with any output:

```
06 15 * * * /prod_serv/scripts/prod_daily_reports
```

Set the time fields so that the job runs again and see whether any output is generated.

Scenario 10-2: Using pstree to Find a Hanging cron Job

Ted, a software engineer, complains that his code sweep didn't run. Using the troubleshooting steps from the first scenario, we verify that Ted's job should have been run at 7:47 a.m.:

```
# crontab -u ted -l
# DO NOT EDIT THIS FILE - edit the master and reinstall.
# (/tmp/crontab.5691 installed on Mon Aug 16 07:45:59 2004)
# (Cron version -- $Id: crontab.c,v 2.13 1994/01/17 03:20:37 vixie Exp $)
47 07 * * * /home/ted/sweep.sh
```

The job was started according to the cron log:

```
Aug 16 07:47:00 sawnee CROND[5697]: (ted) CMD (/home/ted/sweep.sh)
```

The user ted has not received email from cron. We know the job was started but never finished. Thus, it is probably still running. The pstree command is a good way to see what cron is doing. pstree shows process parent-child relationships in a tree format. Here is the entry for ted's job:

```
├─crond ── crond ─┬─ sendmail
│                 └─ sh ── find ── sh ── sleep
```

If necessary, we could look at the output from ps -ef to see more detail. We can see from the cron log that the process ID for the job is 5697. The process might be working normally or could be hanging, but cron is doing its job.

Scenario 10-3: Jobs Not Started Because cron Daemon Is Not Running

Ted's back. He says his code sweep didn't run. Running through the steps, we check the crontab and cron log.

The crontab has a job that should have run at 9:15 a.m.

```
[root@sawnee root]# crontab -u ted -l
# DO NOT EDIT THIS FILE - edit the master and reinstall.
# (/tmp/crontab.5962 installed on Mon Aug 16 09:13:24 2004)
# (Cron version -- $Id: crontab.c,v 2.13 1994/01/17 03:20:37 vixie Exp $)
15 09 * * * /home/ted/sweep.sh
```

Ted modified his crontab this morning but was finished before 9:15. cron should have run the job but apparently did not because there is no line in the cron log indicating that the job was started.

```
Aug 16 09:12:48 sawnee crontab[5962]: (ted) BEGIN EDIT (ted)
Aug 16 09:13:24 sawnee crontab[5962]: (ted) REPLACE (ted)
Aug 16 09:13:24 sawnee crontab[5962]: (ted) END EDIT (ted)
```

Next, we check whether crond is running:

```
# ps -ef|grep cron
root      5977  5832  0 09:23 pts/7    00:00:00 grep cron
```

The crond binary is not running. Let's restart it and then try to figure out what happened.

```
# /etc/init.d/crond start
Starting crond:                                        [  OK  ]
```

We can see crond is now running.

```
# ps -ef|grep cron
root      6001     1  0 09:31 ?        00:00:00 crond
root      6005  5832  0 09:31 pts/7    00:00:00 grep cron
```

We check /var/log/cron, and it seems crond is working:

```
Aug 16 09:31:14 sawnee crond[6001]: (CRON) STARTUP (fork ok)
```

We probably need to run a test cron job just to confirm that cron is working. If so, we move on and try to determine what happened. We check /var/log/messages for system messages that may show a problem. We verify that the cron packages are installed properly.

What cron packages can we find?

```
# rpm -q -a|grep cron
crontabs-1.10-5
vixie-cron-3.0.1-74
anacron-2.3-25
```

The crond binary is probably delivered with vixie-cron. We confirm this suspicion:

```
# rpm -q -filesbypkg vixie-cron-3.0.1-74
vixie-cron           /etc/cron.d
vixie-cron           /etc/rc.d/init.d/crond
vixie-cron           /usr/bin/crontab
```

```
vixie-cron              /usr/sbin/crond
vixie-cron              /usr/share/man/man1/crontab.1.gz
vixie-cron              /usr/share/man/man5/crontab.5.gz
vixie-cron              /usr/share/man/man8/cron.8.gz
vixie-cron              /usr/share/man/man8/crond.8.gz
vixie-cron              /var/spool/cron
```

We see /usr/sbin/crond is delivered with vixie-cron. Now, we just make sure vixie-cron-3.0.1-74 is installed properly:

```
# rpm -V vixie-cron-3.0.1-74
```

No output means that the package is installed properly. Maybe someone with root access killed crond by accident. We could also check for updates to the package that might correct a new bug.

See Chapter 8, "Linux Processes: Structure, Hangs, and Core Dumps," for further troubleshooting guidance.

Scenario 10-4: cron Log Not Updating

Users say cron is working fine, but a system administrator notices that the cron log isn't being updated. The cron log is zero bytes in size.

```
# ls -l /var/log/cron
-rw-------    1 root     root              0 Aug 31 20:26 /var/log/cron
```

Let's run a command to generate a cron log update.

```
# crontab -l
no crontab for root
```

That should have generated an entry in the cron log even though root has no crontab file, but it didn't.

```
# ls -l /var/log/cron
-rw-------    1 root     root              0 Aug 31 20:26 /var/log/cron
```

We know cron uses syslogd to do its logging. Let's make sure syslogd is running and working:

```
# ps -ef|grep syslog
root      1566     1  0 Aug23 ?        00:00:00 syslogd -m 0
root     28889 28848  0 20:21 pts/3    00:00:00 grep syslog
```

We can see syslogd is running. Is it still logging messages?

```
# tail -3 /var/log/messages
Aug 31 17:36:59 sawnee sshd(pam_unix)[28511]: session closed for user
root
Aug 31 20:19:36 sawnee sshd(pam_unix)[28846]: session opened for user
root by (uid=0)
```

From the previous output, we can see syslogd was working as of Aug 31 8:19 p.m. If there were no recent entries in the messages log, we could use the logger command to generate a test message:

```
# logger -p kern.info "test from sysadmin"
# tail -1 /var/log/messages
Aug 31 20:30:47 sawnee root: test from sysadmin
```

Where do cron messages go?

```
# grep cron /etc/syslog.conf
*.info;mail.none;news.none;authpriv.none;cron.none
/var/log/messages
# Log cron stuff
cron.*                                          /var/log/cron
```

Messages should be routed to /var/log/cron. Because syslogd is doing its job, something must be wrong with the cron file itself.

Someone with root access might have tried to trim the file incorrectly by removing or moving it and then touching cron to start a new log. If we look for cron files, we can see a cron.bkup that seems out of place.

```
# ls -l /var/log/cron*
-rw-------    1 root      root              0 Aug 31 20:26 /var/log/cron
-rw-------    1 root      root          19795 Aug 29 04:02 /var/log/cron.1
-rw-------    1 root      root          13506 Aug 22 04:02 /var/log/cron.2
-rw-------    1 root      root          19512 Aug 15 04:02 /var/log/cron.3
-rw-------    1 root      root          12288 Jul 28 22:01 /var/log/cron.4
-rw-------    1 root      root          10254 Aug 31 20:27 /var/log/cron.bkup
```

Sure enough, our `crontab` entry went to the old file.

```
# til -1 /var/log/cron.bkup
Aug 31 20:27:19 sawnee crontab[28906]: (root) LIST (root)
```

Moving a file using the `mv` command within the same filesystem while a file is open for writing generally causes problems. The program attached to the open file descriptor continues writing to the old file until the file descriptor is closed. This happens even though the filename has changed. The file descriptor points to the open inodes on the disk. In this instance, even though the file has a new name, `syslogd` keeps writing to it. The solution is to restart `syslogd` or put the file back. The `syslogd(8)` man page tells us to restart `syslogd` with:

```
kill -SIGHUP 'cat /var/run/syslogd.pid'
```

This command tells `syslog` to close and open the files again and fixes the logging issue. More `syslog` information can be found in the `syslogd(8)` and `syslog.conf(5)` man pages.

```
# crontab -l
no crontab for root
```

```
# tail -1 /var/log/cron
Aug 31 20:39:49 sawnee crontab[28949]: (root) LIST (root)
```

The `cron` log is updating properly.

Methodology

The flow chart in Figure 10-2 shows the troubleshooting methodology that was used in the examples.

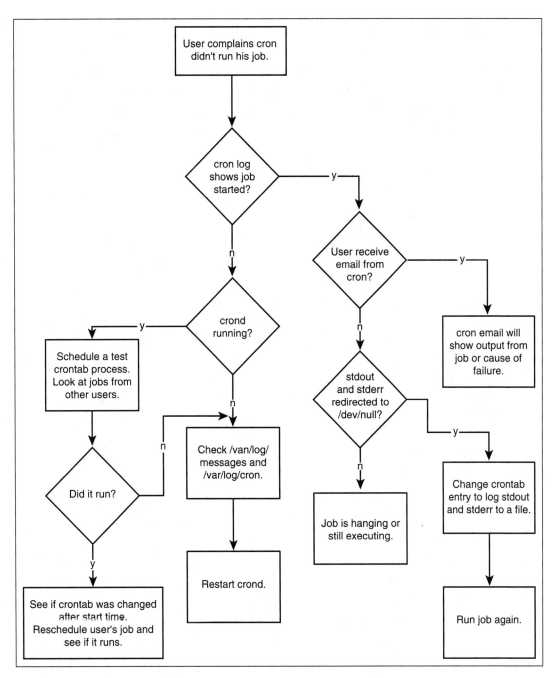

Figure 10-2 Troubleshooting methodology flow chart

Summary

It is necessary to understand how applications work before they can be effectively troubleshot. Our goal for this chapter was to explain how cron, at, anacron, and kcron work so that you will be ready when problems occur. The scenarios build on the foundation provided by the earlier sections. They present step-by-step resolutions for some common problems.

11

Printing and Printers

Printing is easy to overlook. Many people dismiss it as a minor subsystem in Linux. I learned that was not the case one Friday. I received an urgent call for assistance from the payroll department. It was payday, and the payroll system was unable to print. Hundreds of people in that company were praying for the printing subsystem to be fixed. In this chapter, we discuss the major types of printer hardware, the major spooler software available, and ways to troubleshoot both.

What Is a Spooler?

Generally speaking, a spooler is a queue for a limited resource. It is a way of throttling and controlling access to these resources. In the long-forgotten dark days of yore, computers were extremely expensive. They were held in big rooms and operated by nice men in sparkling white coats. The peripherals were also expensive. Access to things such as printing, communications, and so on needed to be rationed and controlled. One way to do this is via spooling. Spooling uses a queue to buffer requests for a physical resource. This allows multiple users to leverage use of this scarce physical resource. Spooling also enables devices that communicate at different rates to exchange data (buffering). A spooler allowed for not only job queuing but also prioritization. A spooler also allows for the service to be run by a privileged user and enables queued jobs to run after a user has submitted a request but is no longer accessing the system.

A good example of spooling is the line at the bank. There is a finite number of tellers, and the customers must wait for their turn in a queue. This is an efficient and equitable way to enable access to the scarce resource of tellers.

In this chapter, we discuss troubleshooting the print spoolers used under Linux. The three major spooler types are

- The System V-style spooler
- The Berkeley-style spooler
- CUPS-based spoolers

The concepts could be applied to other print spoolers as well. We discuss the LPRng (a modified Berkeley-style spooler) and CUPS spoolers in depth.

LPRng is a rewrite and extension of the original Berkeley spooler. It also enables System V commands to control the spooler.

CUPS (Common UNIX Printing System) is a new type of spooler. It was designed to work across most UNIX- and Linux-based systems. It is also standards based. It enables printing through RFC1179 (`lpr`), IPP, CIFS/SMB, Raw socket (JetDirect), and through local printing. CUPS uses network printer browsing and PostScript Printer Description (PPD) files to ease the common tasks of printing.

You can determine which spooler you have by querying your operating system. On RPM-based systems, run `rpm -qa |grep -i "cups\|lp"`. This command should return either CUPS or LPRng RPMs. If it returns both, you must confirm which is running (with `ps`). You can also use `chkconfig` to confirm which of the two is started on system reboot. On a Debian-based system, you must use `dpkg -l` to verify which spooler is installed.

Spoolers can be managed through graphical interfaces or from the command line. Generally, the GUI is easier for day-to-day usage, but for troubleshooting, it is best to know how to use the command-line interfaces. We explore them in depth in this chapter.

Print spoolers generally consist of a daemon, spool directories, and a series of configuration files. The daemon accepts the print requests, spools them, monitors the queues, enables changes to print order, cancels print requests, monitors the hardware, formats the print requests, and transfers them to the print device. The spool directories hold the files to be printed until they are formatted and transferred. The configuration files hold the general spooler configuration, printer-specific data, transfer scripts, and so on. The jobs can be sent unformatted (raw) or formatted (cooked). The formatting is generally per-formed by a Page Description Language (PDL) such as PCL or PostScript.

In some instances, a print queue might not actually be connected to an output device. For example, a print queue can be used to output a PDF file instead of printed paper.

Using the Spooler Commands

lp is the standard command used by System V-style spoolers to submit print requests. CUPS and LPRng also support lp through emulation. Table 11-1 lists the tasks you can accomplish with various lp commands.

Table 11-1   Various Printing Needs and the Corresponding lp Commands

Printing Need	Command
Submit a print request to the default printer	lp/etc/hosts
Submit a print request to a specific printer	lp -d printera/etc/hosts
Submit two copies of a print request	lp -n 2 /etc/hosts
Submit a print request to print landscape	lp -o landscape/etc/hosts
Send mail after printing	lp -m /etc/hosts
Omit printing the banner page	lp -o nb /etc/hosts
Print a banner page	lp -o yb/etc/hosts
Print two pages side by side on the paper	lp -o 2up /etc/hosts
Print on both sides of the paper	lp -o duplex /etc/hosts
Print raw output to the printer	lp -o raw /home/user/afile.pcl
Print request from paper tray 2	lp -o tray2/etc/hosts

lpr is the standard command used by BSD-style spoolers to submit print requests. CUPS supports lpr through emulation, and LPRng supports it natively. Table 11-2 lists lpr uses and commands.

Table 11-2   Various Printing Needs and the Corresponding `lpr` Commands

Printing Need	Command
Submit a print request to the default printer	`lpr /etc/hosts`
Submit a print request to a specific printer	`lpr -p printqueue /etc/hosts`
Submit two copies of a print request	`lpr -# 2 /etc/hosts`
Submit a print request to print landscape	`lpr -Zlandscape /etc/hosts`
Send mail after printing	`lpr -m /etc/hosts`
Omit printing the banner page	`lpr -h /etc/hosts`
Print two pages side by side on the paper	`lpr -Z2up /etc/hosts`
Print on both sides of the paper	`lpr -Zduplex /etc/hosts`
Print raw output to the printer	`lpr -Ztype=raw /home/user/afile.pcl`
Print request from paper tray 2	`lpr -Ztray=2/etc/hosts`

`lpadmin` is the standard command used by System V-style spoolers to configure printers and classes. It is used in CUPS and System V spoolers. There is no BSD equivalent of `lpadmin`. With BSD spoolers, you just manually edit the `/etc/printcap` file. Table 11-3 lists `lpadmin` uses and commands.

`lpstat` is the standard command used by System V-style spoolers to query the status of the spooler, print queues, and jobs.

Table 11-3   Various Printing Needs and the Corresponding `lpadmin` Commands

Printing Need	Command
Change the system default printer	`lpadmin -d printqueue`
Remove a print queue	`lpadmin -xprintqueue`

```
$ lpstat -t
scheduler is running
system default destination: dj5
device for dj5: usb://hp/deskjet%205550
device for Laser: ipp://localhost/ipp
dj5 accepting requests since Jan 01 00:00
Laser accepting requests since Jan 01 00:00
printer dj5 disabled since Jan 01 00:00 -
        Unable to open USB device "usb://hp/deskjet%205550": No such device
        printer Laser is idle.  enabled since Jan 01 00:00
dj5-1               jtk10        11724800    Fri 21 Jan 2005 10:12:22 PM
EST
```

lpq is the standard command used by BSD-style spoolers to query the status of the spooler, print queues, and jobs.

```
$ lpq
dj5 is not ready
Rank    Owner   Job     File(s)                 Total Size
1st     jtk10   1       (stdin)                 11724800 bytes
```

lpoptions is the CUPS command to display or set printer options and defaults. This command is only available in CUPS. For example, you could create two queues for a printer and use lpoptions to set the second queue to print in landscape mode by default.

```
$ lpoptions
job-sheets=none,none cpi=12 lpi=7 page-bottom=86 page-left=57 page-right=57 \
page-top=72 scaling=100 wrap=true
$ lpoptions -o scaling=150
[jtk10@sanctus ~]$ lpoptions
job-sheets=none,none cpi=12 lpi=7 page-bottom=86 page-left=57 page-right=57 \
page-top=72 scaling=150 wrap=true
```

The options for the print queues are saved in the following locations (from the man page):

```
~/.lpoptions - user defaults and instances created by non-root users.
/etc/cups/lpoptions - system-wide defaults and instances created by the
root user.
```

Spooler Plumbing

Think of the spooler as the plumbing in your house and the capability to turn taps on or off as the capability to control job flow to the queues (see Figure 11-1). A main spooler function is the capability to control the flow of jobs through it. It is important to be able to do the following:

* Move a job to another device
* Reject or accept requests from queuing or printing
* Cancel queued requests
* Disable or enable requests to print but still allow them to queue
* Redirect new print requests to another device

The commands used to control the job flow plumbing are:

* lpc—The BSD spooler command that encompasses the functionality of accept, reject, disable, enable, lpmove, and also some functionality of lpstat. CUPS implements a limited subset of this command.

```
usage: lpc [-Ddebuglevel][-Pprinter][-Shost][-Uusername][-V] [command]
    with no command, reads from stdin
        -Ddebuglevel - debug level
        -Pprinter    - printer or printer@host
        -Shost       - connect to lpd server on host
        -Uuser       - identify command as coming from user
        -V           - increase information verbosity
```

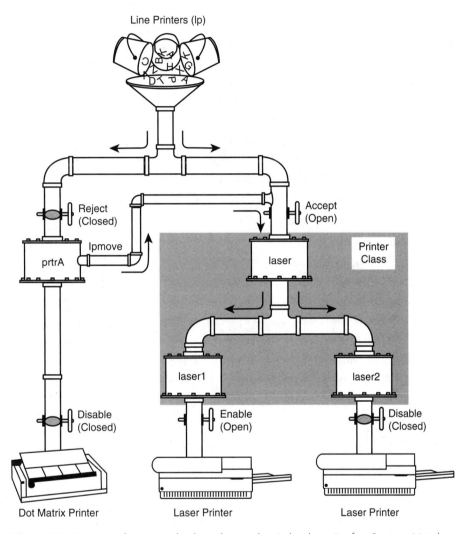

Figure 11-1 A simple example that shows the "plumbing" of a System V-style print spooler

```
commands:
active  (printer[@host])        - check for active server
abort   (printer[@host] | all)  - stop server
class   printer[@host] (class | off) - show/set class printing
disable (printer[@host] | all)  - disable queueing
debug   (printer[@host] | all) debugparms - set debug level for printer
```

```
down    (printer[@host] | all)  - disable printing and queueing
enable  (printer[@host] | all)  - enable queueing
hold    (printer[@host] | all) (name[@host] | job | all)* - hold job
holdall (printer[@host] | all)  - hold all jobs on
kill    (printer[@host] | all)  - stop and restart server
lpd     (printer[@host]) - get LPD PID
lpq     (printer[@host] | all) (name[@host] | job | all)*    - run lpq
lprm    (printer[@host] | all) (name[@host]|host|job| all)* - run lprm
msg printer message text- set status message
move printer (user¦jobid)* target - move jobs to new queue
noholdall (printer[@host] | all)- hold all jobs off
printcap(printer[@host] | all)  - report printcap values
quit                            - exit LPC
redirect(printer[@host] | all) (printer@host | off )*    - redirect jobs
redo    (printer[@host] | all) (name[@host] | job | all)* - redo jobs
release (printer[@host] | all) (name[@host] | job | all)* - release jobs
reread  (printer[@host])        - LPD reread database information
start   (printer[@host] | all)  - start printing
status  (printer[@host] | all)  - status of printers
stop    (printer[@host] | all)  - stop  printing
topq    (printer[@host] | all) (name[@host] | job | all)* - reorder job
up      (printer[@host] | all) - enable printing and queueing
diagnostic:
defaultq                - show default queue for LPD server
defaults                - show default configuration values
client  (printer | all) - client config and printcap information
server (printer | all) - server config and printcap
```

- lprm—The standard command used by BSD-style spoolers to cancel print requests.

```
$ lpq
dj5 is ready and printing
Rank     Owner    Job    File(s)               Total Size
1st      jtk10    3      hosts                 1024 bytes
2nd      jtk10    4      hosts                 1024 bytes
```

```
[jtk10@sanctus ~]$ lprm 3
[jtk10@sanctus ~]$ lpq
dj5 is ready and printing
Rank     Owner    Job     File(s)                          Total Size
1st      jtk10    4       hosts                            1024 bytes
```

- cancel—The standard command used by System V-style spoolers to remove pending print requests.

- accept—The standard command used by System V-style spoolers to tell a print queue to begin spooling print requests.

- reject—The standard command used by System V-style spoolers to stop spooling print requests.

- disable—The standard command used by System V-style spoolers to stop printing print requests.

- enable—The standard command used by System V-style spoolers to begin printing print requests.

- lpmove—The standard command used by System V-style spoolers to move a print request from one print queue to another.

One key concept is the difference between spooling requests and printing them. The reject command enables you to stop jobs from printing and spooling. If a user tries to print to a queue that is set to reject, the following occurs:

```
$ reject dj5
$ lpstat -p
printer dj5 disabled since Jan 01 00:00 -
        Rejecting Jobs
$ lp -d dj5 /etc/hosts
lp: unable to print file: server-error-not-accepting-jobs
$ accept dj5
```

The disable command stops jobs from printing, but they still spool up in the queue.

```
$ accept dj5
$ disable dj5
$ lpstat -p
```

```
printer dj5 disabled since Jan 01 00:00 -
        Paused
$ lp -d dj5 /etc/hosts
request id is dj5-2 (1 file(s))
$ lpstat -t
scheduler is running
system default destination: dj5
device for dj5: usb://hp/deskjet%205550
device for Laser: ipp://localhost/ipp
dj5 accepting requests since Jan 01 00:00
Laser accepting requests since Jan 01 00:00
printer dj5 disabled since Jan 01 00:00 -
        Paused
printer Laser is idle.  enabled since Jan 01 00:00
dj5-2            jtk10         1024      Sat 29 Jan 2005 11:31:05 AM EST

$ enable dj5
```

After the print queue is enabled, the print requests begin printing on the printer.

Term Definitions

It is important to further clarify spooling and printing terms. They are very specific, and using them incorrectly can lead to creating, fixing, or deleting the wrong resource. Let's take time out for a second and make sure we understand the terminology.

* **Queue**—A queue is a fancy name for a line. It is the line in which requests wait for a particular resource. A queue can be attached to a printer, a class, or other devices.

* **Class**—A class is grouping of print queues based on the function of the printers in the class. This grouping could be based on job function (for example, accounting department printers), location, device type (for example, all laser printers), or other classifications.

- **Job**—A job is another name for a request for a service. It is the smallest unit into which you can break a request.

- **User disassociation**—Because requests are queued where they can be controlled and printed by the daemon, you can perform other operations on the computer while the printing takes place in the background. By passing the job through a daemon, you can disassociate it from the specific user. The job becomes owned by the daemon's user instead of the user who submitted it. Usually the submitting user is noted in some control file or log. For example, this process can be performed by passing the request files through a named pipe. The daemon picks up the files on the other side and processes them.

- **Abstraction**—There are many (sometimes conflicting) definitions of abstraction. It is a programming technique that hides complexity. The best example is the VFS portion of the Linux kernel. VFS is a virtual filesystem layer that sits on top of the filesystem drivers. When using VFS, a programmer doesn't need to know the intricacies of each driver to work with them.

- **Spool directory**—This is the directory that stores the files for queued-up jobs. There is either one big directory or a separate directory for each queue or class.

- **Print filters**—A print filter is a program that inserts control codes for a printer into a document before it is transferred to the printer. An example is inserting the PCL code for landscape output into the beginning of a document to tell the printer to print the page in landscape format. Filters can also be used to translate a job from one printer language to another. For example, a Ghostscript print filter could be used to change an ASCII text file into PostScript.

- **Banner or header page**—A banner is a page that prints before a print request to delineate jobs and identify the characteristics specific to that job.

- **Transfer script (backend)**—A script or program used to transfer a print request to a print device. These can be simple transfer programs, or they can have more complex features such as device status checking.

- **Footer page**—A footer is a page that prints after a print request to delineate jobs and identify the characteristics specific to that job.

- **Contention**—Depending on the printer type, device contention can be a major issue. With local printers, only one print request can be printed at a time. If two print requests were trying to print on a serial printer at the same time, you would either have interleaved jobs or missing pages. A spooler allows jobs to wait serially for the printer resource to become free. For local printers (serial, USB, parallel), you should define only one queue for each printer. If you have more than one queue for a local printer, the queues can interfere with each other's print requests. With remote, IPP, and network printing, you can define multiple print queues for each printer because these devices are built to handle requests from multiple systems at the same time.

- **Vector vs. raster graphics**—Raster graphics are more commonly know as bitmaps. This graphics format assembles the data in a rectangular grid of pixels, each with an assigned color. Common file formats that use raster graphics include GIF, TIFF, BMP, and JPEG, among others. They are generally considered photorealistic, but resizing them can cause jaggedness as the pixel size increases. Most printers are raster-based, so any vector-based graphic is usually translated into a bitmap before printing. Suppose the smiley face in the top-left corner of Figure 11-2 is an RGB bitmap image. When zoomed in, it might look like the big smiley face to the right. Every square represents a pixel. Zoomed in further, we see three pixels whose colors are constructed by adding the values for red, green, and blue.

  Vector graphics use geometric shapes to build an image. All the images are composed of lines that are defined by a series of mathematical equations. Vector graphics files are generally smaller than raster files. Vector graphics can be resized to almost any size without jaggedness because they are formula-based. Common file formats for vector graphics include PDF, EPS, and others. Plotters can directly print vector graphics. In Figure 11-3, the image on the right is stripped of color and shows the raw geometric shapes. Each shape is represented by a distinct mathematical equation.

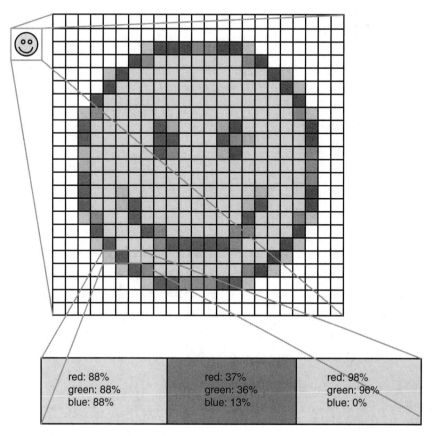

Figure 11-2 An example of raster graphics

Figure 11-3 An example of vector graphics

Printer Types

You can print to many different printer types from your Linux system, and each has its own quirks. The four most common printer classes are

* Dot matrix / line printer
* Laser
* Inkjet
* Plotter

Serial line printers generally accept only ASCII text (these printers are sometimes called dumb printers), but there are exceptions. Some higher-end line printers accept PCL or PostScript. These printers are usually connected through serial or parallel interfaces, but they also can be connected through a terminal server or other network device. Line printers print a page one line at a time. Serial character printers print one character at a time. These printers have tractors that feed the paper through the printer using holes along the sides of the paper. Thus, one of the complications of these printers is paper alignment and jams.

Serial character and line printers accept carbon or duplicate forms, which are commonly used in printing forms, checks, and POS applications. High-speed line printers such as band printers are also used for batched reports from computer systems. They are exceptionally fast and efficient.

One of the great joys of tractor-feed printers is bursting the pages. Because the pages are all connected in a continuous feed, they must be burst apart at their perforations, and the tractor feed holes must be removed from either side.

Laser printers are known for their speed and print quality. These printers print a page at a time rather than a line at a time. They use a heated drum and toner (similar to a copier). Color laser printers are available, but most print in black and white. They can also experience jams in the feeding mechanism, but they occur less frequently than tractor-feed printers. The print quality is generally higher than other printing methods.

The printing speed varies depending on the printer but can range from 3 to more than 750 pages per minute.

Most laser printers accept a variety of PDLs. PCL is the generally accepted standard, but PostScript is common on laser printers as well. Fonts and other PDLs can be loaded into many printers with DIMMs inserted into memory slots in the printer. Due to their cost, laser printers are more common in businesses, although the cost has decreased markedly in the last few years.

Laser printers can be printed to by most of the connectivity types depending on the model. The most common is through the network. This method enables many systems to access the printer. It is common to have one laser printer shared in a work area. This approach spreads the cost more efficiently than having one printer per system.

Another big plus of laser printers is the wide range of accessories that can be attached to them, such as sheet feeders and extra trays, duplexers, stackers, collators, mailboxes, and staplers. Although some of these options are available on other printer types, none can match the range and versatility of a laser printer. Other options include pages sizes (8.5 × 11, A4, legal, card stock, envelopes, labels) and different media types such as transparencies.

Inkjets are generally found on individual systems, although they can be shared. They are common for home printing and small office printing because of their capability to print high-quality color pages. They are often used to print color photographs and overheads for presentations. They work by using a fine spray of super-heated ink from a small print head. They can print on a good range of paper sizes and a great range of media including CDs, cloth, transparencies, and many others. Inkjets are usually connected locally to a computer through USB or parallel interfaces.

Plotters are very high-end print devices that use a pen to essentially draw the image on the paper. Older plotters could only print line-based vector graphics. The newest generations of plotters have switched to other technologies such as thermal inkjet printing. These are usually used in CAD/CAM/CAE environments for schematics and blueprints or for large-format printing. The newest plotters offer exceptionally high quality and can print photo-quality raster graphics on large rolls of paper (60-inch-wide rolls, for example). Plotters are usually either USB, parallel, or networked.

There are many other types of printers such as solid ink, electron beam, thermal wax transfer, electrostatic transfer, and dye sublimation that we do not cover here.

Connectivity Types

To understand printing and troubleshoot it, you need to know details about the various methods of connectivity to printers. Without this information, any problems specific to a connectivity method are a mysterious black box.

Local Serial Printing

Serial communication (through RS-232) is often used for terminals, modems, and other data communication devices. It is flexible and solid but relatively slow. Serial printing is one of the older printing methods, but it gives us a great chance to discuss in depth how local printing works. You can use RS-232 reliably with a cable up to about 15 meters (about 50 feet). This length depends on the quality of the cable, the amount of electromagnetic interference, and the baud rate (speed) at which you are communicating. The slower you communicate, the more reliable the data transmission. 9600 seems to be the best combination of reliability and speed for longer cables, but you can drop to 2400 or 1200 if needed.

Serial ports can communicate to both DTE (data terminal equipment) and DCE (data circuit equipment) devices. DTEs are devices where data terminates such as a printer, terminal, PC, and so on. DCEs are devices that transmit data such as modems, CSUs, DSUs, and so on. This distinction is important because the primary problem with any serial communication is getting the right cable. Without the correct cabling, serial printing does not work. Cable quality is also an issue. Don't just pick up a cable out of a box in a storage room and assume it will work correctly.

There are many types of cables, and each has a different pinout. The pins are the wires over which electrical signals travel. The pinout is the map that shows which pins on one end of the cable map to which pins on the other end. There are three main types of serial connection. They are DB-25 (25 pins), DB-9 (9 pins), and RJ-45 (8 pins, which is essentially a 4-pair network cable). A cable hood for DB-25 and DB-9 can either be male or female. Examples of male and female connectors are shown in Figures 11-4 and 11-5. Male hoods have the pins sticking out, and female hoods have holes to accept the male pins. Typically, cables have one male and one female end.

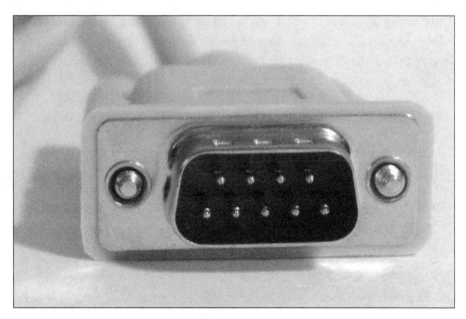

Figure 11-4 A male DB-9 serial connector

Figure 11-5 A female DB-9 serial connection

There are usually at least three active pins in a serial cable. They are Rx (receive), Tx (transmit), and Gnd (ground). An example pinout is shown in Figure 11-6. In a DB-9 connector, DCE devices use pin 2 for Rx, pin 3 for Tx, and pin 5 for Gnd, and DTE devices use pin 3 for Rx, pin 2 for Tx, and pin 5 for Gnd.

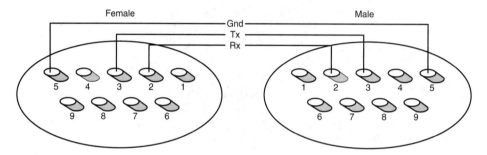

Figure 11-6 Simple DB-9 DCE to DB-9 DTE pinout

The serial device receiving the data uses flow control to let the sending device know that it has received all the data it can handle (for example, in a print buffer on a printer). This functionality is needed because a computer can send a print request faster than the printer can print it. The job is stored in buffer memory on the printer while it is printing. If the print job is bigger than the buffer, the printer needs to be able to tell the computer to stop sending more characters until it has freed space in the buffer.

Serial printers usually use either hardware flow control (RTS/CTS) or software-based flow control (XON/XOFF). There are pins on a serial connection that can be used for hardware data flow control when printing such as RTS (request to send) or CTS (clear to send). When the receiving device is ready to accept data, it raises (sends an electric signal on) its RTS pin. This signal comes across to the other end of the cable on the CTS pin and indicates that it is ok to transmit data. If the print buffer in the printer fills up, the printer drops the CTS signal, and the computer holds additional data until the CTS is raised again. Figure 11-7 shows how the pins connect to the wires when the housing is opened.

We will not discuss the other pins not commonly used in printing such as CD (carrier detect), DSR (dataset ready), DTR (data terminal ready), and others.

To communicate with a local serial printer, you use a device file. An example of a serial device file is the following:

```
crw-rw----  1 root uucp 4, 64 Jan  2 07:31 ttyS0
```

Figure 11-7 A serial connector dismantled

You can get information about a serial port by using the `setserial` command:

```
# setserial /dev/ttyS0
/dev/ttyS0, UART: 16550A, Port: 0x03f8, IRQ: 4
```

You can gather additional settings data about a serial port by using the `stty` command. The `stty` command enables you to print and manipulate serial line settings such as speed, the bit setting, parity, character translation, number of columns, and so on. Here is an example output from `stty` that reports all the current settings on a serial port:

```
# stty -F /dev/ttyS0 -a
speed 9600 baud; rows 0; columns 0; line = 0;
intr = ^C; quit = ^\; erase = ^?; kill = ^U; eof = ^D; eol = <undef>;
eol2 = <undef>; start = ^Q; stop = ^S; susp = ^Z; rprnt = ^R; werase = ^W;
lnext = ^V; flush = ^O; min = 1; time = 0;
-parenb -parodd cs8 hupcl -cstopb cread clocal -crtscts
-ignbrk -brkint -ignpar -parmrk -inpck -istrip -inlcr -igncr icrnl ixon \
-ixoff
-iuclc -ixany -imaxbel
opost -olcuc -ocrnl onlcr -onocr -onlret -ofill -ofdel nl0 cr0 tab0 bs0 \
vt0 ff0
```

```
isig icanon iexten echo echoe echok -echonl -noflsh -xcase -tostop -echoprt
echoctl echoke
```

If the printer is connected and set up correctly, you should be able to send a file using `cat` to the device, and it should come out on the printer. It may look funny because of formatting or line feed issues.

```
# cat afile > /dev/ttyS0
```

This command opens the serial port and transmits the data across the transmit pin to the printer. The printer then takes the data and prints it. However, the data might be stair-stepped, which looks like this:

See Dick run.

     See Jane run.

          See Dick and Jane run.

This error happens because of a mismatch in end of line characters. In Linux and UNIX, the end of line is signaled in text streams by a line feed (LF). You will sometimes also see this notated with a \n character. With DOS, Windows, and other systems, an end of line comprises a carriage return and a line feed (CR/LF). If you look at the `stty` options, you can see that the `onlcr` option specifies whether an LF should be changed into CR/LF. To set the `onlcr` flag, run this command:

```
# stty -F /dev/ttyS0 onlcr
```

To unset the `onlcr` flag, use:

```
# stty -F /dev/ttyS0 -onlcr
```

To set a baud rate for a serial line to 9600 baud, issue the following command:

```
# stty -F /dev/ttyS0 9600
```

Flow control is primarily an issue with slower printers and longer cables. Flow control problems can cause characters or strings of characters to be dropped in job. The characters can be dropped from the middle or end of the job. This problem can be addressed in three ways. The first solution is to slow the baud rate over the serial line. This solution is imperfect, but it works well in a lot of cases. Second, you can switch the printer from software flow control to hardware flow control. The signaling on hardware flow control is more precise, so timing issues and missed signals are less likely. Last, you can adjust the `closing_wait` setting on the serial port with the `set_serial` command. This option is volatile, meaning that it only lasts until the next reboot. The way around this issue is to place the `set_serial` command in an `rc` script such as `/etc/rc.serial`. This method changes the amount of time after close before the serial port buffer is flushed. The default time is 30 seconds. If you don't have a copy of `rc.serial`, look for a template under `/usr/share/doc/setserial*/rc.serial`.

These and other settings can usually be controlled from the spooler's configuration files or `rc` files. We discuss this subject in further detail in the sections on each spooler type.

Local USB Printing

USB has quickly become the default for attaching peripherals to a computer. It is easy to use and fast. It has supplanted parallel (ISEE 1284) as the default method for printing. Most inkjet printers come with at least one USB port. Some have both USB and parallel ports. There are two current standards for USB devices. USB 1.1 runs at 12Mbps, and USB 2.0 runs at 480Mbps. Both standards accept up to 127 peripherals per bus. USB also supports Plug-and-Play installation and hot plugging. The maximum length for a USB cable according to the standard is 16 feet. USB devices can either draw power from the USB bus or be externally powered. This choice depends on the power needs of the device.

There are two types of connectors on a USB cable. They are referred to as type A and type B connectors. The connectors can either be mini- or standard-sized. The type A connector is male and plugs into the female port on the computer. The type B connector is male and connects into the peripheral. You can see examples of connectors in Figure 11-8.

To effectively use USB printing, you should have at least a 2.4 kernel. To use USB 2.0, you should have a late 2.4 or 2.6 kernel. The USB printers use device files similar to `/dev/usb/lp0`. The last digit increments with each printer added.

Non-CUPS spoolers can be confused by the printer device files because USB device files are assigned and removed dynamically. If they are powered on or detected in different orders, the device files could reverse, which could cause print requests to go to the

Figure 11-8 Standard-sized type A and type B USB connectors

wrong printer. CUPS uses a USB abstraction layer and the printer's manufacturer, model, and printer serial number to send the print job to the correct printer.

To gather more information about what USB devices are attached to a system, you can run the following command:

```
# lspci -v
00:10.0 USB Controller: VIA Technologies, Inc. VT82xxxxx \
UHCI USB 1.1 Controller
 (rev 80) (prog-if 00 [UHCI])
        Subsystem: Micro-Star International Co., Ltd.: Unknown device 3902
        Flags: bus master, medium devsel, latency 32, IRQ 11
        I/O ports at d800 [size=32]
        Capabilities: [80] Power Management version 2
```

```
00:10.1 USB Controller: VIA Technologies, Inc. VT82xxxxx \
UHCI USB 1.1 Controller
 (rev 80) (prog-if 00 [UHCI])
        Subsystem: Micro-Star International Co., Ltd.: Unknown device 3902
        Flags: bus master, medium devsel, latency 32, IRQ 3
        I/O ports at dc00 [size=32]
        Capabilities: [80] Power Management version 2


00:10.2 USB Controller: VIA Technologies, Inc. VT82xxxxx \
UHCI USB 1.1 Controller
 (rev 80) (prog-if 00 [UHCI])
        Subsystem: Micro-Star International Co., Ltd.: Unknown device 3902
        Flags: bus master, medium devsel, latency 32, IRQ 10
        I/O ports at e000 [size=32]
        Capabilities: [80] Power Management version 2


00:10.3 USB Controller: VIA Technologies, Inc. USB 2.0 (rev 82) (prog-if \
20 [EHC
I])
        Subsystem: Micro-Star International Co., Ltd.: Unknown device 3902
        Flags: bus master, medium devsel, latency 32, IRQ 5
        Memory at ea001000 (32-bit, non-prefetchable) [size=256]
        Capabilities: [80] Power Management version 2
```

And then:

```
# cat /proc/bus/usb/devices


T:  Bus=04 Lev=00 Prnt=00 Port=00 Cnt=00 Dev#=  1 Spd=12  MxCh= 2
B:  Alloc=  0/900 us ( 0%), #Int=  0, #Iso=  0
D:  Ver= 1.10 Cls=09(hub  ) Sub=00 Prot=00 MxPS= 8 #Cfgs=  1
P:  Vendor=0000 ProdID=0000 Rev= 2.06
S:  Manufacturer=Linux 2.6.9-1.681_FC3 uhci_hcd
S:  Product=UHCI Host Controller
S:  SerialNumber=0000:00:10.2
C:* #Ifs= 1 Cfg#= 1 Atr=c0 MxPwr=  0mA
I:  If#= 0 Alt= 0 #EPs= 1 Cls=09(hub  ) Sub=00 Prot=00 Driver=hub
E:  Ad=81(I) Atr=03(Int.) MxPS=   2 Ivl=255ms
```

```
T:  Bus=03 Lev=00 Prnt=00 Port=00 Cnt=00 Dev#=  1 Spd=12  MxCh= 2
B:  Alloc=  0/900 us ( 0%), #Int=  0, #Iso=  0
D:  Ver= 1.10 Cls=09(hub  ) Sub=00 Prot=00 MxPS= 8 #Cfgs=  1
P:  Vendor=0000 ProdID=0000 Rev= 2.06
S:  Manufacturer=Linux 2.6.9-1.681_FC3 uhci_hcd
S:  Product=UHCI Host Controller
S:  SerialNumber=0000:00:10.1
C:* #Ifs= 1 Cfg#= 1 Atr=c0 MxPwr=  0mA
I:  If#= 0 Alt= 0 #EPs= 1 Cls=09(hub  ) Sub=00 Prot=00 Driver=hub
E:  Ad=81(I) Atr=03(Int.) MxPS=   2 Ivl=255ms


T:  Bus=02 Lev=00 Prnt=00 Port=00 Cnt=00 Dev#=  1 Spd=12  MxCh= 2
B:  Alloc=  0/900 us ( 0%), #Int=  0, #Iso=  0
D:  Ver= 1.10 Cls=09(hub  ) Sub=00 Prot=00 MxPS= 8 #Cfgs=  1
P:  Vendor=0000 ProdID=0000 Rev= 2.06
S:  Manufacturer=Linux 2.6.9-1.681_FC3 uhci_hcd
S:  Product=UHCI Host Controller
S:  SerialNumber=0000:00:10.0
C:* #Ifs= 1 Cfg#= 1 Atr=c0 MxPwr=  0mA
I:  If#= 0 Alt= 0 #EPs= 1 Cls=09(hub  ) Sub=00 Prot=00 Driver=hub
E:  Ad=81(I) Atr=03(Int.) MxPS=   2 Ivl=255ms


T:  Bus=01 Lev=00 Prnt=00 Port=00 Cnt=00 Dev#=  1 Spd=480 MxCh= 6
B:  Alloc=  0/800 us ( 0%), #Int=  0, #Iso=  0
D:  Ver= 2.00 Cls=09(hub  ) Sub=00 Prot=01 MxPS= 8 #Cfgs=  1
P:  Vendor=0000 ProdID=0000 Rev= 2.06
S:  Manufacturer=Linux 2.6.9-1.681_FC3 ehci_hcd
S:  Product=EHCI Host Controller
S:  SerialNumber=0000:00:10.3
C:* #Ifs= 1 Cfg#= 1 Atr=e0 MxPwr=  0mA
I:  If#= 0 Alt= 0 #EPs= 1 Cls=09(hub  ) Sub=00 Prot=00 Driver=hub
E:  Ad=81(I) Atr=03(Int.) MxPS=   2 Ivl=256ms
```

You can see that devices that have Spd=12 are USB 1.x and Spd=480 are USB 2.0.

Local Parallel Printing

The IEEE 1284 standard is bidirectional, but Linux drivers are write-only. This means you receive no status or error information from the printer.

Centronics is the de facto standard for parallel cabling. It has a 36-pin hood to connect to the printer and a 25-pin connector to plug into the computer's parallel port.

When the new kernel is booted, the printer should be identified automatically. To check, you can run:

```
cat /proc/sys/dev/parport/parport0/autoprobe
```

```
# dmesg |grep -i lp
```

The device file is of the format /dev/lp0. The last number of the device file increments for each device on a parallel port.

Parallel ports can be configured as Standard Parallel Port (SPP), Bidirectional Parallel Port (BPP), Enhanced Parallel Port (EPP), or Enhanced Capabilities Port (ECP). EPP and ECP are the most common on modern computers. They are extensions on Centronics and SPP. EPP and ECP are much faster than the original Centronic/SPP standard and have improved handshaking and flow control. The mode is generally set in the computers BIOS. The best setting is a combination of EPP/ECP (if it is offered). If EPP/ECC is not available, you can try to fall back to ECP.

Several versions of EPP are available. If possible, you should select EPP 1.9. This selection sometimes requires experimentation, though. If you are still having problems, you might also try SPP and see how that works for you. Because the Linux driver is not bidirectional, you only lose the speed and handshaking advantages of the other modes.

As with RS-232, parallel printing is extremely sensitive to cabling issues. Make sure the cable is a good-quality IEEE 1294 cable. Also try to minimize the cable length. It is possible to make parallel printing work up to 50 meters, but it becomes problematic past 15 meters.

Remote Printing

Remote printing over port 515 is based on the computing standard RFC1179 created by the Internet Engineering Task Force (IETF). RFC stands for Request For Comment. This method is how a proposed standard is documented and published to the Internet community for feedback. These standards form the communication protocols that make up the Internet (such as HTTP). RFC1179 and other RFCs are available from http://www.ietf.org/rfc. The technology specified by RFC1179 can be used for printing to another system's spooler. This functionality enables you to print remotely to printers that are locally attached to another system. The other system could be a terminal server, a print server, or a computer.

It is important to understand what format is used for RFC1179 printing. The RFC states the following:

3.1 Message formats

LPR is a TCP-based protocol. The port on which a line printer daemon listens is 515. The source port must be in the range 721 to 731, inclusive. A line printer daemon responds to commands sent to its port. All commands begin with a single octet code, which is a binary number which represents the requested function. The code is immediately followed by the ASCII name of the printer queue name on which the function is to be performed. If there are other operands to the command, they are separated from the printer queue name with white space (ASCII space, horizontal tab, vertical tab, and form feed). The end of the command is indicated with an ASCII line feed character.

One disadvantage to RFC1179-style printing is that many of the command-line options are not passed between the two systems. The options passed are very limited. For example, the landscape option would not be passed.

The spooler sends two files for each remote print request. The first is a control file, and the second is a data file. The files can be sent in any order to the remote spooler.

The control file contains information about the print request (such as user ID, queue name, and so on). The control filename is in the format *cfAzzzhostname*, where the *zzz* is a three-digit job number and *hostname* is the hostname of the sending system. These files are stored in the spooler's temporary directories. The print request transfer begins by sending a control string to the remote spooler. This is generally one of three strings. The first is an abort string. The second lets the spooler know that a control file is being transferred, and the last lets the spooler know that a data file is being sent.

The control file contains multiple lines of data. Each line is a separate parameter. The first character of each line is a command character followed by the variable data.

RFC1179 also provides for requesting the status of a print queue, limited control over changing queue status, and canceling a print request.

Control Files

A typical control file contains the following data:

```
Hhost.domain.tld
J/home/usera/afile /home/usera/bfile
CA
Lusera
Pusera
fdfA003host.domain.tld
N/home/usera/afile
UdfA003host.domain.tld
fdfB003host.domain.tld
N/home/usera/bfile
UdfB003host.domain.tld
```

This is not gibberish. All it takes is the secret decoder ring. It is a series of commands to the remote spooler. Each line is executed one after another. In this example, usera on system host.domain.tld has printed two files (/home/usera/afile and /home/usera/bfile).

* Hhost.domain.tld—H is the key for the hostname. The hostname in this case is host.domain.tld.
* J/home/usera/afile /home/usera/bfile—J is the key for job name. The default value is a list of filenames printed. It is possible to specify a job name with lpr -J *jobname* or lp -t *jobname*. The files submitted for printing are /usera/afile and /home/usera/bfile.
* CA—C is the key for printer class. You can specify a class through lpr -C *class*.

- Lusera—L is the key for banner page. The user name can be omitted. Without this, a banner page will be suppressed. Some printers or spoolers create their own banner pages and ignore this flag.

- Pusera—P is the key for the user name to be printed on the banner page. The default is the user who submitted the request. It can also be specified through lpr -U *username* or lp -u *username*. The user name in this case is usera.

- fdfA003host.domain.tld—f is the key for print formatted file. The filename in this case is the first data file: dfB003host.domain.tld.

- N/home/usera/afile—N is the key for the name of the source file. The filename in this case is /home/usera/afile.

- UdfB003host.domain.tld—U is the key for unlink data file. This command causes the temporary data file to be removed from the spooler directories.

The f, N, and U commands are repeated again for the second file.

There are many other possible control characters in a control file. They are all defined in RFC1179. Also be aware that some spoolers also add their own proprietary extensions to the control file. These are used when printing between two spoolers of the same type.

Data Files

The data file contains the file or text stream that was submitted to be printed. Data is usually submitted by specifying a file to be printed or by redirecting STDIN to the print command. The data filename is in the format *dfAzzzhostname*, where the *zzz* is a three-digit job number and *hostname* is the hostname of the sending system. There can be more than one data file if more than one were submitted to be printed in one job.

After the control and data files are transferred, the remote spooler should return a status code. For example, \000 indicates success. Anything else indicates an error.

Contention

How does remote printing handle contention? The jobs are accepted and spooled to the remote print queue. There, the jobs wait in the queue until it is their turn to print on the printer.

Troubleshooting Tools

Remote printing troubleshooting tools include the following:

* Logs in /var/log such as the syslog can contain network errors.
* tcpdump of traffic to port 515 enables you to monitor the packets in and out of a system if you think they are being mangled.
* nmap can be used to verify that port 515 is open and accepting connections.

Scenario 11-1: Unable to Print to Remote Printer

A user received the following error:

```
$ lpr /home/user/Billy.txt
$ lpq
could not talk to print service at germany
```

To troubleshoot this situation, you would do something like the following:

1. Confirm that local and remote queue names are correct. The network is shown in Figure 11-9.

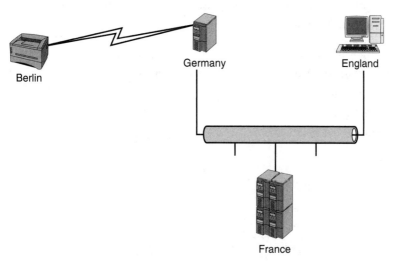

Figure 11-9 The network

In this example, a local serial print queue (Berlin) is defined on the host Germany. If the administrator of the host France wants to print through remote printing, he needs to add it. To do this, he must define four pieces of information in his spooler:

- Remote host name (Germany in this case)
- Remote queue name (Berlin in this case)
- Remote port (515 by default)
- Local queue name (Paris in this case)

The local queue name on France could be Berlin as well, or something else. In this example, the administrator defined it as Paris. The administrator on England might also add the printer with the following values:

- Remote host name (France)
- Remote queue name (Paris)
- Remote port (515)
- Local queue name (London)

As you can see, a print request submitted to London would then go to Paris and then would be forwarded to Berlin for printing. This might happen if France were a print server. You could also define the printer on England to print directly to Germany.

2. Confirm that the server print daemon is accepting connections on port 515 from the client. You would expect to see the following:

```
# telnet germany  515
Trying 127.0.0.1...
Connected to germany.
Escape character is '^]'.
```

An error might look like this:

```
$ telnet 192.168.2.55 515
Connecting To 192.168.2.55...
Could not open connection to the host, on port 515:
Connect failed
```

3. Confirm that outbound connections are allowed from the client on ports 721–731. Some systems have firewalls that restrict connections. You can verify this by looking at the firewall configuration. Run `iptables -L` or `ipchains -L` (for an older firewall) to list the firewall configuration.

4. Confirm that the entry in `/etc/services` for the service is correct.

```
cat /etc/services  |grep 515
printer          515/tcp        spooler    # line printer spooler
printer          515/udp        spooler    # line printer spooler
```

5. Confirm that the remote spooler (on Germany) can print locally.

   Log into Germany and print a file to Berlin. If this works, we know that the local spooler on Germany is working correctly.

Other possible causes of this type of error include the following:

- The remote spooler is not RFC1179 compliant.
- The hostname is longer than eight characters, which can sometimes cause problems.
- Job numbering is above 9999, which can also cause problems with some spoolers.

Raw Network Socket Printing

This type of printing was pioneered by Hewlett-Packard, but most printers with network connections support raw network printing. The main port for these transfers is port 9100, but on multiport print servers, it is also possible to send print jobs to ports 9101 and 9102. This is called raw printing because the port is opened and the raw text stream is then transferred to the device. There is no queue or spooler on the other end to receive the print request. Any formatting or other control characters must be embedded into the raw text stream. The network device can also send back status or error messages while the connection is open. The connection is kept open until the request finishes transferring.

note

Microsoft calls this Standard TCP/IP port printing.

These print servers can be cards inside the printer that allow connection to the network or external boxes with ports to connect the printer to a network connection. Just to confuse things further, many networked printers support printing to both ports 515 and 9100. For example, Hewlett-Packard JetDirect print servers also accept RFC1179 print requests to the queues *raw* and *text*.

One important question is: "How does the print device obtain its IP address and netmask?" Most network printers can obtain their configuration in several ways. The configuration can be hard coded through the front panel or a network interface (TELNET or HTTP), or dynamically through DHCP and bootp. Bootp and DHCP (which is newer and more capable) both are used to dynamically assign networking information to network devices.

The vast majority of printing through port 9100 is done to print servers, but it is possible to set up a UNIX or Linux system to accept print requests this way. This is done by adding a new service line to /etc/inetd.conf. Two examples of this are

- Directing the input to the spooler:

    ```
    9100 stream tcp nowait lp /usr/bin/lp lp -d queuename
    ```

- Redirecting the raw data stream to a device:

    ```
    9100 stream tcp nowait lp /bin/dd dd of=/dev/lp0
    ```

Contention

How does a print server such as HP's JetDirect handle device contention? They are relatively simple devices and have no spooler. They just have a print buffer. When the print device is busy printing, all the other hosts must retry until the print server is free.

Troubleshooting Tools

Troubleshooting tools for working on raw network socket printing problems include the following:

- Netcat (nc):

```
cat <filename> | nc -w 1 <host> <port>
```

    This command transfers a file to the network printer and bypasses the spooler. If this works, you have device connectivity, and the problem is with the spooler.

- TELNET to port 9100:

```
telnet hostname 9100
```

    If you receive a connection on this port, then the printer is online and is accepting connections.

- Syslog: Check syslog for errors

IPP

"The Internet Printing Protocol (IPP) is an application level protocol that can be used for distributed printing using Internet tools and technologies."

[RFC2911]

IPP is a new client/server print protocol that was designed in cooperation with the IETF. IPP is designed with networks and shared resources in mind. All printer and job objects are defined using a Uniform Resource Locator (URL), just like what is used for other Internet-based services such as HTTP, FTP, and so on. Unlike other protocols, IPP also supports access controls, Basic, Digest, and Certificate authentication, LDAP integration, and SSL and TLS encryption. Many new network printers and print servers include built-in IPP capabilities.

The IPP standard is defined in the following documents from the IETF:

- Design Goals for an Internet Printing Protocol [RFC2567]
- Mapping Between LPD and IPP Protocols [RFC2569]

- Rationale for the Structure of the Model and Protocol for the Internet Printing Protocol [RFC2568]
- Internet Printing Protocol/1.1: Encoding and Transport [RFC2910]
- Internet Printing Protocol/1.1: Model and Semantics [RFC2911]
- Internet Printing Protocol/1.1: Implementer's Guide [IPP-IIG]

Five key terms are needed to understand IPP. They are IPP printer, IPP client, privileged operator, job, and notification service. IPP can use port 631 or port 80. Port 631 is the most commonly used. Here is an example of a URL for an IPP print device:

```
# lpstat -v Laser
device for Laser: ipp://localhost/ipp
```

IPP uses standard HTTP POST and GET commands to enable bidirectional communication with print devices. It uses a special "application/ipp" MIME Content-Type. IPP allows normal push printing, but it also has the capability to perform pull printing, in which a server or printer is told the URL of a document, which is then pulled from that URL and printed.

The IPP RFC breaks down the capabilities of IPP printing into six categories:

- Finding a printer
- Creating a local instance of the printer
- Viewing the printer status and capabilities
- Submitting a print job
- Viewing print status
- Altering the print job

Next is an example of a POST-based communication with an IPP device.

```
POST /ipp/ HTTP/1.1
Content-Length: 285
Content-Type: application/ipp
Host: 192.168.2.33
```

Terminal Servers (Networked Serial)

A terminal server (see Figure 11-10) is a piece of networked hardware that provides multiple users with access to terminal and console ports, modems, printers, and other serial devices. A terminal server can be either a piece of custom hardware or a standard computer system with a large number of serial ports. In either case, a terminal server provides a way to enable hardware to be accessed from multiple systems, and it provides network access to devices that don't ordinarily have it. There are two main ways to access devices connected to terminal servers. The first is a direct network connection through specific ports. The other is to use drivers on the client to packetize communication to local device files and forward it to the terminal server. Configuration varies between terminal server manufacturers.

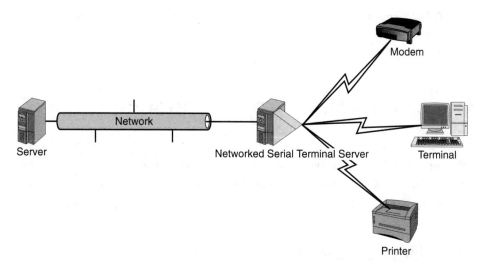

Figure 11-10 A terminal server

Page Description Languages

A Page Description Language (PDL) is a series of commands used for controlling printed page layout. Think of a PDL as a markup language like HTML. A PDL is a series of commands and escape sequences that are embedded into the print data.

A Printer Job Language (PJL) controls job separation, changing and reporting the printer status, changing of printer settings, and PDL language changing between jobs. PJL acts as a wrapper around the PDL(s).

Several examples of PDLs are shown in the following list:

- **PostScript**—PostScript was developed by Adobe. It is a tagged markup language that is rendered into raster by the print driver, filter script, or printer hardware.

- **PCL**—PCL was developed by Hewlett-Packard. It is also a tagged language. It uses escape sequences.

- **HP/GL**—HP/GL was developed by Hewlett-Packard. It is the industry standard PDL for plotters.

- **Other formats**—Raw graphics such as TIFF and JPEG can be interpreted by some printers.

General Printing Troubleshooting

There are many troubleshooting techniques that are useful no matter which spooler you are using. These techniques enable you to understand the printing environment and the general points of failure. When you know these pieces of data, you can use the troubleshooting tools specific to each spooler to figure out what is causing the failure.

Mapping the Spooling Environment

This technique might be the least often used, but in many cases, it can be the most useful. Figure 11-11 shows an example of a map. It is best to have a map completed before printing problems occur so that you can refer to it when troubleshooting.

Figure 11-11 shows multiple types of printers and their connection methods. Keep in mind that a printer that might be local to one system could also be configured as a remote printer on another system. You must know not only the absolute location of a device but also its relationship to other devices. It is best to have this map completed and maintained before you have printing problems because it enables you to immediately

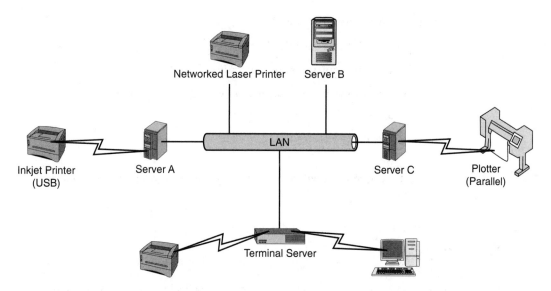

Figure 11-11 An example of mapping the spooling environment

understand the host/printer relationships instead of having to figure them out under duress. If you are not sure about the specifics of a printer's configuration (such as an IP address), you can always go to the printer and attempt to print a test or configuration page from the printer's front panel.

Breakpoints

The common breakpoints for printing are listed here:

1. Can other systems print to the printer?
2. Can you print to the printer by bypassing the spooler?
3. What do you find when you put the spooler in verbose or debug mode and look at log file entries?
4. What is the scope of the problem?

   A. Can't print to one printer?

B. Can't print to several printers?

   a. Cannot print to a specific class or type?

   b. Cannot print to printers in a specific location?

   c. Cannot print to printers with a network device or server in common?

   d. Cannot print to all printers?

The answers to these questions will direct you to the area you will need to troubleshoot further.

Summary

By breaking printing into its component parts, it is relatively easy to troubleshoot. Without knowledge of spooler types, printer connection types, printer types, and so on, printing problems are difficult to fix. It is important to remember to map your environment, be specific about connection types, and test breakpoints to find where the problem lies.

12

System Security

System security is about as important an IT topic as there is these days. A key responsibility of a system administrator is keeping data secure and safe. In the Internet age, this requires more diligence and preparation that ever before. Even on systems inside a firewall, it is urgent to prepare and monitor for intrusions. This chapter begins by defining system security. It then tackles the issue of prevention, focusing on troubleshooting SSH and system hardening issues.

What Is System Security?

The word "security" in general usage is synonymous with "safety," but as a technical term, "security" means not only that something *is secure* but that it *has been secured*. Systems security is a process by which the physical host and the data on it are made safe from unauthorized access, but just as important, they are available to those who need access.

One thing that we must understand is that security through obscurity is not security. It is just luck. Many system administrators rely on the fact that they are behind a firewall or that their system is one of many. This is just perceived security, not real security.

Host Versus Network Security

Two major categories of security exist: host-based and network-based. Host-based security is used to ensure the safety of individual computer systems and their data. Network security is used to ensure the security of the network connections between internal hosts and also between the internal and external networks.

The two are necessarily intertwined. An insecure network unnecessarily exposes the hosts to testing and attacks. Likewise, insecure systems can provide an initial path into a network and give a safe haven to bad guys. The scope of this chapter is mainly host security, not network security, but network security is vital, and more information can be found in such titles as *The Tao of Network Security Monitoring: Beyond Intrusion Detection* by Richard Bejtlich (Boston: Addison-Wesley, 2004).

What Is Vulnerability?

Vulnerability is a weakness that can be exploited and used to attack a host. There are many forms of vulnerabilities. An example is a defect in the software running on a host that allows unintended access to the system. Mitre.org defines vulnerability as follows (from http://cve.mitre.org/about/terminology.html):

> A "universal" vulnerability is one that is considered a vulnerability under any commonly used security policy which includes at least some requirements for minimizing the threat from an attacker. (This excludes entirely "open" security policies in which all users are trusted, or where there is no consideration of risk to the system.)

The following guidelines, while imprecise, provide the basis of a "universal vulnerability" definition. A universal vulnerability is a state in a computing system (or set of systems) which either

- Allows an attacker to execute commands as another user
- Allows an attacker to access data that is contrary to the specified access restrictions for that data
- Allows an attacker to pose as another entity
- Allows an attacker to conduct a denial of service

The following guidelines provide the basis for a definition of an "exposure." An exposure is a state in a computing system (or set of systems) that is not a universal vulnerability, but either:

- Allows an attacker to conduct information-gathering activities
- Allows an attacker to hide activities

- Includes a capability that behaves as expected, but can be easily compromised
- Is a primary point of entry that an attacker may attempt to use to gain access to the system or data
- Is considered a problem according to some reasonable security policy

So an exposure is less severe than a vulnerability but is still of concern. Using a password-less user login would be a vulnerability, whereas running an insecure service such as TELNET or FTP would be an exposure.

Classes of Host Vulnerabilities

Two main classes of host vulnerabilities exist: local and remote vulnerabilities. A local vulnerability can only be exploited by a user who is authenticated and logged into the system. A remote vulnerability can be exploited without a user being logged in, and it is usually executed from another host system that is already compromised.

A local vulnerability is dangerous, but the attacker must obtain a level of penetration to use it, which somewhat lessens the risk. Remote vulnerabilities are much more risky and should be closed immediately. Both involve risk, but remote vulnerabilities are inherently riskier and therefore should be addressed immediately.

In Figure 12-1, you can see a sample network diagram. This is a fairly common configuration, including a connection to the Internet, a DMZ network, and an intranet. A DMZ network is a network that is open to inbound traffic from the Internet. Public mail and Web servers reside in a DMZ. This setup enables you to limit public access to your internal networks. The host security is much tighter on a host deployed in a DMZ than one on an intranet because of the greater risk involved in the DMZ. In a perfect world, all systems would be invulnerable to attack, but this provision would take unlimited resources (or a system that is powered off and locked in a cabinet). Unfortunately, all systems must balance risk with cost (see Figure 12-2). There must be just enough security to decrease the risk to an acceptable level. That level is different for each situation. The cost to reduce the risk to an acceptable level varies depending on the amount of risk to which the host is exposed. The goal is to invest enough in security to reach the point where security and cost are equally balanced.

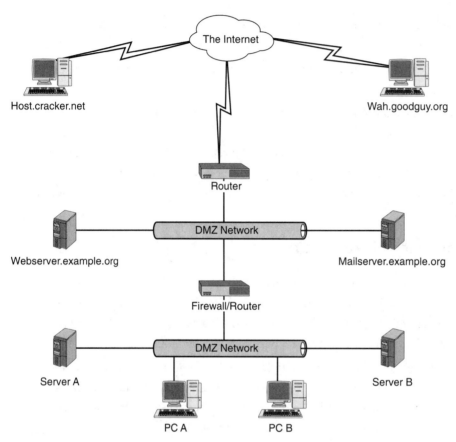

Figure 12-1 A sample network diagram

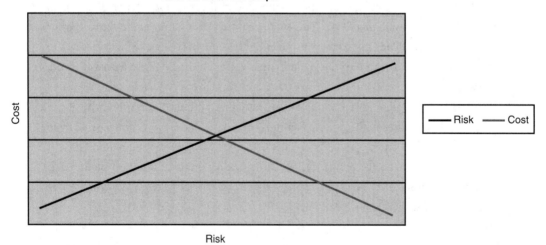

Figure 12-2 Risk versus cost

Types of Vulnerabilities and Exposures

Multiple types of vulnerabilities and exposures must be defined so that we can understand the common risk types. The vulnerabilities and exposures include the following:

- **Software defect**—This is by far the most common risk you will encounter. A defect can be in operating system software or application software. Defects in the OS are typically more worrisome, but an application defect can be just as troublesome. For example, a defect in a database management system (DBMS) that allows customers' data to be viewed by unauthorized people on the Web is just as damaging as revealing that same data through an OS defect. Examples of software defects that typically cause these types of problems are buffer overflows, design problems that allow access to functions that should be disallowed, allowing malformed input, allowing access to files or data that should be disallowed, and so on.

- **Clear text data captured**—With the advent of WiFi, this risk has become more common. If user, password, or other data is transmitted across open networks in clear text, it can be intercepted and used. A classic example is the difference between TELNET and SSH. TELNET transmits all data including passwords and login names in clear text. If bad guys are on the network and have their network card in promiscuous mode, they can sniff out the login information and gain access to a system. SSH uses encryption on all traffic and is inherently more secure. The same issues arise when using FTP instead of SFTP.

- **Weak passwords**—Crackable or easily guessable passwords are a common way for hackers to gain initial access to a system. This vulnerability allows them to peel back one layer of the security onion and makes it much easier for them to use other methods to gain unauthorized super user access.

- **Spoofing**—Spoofing occurs when an attacker pretends to be an entity and takes over communication between systems. For example, if SystemA and SystemB are communicating, the attacker could set up SystemC to use SystemB's IP address, hostname, and so on. The hacker could then use a DoS attack to knock SystemB offline and take over the "conversation" with SystemA.

- **Social engineering attack**—This attack consists of an insider who unknowingly gives out sensitive data to a hacker (phishing). This can take place through email, phone, the Web, and so on. The end goal is for the hacker to obtain account information or personal data for illicit use. Many times this is accomplished when the hacker impersonates a person in authority or a trusted entity (such as a bank).

- **Physical attack**—Security personnel don't always adequately address this type of vulnerability. It is easy to boot a host off a floppy and take control of it. A hacker can also just steal a system. Another overlooked possibility is to buy decommissioned systems and then use tools to recover deleted data from a hard drive.

- **Carelessness**—Carelessness is a human error that hackers exploit to gain access to a system that is exposed through negligence or stupidity. Two classic examples are using the default password and writing down a password.

- **Denial of service**—"A denial-of-service attack (also, DoS attack) is an attack on a computer system or network that causes a loss of service to users, typically the loss of network connectivity and services by consuming the bandwidth of the victim network or overloading the computational resources of the victim system" (from http://en.wikipedia.org/wiki/Denial_of_service). Examples are invalid packet floods, valid packet floods, and service floods such as HTTP attacks.

- **Access controls not restricted enough**—This condition occurs when permission to access a resource (a service, file, directory, system, etc.) is not properly restricted.

- **Espionage**—This attack consists of an insider knowingly working with a hacker to obtain account information or personal data for illicit use.

General Steps to Increase Host Security

We recommend four general steps to increase host security.

1. **Preparation**—The first step is to obtain the knowledge necessary to understand security and then use that to plan a defense in depth.

2. **Planning**—Security should be an ongoing process, not just something you do once. Planning and education should be continual. Any security plan is only as good as its weakest point. After an attacker breaches a single point of defense, the other points become easier to breach. The security plan should also include training for employees, auditing, and so on. It should also include steps to report and repair hosts after a breach. The quicker a breach is caught and corrected, the less time an attacker has to compromise other systems.

3. **Prevention**—We discuss this topic in much more depth later, but it is much easier to prevent an attack than to recover from one. We can use multiple strategies to accomplish prevention:

   * Encryption
   * System hardening
   * Password hardening
   * Physical security
   * Monitoring for unsuccessful attack patterns
   * Vetting and verification of identity
   * Patching
   * System probing

4. **Postvention**—This is a strange term, but there are some good techniques that can't be called prevention. Looking for signatures of a successful attack, notifying authorities, closing a discovered vulnerability, and fixing the affected systems are examples of postvention.

   Monitoring for breaches is very important. It can be accomplished using tools such as Chkrootkit, Rkhunter, Tripwire, and Logwatch.

Prevention

As the old saying goes, "An ounce of prevention is worth a pound of cure." It is much easier and cheaper to prevent security incursions than it is to repair them after the fact. A glance at the headlines reveals a parade of companies who realized too late that they had security problems and had exposed customer data at risk. Even systems behind "secure" firewalls can be at risk and need to have preventative plans in place.

Encryption with SSH

The Secure Shell protocol (SSH) is a method to connect to remote machines through an encrypted network stream. This method prevents packets of data, such as your password, from being intercepted as they travel across the network. SSH provides remote shell access, file transfer, key-based user and host authentication, X11 sessions through the open SSH tunnel, and TCP/IP tunneling through port redirection.

Two SSH versions are available for use: version 1 and version 2. It is recommended that you use only version 2 clients because version 1 has known security vulnerabilities. Version 2 also includes Secure FTP (SFTP), which provides an interface that is easier to use for transferring files than secure copy (SCP).

SSH has four main key types: public host keys, private host keys, public user keys, and private user keys.

The SSH server that runs on most Linux systems is OpenSSH (http://www. openssh.org/). OpenSSH is a free version of the SSH protocol suite of network connectivity tools. In SSH version 1 mode, OpenSSH only supports 3DES and Blowfish encryption standards. In SSH version 2 mode, OpenSSH 3DES, Blowfish, CAST128, Arcfour, and AES encryption standards are supported.

OpenSSH also provides the client binaries for Linux, shown in Table 12-1.

Table 12-1   OpenSSH Client Binaries

Binary	Function
/usr/bin/scp	Secure copy (replaces rcp).
/usr/bin/slogin	Secure login (replaces rlogin and rsh).
/usr/bin/ssh-add	Adds SSH keys to the ssh-agent.
/usr/bin/ssh-keyscan	Gathers SSH public keys.
/usr/bin/ssh-agent	SSH authentication agent. It holds private keys for users.
/usr/bin/ssh	SSH remote login program (replaces telnet).
/usr/bin/sftp	Secure file transfer (replaces ftp).

The output from a system installed with Red Hat Enterprise Linux 3.0 and OpenSSH 3.6.1 looks like this:

```
# rpm -qa |grep -i ssh
openssh-config-3.6.1p2-18c
openssh-3.6.1p2-33.30.3
openssh-clients-3.6.1p2-33.30.3
openssh-server-3.6.1p2-33.30.3
```

OpenSSH's RSA/DSA key authentication system is one of its biggest features. It is an alternative to the regular password authentication system used by OpenSSH.

OpenSSH key pair authentication uses a pair of specially generated cryptographic keys: the *private key* and the *public key*. These key-based authentication systems make it possible to initiate secure connections without having to type in a password. Instead, you type in the key password. The keys are generated with ssh-keygen.

You can also use ssh-agent to cache the key and its password in memory, enabling you to log into any system containing your public key with no password at all. RSA and DSA keys are also used to identify each host.

OpenSSH keeps system configuration files in several locations. It is important to know these files and what they do. The location varies based on the distribution. They are generally in either /etc/ssh or /etc/sshd, but a few older distributions put the files directly in the /etc directory. Table 12-2 lists the OpenSSH configuration files.

A user's configuration files are typically kept in the ~/.ssh directory (see Table 12-3).

PuTTY (http://www.chiark.greenend.org.uk/~sgtatham/putty/) is a commonly used SSH client for both Microsoft Windows and Linux systems (see Figure 12-3). It makes port forwarding and setting SSH options much easier. It gives the user the same functionality as the OpenSSH client except for file transfer. WinSCP (http://winscp.net/eng/index.php) is a good client to fill this file transfer functionality gap.

Figure 12-4 shows the PuTTY options for configuring SSH tunneling.

A tunnel is an encrypted connection that connects two computers across an open network (see Figure 12-5). This is one of the most useful features of SSH. Tunneling enables insecure network traffic between systems to be encrypted and encapsulated without having to change how the overlaying applications or protocols work.

Table 12-2   OpenSSH System Configuration Files

File	Function
ssh_config	OpenSSH SSH client configuration file.
sshd_config	OpenSSH SSH daemon configuration file.
ssh_host_dsa_key	The SSH host Version 2 DSA-based private key.
ssh_host_dsa_key.pub	The SSH host Version 2 DSA-based public key.
ssh_host_key	The SSH host Version 1 RSA-based private key.
ssh_host_key.pub	The SSH host Version 1 RSA-based public key.
ssh_host_rsa_key	The SSH host Version 2 RSA-based private key.
ssh_host_rsa_key.pub	The SSH host Version 2 RSA-based public key.
banner	Optional banner file similar to motd.
moduli	This file contains the system-wide prime moduli for sshd used to generate keys.

Table 12-3   User Configuration Files

File	Function
Config	OpenSSH SSH client configuration file.
identity	SSH Version 1 RSA-based private key.
identity.pub	SSH Version 1 RSA-based public key.
authorized_keys	SSH Version 1 allowed servers' public keys.
authorized_keys2	SSH Version 2 allowed servers' public keys.
known_hosts	Keys for hosts to which you have connected.
id_dsa.pub	SSH Version 2 DSA-based public key.
id_dsa	SSH Version 2 DSA-based private key.
id_rsa.pub	SSH Version 2 RSA-based public key.
id_rsa	SSH Version 2 RSA-based private key.

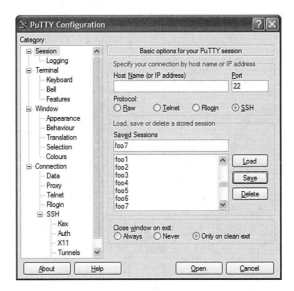

Figure 12-3 The PuTTY configuration tool

Figure 12-4 Configuring SSH tunnels

So in the example in Figure 12-5, you can establish the session by issuing the following command:

```
ssh -L 110:mailserver:110 -L 515:Printer:515 -l username -N firewall
```

An Example of SSH Tunnels in Action

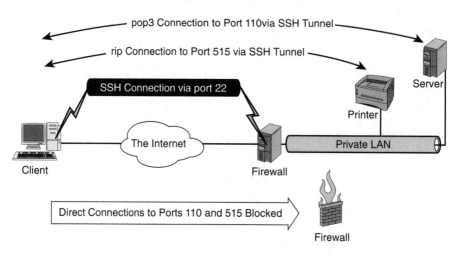

Figure 12-5 SSH Tunnel example

You can also map remote ports to nonstandard local ports. This enables you to continue using these ports to communicate to other systems on these ports. Otherwise all traffic to these ports is intercepted by SSH. If you want the POP3 traffic to be transported through a non-privileged port, you can run the following command:

```
ssh -L 1610:mailserver:110 -L 515:Printer:515 -l username -N firewall
```

The email program on the client now can grab POP3 mail from the mailserver through port 1601 and can leave port 110 free for non-SSH tunneled POP3 traffic. You can also forward SMTP for outgoing mail through port 25.

The user can then test the connection:

```
# telnet localhost 1601
Trying 127.0.0.1...
Connected to localhost.
Escape character is '^]'.
+OK mailserver.example.org Cyrus POP3 v2.2.10-Invoca-RPM-2.2.10-3.fc3
server ready <2107198432.1112551972@ mailserver.example.org>
```

```
# telnet localhost 515
Trying 127.0.0.1...
Connected to localhost.
Escape character is '^]'.
```

This output shows that both tunnels are working.

X11 traffic can also be forwarded through the tunnel, but SSH has integrated this into the daemon. A detailed description from the ssh(1) man page follows:

```
X11 and TCP forwarding
If the ForwardX11 variable is set to 'yes' (or see the description of the
-X and -x options described later) and the user is using X11 (the DISPLAY
environment variable is set), the connection to the X11 display is
automatically forwarded to the remote side in such a way that any X11
programs started from the shell (or command) will go through the
encrypted channel, and the connection to the real X server will be made
from the local machine.  The user should not manually set DISPLAY.
Forwarding of X11 connections can be configured on the command line or in
configuration files.
```

Troubleshooting Typical SSH Problems

One crucial task is gathering logs and data from SSH failures. You can perform this task in several ways. You can increase the verbosity of both the SSH server and client. The nodes /var/log/messages and /var/log/secure should give you some other details as to what is causing issues.

From the ssh(1) man page:

```
-v      Verbose mode.  Causes ssh to print debugging messages about its
progress.  This is helpful in debugging connection, authentication, and
configuration problems.  Multiple -v options increases the verbosity.
Maximum is 3.
```

From the sshd(8) man page:

```
-d      Debug mode.  The server sends verbose debug output to the system
log, and does not put itself in the background.  The server also will not
fork and will only process one connection.  This option is only intended
for debugging for the server.  Multiple -d options increase the debugging
level.  Maximum is 3.
```

Newer versions of sshd might also have a -v debug option as well. You also should confirm that sshd is actually running.

```
# ps -ef |grep ssh


root      7714    1  0 Dec02 ?          00:00:00 /usr/sbin/sshd -o
PidFile=/var/run/sshd.init.pid
```

Connection and Login Failures

You might encounter several connection and login failure scenarios using SSH. They are easily corrected if you know what to look for. Generally they can be addressed by looking at /var/log/messages and setting ssh into verbose mode.

Scenario 12-1: Host Key Mismatch

The user tries to SSH to the host stapler.example.org, but it fails with the following message:

```
# ssh stapler
Host key verification failed.
```

The entry in the ~/.known_hosts for stapler is:

```
stapler,192.168.48.127 ssh-rsa
3NzaC1yc2EAAAABIwAAAIEA1OOYLo55uYHeG0aYoXQpMVgCmOtydMgolYI7rM3dDAgvorAmEi
pcDU5cDtr7n51L5ykwv/N5nt74fDC+sjwDLKYiXW7KYLLWcnpIC3WWOI3zKa8sQRQ7z2Es6Fg
ahYOa1FpDOQQiKUCbFScOfUNwBrRpWQgZMgPjf94IqENdhx8=
```

On stapler, the contents of /etc/ssh/ssh_host_rsa_key.pub are:

```
ssh-rsa
CCCCZ3NzaC1yc2EAAAABIwAAAIEA1OOYLo55uYHeG0aYoXQpMVgCmOtydMgolYI7rM3dDAgvo
rAmEipcDU5cDtr7n51L5ykwv/N5nt74fDC+sjwDLKYiXW7KYLLWcnpIC3WWOI3zKa8sQRQ
7z2Es6FgahYOa1FpDOQQiKUCbFScOfUNwBrRpWQgZMgPjf94IqENdhx8=
```

The mismatch between these two entries is causing the problem. A typical cause is that stapler might have been reinstalled or changed. If you know the cause of the change and are satisfied, you can delete the entry in known_hosts and reconnect. You receive the following message:

```
# ssh stapler
The authenticity of host 'stapler (192.168.48.127)' can't be established.
RSA key fingerprint is dd:4f:gg:e0:69:1e:a7:c2:d1:6f:0f:ff:a5:ac:47:74.
Are you sure you want to continue connecting (yes/no)? yes
Warning: Permanently added 'stapler,192.168.48.127' (RSA) to the list of known hosts.
```

Scenario 12-2: The User Put His or Her Public Key into authorized_keys But Key-Based Authentication Still Doesn't Work

This problem can be caused by open permissions on ~/.ssh or files underneath it. For example,

```
# ) ssh -v stapler
OpenSSH_3.6.1p2, SSH protocols 1.5/2.0, OpenSSL 0x0090701f
debug1: Reading configuration data /etc/ssh/ssh_config
debug1: Applying options for *
debug1: Rhosts Authentication disabled, originating port will not be
    trusted.
debug1: Connecting to stapler [192.168.48.127] port 22.
debug1: Connection established.
debug1: identity file /home/jxk/.ssh/identity type 1
debug1: identity file /home/jxk/.ssh/id_rsa type -1
debug1: identity file /home/jxk/.ssh/id_dsa type -1
debug1: Remote protocol version 1.99, remote software version
    OpenSSH_3.6.1p2
debug1: match: OpenSSH_3.6.1p2 pat OpenSSH*
debug1: Enabling compatibility mode for protocol 2.0
debug1: Local version string SSH-2.0-OpenSSH_3.6.1p2
debug1: SSH2_MSG_KEXINIT sent
debug1: SSH2_MSG_KEXINIT received
```

```
debug1: kex: server->client aes128-cbc hmac-md5 none
debug1: kex: client->server aes128-cbc hmac-md5 none
debug1: SSH2_MSG_KEX_DH_GEX_REQUEST sent
debug1: expecting SSH2_MSG_KEX_DH_GEX_GROUP
debug1: SSH2_MSG_KEX_DH_GEX_INIT sent
debug1: expecting SSH2_MSG_KEX_DH_GEX_REPLY
debug1: Host 'stapler' is known and matches the RSA host key.
debug1: Found key in /home/jxk/.ssh/known_hosts:40
debug1: ssh_rsa_verify: signature correct
debug1: SSH2_MSG_NEWKEYS sent
debug1: expecting SSH2_MSG_NEWKEYS
debug1: SSH2_MSG_NEWKEYS received
debug1: SSH2_MSG_SERVICE_REQUEST sent
debug1: SSH2_MSG_SERVICE_ACCEPT received
debug1: Authentications that can continue: publickey,password,keyboard-
        interactive
debug1: Next authentication method: publickey
debug1: Offering public key: /home/jxk/.ssh/identity
debug1: Authentications that can continue: publickey,password,keyboard-
        interactive
debug1: Trying private key: /home/jxk/.ssh/id_rsa
debug1: Trying private key: /home/jxk/.ssh/id_dsa
debug1: Next authentication method: keyboard-interactive
debug1: Authentications that can continue: publickey,password,keyboard-
        interactive
debug1: Next authentication method: password
        jxk@stapler's password:
debug1: Authentication succeeded (password).
debug1: channel 0: new [client-session]
debug1: Entering interactive session.
debug1: channel 0: request pty-req
debug1: channel 0: request shell
debug1: channel 0: open confirm rwindow 0 rmax 32768
```

In this case, the problem can be solved by executing the following on both the server and your local computer. Permissions are enforced by sshd. There also must be one key per line in the authorized_keys files. Line breaks are not allowed in a key.

```
# chmod -R 600 ~/.ssh/*
# chmod 700 ~/.ssh


# ssh -v stapler
OpenSSH_3.6.1p2, SSH protocols 1.5/2.0, OpenSSL 0x0090701f
debug1: Reading configuration data /etc/ssh/ssh_config
debug1: Applying options for *
debug1: Rhosts Authentication disabled, originating port will not be
        trusted.
debug1: Connecting to stapler [192.168.48.127] port 22.
debug1: Connection established.
debug1: identity file /home/jxk/.ssh/identity type 1
debug1: identity file /home/jxk/.ssh/id_rsa type -1
debug1: identity file /home/jxk/.ssh/id_dsa type -1
debug1: Remote protocol version 1.99, remote software version
        OpenSSH_3.6.1p2
debug1: match: OpenSSH_3.6.1p2 pat OpenSSH*
debug1: Enabling compatibility mode for protocol 2.0
debug1: Local version string SSH-2.0-OpenSSH_3.6.1p2
debug1: SSH2_MSG_KEXINIT sent
debug1: SSH2_MSG_KEXINIT received
debug1: kex: server->client aes128-cbc hmac-md5 none
debug1: kex: client->server aes128-cbc hmac-md5 none
debug1: SSH2_MSG_KEX_DH_GEX_REQUEST sent
debug1: expecting SSH2_MSG_KEX_DH_GEX_GROUP
debug1: SSH2_MSG_KEX_DH_GEX_INIT sent
debug1: expecting SSH2_MSG_KEX_DH_GEX_REPLY
debug1: Host 'stapler' is known and matches the RSA host key.
debug1: Found key in /home/jxk/.ssh/known_hosts:40
debug1: ssh_rsa_verify: signature correct
debug1: SSH2_MSG_NEWKEYS sent
debug1: expecting SSH2_MSG_NEWKEYS
debug1: SSH2_MSG_NEWKEYS received
debug1: SSH2_MSG_SERVICE_REQUEST sent
debug1: SSH2_MSG_SERVICE_ACCEPT received
```

```
debug1: Authentications that can continue: publickey,password,keyboard-
        interactive
debug1: Next authentication method: publickey
debug1: Offering public key: /home/jxk/.ssh/identity
debug1: Server accepts key: pkalg ssh-rsa blen 148 lastkey 0x8718d38 hint 0
debug1: PEM_read_PrivateKey failed
debug1: read PEM private key done: type <unknown>
Enter passphrase for key '/home/jxk/.ssh/identity':
debug1: read PEM private key done: type RSA
debug1: Authentication succeeded (publickey).
debug1: channel 0: new [client-session]
debug1: Entering interactive session.
debug1: channel 0: request pty-req
debug1: channel 0: request shell
debug1: channel 0: open confirm rwindow 0 rmax 32768
```

You could also change the value of `StrictModes` to `no` in the `sshd_config` file, but this approach is insecure and not recommended.

Scenario 12-3: SSH Is Receiving Connection Refused Messages

This problem has several possible causes. The most common is that `iptables` is blocking access to the ports needed by SSH. You can check with the following command:

```
# iptables -L | grep -i ssh
DROP      tcp  --  anywhere             anywhere            tcp dpt:ssh
flags:SYN,RST,ACK/SYN
```

As you can see in this example, TCP packets going to port 22 (the SSH port) are set to drop. You can edit the `iptables` configuration file in `/etc/sysconfig/iptables` and change the line for port 22. In this case,

```
-A RH-Lokkit-0-50-INPUT -p tcp -m tcp --dport 22 -j DROP --syn
```

would be changed to

```
-A RH-Lokkit-0-50-INPUT -p tcp -m tcp --dport 22 -j ACCEPT -syn
```

If there is no line for port 22, you could append one to add the ACCEPT syntax. iptables would need to be restarted for any changes to take effect.

Scenario 12-4: Correct Password Generates Error

A user is trying to connect to a system using SSH, and she receives the following error:

```
Password (incorrect) for user on host hostname:
```

The password has been verified as correct. The server to which the user is trying to connect has SSH password authentication turned off. The daemon is configured to use alternate forms of authentication such as PAM or keys. For OpenSSH, in the /etc/ssh/sshd_config file on the server, the PasswordAuthentication option is set to no.

Functionality Failures

After you have your connection and login problems solved, you can run into a couple of functionality-related problems.

Scenario 12-5: X11 and/or Agent Forwarding Does Not Work

Check your ssh_config and sshd_config files. The default configuration files disable authentication agent and X11 forwarding. To enable this forwarding, put the following line in sshd_config:

```
X11Forwarding yes
```

Then place the following lines in ssh_config:

```
ForwardAgent yes
ForwardX11 yes
```

If this is set and X11 forwarding is still not working, check whether your DISPLAY variable is set correctly. Sometimes it doesn't map correctly. This problem is usually caused by either not having the X11 server running before you SSH into the remote system or by having a line in your login scripts (such as .bashrc or .bash_profile) that manually sets the DISPLAY variable (such as export DISPLAY=hostname.example.org:0.0). The display number changes based on how many other displays are in use.

It usually starts at 10. If you run the following example, you should see the window shown in Figure 12-6 appear.

```
$ echo $DISPLAY
$ xclock
Error: Can't open display:
$ export DISPLAY=localhost:0
$ xclock
Error: Can't open display: localhost:0
$ export DISPLAY=localhost:10
$ xclock
```

Figure 12-6 xclock

Scenario 12-6: The User Created a Tunnel and the Application Won't Connect

The most common cause of this problem is that the user is trying to connect using the remote host name instead of `localhost`.

```
# ssh -L 110:mailserver:110 -L 515:Printer:515 -l username -N firewall


# ftp ftp.example.org
ftp: ftp.example.com: Name or service not known
ftp>


# ftp localhost
Trying 127.0.0.1...
```

```
Connected to ftp.example.org (192.168.22.105).
220 ftp.example.org  FTP server (example.com version w02) ready.
Name (ftp.example.com:jxk):
```

System Hardening with netfilter/iptables

netfilter and iptables together make up the standard firewall software for the Linux 2.4 and 2.6 kernels. They are the replacement for the 2.2 kernel ipchains, nat, and proxying facilities. netfilter is the kernel portion of the firewall software, and iptables consists of the user utilities used to manage the firewall.

netfilter enables the system administrator to define rules for dealing with network packets. A packet is the fundamental unit of information transmission in TCP/IP networking.

The netfilter rules are then grouped into chains. A chain is an ordered list of rules. The chains are then grouped into tables. Each table is associated with a different class of packet processing. Each chain is responsible for filtering or modifying packets as they come through the chain. Filtering is the process of either blocking or allowing the packets as they travel through the system.

Each chain contains a manifest of rules. When a packet is sent to a chain, it is compared against each rule in the chain in order. The rules provide a specification that shows which packets match it and a target that shows iptables what to do with the packet if it is matched by that rule. Every network packet arriving at or leaving from the computer traverses at least one chain, and each rule on that chain attempts to match the packet. If the rule matches the packet, the traversal stops, and the rule's target dictates what to do with the packet. If a packet reaches the end of a chain without being matched by any rule on the chain, the chain's policy target dictates what to do with the packet.

There are three statically defined tables. Users cannot change the tables, but they can modify the chains that each table contains. The three tables are described in Table 12-4.

The man page for iptables(8) gives a good description of targets of chains. This is further illustrated by Figure 12-7.

Table 12-4   iptables

Table Name	Predefined Chains	Description
FILTER table		This table is the default table and is the main table responsible for filtering packets.
	Input	All incoming packets go through this chain.
	Output	All outgoing packets go through this chain.
	Forward	All packets being routed through the system use this chain.
NAT table		This table is responsible for rewriting packet addresses or ports.
	Prerouting	Incoming packets pass through this chain before the local routing table is consulted, primarily for DNAT (destination-NAT).
	Postrouting	Outgoing packets pass through this chain after the routing decision has been made, primarily for SNAT (source-NAT).
MANGLE table		This table is used for specialized packet alteration.
	Input	Added in kernel 2.4.18 for packets coming into the box itself.
	Output	Used for altering locally generated packets before routing.
	Forward	Added in kernel 2.4.18 for altering packets being routed through the box.
	Prerouting	Used for altering incoming packets before routing.
	Postrouting	Added in kernel 2.4.18 for altering packets as they are about to go out.

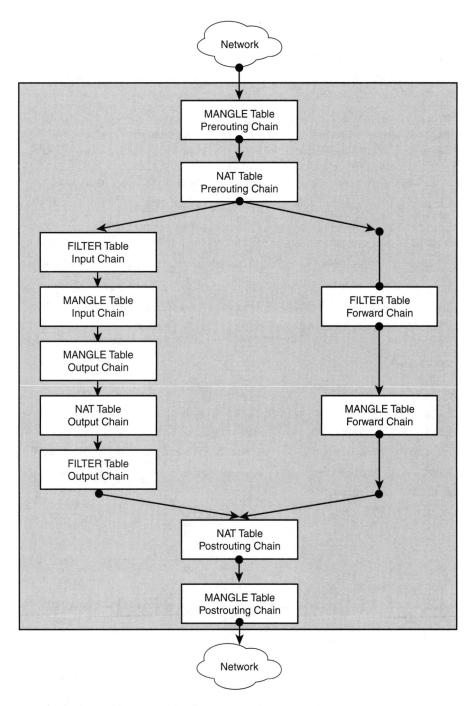

Figure 12-7 *netfilter/iptables* flow example

A firewall rule specifies criteria for a packet, and a target. If the
packet does not match, the next rule in the chain is the examined; if it
does match, then the next rule is specified by the value of the target,
which can be the name of a user-defined chain or one of the special
values ACCEPT, DROP, QUEUE, or RETURN.

ACCEPT means to let the packet through. DROP means to drop the packet on
the floor. QUEUE means to pass the packet to userspace (if supported by
the kernel). RETURN means stop traversing this chain and resume at the
next rule in the previous (calling) chain. If the end of a built-in
chain is reached or a rule in a built-in chain with target RETURN is
matched, the target specified by the chain policy determines the fate of
the packet.

An example of a user-defined target is RH-Firewall-1-INPUT. This target is used by
default on Red Hat Enterprise Linux 3.0. It is used like a subroutine to the Input chain.

There are a few additional special values beyond ACCEPT, DROP, QUEUE, or
RETURN. They are LOG, MARK, MASQUERADE, MIRROR, QUEUE, REDIRECT,
REJECT, TOS, TTL, ULOG, SNAT, and DNAT.

What Is NAT?

Network Address Translation (NAT) is commonly used to enable multiple systems on a
private network to share one public IP address. The public IP address is owned by a dual-
homed device that commonly acts as a router and firewall. NAT enables the user to shield
addresses on the internal network from addresses on the Internet network. NAT rewrites
the source and/or destination addresses of IP packets as they pass through the
router/firewall (see Figure 12-8).

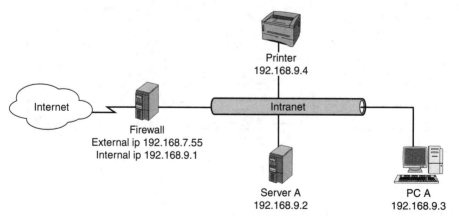

Figure 12-8 NAT

MANGLE Table

Whereas the NAT table enables you to change the source and destination IP addresses to do site hiding, the MANGLE table enables you to change other characteristics within the TCP/IP packet. There are only a few targets that are only valid in the MANGLE table. These are TOS (Type Of Service), TTL (Time To Live), and MARK (used to set special mark values in the packets).

So why would a system administrator use mangling? It is most common in load balancing and QoS (Quality of Service) applications. An example of this might be these rules:

```
iptables -A PREROUTING -t mangle -p tcp --dport 29005 -j TOS --set-tos
Maximize-Throughput

iptables -A PREROUTING -t mangle -p udp --sport 29015 -j TOS --set-tos
Minimize-Delay
```

Configuration with iptables

The first decision most system administrators make when configuring iptables is the default policy for the FILTER table. This is one of the most important decisions and many times is the least considered. Should all packets that do not match any rule be accepted, dropped, or handled in some other way? If you set the default to accept the packets, it is much easier on the system administrator, but it is inherently insecure. If you drop the packets by default, any network service troubleshooting must include iptables as a consideration.

The most-used commands to tell the state of iptables are iptables -L and iptables --list. You can specify a particular chain to any of the -list commands, or you can use no other options, in which case it prints all the chains. Adding -n to this command changes the output from hostnames to IP addresses. By default, iptables only reports on the FILTER table. You must use the -t option to specify a different table. Finally, the -v option provides statistics on the output.

```
# iptables -L

Chain INPUT (policy ACCEPT)
target     prot opt source             destination
LOG        all  -- anywhere            anywhere           LOG level \
debug pre
fix 'BANDWIDTH_IN:'
RH-Lokkit-0-50-INPUT  all  -- anywhere              anywhere


Chain FORWARD (policy ACCEPT)
target     prot opt source             destination
LOG        all  -- anywhere            anywhere           LOG level \
debug pre
fix 'BANDWIDTH_OUT:'
LOG        all  -- anywhere            anywhere           LOG level \
debug pre
fix 'BANDWIDTH_IN:'
RH-Lokkit-0-50-INPUT  all  -- anywhere              anywhere


Chain OUTPUT (policy ACCEPT)
target     prot opt source             destination
LOG        all  -- anywhere            anywhere           LOG level \
debug pre
fix 'BANDWIDTH_OUT:'
Chain RH-Lokkit-0-50-INPUT (2 references)
target     prot opt source             destination
ACCEPT     udp  -- router              anywhere           udp \
spt:domain dpts
:1025:65535
ACCEPT     udp  -- router              anywhere           udp \
spt:domain dpts
:1025:65535
DROP       all  -- 192.168.6.6         anywhere
DROP       all  -- 197.15.43.3         anywhere
DROP       all  -- 198.229.244.130     anywhere
ACCEPT     udp  -- anywhere            anywhere           udp dpt:ntp
```

```
ACCEPT      tcp  --  anywhere            anywhere            tcp dpt:smtp \
flags:
SYN,RST,ACK/SYN
ACCEPT      tcp  --  anywhere            anywhere            tcp \
dpts:netbios-ns
:netbios-ssn
ACCEPT      tcp  --  anywhere            anywhere            tcp dpt:http \
flags:
SYN,RST,ACK/SYN
ACCEPT      tcp  --  anywhere            anywhere            tcp dpt:ssh \
flags:S
YN,RST,ACK/SYN
ACCEPT      tcp  --  anywhere            anywhere            tcp dpt:https
ACCEPT      tcp  --  anywhere            anywhere            tcp dpt:imaps
ACCEPT      tcp  --  anywhere            anywhere            tcp dpt:imap
ACCEPT      all  --  anywhere            anywhere
DROP        tcp  --  anywhere            anywhere            tcp \
dpts:0:1023 fla
gs:SYN,RST,ACK/SYN
DROP        tcp  --  anywhere            anywhere            tcp dpt:nfs
flags:S
YN,RST,ACK/SYN
DROP        udp  --  anywhere            anywhere            udp \
dpts:0:1023
DROP        udp  --  anywhere            anywhere            udp dpt:nfs
DROP        tcp  --  anywhere            anywhere            tcp \
dpts:x11:6009 f
lags:SYN,RST,ACK/SYN
DROP        tcp  --  anywhere            anywhere            tcp dpt:xfs \
flags:S
YN,RST,ACK/SYN


# iptables -L OUTPUT
Chain OUTPUT (policy ACCEPT)
target     prot opt source              destination
LOG        all  --  anywhere
```

```
# iptables -L OUTPUT -v
Chain OUTPUT (policy ACCEPT 1907K packets, 1110M bytes)
 pkts bytes target      prot opt in      out      source \
destination
1754K 1040M LOG         all  -- any     eth0     anywhere \
anywhere                LOG level debug prefix 'BANDWIDTH_OUT:'

# iptables -L -t mangle
Chain PREROUTING (policy ACCEPT)
target      prot opt source              destination
TOS         tcp -- anywhere              anywhere              tcp \
dpt:29005 TOS set Maximize-Throughput

Chain INPUT (policy ACCEPT)
target      prot opt source              destination

Chain FORWARD (policy ACCEPT)
target      prot opt source              destination

Chain OUTPUT (policy ACCEPT)
target      prot opt source              destination

Chain POSTROUTING (policy ACCEPT)
target      prot opt source              destination
```

If the netfilter/iptables is disabled, you will likely see this type of output:

```
# iptables -L
Chain INPUT (policy ACCEPT)
target      prot opt source              destination

Chain FORWARD (policy ACCEPT)
target      prot opt source              destination

Chain OUTPUT (policy ACCEPT)
target      prot opt source              destination
```

```
[root@sanctus net]# service iptables status
Firewall is stopped.
```

If you are not sure what a port maps to or what port a service is on, you can grep it out of /etc/services:

```
# grep 25 /etc/services
smtp            25/tcp          mail
smtp            25/udp          mail
```

So in this case, the service running on port 25 was SMTP (Simple Mail Transport Protocol).

The next diagnostic command of note is conntrack. conntrack contains all the different connections currently tracked by netfilter. It serves as a basic reference for the current state of a connection. This table is read-only.

```
# less /proc/net/ip_conntrack
tcp       6 163770 ESTABLISHED src=192.168.5.54 dst=200.157.35.3 sport=80
dport=41057 packets=3 bytes=4260 [UNREPLIED] src=200.157.35.3
dst=192.168.5.54 sport=41057 dport=80 packets=0 bytes=0 mark=0 use=1

tcp       6 163783 ESTABLISHED src=192.168.5.54 dst=200.157.35.3 sport=80
dport=41029 packets=3 bytes=4260 [UNREPLIED] src=200.157.35.3
dst=192.168.5.54 sport=41029 dport=80 packets=0 bytes=0 mark=0 use=1

tcp       6 307635 ESTABLISHED src=192.168.5.54 dst=216.230.44.66 sport=80
dport=20641 packets=3 bytes=4260 [UNREPLIED] src=216.230.44.66
dst=192.168.5.54 sport=20641 dport=80 packets=0 bytes=0 mark=0 use=1

tcp       6 21086 ESTABLISHED src=192.168.2.63 dst=192.168.5.54 sport=1067
dport=143 packets=1 bytes=46 src=192.168.5.54 dst=192.168.2.63 sport=143
dport=1067 packets=0 bytes=0 mark=0 use=1

tcp       6 431988 ESTABLISHED src=192.168.2.26 dst=192.168.5.54
sport=2186 dport=22 packets=27360 bytes=2221935 src=192.168.5.54
dst=192.168.2.26 sport=22 dport=2186 packets=31472 bytes=2971402
[ASSURED] mark=0 use=1

tcp       6 56 TIME_WAIT src=127.0.0.1 dst=127.0.0.1 sport=33591 dport=25
packets=17 bytes=1104 src=127.0.0.1 dst=127.0.0.1 sport=25 dport=33591
packets=12 bytes=1012 [ASSURED] mark=0 use=1

udp       17 116 src=192.168.5.54 dst=192.168.2.1 sport=47997 dport=53
packets=13 bytes=958 src=192.168.2.1 dst=192.168.5.54 sport=53
dport=47997 packets=13 bytes=1593 [ASSURED] mark=0 use=1
```

Example iptables Commands

This section presents several examples of commonly used `iptables` commands. It walks you through listing, flushing, deleting, and creating `iptables` configurations through the command line.

Note that for Red Hat and Debian, the `iptables` binaries are located in `/sbin`. With SUSE, the binaries are located in `/usr/sbin`.

Look at the examples of the following commands.

Clearing `iptables` configuration:

```
# iptables --flush
# iptables --delete-chain
```

Setting the default policy to drop for the input chain:

```
# iptables -P INPUT DROP
```

Setting `iptables` to accept all connections on the loopback address:

```
# iptables -I INPUT 1 -i lo -j ACCEPT
```

Changing `iptables` to drop traffic on certain ports to stop unauthorized access:

```
# iptables -A RH-Lokkit-0-50-INPUT -p tcp -m tcp --dport 137:139 -j ACCEPT
# iptables -A INPUT -p TCP --dport 135 -s 0/0 -j DROP
```

Change `iptables` to allow outgoing traffic from certain hosts:

```
# iptables -A FORWARD -p ALL -s 192.168.9.3 -j ACCEPT
```

Deleting a rule:

From the `iptables(8)` man page:

```
-D, --delete
Delete one or more rules from the selected chain. There are two versions
of this command: the rule can be specified as a number in the chain
(starting at 1 for the first rule) or a rule to match.
```

A couple examples follow:

```
# iptables -D 1
# iptables -D 2
```

Saving the Configuration

Any changes to `netfilter/iptables` are volatile—they only last until the next system reboot. The only way around this is to save the rules into the system configuration file. This file resides in different places on different distributions.

The SUSE configuration file typically resides in `/etc/sysconfig/SuSEfirewall2`. The Debian configuration file typically resides in `/etc/default/iptables`. The Red Hat configuration file typically resides in `/etc/sysconfig/iptables`. The `/etc/sysconfig/iptables` file is actually the location for the Gnome Lokkit version of the configuration file. This is what Red Hat uses, but it could also be used on other distributions.

```
# iptables-save > /etc/sysconfig/iptables
# iptables-restore > /etc/sysconfig/iptables
```

Stopping, Verifying Status, and Starting iptables

The `chkconfig` command updates and queries runlevel information for system services. This is the first step in verifying that a service is running. This command is covered in depth in Chapter 1, "System Boot, Startup, and Shutdown Issues," but some differences are covered here for `iptables`.

```
# chkconfig --list iptables

iptables 0:off   1:off   2:on   3:on   4:on   5:on   6:off
```

You can also use `chkconfig` to enable or disable a system service from running at boot.

```
# chkconfig iptables on
# chkconfig iptables off
```

You can use the scripts in /etc/init.d or the service command to stop, verify status, and start a service between system boots.

```
# /etc/init.d/iptables stop
# /etc/init.d/iptables start
# /etc/init.d/iptables restart
# /etc/init.d/iptables status


Aborting iptables initd: unknown command(s): "status".
ls: /var/lib/iptables: Permission denied
/etc/init.d/iptables options:
  start|restart|reload|force-reload
     load the "active" ruleset
  save <ruleset>
     save the current ruleset
  load <ruleset>
     load a ruleset
  stop
     load the "inactive" ruleset
  clear
     remove all rules and user-defined chains, set default policy to \
     ACCEPT
  halt
     remove all rules and user-defined chains, set default policy to DROP
```

Troubleshooting Examples

How do you tell whether the system is accepting or rejecting connections on certain ports? How do you know whether a daemon is listening or talking over a port? The following examples assist you in making these determinations.

Scenario 12-7: Open Ports

nmap enables you to scan a host for open ports.

```
# nmap hostname

Starting nmap 3.81 (http://www.insecure.org/nmap/) at 2005-04-17 13:43 EDT
Interesting ports on hostname (192.168.5.54):
(The 1644 ports scanned but not shown below are in state: closed)
PORT        STATE SERVICE
22/tcp      open  ssh
25/tcp      open  smtp
80/tcp      open  http
110/tcp     open  pop3
111/tcp     open  rpcbind
139/tcp     open  netbios-ssn
143/tcp     open  imap
443/tcp     open  https
445/tcp     open  microsoft-ds
515/tcp     open  printer
555/tcp     open  dsf
631/tcp     open  ipp
783/tcp     open  hp-alarm-mgr
993/tcp     open  imaps
995/tcp     open  pop3s
2000/tcp    open  callbook
2500/tcp    open  rtsserv
3306/tcp    open  mysql
10000/tcp   open  snet-sensor-mgmt
```

Scenario 12-8: Closed Ports

Problems with closed ports (SNMP, for example) also can be detected by using nmap and
netstat to determine which ports are being listened to, as opposed to iptables, which
shows which ports are open.

```
# nmap -sT -O localhost

Starting nmap 3.81 (http://www.insecure.org/nmap/) at 2005-04-17 13:45 EDT
```

```
Interesting ports on localhost (127.0.0.1):
(The 1644 ports scanned but not shown below are in state: closed)
PORT       STATE SERVICE
22/tcp     open  ssh
25/tcp     open  smtp
80/tcp     open  http
110/tcp    open  pop3
111/tcp    open  rpcbind
139/tcp    open  netbios-ssn
143/tcp    open  imap
443/tcp    open  https
445/tcp    open  microsoft-ds
515/tcp    open  printer
555/tcp    open  dsf
631/tcp    open  ipp
783/tcp    open  hp-alarm-mgr
993/tcp    open  imaps
995/tcp    open  pop3s
2000/tcp   open  callbook
2500/tcp   open  rtsserv
3306/tcp   open  mysql
10000/tcp open   snet-sensor-mgmt
Device type: general purpose
Running: Linux 2.4.X|2.5.X|2.6.X
OS details: Linux 2.5.25 - 2.6.3 or Gentoo 1.2 Linux 2.4.19 rc1-rc7),
Linux 2.6.3 - 2.6.8
Uptime 4.833 days (since Tue Apr 12 17:47:12 2005)


Nmap finished: 1 IP address  (1 host up) scanned in 2.300 seconds
```

You can then run the following:

```
# netstat -anp | grep 10000
tcp       0       0 0.0.0.0:10000       0.0.0.0:*     LISTEN      4546/perl
udp       0       0 0.0.0.0:10000       0.0.0.0:*                 4546/perl
```

```
# lsof -i | grep 10000
miniserv.  4546    root    5u   IPv4   11329      TCP *:10000 (LISTEN)
miniserv.  4546    root    6u   IPv4   11330      UDP *:10000


# netstat -ln
Active Internet connections (only servers)
Proto Recv-Q Send-Q Local Address           Foreign Address         State
tcp        0      0 0.0.0.0:32769           0.0.0.0:*               LISTEN
tcp        0      0 0.0.0.0:32772           0.0.0.0:*               LISTEN
tcp        0      0 0.0.0.0:743             0.0.0.0:*               LISTEN
tcp        0      0 0.0.0.0:111             0.0.0.0:*               LISTEN
tcp        0      0 0.0.0.0:21              0.0.0.0:*               LISTEN
tcp        0      0 127.0.0.1:631           0.0.0.0:*               LISTEN
tcp        0      0 0.0.0.0:23              0.0.0.0:*               LISTEN
tcp        0      0 127.0.0.1:25            0.0.0.0:*               LISTEN
tcp        0      0 :::22                   :::*                    LISTEN
udp        0      0 0.0.0.0:32768           0.0.0.0:*
udp        0      0 0.0.0.0:32769           0.0.0.0:*
udp        0      0 0.0.0.0:514             0.0.0.0:*
udp        0      0 0.0.0.0:651             0.0.0.0:*
udp        0      0 0.0.0.0:740             0.0.0.0:*
udp        0      0 0.0.0.0:111             0.0.0.0:*
udp        0      0 0.0.0.0:631             0.0.0.0:*
udp        0      0 0.0.0.0:633             0.0.0.0:*
Active UNIX domain sockets (only servers)
Proto RefCnt Flags       Type       State         I-Node Path
unix  2      [ ACC ]     STREAM     LISTENING     7311   /tmp/.ICE- \
unix/2790
unix  2      [ ACC ]     STREAM     LISTENING     6599   /tmp/.X11- \
unix/X0
unix  2      [ ACC ]     STREAM     LISTENING     7365   @/tmp/fam-root-
unix  2      [ ACC ]     STREAM     LISTENING     6536   /tmp/.gdm_socket
unix  2      [ ACC ]     STREAM     LISTENING     7644   /tmp/mapping-root
unix  2      [ ACC ]     STREAM     LISTENING     4666   /var/run/ \
acpid.socket
```

```
unix  2     [ ACC ]     STREAM     LISTENING     5108    /var/run/ \
dbus/system_bus_socket
unix  2     [ ACC ]     STREAM     LISTENING     1923392 /tmp/orbit- \
root/linc-e2f-0-bbfff546128b
unix  2     [ ACC ]     STREAM     LISTENING     7147    /tmp/orbit- \
root/linc-ae6-0-4dad07126929d
unix  2     [ ACC ]     STREAM     LISTENING     7330    /tmp/orbit- \
root/linc-b30-0-58a7a2fcd05ba
unix  2     [ ACC ]     STREAM     LISTENING     4932    /dev/gpmctl
unix  2     [ ACC ]     STREAM     LISTENING     7350    /tmp/orbit- \
root/linc-b32-0-2655db2aeda0a
unix  2     [ ACC ]     STREAM     LISTENING     7460    /tmp/orbit- \
root/linc-b58-0-621592d496fed
unix  2     [ ACC ]     STREAM     LISTENING     7490    /tmp/orbit- \
root/linc-b5c-0-3d2be190ec0ee
unix  2     [ ACC ]     STREAM     LISTENING     7512    /tmp/orbit- \
root/linc-b60-0-3d2be190f2ac4
unix  2     [ ACC ]     STREAM     LISTENING     7533    /tmp/orbit- \
root/linc-b5e-0-6fdfda4710351
unix  2     [ ACC ]     STREAM     LISTENING     7573    /tmp/orbit- \
root/linc-b62-0-6fdfda475dd4e
unix  2     [ ACC ]     STREAM     LISTENING     7613    /tmp/orbit- \
root/linc-b6b-0-42041c2cbc4d6
unix  2     [ ACC ]     STREAM     LISTENING     7669    /tmp/orbit- \
root/linc-b66-0-592c61f838cde
unix  2     [ ACC ]     STREAM     LISTENING     7690    /tmp/orbit- \
root/linc-b79-0-4b667834a27c1
unix  2     [ ACC ]     STREAM     LISTENING     7718    /tmp/orbit- \
root/linc-b7b-0-4b667834f2d60
unix  2     [ ACC ]     STREAM     LISTENING     7752    /tmp/orbit- \
root/linc-b7d-0-349f4c4e688f5
unix  2     [ ACC ]     STREAM     LISTENING     7781    /tmp/orbit- \
root/linc-b7f-0-349f4c4e8bd45
unix  2     [ ACC ]     STREAM     LISTENING     7813    /tmp/orbit- \
root/linc-b81-0-281c194d3e01
unix  2     [ ACC ]     STREAM     LISTENING     5032    /tmp/.font- \
unix/fs7100
unix  2     [ ACC ]     STREAM     LISTENING     7320    /tmp/keyring- \
b4Tynh/socket
```

```
unix  2      [ ACC ]     STREAM     LISTENING     7057   /tmp/ssh- \
ifzjtp2817/agent.2817
unix  2      [ ACC ]     STREAM     LISTENING     7114   @/tmp/dbus- \
q34OAqqJlD
```

Scenario 12-9: iptables Rules Not Showing Up on Boot or Disappearing

This problem typically happens when someone shuts down iptables. You can diagnose this issue with the following command.

```
# /etc/init.d/iptables status


Table: filter
Chain INPUT (policy ACCEPT)
target       prot opt source              destination
RH-Firewall-1-INPUT  all  --  0.0.0.0/0           0.0.0.0/0


Chain FORWARD (policy ACCEPT)
target       prot opt source              destination
RH-Firewall-1-INPUT  all  --  0.0.0.0/0           0.0.0.0/0


Chain OUTPUT (policy ACCEPT)
target       prot opt source              destination


Chain RH-Firewall-1-INPUT (2 references)
target       prot opt source              destination
ACCEPT       all  --  0.0.0.0/0           0.0.0.0/0
ACCEPT       icmp --  0.0.0.0/0           0.0.0.0/0           icmp type 255
ACCEPT       all  --  0.0.0.0/0           0.0.0.0/0           state \
RELATED,ESTABLISHED
ACCEPT       tcp  --  15.45.88.52         0.0.0.0/0           state NEW \
tcp dpt:382
ACCEPT       tcp  --  0.0.0.0/0           0.0.0.0/0           state NEW \
tcp dpt:135
```

```
ACCEPT     tcp  --  0.0.0.0/0              0.0.0.0/0             state NEW \
tcp dpt:25
ACCEPT     tcp  --  0.0.0.0/0              0.0.0.0/0             state NEW \
tcp dpt:22
REJECT     udp  --  0.0.0.0/0              0.0.0.0/0             state NEW \
udp dpts:0:1023 reject-with icmp-port-unreachable
REJECT     tcp  --  0.0.0.0/0              0.0.0.0/0             state NEW \
tcp dpts:0:1023 reject-with icmp-port-unreachable
REJECT     udp  --  0.0.0.0/0              0.0.0.0/0             state NEW \
udp dpt:2049 reject-with icmp-port-unreachable
REJECT     tcp  --  0.0.0.0/0              0.0.0.0/0             state NEW \
tcp dpt:2049 reject-with icmp-port-unreachable
REJECT     tcp  --  0.0.0.0/0              0.0.0.0/0             state NEW \
tcp dpts:6000:6009 reject-with icmp-port-unreachable
REJECT     tcp  --  0.0.0.0/0              0.0.0.0/0             state NEW \
tcp dpt:7100 reject-with icmp-port-unreachable
ACCEPT     tcp  --  0.0.0.0/0              0.0.0.0/0             state NEW \
tcp dpt:5555
REJECT     all  --  0.0.0.0/0              0.0.0.0/0             reject-with \
icmp-host-prohibited
```

Show output

Scenario 12-10: Rule Order Issues

One important concept that causes trouble for many administrators is rule order. For example, if you set all TCP packets to REJECT as the first rule in a chain, any subsequent rules that try to ACCEPT packets are ignored.

A good idea is to structure the chain similarly to the following:

accept (unlogged)

drop (unlogged)

log

accept

default policy

TCP wrappers

UNIX permissions

Patching

Patching is not a replacement for good security, but it is important. Make sure to verify that packages are genuine and come from the vendor. You should also verify their md5sum.

```
# md5sum VMware-workstation-5.5.0-18007.i386.rpm
df4fe57c8e8650b529f8cbb1226b6b2d   VMware-workstation-5.5.0-18007.i386.rpm
```

The md5sum supplied by the software vendor for the RPM file is:

```
md5sum:df4fe57c8e8650b529f8cbb1226b6b2d
```

It is common for hackers to dummy a package up to look authentic and include compromised binaries in the package.

Recovery After Being Hacked

Unfortunately the best way to recover after being hacked is to disconnect the network cable and reinstall the system. It might be possible to salvage some files from the system before reinstalling, but you must be very careful because you might inadvertently place a file back on the system that could re-compromise it. Reinstall instead!

Summary

System security is a vocation. I hope that this introduction to the topic and how to troubleshoot it under Linux gives you a jumping off point. It is key that you understand how the Linux networking, filesystem, authentication, and other subsystems work to truly understand the security implications of each. It is also crucial that you treat security as a continuum. There is no state of complete security, only states of relative insecurity.

13

Network Problems

I t goes without saying that a networking problem can really put a kink in your day. That is why we devote an entire chapter to Linux network troubleshooting. Although this chapter is not intended to teach the fundamentals of networking, a brief overview is justified. Therefore, we begin by explaining the ISO (International Standard Organization) OSI (Open System Interconnect) networking interconnect model. After we cover this subject, we move on to discussing identification of the perceived network problem and isolation of the subsystem involved. We then discuss options for resolution.

Many protocols and network types exist; however, this chapter deals only with troubleshooting the Ethernet Carrier Sense Multiple Access/Collision Detection (CSMA/CD) standard with the Transmission Control Protocol/Internet Protocol (TCP/IP) suite. Various models and protocol suites are available; however, the most widely used in homes and offices is the Ethernet TCP/IP model.

An Introduction to the OSI and TCP/IP Layers

We discuss two networking models in this chapter: OSI and TCP/IP. The OSI networking model is not the only interconnect model out there; however, it is the ISO's adopted model. This model defines networking as consisting of seven layers. In addition to the OSI model, there is the TCP/IP model. This is the model that is most commonly referenced in today's IT world, and it should be mentioned that the TCP/IP model was around before the OSI model. The TCP/IP model originally was named the DOD model after its creator, the Department of Defense. It consists of the same initial layers that make up the OSI model; however, it combines the last four layers.

A comparison of these layers is shown in Table 13-1.

Table 13-1   OSI Layers, Descriptions, and Corresponding TCP/IP Layers

OSI Layers	Description	TCP/IP Layers
Application	This is where the user process resides: NIS, NFS, DNS, TELNET, mail, and other network applications.	
Presentation	In the TCP/IP model, the representation of the data is defined by the application. However, in new TCP/IP protocols such as External Data Representation (XDR), this data representation is handled by the protocol at this layer.	Application Programming Interface
Session	RPC is one example of a session protocol. An application can be built on top of TCP or UDP, but the management of cooperating applications is controlled by the RPC. NFS is a program that uses RPC for its session protocol, while the underlying layer is UDP. The latest versions of NFS can use either UDP or TCP. For a list of applications that use RPC, run this command: `cat /etc/rpc`.	
Transport (TCP and UDP)	Transmission Control Protocol (TCP) and User Datagram Protocol (UDP) are two transport protocols that sit at this layer. TCP requires a "handshake" socket connection, which allows for keeping track of packet delivery and packets that need to be re-sent. UDP uses less of this overhead for better performance at the cost of error checking (which is done within the application).	Transport (TCP and UDP)

Network (IP)	The Internet Protocol (IP), which routes packets from one location to another. This layer also handles the breaking up of large datagrams into smaller units if the datagrams exceed the Maximum Transmission Unit (MTU) size defined in the lower level. Commonly referred to as the TCP/IP network layer.	Internetwork layer (IP, AppleTalk, IPX)
Data link	Handles the transmission and reception of data and passes the packets to the network interface (Ethernet, FDDI, and so on). Addresses the physical interface for the network. An Ethernet interface has a unique 48-bit MAC address. Additionally, this layer includes the MTU, checksums, source address, and destination address.	Physical network access layer For example, Ethernet, 802.11 (wireless), Token Ring, and so on.
Physical	The physical medium: cables, switches, pin locations, and converters, which convert one media type to another.	

Troubleshooting the Network Layers

When you understand the layers involved in the applicable network, you can focus upon layers as needed to find and remedy the networking problem. The most fundamental place to begin looking for a networking problem is in the lowest layer. Then you work your way up through the subsequent layers. Therefore, problem solving typically begins at the first, or physical (also known as "hardware"), layer. Thus, our discussion begins there too. We then discuss troubleshooting at the subsequent layers. Note that although other suites exist, this discussion of layers centers upon the TCP/IP suite of protocols. Also be aware that unless otherwise noted, this discussion of troubleshooting in the network layers refers to the TCP/IP model, so any references to layers refer to the four layers of that model. References to the OSI model are noted expressly as such in this discussion.

Troubleshooting the TCP/IP Physical Network Access Layer

Because this layer consists of several aspects encompassing everything from the hardware to the MAC protocol, we have divided this discussion into smaller sections. We begin by discussing the physical connection and then move through the process before ending with a discussion of Address Resolution Protocol (ARP).

Physical Aspects

At the outset, note that this layer usually is external to the box (except the network adaptor) and is independent of the Linux kernel itself. However, a problem with this layer can cause significant disruption of subsequent layer functioning. As mentioned previously, the hardware layer defines the characteristics of the physical medium used for the network. This includes not only cable type and pinouts but also power modulation, bit encoding, carrier signals, and bit synchronization, among other elements. The hardware also includes switches, routers, and even converters.

The first step in determining whether there is a problem at the hardware layer is to look for the link light. If the light is not on, there is a problem at the physical layer. The physical layer incorporates cooperation between the driver and the interface card to bring the interface online.

If the light is on, a problem at the physical layer still might exist because there could be cross-talk on the wire due to pins not being on the correct pair of the copper twisted-pair (cross-talk can also be due to the quality of the wire) or because an incorrect driver is being used, lighting the link light but not performing other necessary functions.

If you suspect a problem at the hardware layer, the culprit could be a number of things, some internal and some external. Externally, a problem can occur because of a bad cable, switch, or hub. A system administrator normally would engage a network engineer to assist in troubleshooting this type of problem.

Internally, an incorrect driver might be bound to the interface card, or the interface card simply might be bad. Confirm that the hardware and the operating system's driver support the card before proceeding. Then try another network card. Confirm that other network adapters can use the same cable and switch ports. If the hardware is the problem, replace it. If the problem is not resolved after troubleshooting different cards, and the card and the driver required to operate the device are supported by both the computer vendor and the Linux kernel, you must engage assistance from the network engineers who maintain the network hardware. You can also contact the vendor to determine whether a patch is necessary.

Finally, note that it is possible to experience symptoms in higher layers of the TCP/IP model caused by switch firmware issues at the hardware layer. Later in this chapter, we give an example of such a case.

Link Aspects: Network Interfaces

After the cables and switches have been successfully tested, we move on to troubleshooting the link. Under the OSI model, this is the second layer; however, both the OSI physical and link layers are contained within the physical layer of the TCP/IP model. In either case, this is the layer at which the magical link light appears on the interface.

The next step in troubleshooting a link problem is to verify that the link light is on and that the kernel sees the card. Confirm that the kernel recognizes the Ethernet adapter(s) on the system and that drivers are bound to the interface(s). Some examples of such a confirmation process follow.

An IA-32 machine with a Broadcom network interface yields something like the following:

```
#dmesg | grep eth
eth0: Tigon3 [partno(N/A) rev 1002 PHY(5703)] (PCI:33MHz:32-bit)
10/100/1000BaseT Ethernet 00:0e:7f:b4:27:aa
tg3: eth0: Link is up at 100 Mbps, full duplex.
tg3: eth0: Flow control is on for TX and on for RX
```

In this situation, eth0 is using the Tigon3 driver.

If the kernel message buffer has been overwritten with other messages already, use lspci or the /proc filesystem, as shown next. Note that in this example, we display the same hardware as previously; however, lspci does not show the driver binding.

```
# lspci
00:00.0 Host bridge: ServerWorks CNB20-HE Host Bridge (rev 32)
00:00.1 Host bridge: ServerWorks CNB20-HE Host Bridge
00:00.2 Host bridge: ServerWorks CNB20-HE Host Bridge
```

```
00:01.0 Communication controller: Conexant HCF 56k Data/Fax/Voice Modem
(Worldwide) (rev 08)
00:02.0 SCSI storage controller: Adaptec AHA-3960D / AIC-7899A U160/m
(rev 01)
00:02.1 SCSI storage controller: Adaptec AHA-3960D / AIC-7899A U160/m
(rev 01)
00:03.0 VGA compatible controller: ATI Technologies Inc Rage XL (rev 27)
00:04.0 Ethernet controller: Broadcom Corporation NetXtreme BCM5702
Gigabit Ethernet (rev 02)
00:05.0 System peripheral: Compaq Computer Corporation Advanced System
Management Controller
00:0f.0 ISA bridge: ServerWorks CSB5 South Bridge (rev 93)
00:0f.1 IDE interface: ServerWorks CSB5 IDE Controller (rev 93)
00:0f.2 USB Controller: ServerWorks OSB4/CSB5 OHCI USB Controller (rev
05)
00:0f.3 Host bridge: ServerWorks GCLE Host Bridge
00:11.0 Host bridge: ServerWorks: Unknown device 0101 (rev 05)
00:11.2 Host bridge: ServerWorks: Unknown device 0101 (rev 05)
```

With older kernels, the only location that depicts the device along with the driver bound to that device is dmesg or the log file /var/log/dmesg. With the newer kernels built for the IA-64 platform, the file /proc/ioports does a great job of showing the Domain:Bus:slot.function and the driver for the device.

The following is an example of lspci and cat /proc/ioports on an IA-64 machine running the 2.6.5 kernel release. Notice that by using these two commands, we can determine the hardware address of the interface and the driver that is bound to the hardware path.

```
# lspci
0000:00:00.0 Serial controller: Hewlett-Packard Company Diva Serial
[GSP] Multiport UART (rev 02)
0000:00:01.0 Ethernet controller: Digital Equipment Corporation DECchip
21142/43 (rev 41)

...
```

```
# cat /proc/ioports
00000000-00000fff : PCI Bus 0000:00
  00000060-0000006f : i8042
  00000d00-00000d7f : 0000:00:01.0
    00000d00-00000d7f : tulip
...
```

Link Aspects: Configuration

Now that we have a list of the Ethernet adapters, we can confirm their link states by using user-level applications, which perform the necessary ioctls. A couple commands that provide this functionality are mii-tool and ethtool. These tools do not support every network adapter, but they support many.

You must note some caveats about these tools. Network drivers detect link status in a couple ways. Some drivers use the Media Independent Interface (MII) to detect the link status by reading an interface register. Others, such as the driver in the previous example (tg3), use the adapter's last known state. In short, performing an ifdown on an interface with the tg3 driver results in no link detected. In this case, that means only that the interface has been disabled, not that a cable is not present. The interface might never have been enabled; therefore, you would not know whether a cable was connected to the interface. The cable presence could be confirmed by simply attempting to bring the interface online with ifup.

An example of link detection follows:

```
# mii-tool eth0
SIOCGMIIPHY on 'eth0' failed: Operation not supported
```

This failed because the driver of this interface does not support the mii-tool's query. However, using ethtool on the same device, we see the following:

```
# ethtool eth0
Settings for eth0:
        Supported ports: [ MII ]
        Supported link modes:   10baseT/Half 10baseT/Full
                                100baseT/Half 100baseT/Full
                                1000baseT/Half 1000baseT/Full
```

```
        Supports auto-negotiation: Yes
        Advertised link modes:  10baseT/Half 10baseT/Full
                                100baseT/Half 100baseT/Full
                                1000baseT/Half 1000baseT/Full
        Advertised auto-negotiation: Yes
        Speed: 100Mb/s
        Duplex: Full
        Port: Twisted Pair
        PHYAD: 1
        Transceiver: internal
        Auto-negotiation: on
        Supports Wake-on: g
        Wake-on: d
        Current message level: 0x000000ff (255)
        Link detected: yes
```

Bringing the device down can give you misleading results if you do not know what to expect. With the `tg3` driver, as mentioned previously, `ethtool` can detect only the interface's last configuration, unlike `mii-tool`, which can read the interface register to determine whether the carrier signal is present. See the following example:

```
# ifdown eth0
# ethtool eth0
Settings for eth0:
        Supports Wake-on: g
        Wake-on: d
        Current message level: 0x000000ff (255)
        Link detected: no
```

Here we know that the link is valid and that the cable is in good working order. However, when the user-level command takes the card offline, it sets the link status to "not present." Note that other drivers behave differently, and some drivers still are not supported with these tools.

After the cable is confirmed, it is up to the interface's chipset and the adaptor's driver to bring the network card online. The physical layer accomplishes this task by placing a carrier signal on a wire (pin). When the cable is connected to the Ethernet card, the chipset generates an external interrupt. This is when the kernel driver initiates a netif_carrier_ok(), causing the driver to bring the interface online. If the hardware layer is not set up properly (that is, the wires are not aligned properly), the link might come online, yet you might experience high network traffic loss. An example of this would occur if the twisted pairs were not aligned properly with the other end of the cable, resulting in cross-talk. For example, pins 2 and 5 should be a twisted pair for standard Ethernet.

After the link is brought online, the next step is for the driver to negotiate speed and duplex. Most drivers leave this task to an auto-negotiation between the driver and the device at the other end. However, the duplex and speed of the connection can be changed during driver module installation or at the user level by running tools such as the aforementioned mii-tool and ethtool.

Next is an illustration of changing the interface's speed and duplex with mii-tool:

```
# mii-tool -v
eth0: 100 Mbit, full duplex, link ok
  product info: TDK 78Q2120 rev 11
  basic mode:   100 Mbit, full duplex
  basic status: link ok
  capabilities: 100baseTx-FD 100baseTx-HD 10baseT-FD 10baseT-HD
  advertising:  100baseTx-FD 100baseTx-HD 10baseT-FD 10baseT-HD


# mii-tool -F 10baseT-FD

# mii-tool -v
eth0: 10 Mbit, full duplex, link ok
  product info: TDK 78Q2120 rev 11
  basic mode:   10 Mbit, full duplex
  basic status: link ok
  capabilities: 100baseTx-FD 100baseTx-HD 10baseT-FD 10baseT-HD
  advertising:  100baseTx-FD 100baseTx-HD 10baseT-FD 10baseT-HD
```

An example of using a similar approach with the ethtool command with an interface that uses the tg3 driver follows.

First we confirm the interface and driver used by the interface.

```
# grep eth0 /var/log/dmesg
eth0: Tigon3 [partno(N/A) rev 1002 PHY(5703)] (PCI:33MHz:32-bit)
10/100/1000BaseT Ethernet 00:0e:7f:b4:27:aa
```

Using ethtool, we determine the driver's capabilities.

```
# ethtool eth0
Settings for eth0:
        Supported ports: [ MII ]
        Supported link modes:   10baseT/Half 10baseT/Full
                                100baseT/Half 100baseT/Full
                                1000baseT/Half 1000baseT/Full
        Supports auto-negotiation: Yes
        Advertised link modes:  10baseT/Half 10baseT/Full
                                100baseT/Half 100baseT/Full
                                1000baseT/Half 1000baseT/Full
        Advertised auto-negotiation: Yes
        Speed: 100Mb/s
        Duplex: Full
        Port: Twisted Pair
        PHYAD: 1
        Transceiver: internal
        Auto-negotiation: on
        Supports Wake-on: g
        Wake-on: d
        Current message level: 0x000000ff (255)
        Link detected: yes
```

We change the interface to HD, 10Mbps, and turn auto-negotiation off.

```
# ethtool -s eth0 speed 10 duplex half autoneg off
```

We check dmesg for driver messages.

```
# dmesg
...
tg3: eth0: Link is down.
tg3: eth0: Link is up at 10 Mbps, half duplex.
tg3: eth0: Flow control is on for TX and on for RX.
```

Now that the users are complaining that the machine is slow, we can take it back to 100Mbps, using auto-negotiation.

```
# ethtool -s eth0 autoneg on
```

We confirm with dmesg that the driver took the card back to 100Mbps, full duplex.

```
# dmesg
...
tg3: eth0: Link is down.
tg3: eth0: Link is up at 100 Mbps, full duplex.
tg3: eth0: Flow control is on for TX and on for RX.
```

Changing the speed and duplex of a Linux network interface is easy with these user-level commands; however, these changes are not persistent. Making the changes persist across reboots can be accomplished in several ways. One way is to create a startup script that calls these user-level tools to make the changes to the interface. Some distributions have modified the ifup script to read variables such as ETHTOOL_OPTS="speed 1000 duplex full"; however, this is the case with neither all distributions nor all versions of those distributions. If the interface's driver is a module, configuring the interface's speed and duplex can be done by modifying /etc/modules.conf with the 2.4 kernel release and /etc/modprobe.conf with the 2.6 kernel release.

The following is an example of the default modules.conf file on a 2.4 kernel release using the tg3 driver.

```
# cat /etc/modules.conf
probeall scsi_hostadapter aic7xxx imm ppa
probeall usb-interface usb-ohci
alias eth0 tg3
```

To configure the interface to auto-negotiation off, speed 100Mbps, and full duplex, all that is required is the following:

```
# cat /etc/modules.conf
probeall scsi_hostadapter aic7xxx imm ppa
probeall usb-interface usb-ohci
alias eth0 tg3
post-install tg3 /usr/sbin/ethtool -s eth0 speed 100 duplex full
autoneg off
```

Following are the same interface and driver with the 2.6 kernel release using the modprobe.conf file.

```
# cat /etc/modprobe.conf
...
install eth1            /bin/true
install tg3 /sbin/modprobe --ignore-install tg3 && /bin/sleep 2 &&
/usr/sbin/ethtool -s eth1 speed 100 duplex full autoneg off
```

Note that the sleep statement was added to allow time for the driver to establish communication with the device before trying to change its speed and duplex.

Test this modprobe setup with the following commands.

```
# modprobe -r tg3
```

note

> # modprobe -r tg3 removes the driver, so you must be on the console or communicating over another network interface that does not need this driver; otherwise, you can no longer communicate with this system.

```
# modprobe -v tg3
install /sbin/modprobe --ignore-install tg3 && /bin/sleep 2 &&
/usr/sbin/ethtool -s eth1 speed 100 duplex full autoneg off
insmod /lib/modules/2.6.5-7.97-default/kernel/drivers/net/tg3.ko
```

Now we can view the settings with `ethtool` to see whether auto-negotiation is disabled.

```
# ethtool eth1
Settings for eth1:
        Supported ports: [ MII ]
        Supported link modes:    10baseT/Half 10baseT/Full
                                 100baseT/Half 100baseT/Full
                                 1000baseT/Half 1000baseT/Full
        Supports auto-negotiation: Yes
        Advertised link modes:   10baseT/Half 10baseT/Full
                                 100baseT/Half 100baseT/Full
                                 1000baseT/Half 1000baseT/Full
        Advertised auto-negotiation: Yes
        Speed: 100Mb/s
        Duplex: Full
        Port: Twisted Pair
        PHYAD: 1
        Transceiver: internal
        Auto-negotiation: off
        Supports Wake-on: g
        Wake-on: d
        Current message level: 0x000000ff (255)
        Link detected: yes
```

In addition to specifying an additional command inside the module's configuration files, it also is possible to pass arguments along to some drivers. Of course, not all drivers support the use of options, which are very similar to command arguments. The `tg3` driver is an example of such a driver. Other vendors have made their drivers accept options at load time, which can define speed and duplex. We recommend using the user-level commands; however, if the drivers do not support these commands, you have little choice but to use the driver options.

Using the `modinfo` command, we can see a driver's supported options and their meanings as illustrated next. This first example shows a driver that has no options:

```
# modinfo tg3
filename:     /lib/modules/2.4.19-16glt1/kernel/drivers/net/tg3.o
description: "Broadcom Tigon3 ethernet driver"
author:       "David S. Miller (davem@redhat.com) and Jeff Garzik
              (jgarzik@mandrakesoft.com)"
license:      "GPL"
parm:         tg3_debug int, description "Tigon3 bitmapped debugging
              message enable value"
```

From the previous output, we can determine that the driver has no driver options to set, so we must use the user-level tools to configure the interface.

Next let's look at a driver that has options:

```
# modinfo eepro100
filename:     /lib/modules/2.4.19-16glt1/kernel/drivers/net/eepro100.o
description: "Intel i82557/i82558/i82559 PCI EtherExpressPro driver"
author:       "Maintainer: Andrey V. Savochkin <saw@saw.sw.com.sg>"
license:      "GPL"
parm:         debug int, description "debug level (0-6)"
parm:         options int array (min = 1, max = 8), description "Bits 0-3:
              tranceiver type, bit 4: full duplex, bit 5: 100Mbps"
parm:         full_duplex int array (min = 1, max = 8), description "full
              duplex setting(s) (1)"
parm:         congenb int, description "Enable congestion control (1)"
parm:         txfifo int, description "Tx FIFO threshold in 4 byte
              units, (0-15)"
parm:         rxfifo int, description "Rx FIFO threshold in 4 byte
              units, (0-15)"
parm:         txdmacount int
parm:         rxdmacount int
parm:         rx_copybreak int, description "copy breakpoint for copy-
              only-tiny-frames"
parm:         max_interrupt_work int, description "maximum events handled
              per interrupt"
parm:         multicast_filter_limit int, description "maximum number of
              filtered multicast addresses"
```

The e100 driver's options include the following:

```
# modinfo e100
filename:      /lib/modules/2.4.19-16glt1/kernel/drivers/net/e100/e100.o
               description: "Intel(R) PRO/100 Network Driver"
author:        "Intel Corporation, <linux.nics@intel.com>"
license:       "Dual BSD/GPL"
parm:          TxDescriptors int array (min = 1, max = 16), description
               "Number of transmit descriptors"
parm:          RxDescriptors int array (min = 1, max = 16), description
               "Number of receive descriptors"
parm:          XsumRX int array (min = 1, max = 16), description "Disable
               or enable Receive Checksum offload"
parm:          e100_speed_duplex int array (min = 1, max = 16), description
               "Speed and Duplex settings"
parm:          ucode int array (min = 1, max = 16), description "Disable or
               enable microcode loading"
parm:          ber int array (min = 1, max = 16), description "Value for
               the BER correction algorithm"
parm:          flow_control int array (min = 1, max = 16), description
               "Disable or enable Ethernet PAUSE frames processing"
parm:          IntDelay int array (min = 1, max = 16), description "Value
               for CPU saver's interrupt delay"
parm:          BundleSmallFr int array (min = 1, max = 16), description
               "Disable or enable interrupt bundling of small frames"
parm:          BundleMax int array (min = 1, max = 16), description
               "Maximum number for CPU saver's packet bundling"
parm:          IFS int array (min = 1, max = 16), description "Disable or
               enable the adaptive IFS algorithm"
parm:          RxCongestionControl int array (min = 1, max = 16),
               description "Disable or enable switch to polling mode"
parm:          PollingMaxWork int array (min = 1, max = 16), description
               "Max number of receive packets processed on single polling
               call"
```

Drivers have different ways of listing their options and different means of implementing them. You can try these examples; however, if they fail, check the vendor Web site for example interface card and driver configurations.

According to the header file e100.h, the driver option values are as follows:

```
#define E100_AUTONEG        0
#define E100_SPEED_10_HALF  1
#define E100_SPEED_10_FULL  2
#define E100_SPEED_100_HALF 3
#define E100_SPEED_100_FULL 4
```

Therefore, when using insmod to install the driver or when modifying the modules.conf file, you add the following entry to configure the interface at 100 full duplex:

```
# cat /etc/modules.conf
...
options e100 e100_speed_duplex=4
...
```

Communication at the Physical Level

Communication at the physical level is made possible by the physical address of the interface and the IP address assigned to it. The IP actually is assigned at a higher layer; however, we mention it here to assist with discussion of link-level communication. The association between the IP address and the Media Access Control (MAC) address is made possible by the Address Resolution Protocol (ARP). It is crucial to understand the interface, its MAC address, and the IP address assigned to it to troubleshoot this area. The question is whether Ethernet frames can traverse the network. The goal is to see whether this interface can see other interfaces.

Before we begin discussing the particulars of troubleshooting, we need to discuss some items to provide a background for understanding some critical components. Included within the physical layer is Ethernet's Logical Link Control (LLC) and MAC protocol. In short, the LLC deals with error correction and flow control, whereas the MAC protocol encapsulates the network packet with the destination MAC address, source MAC address, and a cyclic redundancy check (CRC), creating the network frame.

If the CRC values do not match, the frame is discarded, and communication between the source and destination might not be possible. The destination and source mentioned previously are self-explanatory; however, the CRC value is determined after performing a modulo-2 division of the data bits by a polynomial. The remainder of this division provides the CRC value. The importance of this is that after the frame reaches its destination, the Link layer of that interface performs the same algorithm and compares the results stored in this 4-byte address.

As mentioned previously, the MAC address is a network interface's unique identifier. With Ethernet interfaces, vendors assign a unique address to each card. The IEEE assigns the vendor a unique ID, which is represented by the first 24 bits of the address (XX:XX:XX). Then the vendor must come up with the remaining unique 24 bits (YY:YY:YY).

Each frame that traverses the TCP/IP network has this MAC header. The destination MAC is simply the next hop for the frame, which may or may not be the frame's final destination. If it is not the frame's final destination, the source MAC is set to the new interface's MAC address, and the destination MAC is set to the next hop. This setting, of course, does not affect the IP header and TCP headers stored within the frame because only the MAC addresses are manipulated. An example is a frame that must travel outside of its subnet, traveling through a router before arriving at its final destination.

Higher layers, however, do not work with these MAC addresses and instead work with network addresses—in our case, the IP addresses. When the transport layer sends a TCP packet down to the network layer, an IP header is added with the source and destination IP. However, for the IP packet to get to the destination, it must first determine its route, which is handled at the network layer. The route determines the interface from which the IP packet departs and the next interface that will receive the packet. We discuss routes in the next section; however, for the IP packet to reach its destination, the machine must be able to translate an IP to the physical interface address, which is where ARP and Reverse ARP play a role.

ARP and RARP provide the link between the IP address of a card and its MAC address. In troubleshooting whether a machine can get to its gateway, checking the kernel's ARP cache can be of assistance. For example, if a machine cannot communicate on the network, a simple check of the ARP cache will determine whether any frames have been received from the gateway device. The following example illustrates this idea.

First, confirm that the interface is up and has an IP assigned.

```
# ifconfig eth1
eth1      Link encap:Ethernet  HWaddr 00:06:25:AC:C5:25
          inet addr:15.50.74.104  Bcast:15.50.74.255  Mask:255.255.255.0
          UP BROADCAST RUNNING MULTICAST  MTU:1500  Metric:1
          RX packets:125 errors:0 dropped:0 overruns:0 frame:0
          TX packets:65 errors:0 dropped:0 overruns:0 carrier:0
          collisions:0 txqueuelen:100
          RX bytes:18398 (17.9 Kb)  TX bytes:9354 (9.1 Kb)
          Interrupt:3 Base address:0x100
```

Next, using the `route` command, we can determine that if any traffic from this machine needs to leave the local network, it must leave out device `eth1` and go through a gateway of 15.50.74.40.

```
# route
Kernel IP routing table
Destination   Gateway       Genmask         Flags Metric Ref    Use Iface
15.50.74.0    *             255.255.255.0   U     0      0        0 eth1
127.0.0.0     *             255.0.0.0       U     0      0        0 lo
default       15.50.74.40   0.0.0.0         UG    0      0        0 eth1
```

Finally, we confirm that the kernel can populate the gateway's MAC address. This will confirm that communication to that interface is operational at this layer.

```
# arp -v
Address                 HWtype  HWaddress          Flags Mask
Iface
15.50.74.40             ether   00:09:5B:24:65:3A  C
eth1
Entries: 1      Skipped: 0      Found: 1
```

This example confirms that the interface (`eth1`) has received an ARP reply from the gateway device. Note that the ARP entry is cached and will timeout. A quick `ping` can repopulate the ARP cache.

Ethernet Frames

Illustrated in Figures 13-1 through 13-4 are some Ethernet frames with the MAC encapsulation highlighted. There are essentially four types of Ethernet frames, which include

Ethernet II (Figure 13-1), IEEE 802.3/802.2 (Figure 13-2), Novel 802.3 (Figure 13-3), and IEEE 802.3/802.2 SNAP (Figure 13-4). Note that we are using the TCP/IP protocol suite in our discussion, so these examples contain the MAC encapsulation. In addition, Ethernet frames have a maximum size, so bytes are taken from the payload to create room for the other protocols.

7 Bytes	1	6	6	2	46-1500 Bytes	4
Preamble	Start of Frame Delivery	Destination	Source	Length	IPX	CRC

Figure 13-1 A Novel 802.3 frame

7 Bytes	1	6	6	2	1	1	1	3	2	38-1492	4
Preamble	Start of Frame Delivery	Destination	Source	Length	LLC			Organization Code	Ethernet Type	Data	CRC
					Destination Service Access Point (DSAP)	Source Service Access Point (SSAP)	High-Level Data Link Control (HDLC)	SNAP (Used with AppleTalk and token ring networks)			

Figure 13-2 The Ethernet Sub Network Access Protocol (SNAP) frame

8 Bytes	6	6	2	46-1500	4
Preamble	Destination	Source	Type	Service Data Unit (DATA)	CRC

Figure 13-3 The Ethernet II frame. (Note that this example contains Type instead of Length. For example, IP is a protocol type.)

					46-1500 Bytes				4
7 Bytes	1	6	6	2	1	1	1	43-1492	4
Preamble	Start of Frame Delivery	Destination	Source	Number of Data Bytes (Length)	LLC			Service Data Unit (DATA)	CRC
					Destination Service Access Point (DSAP)	Source Service Access Point (SSAP)	High-Level Data Link Control (HDLC)		

Figure 13-4 An IEEE 802.3 with LLC Ethernet frame

As Figure 13-5 shows, at each layer the data packet gets the new layer's header prepended to the frame.

Application Layer ------------				Application Data
Transport Layer -------------			TCP Header	Application Data
IP Layer ------------------------		IP Header	TCP Header	Application Data
Link -------------------------	Mac Header	IP Header	TCP Header	Application Data

Figure 13-5 The new layer's header is prepended to the frame.

The main point of these figures is to show each layer's header as it is added to the packet. Each layer prepends its header to the preceding layer's packet, resulting in an Ethernet frame when it reaches the physical layer. Even though the details of the IP and transport layers are not included in the figures, the IP and TCP headers are present but are buried in the data portion of the frame.

Internet sites are available that can determine the manufacturer of a network interface. As mentioned earlier, IEEE has set up rules that require every network adapter to have a unique identifier, and they supply the manufacturer with the first 24 bits. Given this, we can do a quick search on www.google.com and get a URL that can decode a MAC address to a vendor.

The following is a list of MAC addresses used in this section of the book with the vendor that manufactures the interface.

- 00:04:75—3COM
- 00:06:25—The Linksys Group
- 00:30:6E—Hewlett-Packard
- 00:09:5B—Netgear

Troubleshooting the Network Layer (OSI Third Layer, TCP/IP Second Layer)

The internetwork layer is the point at which an IP header is added to the transport layer's datagram and routing of the network packet takes place; therefore, it is the next logical place to look for network problems in many cases. Both the OSI model and the TCP/IP model include this layer. This section starts with a brief overview of the protocols at this layer. It then takes a deeper look into the IP protocol before concluding with an overview of the IP address model and IP routing.

The TCP/IP internetwork layer covers several protocols, namely the IP, ICMP, RIP, ARP, and RARP protocols. This section covers mainly the IP protocol because it is primarily used by the upper layers; however, we also touch on these other protocols because they sometimes are used in the troubleshooting arena.

ARP and RARP

As mentioned in the previous layer's discussion, ARP enables mapping of an IP address to a station's physical address. Even though we have mentioned this in the previous layer, we mention it again here to clarify that the ARP and RARP functionality exists essentially between the physical and network layers of the TCP/IP model (or even the OSI model). Because communication between the interfaces only takes place at the link level, and because the higher layers only talk to the IP layer, the ARP and RARP protocols provide the necessary connection to make communication possible. It should be noted that the MAC addresses are encapsulated in the MAC header, which is applied to the datagram when it reaches the physical layer. To display a host's ARP cache, just use the arp command or cat /proc/net/arp, but bear in mind that the arp command has better formatted output.

The following is an example of how the ARP cache is populated on a system.

```
# arp -vn
Address                 HWtype  HWaddress          Flags Mask
Iface
15.50.74.40             ether   00:09:5B:24:65:3A  C
eth1
Entries: 1     Skipped: 0     Found: 1

# ping 15.50.74.20
```

Note that before the ping takes place, we must know where to send the Ethernet frame (link communication is done at the MAC level). This is where routing comes in; however, we cover routing later in this section. For now, let us just say that 15.50.74.20 is on the local network; therefore, an ARP broadcast will be sent out, and any device that knows the MAC of the IP being requested will respond with the information required. In this case, 15.50.74.40 is the local router/switch for this test network.

Using a network troubleshooting tool such as ethereal and tracing the network ping request, we can see the ARP functionality taking place, as shown in the next listing. Note that we saved ethereal's output to /tmp/ping.trace.

Review each frame of the trace:

```
# cat /tmp/ping.trace
```

The following shows the ARP broadcast in frame one.

```
Frame 1 (42 bytes on wire, 42 bytes captured)
Ethernet II, Src: 00:06:25:ac:c5:25, Dst: ff:ff:ff:ff:ff:ff
    Destination: ff:ff:ff:ff:ff:ff (Broadcast)
    Source: 00:06:25:ac:c5:25 (LinksysG_ac:c5:25)
    Type: ARP (0x0806)
Address Resolution Protocol (request)
    Hardware type: Ethernet (0x0001)
    Protocol type: IP (0x0800)
    Hardware size: 6
    Protocol size: 4
    Opcode: request (0x0001)
    Sender MAC address: 00:06:25:ac:c5:25 (LinksysG_ac:c5:25)
    Sender IP address: 15.50.74.104 (15.50.74.104)
    Target MAC address: 00:00:00:00:00:00 (00:00:00_00:00:00)
    Target IP address: 15.50.74.20 (15.50.74.20)
```

The following shows the ARP reply in frame two.

```
Frame 2 (60 bytes on wire, 60 bytes captured)
Ethernet II, Src: 00:0e:a6:78:e3:d6, Dst: 00:06:25:ac:c5:25
    Destination: 00:06:25:ac:c5:25 (LinksysG_ac:c5:25)
    Source: 00:0e:a6:78:e3:d6 (00:0e:a6:78:e3:d6)
```

```
    Type: ARP (0x0806)
    Trailer: 000000000000000000000000000000000...
Address Resolution Protocol (reply)
    Hardware type: Ethernet (0x0001)
    Protocol type: IP (0x0800)
    Hardware size: 6
    Protocol size: 4
    Opcode: reply (0x0002)
    Sender MAC address: 00:0e:a6:78:e3:d6 (00:0e:a6:78:e3:d6)
    Sender IP address: 15.50.74.20 (15.50.74.20)
    Target MAC address: 00:06:25:ac:c5:25 (LinksysG_ac:c5:25)
    Target IP address: 15.50.74.104 (15.50.74.104)
```

Check the host's ARP cache to make sure that the host's MAC shows up, as per the following.

```
# arp -vn
Address               HWtype   HWaddress          Flags Mask    Iface
15.50.74.20           ether    00:0E:A6:78:E3:D6  C              eth1
15.50.74.40           ether    00:09:5B:24:65:3A  C              eth1
Entries: 2    Skipped: 0      Found: 2
```

To clarify, if this destination IP were not on the same subnet (discussed later), the MAC of the destination IP would not be in our host's ARP cache. The cache only includes devices on the same physical network. If the IP were on another network, the ARP cache would be populated with the MAC of the gateway device required to leave this network to get to the destination IP. In the previous example, the gateway (15.50.74.40) would be the hop required to get to any other network.

ICMP

One of the most recognized protocols other than IP is the Internet Control Message Protocol (ICMP), mainly because everyone's first method of troubleshooting a network problem is to ask whether they can ping the desired destination. After the cables are run and the IP addresses are assigned, the first thing usually done is a ping test. This is nothing more than an application that uses ICMP, which is located at this layer. ping builds

ICMP control messages and sends them out over the wire, awaiting a reply from the destination machine. The replies provide some very useful information, including the time it took to receive the reply message and whether any packets are being dropped. Note that in today's IT world, most companies disable ICMP messages from coming into their environments from the Internet to prevent unwanted or malicious communications.

Continuing with the previous ARP cache example, we can see the ICMP messages with frames three and beyond.

```
Frame 3 (ICMP)
Frame 3 (98 bytes on wire, 98 bytes captured)
Ethernet II, Src: 00:06:25:ac:c5:25, Dst: 00:0e:a6:78:e3:d6
    Destination: 00:0e:a6:78:e3:d6 (00:0e:a6:78:e3:d6)
    Source: 00:06:25:ac:c5:25 (LinksysG_ac:c5:25)
    Type: IP (0x0800)
Internet Protocol, Src Addr: 15.50.74.104 (15.50.74.104), Dst Addr:
15.50.74.20 (15.50.74.20)
    Version: 4
    Header length: 20 bytes
    Differentiated Services Field: 0x00 (DSCP 0x00: Default; ECN: 0x00)
    Total Length: 84
    Identification: 0x0000 (0)
    Flags: 0x04
    Fragment offset: 0
    Time to live: 64
    Protocol: ICMP (0x01)
    Header checksum: 0x87c9 (correct)
    Source: 15.50.74.104 (15.50.74.104)
    Destination: 15.50.74.20 (15.50.74.20)
Internet Control Message Protocol
    Type: 8 (Echo (ping) request)
    Code: 0
    Checksum: 0x8dd8 (correct)
    Identifier: 0x9a0a
    Sequence number: 0x0001
    Data (56 bytes)
```

The reply to `ping` was in the very next frame received on that interface!

```
Frame 4 (98 bytes on wire, 98 bytes captured)
Ethernet II, Src: 00:0e:a6:78:e3:d6, Dst: 00:06:25:ac:c5:25
    Destination: 00:06:25:ac:c5:25 (LinksysG_ac:c5:25)
    Source: 00:0e:a6:78:e3:d6 (00:0e:a6:78:e3:d6)
    Type: IP (0x0800)
Internet Protocol, Src Addr: 15.50.74.20 (15.50.74.20), Dst Addr:
15.50.74.104 (15.50.74.104)
    Version: 4
    Header length: 20 bytes
    Differentiated Services Field: 0x00 (DSCP 0x00: Default; ECN: 0x00)
    Total Length: 84
    Identification: 0x8045 (32837)
    Flags: 0x00
    Fragment offset: 0
    Time to live: 64
    Protocol: ICMP (0x01)
    Header checksum: 0x4784 (correct)
    Source: 15.50.74.20 (15.50.74.20)
    Destination: 15.50.74.104 (15.50.74.104)
Internet Control Message Protocol
    Type: 0 (Echo (ping) reply)
    Code: 0
    Checksum: 0x95d8 (correct)
    Identifier: 0x9a0a
    Sequence number: 0x0001
    Data (56 bytes)
```

In the following example, we show a `ping` test that fails. We use hp.com as the test site, knowing that a ping test probably will fail due to ICMP datagrams' being ignored.

```
# ping hp.com
PING hp.com (161.114.22.105) 56(84) bytes of data.

--- hp.com ping statistics ---
9 packets transmitted, 0 received, 100% packet loss, time 8017ms
```

In this case, knowing that a `ping` test failed does not mean that the hp.com site is down; it just means that it does not respond to ICMP requests.

The following is a portion of the network trace of the `ping` test to hp.com using `ethereal`.

```
Frame 1 (98 bytes on wire, 98 bytes captured)
Ethernet II, Src: 00:06:25:ac:c5:25, Dst: 00:09:5b:24:65:3a
    Destination: 00:09:5b:24:65:3a (Netgear_24:65:3a)
    Source: 00:06:25:ac:c5:25 (LinksysG_ac:c5:25)
    Type: IP (0x0800)
Internet Protocol, Src Addr: 15.50.74.104 (15.50.74.104), Dst Addr:
161.114.22.105 (161.114.22.105)
    Version: 4
    Header length: 20 bytes
    Differentiated Services Field: 0x00 (DSCP 0x00: Default; ECN: 0x00)
    Total Length: 84
    Identification: 0x0000 (0)
    Flags: 0x04
        .1.. = Don't fragment: Set
        ..0. = More fragments: Not set
    Fragment offset: 0
    Time to live: 64
    Protocol: ICMP (0x01)
    Header checksum: 0x2934 (correct)
    Source: 15.50.74.104 (15.50.74.104)
    Destination: 161.114.22.105 (161.114.22.105)
Internet Control Message Protocol
    Type: 8 (Echo (ping) request)
    Code: 0
    Checksum: 0x2d82 (correct)
    Identifier: 0x7620
    Sequence number: 0x0001
    Data (56 bytes)
```

Unlike the successful `ping` in the previous example, in this case no reply `ping` completes the ICMP sequence. The following is an example of how to configure a Linux machine to ignore ICMP requests.

```
# ping localhost
PING localhost (127.0.0.1) 56(84) bytes of data.
64 bytes from localhost (127.0.0.1): icmp_seq=1 ttl=64 time=0.102 ms

--- localhost ping statistics ---
1 packets transmitted, 1 received, 0% packet loss, time 0ms
rtt min/avg/max/mdev = 0.102/0.102/0.102/0.000 ms
```

Next you disable ICMP:

```
# echo 1 > /proc/sys/net/ipv4/icmp_echo_ignore_all
```

Repeating the same test as previously, we get the following:

```
# ping localhost
PING localhost (127.0.0.1) 56(84) bytes of data.

--- localhost ping statistics ---
2 packets transmitted, 0 received, 100% packet loss, time 1013ms
```

IP

By far, IP is the most recognized protocol used in this layer. It is even a portion of the name of the protocol suite upon which this chapter focuses: TCP/IP. The Internet Protocol provides, among other things, a logical addressing of the physical interfaces and routing of the data throughout the network. IP addresses are divided into networks and then into subnetworks, which assists in decreasing network congestion and reducing collision rates.

In this section, we begin with an anatomy of the IP header, which, just like the MAC header, is prepended to the transport layer's datagram. Figure 13-6 provides an illustration of the IP header.

The IP header does have a few interesting areas that we should mention before proceeding. For example, the IP version identifies whether the packet is meant for the standard IPv4 (32-bit) network or the newer IPv6 (128-bit) network. In today's IT environments, most network configurations use the IPv4 protocol version; however, use of IPv6 is growing. The newer IPv6 (128-bit IP) protocol essentially eliminates many of

IP Header												
Version	Internet Header Length	Type of Service	Total Length if IP Datagram	Unique ID for Datagram	Flags for Fragments	Flag Offset: Fragment # in the Datagram	TTL	Protocol: ICMP, TCP, UDP, etc	CRC for This Header	Source IP	Destination IP	PAD: Aligns the datagram so that it ends on a 32-bit boundary

Figure 13-6 The IP header broken down

the shortcomings of IPv4, the largest of which is the lack of available addresses. IPv6 also does away with ARP and replaces it with multicast neighbor solicitation messages. Because the majority of users are still connected to IPv4 installations, however, this book only covers troubleshooting with the IPv4 protocol.

Other fields of interest are the Type of Service (TOS), Flags, Fragment offset, Time-To-Live (TTL), Protocol, and the source and destination IP. The 8-bit TOS field refers to the precedence, delay, normal throughput, and normal reliability of the IP datagram. The TOS is a legacy term, which has now been replaced with "differentiated services," which is the new approach for IP Quality of Service (QoS). Upon reviewing an ethereal output of an IP frame, we would see the TOS field as the Differentiated Services Code Point (DSCP), as shown here.

```
# cat /tmp/ethereal.trace
...
Differentiated Services Field: 0x10 (DSCP 0x04: Unknown DSCP; ECN: 0x00)
        0001 00.. = Differentiated Services Codepoint: Unknown (0x04)
        .... ..0. = ECN-Capable Transport (ECT): 0
        .... ...0 = ECN-CE: 0
...
```

Another place that documents the QoS for a packet is located in the man page on ping. See the -Q option, as in the following.

```
...
-Q tos
Set Quality of Service -related bits in ICMP datagrams.  tos can be
either decimal or hex number.  Traditionally (RFC1349), these have been
interpreted as: 0 for reserved (currently being redefined as congestion
```

control), 1-4 for Type of Service and 5-7 for Precedence. Possible
settings for Type of Service are: minimal cost: 0x02, reliability: 0x04,
throughput: 0x08, low delay: 0x10. Multiple TOS bits should not be set
simultaneously. Possible settings for special Precedence range from
priority (0x20) to net control (0xe0). You must be root CAP_NET_ADMIN
capability) to use Critical or higher precedence value. You cannot set
bit 0x01 (reserved) unless ECN has been enabled in the kernel. In
RFC2474, these fields has been redefined as 8-bit Differentiated Services
(DS), consisting of: bits 0-1 of separate data (ECN will be used, here),
and bits 2-7 of Differentiated Services Codepoint (DSCP).

...

The FLAG and Fragment offset fields deal with datagram fragmentation. As covered
earlier, IP datagrams are encapsulated into Ethernet frames, which have a Maximum
Transaction Unit (MTU). Just as the link layer has its MTU, the IP layer has its maximum
length. If an IP datagram exceeds this maximum, then the packet is fragmented. Unlike
IPv6, in which only the host can fragment a packet, in IPv4, the packet can be fragmented at the host or any intermediate routers. The 3-bit flag field indicates whether the
packet is fragmented, and the 64-bit fragmentation offset field indicates the fragment
location so that the receiving host can put the fragments back together and rebuild the
datagram. If a fragment is lost in the transmission, the entire datagram is discarded after
a timeout, and the datagram must be re-sent.

Next is an example of a fragmented ICMP ping request.

```
# ping -s 1472 15.50.74.20  (This allows the packet to align on the MTU
size)
PING 15.50.74.20 (15.50.74.20) 1472(1500) bytes of data.
1480 bytes from 15.50.74.20: icmp_seq=1 ttl=64 time=3.93 ms
1480 bytes from 15.50.74.20: icmp_seq=2 ttl=64 time=3.44 ms
1480 bytes from 15.50.74.20: icmp_seq=3 ttl=64 time=3.22 ms
```

The following is just a fragment of the datagram:

```
Frame 2 (586 bytes on wire, 586 bytes captured)
Ethernet II, Src: 00:06:25:ac:c5:25, Dst: 00:0e:a6:78:e3:d6
Internet Protocol, Src Addr: 15.50.74.104 (15.50.74.104), Dst Addr:
15.50.74.20 (15.50.74.20)
    Version: 4
    Header length: 20 bytes
```

```
    Differentiated Services Field: 0x00 (DSCP 0x00: Default; ECN: 0x00)
    Total Length: 572
    Identification: 0x0000 (0)
    Flags: 0x06
        .1.. = Don't fragment: Set
        ..1. = More fragments: Set
    Fragment offset: 552
    Time to live: 64
    Protocol: ICMP (0x01)
    Header checksum: 0x659c (correct)
    Source: 15.50.74.104 (15.50.74.104)
    Destination: 15.50.74.20 (15.50.74.20)
Data (552 bytes)
```

The last packet that completes this transfer segment is shown next:

```
Frame 3 (410 bytes on wire, 410 bytes captured)
Ethernet II, Src: 00:06:25:ac:c5:25, Dst: 00:0e:a6:78:e3:d6
Internet Protocol, Src Addr: 15.50.74.104 (15.50.74.104), Dst Addr:
15.50.74.20 (15.50.74.20)
    Version: 4
    Header length: 20 bytes
    Differentiated Services Field: 0x00 (DSCP 0x00: Default; ECN: 0x00)
    Total Length: 396
    Identification: 0x0000 (0)
    Flags: 0x04
        .1.. = Don't fragment: Set
        ..0. = More fragments: Not set
    Fragment offset: 1104
    Time to live: 64
    Protocol: ICMP (0x01)
    Header checksum: 0x8607 (correct)
    Source: 15.50.74.104 (15.50.74.104)
    Destination: 15.50.74.20 (15.50.74.20)
Data (376 bytes)
```

The next two fields deal with the duration for which the packet survives on the network before being discarded and the protocol that follows the IP header. The Time-To-Live (TTL) is either measured in hops or seconds depending on the OS and device. The most common protocols for our discussion are TCP, UDP, ICMP, and even Encapsulating Security Payload (ESP for VPN tunnels).

Before we cover the IP address model, we should mention a few Linux kernel parameters, which are listed here.

```
# ls /proc/sys/net/ipv4/ip*
/proc/sys/net/ipv4/ip_autoconfig
/proc/sys/net/ipv4/ip_default_ttl
/proc/sys/net/ipv4/ip_dynaddr
/proc/sys/net/ipv4/ip_forward
/proc/sys/net/ipv4/ipfrag_high_thresh
/proc/sys/net/ipv4/ipfrag_low_thresh
/proc/sys/net/ipv4/ipfrag_time
/proc/sys/net/ipv4/ip_local_port_range
/proc/sys/net/ipv4/ip_nonlocal_bind
/proc/sys/net/ipv4/ip_no_pmtu_disc
```

A brief description of some of the kernel parameters follows.

- ip_autoconfig—This parameter is 1 if the host's IP configuration was done by RARP, DHCP, BOOTP, or some other mechanism; otherwise, it is 0.

- ip_default_ttl—This value sets the timeout previously mentioned. In network hops, it is set to 64 by default.

  Checking the source file, we find that the ip_default_ttl is set to IPDEFTTL:
  ```
  linux/net/ipv4/ip_output.c
  int sysctl_ip_default_ttl = IPDEFTTL;
  ```

  ```
  /usr/include/linux/ip.h
  #define IPDEFTTL        64
  ```

- `ip_dynaddr`—This parameter is for use with dial-on-demand devices.

- `ip_forward`—This parameter causes the kernel to forward packets.

- `ipfrag_high_thresh`—This parameter is the maximum memory used to rebuild incoming IP fragments.

- `ipfrag_low_thresh`—This parameter is the minimum memory used to rebuild incoming IP fragments.

- `ipfrag_time`—This parameter is the amount of time before the datagram is discarded due to a fragment that has yet to be received.

Note that if your system is on a network with a high number of fragmented packets, it will suffer a performance hit as a result of managing the overhead of rebuilding the packets into the originating datagram. Furthermore, your system runs the risk of reaching the timeout before receiving all the fragments, in which case the datagram's must be re-sent.

IP: Address Model and Routing

The next logical step in the ideal network troubleshooting process is determining why a host is having difficulty in communicating with another host. You need the applicable IP address(es), subnet mask, and gateway to troubleshoot at this point. Just as each physical network interface has an address given to it by its manufacturer, for a card to be used on the network, the system administrator or network engineer must assign the interface a logical address. Recall that we focus on the address model of IPv4 here.

First, by way of background, let us quickly cover the IP layout. IPs are composed of two sides: one network and one host. The network side routes IP packets from one network to another, whereas the host side directs packets to the appropriate network interfaces.

When originally developed, IPs were assigned classes, which defined particular network ranges by defining the default network mask. The network mask positions the separator (separation between the network and host portions) for the IP's two parts, assigning n number of bits to the network side and the remaining H number of bits to the host side. These bits are used to calculate the number of networks in an IP range and the number of hosts on each of those networks. If two IPs that are attempting to communicate with each other reside on the same network, packet routing is not required. If routing is not required, yet there remains a problem with IP communication, we know the problem is either an issue previously discussed at the hardware link layer (ARP or lower) or an issue with firewall implementation (discussed later in this chapter). If routing is involved, this is where the gateway IP plays a crucial role because it is the one device tasked with getting the packet to its destination network.

To briefly cover network routing, we begin by providing some background on network classes and their roles. As previously mentioned, the IP has two parts. The network portion is then subcategorized into classes. The first few bits, which form the network portion of the address, distinguish the five network classes. These classes, which originally were designed by the U.S. Department of Defense, range from A to E. Of these five classes, primarily the first three are used. The fourth class, D, is used only as a multicast network range. A multicast network is not common; however, it does provide the capability for a single IP to be assigned to multiple hosts, which in turn enables multiple hosts to receive the same broadcast from a single transmission. The fifth and final class, E, is reserved for future use. In any case, the network class determines the default mask, and as a result, it also determines the ratio of hosts to networks that we can use.

The determination of the IP class falls on which of the first few Big Endian bits are set. Note that the TCP/IP stack is defined in Big Endian order, meaning that the most significant value is stored at the lowest address. An IP address is made up of four integer fields separated by dots (for example, 15.38.28.2). Each field is composed of eight bits, which collectively are referred to as an "octet." Because there are four octets, the sum yields the 32 total bits that make up an IPv4 address.

The following is an IP address and the same address in bit form:

IP address: 123.2.3.4

Bit notation: **01111011**.00000010.00000011.00000100

Figure 13-7 is an illustration of how the first octet (123) is calculated.

A bit is either on (1) or off (0). Sum the on bits as follows: $64+32+16+8+2+1 = 123$. As mentioned earlier, the first octet also determines the IP class. Table 13-2 illustrates how the class is determined. Take note of the **bold** bits.

```
128   64   32   16   8   4   2   1
 |    |    |    |    |   |   |   |
 0    1    1    1    1   0   1   1
```

Figure 13-7 Calculation of the first octet

Table 13-2   Determining the Class

Class	IP Range	Bits
Class A	1-126	**0**0000000–01111110 (Note that 127 = lo and for testing)
Class B	128-191	**10**000000–10111111
Class C	192-223	**110**00000–11011111
Class D	224-239 *	**1110**0000–11101111
Class E	240-255 **	**11110**000–11111111

* Multicast **Reserved

There are default masks for each class of network; however, subnet masks can be modified to create smaller or larger groupings of hosts/networks. Since the mid '90s, the routing protocols have used an "IP network prefix" called Classless Inter-Domain Routing (CIDR) mentioned previously. In either case, the calculation is done in the same manner; however, with CIDR, the mask is no longer restricted to the boundaries set by the IP class. With CIDR, the network prefix is the number of contiguous bits set to "1," which identifies the network. Originally implemented due to the routing overhead caused by the Class C network range, it is now found in many network installations. First, we show an illustration of how a subnet mask is used to calculate the network range, and then we proceed to show the default masks and networks/hosts available for each.

The following is an example of a network calculation using the same IP from earlier (IP = 123.2.3.4). The class is A, so the default subnet is 255.0.0.0. The bit notation of the IP and the mask are as follows:

IP: 01111011.00000010.00000011.00000100

Mask: 11111111.00000000.00000000.00000000

Note that the separation between the network portion and the host portion of the IP is on the octet boundary. So, in this case, the "separator" between the network side and the host side is the decimal between the contiguous 1s and 0s.

Performing a logical AND calculation yields the logical network. The calculation goes like this:

(0 AND 1 = 0), (0 AND 0 = 0), (1 AND 0 = 0), (1 AND 1 = 1)

AND: 01111011.00000000.00000000.00000000

Converting the AND results into IP form yields the IP network:

Network: **123**.0.0.0

The "host" IP range is all possible variations of bit settings between all zeros and all ones in the host portion of the address.

IP range: 123.0.0.0–123.255.255.255

Illustrated next are the primary class layouts in detail:

- **Layout of Class A Network**—The default Class A mask is 255.0.0.0, so the first octet equals the network portion, and the last three octets equal the host portion.

  0 | 0000000 - 0 | 1111111 7 bits for network portion, and because 0.0.0.0 is not a valid IP, and because 127 is reserved for testing and loopback, we must subtract 2 from the network range. Simplifying the calculation $2^7 - 2 = 126$ networks possible. Following the same format for the number of hosts per network, sum the host bits and throw out all 0s value and all 1s value: (32bits – 8bits = 24bits), so $2^{24} - 2 = 16,777,214$ hosts per network.

- **Layout of Class B Network**—The default Class B mask is 255.255.0.0, so the first two octets equals the network portion, and the last two octets equals the host portion.

  10 | 000000.00000000. 14 bits for network portion. The calculation $2^{14} - 2 = 16,382$ networks possible. There are two remaining octets for the host portion, so there is a possible $2^{16} - 2 = 16,534$ hosts/network.

- **Layout of Class C Network**—The default Class C mask is 255.255.255.0, so the first three octets equal the network portion, and the last octet equals the host portion.

  110 | 00000.00000000.00000000. 21 bits for network portion. The calculation $2^{21} - 2 = 2,097,150$ networks possible. There is one remaining octet for the host portion, so there is a possible $2^8 - 2 = 254$ hosts/network

As aforementioned, in network troubleshooting, we need the applicable IP address(es), subnet mask, and the gateway. Determining the logical network in which an IP resides requires a basic understanding of IP classes and network masks. As shown previously, originally the class defined the subnet mask, so it also defined the network. Note that today, however, this is not necessarily the case as with the introduction of CIDR in the mid '90s. The CIDR is represented by a value and the end of an IP address in the form of IP/#, where # is the number of network bits in the netmask.

Let us review an example of CIDR in action. Look at the following IP address:

IP: 15.50.74.64/21

Here we have a Class A address; however, instead of the network mask being 8 bits in length, it is set to 21 (essentially a Class C netmask of 255.255.248.0).

Using the same method as before, we can calculate the network by taking the IP and logically ANDing the mask to it. Again, we use "|" to show where the mask separates the net from the host portion.

| IP: | 15.50.65.104 | 00001111.00110010.01000 | 001.01101000 |
| Mask: | 255.255.248.0 | 11111111.11111111.11111 | 000.00000000 |

The logical AND yields

| Net: | 15.50.64.0 | 00001111.00110010.01000 | 000.00000000 |

Setting all the host bits to 1 yields the broadcast for the network.

| Broadcast: | 15.50.71.255 | 00001111.00110010.01000 | 111.11111111 |

As shown previously, normally a Class A network has millions of hosts and few networks, whereas a Class C network has the opposite. To reduce network congestion, a network engineer can use this type of layout to increase the number of networks contained within a Class A network. Because the class no longer defines the number of networks, we call this "classless inter-domain routing," as mentioned earlier. This calculation can be depicted easily using any number of tools that are packaged with some Linux distributions and other tools simply downloaded off the Internet. An example of such a tool from the Internet is a Perl script called `ipcalc` (by Krischan Jodies GPL) from http://jodies.de/ipcalc (downloaded latest rev .38 05/2005). We like using this tool because it shows the important IPs needed for an IP/mask range while also including the bit notation so that you can see how the calculation was done.

The following is the same IP/CIDR from earlier, passed as an argument to the `ipcalc` program.

```
# ipcalc 15.50.65.104/21
Address:   15.50.65.104        00001111.00110010.01000 001.01101000
Netmask:   255.255.248.0 = 21  11111111.11111111.11111 000.00000000
Wildcard:  0.0.7.255           00000000.00000000.00000 111.11111111
=>
Network:   15.50.64.0/21       00001111.00110010.01000 000.00000000
HostMin:   15.50.64.1          00001111.00110010.01000 000.00000001
HostMax:   15.50.71.254        00001111.00110010.01000 111.11111110
Broadcast: 15.50.71.255        00001111.00110010.01000 111.11111111
Hosts/Net: 2046                Class A
```

As shown previously, the calculation for the number of hosts/net is 2^hostbits – 2. In this case, the number is $2^{11} - 2 = 2046$ hosts/net.

Note that a host cannot be assigned an IP address that has the host bits set to all 0s or all 1s. As shown previously, when all the host bits are set to zero, this defines the network. So the first host IP in this case is 123.0.0.1. In the same manner, not all the host bits can be set to 1. When all the host bits are set to 1, this represents a special IP known as the broadcast IP for the network. Each network range, by this definition, has a broadcast, which is always the highest possible IP for the network range. So, the highest usable host IP must be the broadcast minus one, or in this case, 123.255.255.254. Thus, for any IP range, we have to subtract 2 IPs from the range because they cannot be used.

The broadcast IP is unique in that it can help troubleshoot why a host cannot communicate with a desired interface on the same network. When a host sends a packet with the destination of the network ranges broadcasted, the lower MAC header's destination is set to ff:ff:ff:ff:ff:ff. Thus, after the IP packet is built and passed down to the lower link layer, the packet is not intended for one interface but rather all interfaces on the network. So, for example you could determine whether the troublesome interface can see any interface on the local network by sending a simple `ping` to the broadcast IP. The key here is that this technique is used to troubleshoot a local network because a broadcast IP transmission is not routed, but they are used to populate routing tables.

Generally, router devices or hosts are located at either the lowest or highest IP address of the network, depending on how the network is designed. Usually, however, the same scheme is used throughout a single network design. For an IP packet to leave a network, it must go through a router. The router is the device that knows how to get to subsequent networks or that knows of another device that can get to another network. Note that going from one network to another by way of routing a packet is considered a "hop." Though exceptions exist, even among large networks, such as the World Wide Web, getting to the destination IP generally involves no more than fifteen or sixteen hops.

Scenario 13-1: Unable to Communicate with Other Hosts

After connecting a network cable to an interface and confirming that the link is online, we cannot communicate with other hosts. What do we do? The hosts are at the following IP addresses:

Host A is at 15.50.64.104   Linux

Host B is at 15.50.65.103   HP-UX

Begin by determining the IP and network mask assigned to each interface.

For Host A, `ifconfig` yields the following:

```
# ifconfig eth1
eth1      Link encap:Ethernet  HWaddr 00:30:6E:F4:26:EC
          inet addr:15.50.65.104  Bcast:15.50.1.1  Mask:255.255.248.0
          inet6 addr: fe80::230:6eff:fef4:26ec/64 Scope:Link
          UP BROADCAST RUNNING MULTICAST  MTU:1500  Metric:1
          RX packets:461962 errors:2 dropped:0 overruns:0 frame:0
          TX packets:3447 errors:0 dropped:0 overruns:0 carrier:0
          collisions:0 txqueuelen:1000
          RX bytes:45269857 (43.1 Mb)  TX bytes:278694 (272.1 Kb)
          Interrupt:85
```

For Host B, `ifconfig` yields the following:

```
# ifconfig lan0
lan0: flags=843<UP,BROADCAST,RUNNING,MULTICAST>
        inet 15.228.74.55 netmask fffffe00 broadcast 15.228.75.255
```

A netmask of fffffe00 = 255.255.254.0.

As shown, the crucial pieces of information include the IP address and the network mask. From these two pieces of information, the IP layer of the kernel calculates the broadcast. Of course, all these values can be specified by the administrator, so when troubleshooting the network, double-check these values. The broadcast should be the highest IP in a network range, which most of the time would have a "255" somewhere. Host A's interface, however, does not show the broadcast we would expect. SUSE Linux has its network configuration files under /etc/sysconfig/network/, and the files usually have the interface's MAC located in the filename, such as ifcfg-eth-id-00:30:6e:f4:26:ec. Other distributions follow similar practices: Mandrake and Red Hat place the file in /etc/sysconfig/network-scripts/ and name it ifcfg-eth0, and so forth.

Next, ping the broadcast to see whether there are any other IPs on the local network.

For Host A, ping yields the following:

```
# ping -b 15.50.1.1
WARNING: pinging broadcast address
PING 15.50.1.1 (15.50.1.1) 56(84) bytes of data.
64 bytes from 15.50.65.104: icmp_seq=1 ttl=64 time=0.044 ms
64 bytes from 15.50.65.104: icmp_seq=2 ttl=64 time=0.007 ms
64 bytes from 15.50.65.104: icmp_seq=3 ttl=64 time=0.005 ms
64 bytes from 15.50.65.104: icmp_seq=4 ttl=64 time=0.006 ms
```

Right away, we can tell that something is wrong, unless this is the only interface on the local network. Check the host's ARP cache for entries.

```
# arp -n
#
```

Nothing?

Using the ipcalc tool, we quickly can confirm the IP ranges and broadcast.

```
# ipcalc 15.50.65.104/255.255.248.0
Address:   15.50.65.104         00001111.00110010.01000 001.01101000
Netmask:   255.255.248.0 = 21   11111111.11111111.11111 000.00000000
Wildcard:  0.0.7.255            00000000.00000000.00000 111.11111111
=>
```

```
Network:    15.50.64.0/21      00001111.00110010.01000 000.00000000
HostMin:    15.50.64.1         00001111.00110010.01000 000.00000001
HostMax:    15.50.71.254       00001111.00110010.01000 111.11111110
Broadcast:  15.50.71.255       00001111.00110010.01000 111.11111111
Hosts/Net:  2046               Class A
```

So, the broadcast is wrong? Yet the kernel should have calculated the right broadcast IP. Thus, it sounds like a configuration file mistake.

```
# cat /etc/sysconfig/network/ifcfg-eth-id-00:30:6e:f4:26:ec
BOOTPROTO='static'
BROADCAST='15.50.1.1'
IPADDR='15.50.65.104'
MTU=''
NETMASK='255.255.248.0'
NETWORK='15.50.64.0'
REMOTE_IPADDR=''
STARTMODE='onboot'
UNIQUE='3pA6.sg1D61MCQsA'
_nm_name='bus-pci-0000:be:01.0'
ETHTOOL_OPTS="speed 100 duplex full"
```

Not all network problems are identified so easily, yet the background should prove helpful. After blanking the broadcast line in the config file and reinitializing the interface, we test the ping again.

```
# ifdown eth1
# ifup eth1
# ifconfig eth1
eth1      Link encap:Ethernet  HWaddr 00:30:6E:F4:26:EC
          inet addr:15.50.65.104  Bcast:15.50.71.255
          Mask:255.255.248.0
          inet6 addr: fe80::230:6eff:fef4:26ec/64 Scope:Link
          UP BROADCAST RUNNING MULTICAST  MTU:1500  Metric:1
          RX packets:22 errors:0 dropped:0 overruns:0 frame:0
          TX packets:6 errors:0 dropped:0 overruns:0 carrier:0
          collisions:0 txqueuelen:1000
          RX bytes:1673 (1.6 Kb)  TX bytes:484 (484.0 b)
```

Now that the broadcast is correct, let us retry pinging the broadcast.

```
# ping -b 15.50.71.255
WARNING: pinging broadcast address
PING 15.50.71.255 (15.50.71.255) 56(84) bytes of data.
64 bytes from 15.50.65.104: icmp_seq=1 ttl=64 time=0.046 ms
64 bytes from 15.50.65.214: icmp_seq=1 ttl=255 time=0.381 ms (DUP!)
64 bytes from 15.50.64.217: icmp_seq=1 ttl=255 time=0.412 ms (DUP!)
64 bytes from 15.50.64.216: icmp_seq=1 ttl=255 time=0.498 ms (DUP!)
64 bytes from 15.50.65.102: icmp_seq=1 ttl=64 time=0.657 ms (DUP!)
64 bytes from 15.50.65.35: icmp_seq=1 ttl=255 time=1.01 ms (DUP!)
64 bytes from 15.50.65.106: icmp_seq=1 ttl=64 time=1.12 ms (DUP!)
64 bytes from 15.50.64.209: icmp_seq=1 ttl=255 time=1.95 ms (DUP!)
64 bytes from 15.50.64.108: icmp_seq=1 ttl=64 time=9.10 ms (DUP!)
64 bytes from 15.50.65.6: icmp_seq=1 ttl=255 time=9.21 ms (DUP!)
...
```

It works.

The DUP normally is a *bad* sign because it means duplicate or damaged packets are being received. This is to be expected when sending a ping to the broadcast. Under normal conditions, ping sends out one packet and expects a single reply to that packet (as opposed to multiple replies); however, when sending a ping to a broadcast, we get a reply from everyone on the local network.

Notice that when we can ping the broadcast, we get an ARP entry for every IP in our local network.

```
# arp -n
Address             HWtype  HWaddress          Flags Mask      Iface
15.50.64.19         ether   00:30:6E:0C:80:F9  C               eth1
15.50.64.18         ether   00:30:6E:0C:81:2C  C               eth1
15.50.64.48         ether   08:00:09:8E:0C:E2  C               eth1
15.50.64.108        ether   00:10:83:49:48:80  C               eth1
15.50.64.109        ether   00:10:83:C3:AF:80  C               eth1
15.50.65.180        ether   00:10:83:F7:02:15  C               eth1
15.50.64.216        ether   00:10:83:36:84:D3  C               eth1
15.50.64.217        ether   00:0F:20:1D:8E:44  C               eth1
15.50.64.104        ether   00:01:E7:33:AB:00  C               eth1
```

After confirming that communication on the local network is up and operational, the user still cannot communicate from Host A to Host B or vice versa.

Recall that the Linux kernel has the capability to ignore ICMP packets. It can also just ignore ICMP packets with a destination of broadcast. This is accomplished when the kernel file /proc/sys/net/ipv4/icmp_echo_ignore_broadcasts contains a value of 1. Even a network trace would not help here because the kernel does not reject the packet that would create a reply; the packet simply is dropped.

In the example, the two hosts are on different networks, so for the communication to take place, a router must be involved. Host A is on a network of 15.50.64.0/21, and Host B is on a network of 15.228.74.0/23. For host communication to take place, we must determine whether the routes are set up. As mentioned before, the router must be on the local network because the only thing to which the host can route is on the local network range. If a packet is to leave a network, the router uses its route tables to determine the best path.

Determine route setup on Host A. (Assume the network administrator said that the router for the network is at 15.50.64.1.) There are several ways to gather routing information on a Linux host, including commands such as netstat and route, as well as issuing a cat /proc/net/route. (Note that the output of the cat command reports the entries in HEX as well as Little Endian order, so a destination of 15.50.64.0 would be 0x0F324000 in Big Endian and 0x0040320f in Little Endian.)

```
# netstat -rn                   Kernel IP routing table
Destination     Gateway     Genmask          Flags  MSS Window  irtt Iface
15.50.64.0      0.0.0.0     255.255.248.0    U        0 0          0 eth1
127.0.0.0       0.0.0.0     255.0.0.0        U        0 0          0 lo
```

Determine whether the router can be pinged.

```
# ping 15.50.64.1
PING 15.50.64.1 (15.50.64.1) 56(84) bytes of data.
64 bytes from 15.50.64.1: icmp_seq=1 ttl=255 time=0.271 ms
64 bytes from 15.50.64.1: icmp_seq=2 ttl=255 time=0.281 ms

--- 15.50.64.1 ping statistics ---
2 packets transmitted, 2 received, 0% packet loss, time 999ms
rtt min/avg/max/mdev = 0.271/0.276/0.281/0.005 ms
```

Yes, so add the route to the machine.

```
# route add default gw 15.50.64.1 eth1
# route -n
Kernel IP routing table
Destination     Gateway          Genmask          Flags Metric Ref     Use Iface
15.50.64.0      0.0.0.0          255.255.248.0    U     0      0         0 eth1
127.0.0.0       0.0.0.0          255.0.0.0        U     0      0         0 lo
0.0.0.0         15.50.64.1       0.0.0.0          UG    0      0         0 eth1
```

Now that the route entry has been added and we have confirmed that the interface can communicate on the local network, we see whether it can ping Host B.

```
# ping 15.228.74.55
PING 15.228.74.55 (15.228.74.55) 56(84) bytes of data.

--- 15.228.74.55 ping statistics ---
2 packets transmitted, 0 received, 100% packet loss, time 999ms
```

IP is a two-way street. Not only must the IP configuration be correct on the local host, but it also must be right on the destination host. In this case, we start by checking whether the destination host has a route entry.

```
# netstat -rn
Routing tables
Destination          Gateway          Flags  Refs Interface  Pmtu
127.0.0.1            127.0.0.1        UH        0 lo0         4136
15.228.74.55         15.228.74.55     UH        0 lan0        4136
15.228.74.0          15.228.74.55     U         2 lan0        1500
127.0.0.0            127.0.0.1        U         0 lo0            0
```

Here we see that Host B does not have a network route entry to leave the local network. We could do a network trace to see whether the packet was reaching the host, but the host would not know how to respond. After adding the default route entry for the network, we get a successful ping.

```
# route add default 15.228.74.1 1   <-- HPUX requires # of HOPS which
                                         in this case is 1.
add net default: gateway 15.228.74.1


On Host A attempt to ping Host B
# ping 15.228.74.55
PING 15.228.74.55 (15.228.74.55) 56(84) bytes of data.
64 bytes from 15.228.74.55: icmp_seq=1 ttl=254 time=1.22 ms
64 bytes from 15.228.74.55: icmp_seq=2 ttl=254 time=0.184 ms


--- 15.228.74.55 ping statistics ---
2 packets transmitted, 2 received, 0% packet loss, time 1000ms
rtt min/avg/max/mdev = 0.184/0.704/1.224/0.520 ms
```

In conclusion, when troubleshooting at the IP layer, confirm that the hosts either are on the same IP network or possess a gateway/router that is configured to enable communication between the two hosts, as in the previous example.

Network routing protocols extend beyond the context of this book; however, we mention the subject briefly here. In troubleshooting a network, a system administrator can trace a network interface with `tcpdump` or `ethereal` and discover protocols such as Routing Information Protocol (RIP) or Open Shortest Path First (OSPF). These are used by routers and other hosts posing as routers by running `gated` or `routed`. Gateways perform dynamic route discovery by using RIP. They send RIP queries down the broadcast of a given network. These queries return the information needed to build routing tables, so when a host needs to leave a given network for another one, the gateway device knows the route to take. Routers not only build their own route databases for their own networks, but they also receive routing databases from other routers, so eventually all the routers/gateways on the network will have route tables that can route network traffic throughout their networks while attempting to keep the number of network hops to a minimum. Many documents and books explain the intricacies of network routing.

IP Firewalls: iptables

Before progressing to the next logical layer (transport), note that the Linux kernel has a built-in packet-filtering firewall mechanism that operates at the IP, MAC, and transport layers. If, after confirming that the IP address and routing, are not problems, along with all the hardware in the middle (switches, routers, gateways, and so on), consider the possibility that the problem is being caused by the Linux firewall or, for that matter, another firewall. Some Linux distributions have a firewall scheme in place by default. That firewall scheme disables significant amounts of network communication. For network security, this is a good thing; however, for the person needing to log in to the machine remotely, this can be, to say the least, "a sore point."

`iptables` and the older version called `ipchains` are implemented through a firewall script. Today's Linux kernels 2.4 and higher use `iptables`. Note that some initial 2.4 kernel releases used `ipchains`. Many books and sources on the Web describe how to set up an `iptables` firewall. There are even example scripts, including the scripts that are shipped with some Linux distributions. Of course, this subject is beyond the scope of this book. However, we do offer some information for background purposes only.

`iptables` operates with three chains: INPUT, OUTPUT, and FORWARD. With these chains, the administrator can set the rule for the chain ACCEPT, DENY, and DROP. It is possible to lock down the machine so tightly that not only can packets not get into the machine, but they also cannot leave the machine. If, after troubleshooting a connection, you cannot connect, you might try disabling the firewall and seeing whether the connection is still broken. In a high-security environment, this is not recommended, of course, but it is a fast way to rule it out.

In the next section, we demonstrate the TCP and UDP protocols. If you are dealing with a UDP protocol, the firewall could present a major problem. Because the protocol is connectionless, there is no acknowledgment of the datagram; therefore, unless the program had an embedded timeout, such as an `alarm()`, it would not know whether the packet got to its destination. On the other hand, a network trace would show the packet inbound. In addition, the `iptables` firewall has the capability to log connection attempts such as an inbound UDP datagram. If the `iptables` policy is set to DROP and NOLOG, then the trace is the way to go. If, however, the policy is DENY, the host making the connection request sees an ICMP-3 message returned in a local trace. However, most firewalls do not DENY because that would generate a reply and acknowledge the machine's existence on the network.

You can identify programs attempting to connect to remote machines by utilizing the `netstat` command. For TCP connections, `netstat` might show SYN_SENT, indicating that a TCP connection is trying to become established, but if the firewall has a policy to DROP inbound connections on the destination port, the program must timeout. However, because UDP datagrams are connectionless, the only thing to do is review UDP stats with `netstat`.

Tools that can determine whether a firewall is in place include these:

* `iptables -L`—Lists firewall rules.
* `iptables -F`—If you cannot determine whether the firewall is causing the problem, disable it for a moment during your test. Make sure that you rerun the script that sets it back up.
* `nmap`—A port scanner.
* `strobe`—A port scanner.
* `netstat`—A common network tool used to gather network statistics.

Here is an example of nmap in action:

```
# nmap -sS -P0 15.50.65.104


Starting nmap 3.70 ( http://www.insecure.org/nmap/ ) at 2005-05-13
18:33 EDT
All 1660 scanned ports on atlorca2.atl.hp.com (15.50.65.104) are:
filtered


Nmap run completed -- 1 IP address (1 host up) scanned in 372.664 seconds
```

Troubleshooting at the Transport Layer (TCP and UDP)

There are times when error conditions take place at the higher layers of the network stack and are not easily identified or rectified. Troubles at the lower layers are usually more evident. Examples of lower layer issues are when packets do not get routed or interfaces do not initialize. Attempting to explain why a host cannot communicate with another host or has impaired communication, however, might require troubleshooting at the transport layer.

In this section, we cover two protocols for the IPv4 model: Transmission Control Protocol (TCP) and User Datagram Protocol (UDP). Most administrators already know the significant difference between these two protocols. In short, TCP often is referred to as a "reliable connection," whereas UDP often gets chalked up as "unreliable."

"Unreliable" is kind of a harsh way of putting it. TCP is referred to as "reliable" because of how the protocol performs built-in checks. UDP does not contain these built-in checks; therefore, the overhead of the protocol is reduced. The lack of overhead enables UDP transfers to be several times faster than their TCP counterparts. Another point of note is that some protocols at the application layer contain reliability checks, so the TCP reliability mechanism makes these checks redundant.

In either case, communication at this layer is accomplished through sockets. Whether a transfer is made through TCP or UDP, the client must acquire a local port to depart the machine. Attaching a port to the end of an IP address creates an entity referred to as a "socket." After the client application acquires a local socket, it proceeds with communication to the remote socket.

Client applications are not allowed to use a certain range of ports. This range applies to both TCP and UDP and is referred to as the "well-known" port range. These ports are reserved for services such as TELNET, SSH, FTP, NTP, and so on. The ports that fall into this category are below 1024, and depending on which RFC is applicable, ports 0–255 are "well-known," whereas the ports below 1024 are the "privileged," meaning that only superuser can bind() to them. It is possible for a client application, running as root, to attempt to use some of these ports; however, besides breaking the RFC standard, such an attempt most likely would result in an error stating that the port is already in use.

The "well-known" and privileged ports usually refer to the service (daemon) that is listening for inbound communication. Some client applications bind() to the privileged ports to perform their communications, however. Examples of these include NFS and the Berkley r commands (remsh, rcp, and so on). It is easy to see how NFS does this because it takes a root user to mount a filesystem, but the Berkley r commands get away with it because of the Set UID bit set on the program.

```
# ls -al /usr/bin/rcp

-rwsr-xr-x  1 root root 15964 2004-10-01 21:14 /usr/bin/rcp
```

Because the "S" is on the owner, and the owner is root, this program is executed as superuser.

Other client applications must pick from the unprivileged port range. This range is said to be simply above 1024; however, a lot of these ports have been registered with the Internet Assigned Numbers Authority (IANA). In fact, the ports in the range of

1024–49151 have been registered. That is not to say that they cannot be and are not used by applications as temporary ports, however. Most UNIX kernels have an anonymous port range from which client applications can select a port. In Linux, this range is 32768–61000, which can be dynamically changed. For comparison, HPUX sets this range to 49152–65535. More about the port ranges can be found at http://docs.hp.com/en/ 5990-7252/ch01s01.html?btnNext=next%A0%BB.

The anonymous port range in Linux can be determined with the following command:

```
# cat /proc/sys/net/ipv4/ip_local_port_range
32768    61000
```

To change the port range, you issue a command like this:

```
# echo "49152  65535" > /proc/sys/net/ipv4/ip_local_port_range
```

To view the change, you check it with this command:

```
# cat /proc/sys/net/ipv4/ip_local_port_range
49152    65535
```

UDP

This protocol does not maintain a connection state, nor does it perform any flow control. It is possible for a datagram to be dropped along the way if a portion of the network segment is unable to forward the datagram for some reason. It is up to the application to check for the packet loss and resend if needed.

This connectionless protocol has little overhead. The local machine creates a datagram and sends it out over the wire, and most of the time, it waits for a response. It is up to the application to have built-in timeout and error handling in case a response never returns. In the next trace, the datagram's destination is a machine's time server port. If we are fortunate, the remote machine will have the NTP daemon running, and we will get a response. When the server receives the NTP datagram, it will respond with the destination port set to the original source port for which the client application should be listening for a reply. If the server is not listening for communication on the destination port, or even if the server does respond and the client application has already died, we should receive or generate an ICMP type 3 error message.

Troubleshooting a program utilizing the UDP protocol can be somewhat difficult. When performing network traces, there is no sequence number or acknowledgment to reference. As mentioned previously, the application must be responsible for error checking or for placing a timeout if a response is never returned. An understanding of the fundamentals of how the UDP transfer takes place helps us to know where to begin the troubleshooting process.

Figure 13-8 conveys an illustration of a UDP header.

UDP	
Source Port	Destination Port
Packet Length	Checksum

Figure 13-8 A UDP header

The following `ethereal` trace snippet illustrates a client sending a UDP datagram to a network time protocol server. It demonstrates where the UDP protocol is placed in relation to other layers detailed earlier in this chapter.

```
Frame 34 (90 bytes on wire, 90 bytes captured)
Ethernet II, Src: 00:12:79:3e:09:ec, Dst: 00:09:5b:24:65:3a
Internet Protocol, Src Addr: 15.50.74.105 (15.50.74.105), Dst Addr:
16.54.97.90 (16.54.97.90)
User Datagram Protocol, Src Port: ntp (123), Dst Port: ntp (123)
    Source port: ntp (123)
    Destination port: ntp (123)
    Length: 56
    Checksum: 0xbc5e (correct)
Network Time Protocol
```

Communication at the transportation level requires two end points, whether TCP or UDP is the protocol. As with the previous example NTP trace, an IP.PORT exists for both ends. Of course, these are referred to as "sockets." Just as does TCP, the first thing the server program does is to create a socket file descriptor through the socket() system call. Then the server performs `bind()` to bind that socket descriptor to a socket (IP and PORT). This operation refers to the earlier discussion of port ranges and, if applicable, binds to privileged or unprivileged ports. In this example (NTP), `bind()` uses a privileged port of 123, which is also a "well-known" port. The last step is for the server to listen for datagrams to come in on the port and for the application to process these messages. The application calls `recvfrom()`, which is blocked until data is received.

Next, the client must perform the same `socket()` system call. After doing so, it can perform a `bind()` to set the local interface and port for which to listen for replies. `Bind()` is usually only done by the server, yet some client applications perform this operation (for example, `ntpd`). In addition, if a client program is maintaining the communication to the server, the client uses the `connect()` system call to specify the destination port and IP. This connection does not have the same meaning as with TCP connections: It only stores the target IP and port for future communications. An example of this can be found with the latest `ntpd` daemon. Now that the local socket is ready, the client uses `sendmsg()` or another `send()` system call to send a datagram to the server. After the datagram arrives, the servers `recvmsg()` unblocks on an interrupt and passes the datagram up to the application for further processing. At this point, the communication is up and running. If, however, a client or the server issues a `close()` on the connection, a message is not sent to the other node. Hence, the reliability factor comes into play. This is usually more of a coding issue or the result of someone shutting down the system before the applications are stopped properly.

In troubleshooting UDP issues, start with tracing the application to see exactly what it is doing. Look for obvious things such as the program performing a `recvfrom()` without using an `alarm()` or some other timeout mechanism. Then move on to the `ethereal`, `tcpdump`, and `netstat` programs. Of course, determine whether this is the only machine experiencing the problem because, if so, maybe a network profiling appliance is needed.

TCP

The last protocol at this layer that we cover in this book is the Transmission Control Protocol (TCP). It is referred to as "reliable" because of how it makes its connection to the destination socket. To clarify, a UDP transfer simply creates a datagram and sends it out over the wire hoping that it makes it to the other end point. TCP transfer first establishes a connection to the end points before sending data, however.

TCP has much more overhead than UDP. The key differences between the two protocols primarily are in the Sequence Number, Acknowledgment Number, Window, and TCP Flags. When troubleshooting the TCP protocol, these are the fields to which to pay attention. That is not to say that the others are unimportant; however, most solutions come from the sequence numbers and the flags that are set. These fields enable this protocol to maintain flow control, error handling, full duplex, buffered transfers, and order of delivery.

Figure 13-9 is an illustration of the 32-bit TCP header.

TCP		
Source Port	Destination Port	Sequence Number
Acknowledgment Number		
Offset	Reserved	Flags
Window	Checksum	Urgent Pointer

Figure 13-9 A TCP header

A breakdown of the TCP header includes the following:

* **Source Port: 16 bits**—Same meaning as a UDP port `socket()`, `bind()`, and so on.

* **Destination Port: 16 bits**—Same meaning as UDP port `connect()`...

* **Sequence Number: 32 bits**—The sequence number of the first octet of the TCP data block. It represents the amount of data transferred starting from a random value. This sequence enables the receiving entity to piece the packets back together to form the overall message that is released to the application layer.

* **Acknowledgment Number: 32 bits**—Initial acknowledgment is the received sequence number + 1 (referred to as the TCP "piggy back" confirmation). Informs the sender that it has received the segment. Initially, it is a random value from which the client starts counting to calculate the number of bytes transferred.

* **Offset: 4 bits**—Number of 32-bit words in the header.

- **Reserved: 6 bits**—Reserved for future use.
- **Flags: 6 separate 1-bit flags**—ACK, SYN, FIN, RST, PSH, and URG.

  Flag details:

  - ACK bit—This means that the host acknowledges that it has received the last bit stream. This frame's acknowledgment number is the next expected sequence number for the next frame.
  - SYN bit—Each host sends this at the initialization of the communication. Actually, the first host to send the frame would have a random sequence number, but all subsequent frames should be incremented from this first frame.
  - FIN bit—Finished with data, ready to close() the connection. This causes the destination machine to send an ACK for receiving the FIN and another FIN-ACK notifying the terminating party that they, too, are ready to close down the connection. A final ACK is sent back to close the connection.
  - RST bit—Reset the connection. Both sides reset the connection, usually as the result of an error.
  - PSH bit—Push data through to the application and do not buffer it.
  - URG bit—Urgent delivery, as in real-time event handling.
- **Window: 16 bits**—"Advertisement" of the amount, in bytes, that the sender is willing to accept before receiving an ACK. Note that DATA exchange for TCP is "full duplex," meaning that both ends can send data simultaneously. This would have to be adjusted from the sending host to notify the other end of what sender is willing to accept.
- **Checksum: 16 bits**—Used to confirm that the header was not damaged during the transmission.
- **Urgent Pointer: 16 bits**—When a packet is received with the URG FLAG (described previously) set, this field points to the sequence just after the URG data. This field is not referenced unless the URG flag is set.

Flow control is maintained through the sequence. These sequence numbers are at each end of the data flow. When the ACK flag is set, the acknowledgment number of the sender is the next expected sequence. When the sending host receives an ACK for data sent, it can remove that data from the kernel buffer. Large problems result if either of the hosts starts receiving segments out of order. This causes an ACK to be sent for the last in-order segment; thus, you would have the possibility of at least one more ACK for the one segment. This could stack up, causing congestion on the network and resulting in a considerable network slowdown. An example of this would be to cause a 100Mbps network to run at 10Kbps (see Scenario 13-5, "FTP Slows Down When Transferring from One Machine to Another").

An example of sequence numbers of an FTP data transmission in action follows.

SEQ: 1118533542 ACK: 0

An initial SYN is sent from the server to the client to establish the DATA connection. The server specifies 1118533542 as a random value from which to start counting.

SEQ: 3259969417 ACK: 1118533543

This is the SYN ACK from the client to the server. The ACK is the SEQ value supplied by the server + 1. The incremented value informs the server that the segment was correctly received and not just a guess ("piggy back"). The ACK value is the random value from which the client starts counting for bytes transferred from client to server as mentioned previously.

SEQ: 1118533543 ACK: 3259969418

Notice the ACK from the server to the client, which completes the three-way handshake for establishing the TCP connection. The SEQ value is incremented as per the ACK value from the client, and the ACK value is the recognition of the random value used by the client for counting bytes transferred +1.

At this stage, the DATA connection is now established. The next frame shows the actual file data being transferred from client to server.

SEQ=1118533543 ACK: 3259970878

When data is flowing, the ACK value is increased by 1460, which is the number of bytes sent in the previous packet. This is correct because it is saying that 1460 bytes of data have been sent from client to server.

As in this example, if data were only flowing in one direction (such as a get or put in an FTP transmission), we would expect the SEQ numbers to remain the same and the ACK value to increase.

TCP offers the capability for a host to receive several segments before having to send an acknowledgment. By so doing, it greatly increases the performance of the data flow. Known as "sliding window," the TCP header field "window" controls this feature. In short, the window is an advertisement from the sender informing the destination host that the sending host will accept x bytes of data before having to send an ACK, essentially cutting down on the data transmissions to increase bandwidth. The "window," which is advertised, can be large or small and is always being adjusted by the kernel algorithms. A smaller window informs the sending device to slow down the rate of outbound packets, whereas a larger window informs the sender to ramp up the amount of data sent.

This "window" refers to a receive buffer on the sending host. It is a smaller area inside a large receive kernel buffer. When an ACK has confirmed that the data has been received, the window "slides" down, at which point the sender's kernel can now remove the old transmission from the buffer. An API can set this window by using the `setsock-opt()` system call and `SO_RCVBUF` (see the `socket(7)` man page for more details). Most applications leave this up to the kernel algorithms in the TCP stack, which is recommended.

Besides the obvious difference in the header, this protocol also uses a three-way hand-shake." This is significant because it identifies the originator by the sequence number mentioned previously. Figure 13-10 presents a demonstration of the TCP connection.

Now the data can be sent back and forth . . . ACK . . . ACK . . .

Next, the shutdown of the connection can be represented, as shown in Figure 13-11.

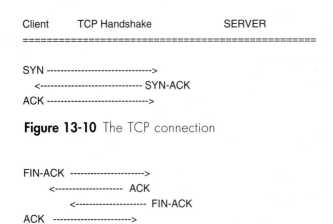

```
Client       TCP Handshake              SERVER
==================================================

SYN ------------------------------->
   <------------------------------ SYN-ACK
ACK ------------------------------->
```

Figure 13-10 The TCP connection

```
FIN-ACK ---------------------->
      <------------------- ACK
            <--------------------- FIN-ACK
ACK  ---------------------->
```

Figure 13-11 Shutdown of the TCP connection

The application that makes use of the TCP protocol appears slightly different from UDP applications. For example, on the server, a socket() call to acquire a socket descriptor and bind() call to assign a network socket to the file descriptor are made. At this point, the similarities stop, and the server application calls the listen() and accept() system calls. This sets up the daemon to listen for incoming connections on a particular port. Next is an example of SSH and how it sets up to listen for connections.

```
# netstat -an | grep LISTEN
tcp        0     0 :::22                   :::*
LISTEN
```

The following is a portion of a trace performed on the same sshd daemon.

```
# Gather a socket Descriptor
578 32728     0.000095 [ffffe410] socket(PF_INET6, SOCK_STREAM,
IPPROTO_TCP) = 3 <0.000011

...

# Next we see the bind() system call bind a socket to the Socket
Descriptor

...

582 32728     0.000066 [ffffe410] bind(3, {sa_family=AF_INET6,
sin6_port=htons(22), inet_pton(AF_INET6, "::", &sin6_add        r),
sin6_flowinfo=0, sin6_scope_id=0}, 28) = 0 <0.000026>

...

# Setup Listen()

...

609 32728     0.000095 [ffffe410] listen(3, 128) = 0 <0.000037>

...

# A connections was made to the daemon, call accept()

...

713 32728      17.001662 [ffffe410] accept(3, {sa_family=AF_INET6,
sin6_port=htons(34732), inet_pton(AF_INET6, "::ffff:12      7.0.0.1",
&sin6_addr), sin6_flowinfo=0, sin6_scope_id=0}, [28]) = 4 <0.000009>

...

# Now the sshd daemon clones a new thread and the connection goes to an
established state.
```

A socket connection can exist in one of several states at any given time. Most users will only ever see a few of these states, however, because transition from one state to another is performed so quickly. A TCP transitional diagram is included with RFC793, located at http://www.cse.ohio-state.edu/cgi-bin/rfc/rfc0793.html. The most common states regarding a new connection are LISTEN, SYN_SENT, SYNC_RECV, and ESTAB-LISH. These states normally can be seen with `netstat`; however, the two SYNCs are harder to catch with `netstat` unless there is a problem with getting packets from one side of the connection to the other.

Listed here are the TCP states right out of the source code in `linux/net/ipv4/tcp.c` source.

```
...

* Description of States:
*
*       TCP_SYN_SENT        sent a connection request, waiting for ack
*
*       TCP_SYN_RECV        received a connection request, sent ack,
*                           waiting for final ack in three-way handshake
*
*       TCP_ESTABLISHED     connection established
*
*       TCP_FIN_WAIT1       our side has shutdown, waiting to complete
*                           transmission of remaining buffered data
*
*       TCP_FIN_WAIT2       all buffered data sent, waiting for remote
*                           to shutdown
*
*       TCP_CLOSING         both sides have shutdown but we still have
*                           data we have to finish sending
*
*       TCP_TIME_WAIT       timeout to catch resent junk before entering
*                           closed, can only be entered from FIN_WAIT2
*                           or CLOSING.  Required because the other end
*                           may not have gotten our last ACK causing it
*                           to retransmit the data packet (which we ignore)
```

```
 *
 *      TCP_CLOSE_WAIT      remote side has shutdown and is waiting for
 *                          us to finish writing our data and to shutdown
 *                          (we have to close() to move on to LAST_ACK)
 *
 *      TCP_LAST_ACK        out side has shutdown after remote has
 *                          shutdown.  There may still be data in our
 *                          buffer that we have to finish sending
 *
 *      TCP_CLOSE           socket is finished
 */
...
```

As with the building of the TCP connection, the teardown states are mostly unseen upon issuing the `netstat` command at arbitrary intervals. If any are seen, such as FIN_WAIT_2, which does not have a timeout value specified in the RFC, they are seen because a FIN was not received from the remote connection. If your system is plagued by this situation, it normally is attributable to an application bug. On some UNIX operating systems, a FIN_WAIT_2 simply would linger around until a system reboot or kernel hack was performed. For example, even though the RFC does not provide for a timeout for a FIN_WAIT2, the Linux kernel provides a way with `/proc/sys/net/ipv4/tcp_fin_timeout`. Review of the source file `linux/net/ipv4/tcp.c` shows this feature in action.

Just as with all the dynamic kernel parameters, Linux's network parameters can be found under the magical `/proc` filesystem. The vast majority of these network kernel tunables are located in the `/proc/sys/net/ipv4` directory and, depending on the kernel release, consist of over 240 files. Of these files, about 40 deal with TCP connections. For details on these parameters, see the kernel source and sites on the Internet such as http://ipsysctl-tutorial.frozentux.net/ipsysctl-tutorial.html#TCPVARIABLES.

Scenario 13-2: UDP and Network Time Protocol

While trying to set up an NTP client, the administrator configures the wrong IP address into the `ntp.conf` file. After the administrator starts the `ntp` daemon, he notices that the time never synchronizes.

Check for the synchronization, as demonstrated here.

```
# ntpq -pn
     remote           refid      st t when poll reach   delay   offset  jitter
=======================================================================
 15.228.74.53    .INIT.          16 u    - 1024     0   0.000    0.000 4000.00
```

Next determine how long the daemon has been running.

```
# ps -ef | grep ntp
ntp      32166      1  0 12:49 ?        00:00:00 /usr/sbin/ntpd


# date
Tue May 10 14:10:54 PDT 2005
```

Note that the daemon has been running for about one hour and twenty minutes. Now determine whether the NTP daemon has sockets that are held open.

```
atlorca2: # lsof -p 32166
COMMAND    PID USER   FD    TYPE          DEVICE     SIZE  NODE NAME
ntpd     32166  ntp  cwd    DIR             8,35      144 82232 \
var/lib/ntp
ntpd     32166  ntp  rtd    DIR             8,35      144 82232 \
/var/lib/ntp
ntpd     32166  ntp  txt    REG             8,35   808340 82110 \
/usr/sbin/ntpd
ntpd     32166  ntp  mem    REG             8,35   209718 19367 \
/lib/ld-2.3.3.so
ntpd     32166  ntp  mem    REG             8,35   659679 19393 \
/lib/tls/libm.so.6.1
ntpd     32166  ntp  mem    REG             8,35    45629 23482 \
/lib/libcap.so.1.92
ntpd     32166  ntp  mem    REG             8,35  2358847 19392 \
/lib/tls/libc.so.6.1
ntpd     32166  ntp  mem    REG             8,35    87223 19381 \
/lib/libnss_files.so.2
```

```
ntpd      32166   ntp    0u   CHR                    1,3         46349 /dev/null
ntpd      32166   ntp    1u   CHR                    1,3         46349 /dev/null
ntpd      32166   ntp    2u   CHR                    1,3         46349 /dev/null
ntpd      32166   ntp    3u   unix 0xe00000408798c380            46262 socket
ntpd      32166   ntp    4u   IPv4               46266           UDP *:ntp
ntpd      32166   ntp    5u   IPv6               46267           UDP *:ntp
ntpd      32166   ntp    6u   IPv4               46268           UDP \
localhost:ntp
ntpd      32166   ntp    7u   IPv4               46269           UDP \
atlorca2.atl.hp.com:ntp
ntpd      32166   ntp    9w   REG                    8,35    220 82246
/var/log/ntp
```

Note that at this point, the application simply is awaiting a response. Performing a network trace, as demonstrated here, can lead us to a solution.

```
No.     Time        Source           Destination        Protocol Info
   234 17.074282    15.50.65.104     15.228.74.53        NTP      NTP


Frame 234 (90 bytes on wire, 90 bytes captured)
Ethernet II, Src: 00:30:6e:f4:26:ec, Dst: 00:d0:04:e2:ab:fc
Internet Protocol, Src Addr: 15.50.65.104 (15.50.65.104), Dst Addr:
15.228.74.53 (15.228.74.53)
User Datagram Protocol, Src Port: ntp (123), Dst Port: ntp (123)
    Source port: ntp (123)
    Destination port: ntp (123)
    Length: 56
    Checksum: 0xb218 (correct)
Network Time Protocol
    Flags: 0xe3
    Peer Clock Stratum: unspecified or unavailable (0)
    Peer Polling Interval: 6 (64 sec)
    Peer Clock Precision: 0.000061 sec
    Root Delay:    0.0000 sec
    Clock Dispersion:    0.0000 sec
    Reference Clock ID: Unindentified reference source 'INIT'
```

```
        Reference Clock Update Time: NULL
        Originate Time Stamp: NULL
        Receive Time Stamp: NULL
        Transmit Time Stamp: 2005-05-10 17:52:02.9955 UTC


No.    Time          Source           Destination           Protocol Info
    237 17.074710    15.228.74.53     15.50.65.104           ICMP
Destination unreachable


Frame 237 (118 bytes on wire, 118 bytes captured)
Ethernet II, Src: 00:10:83:fd:2d:5c, Dst: 00:30:6e:f4:26:ec
Internet Protocol, Src Addr: 15.228.74.53 (15.228.74.53), Dst Addr:
15.50.65.104 (15.50.65.104)
Internet Control Message Protocol
    Type: 3 (Destination unreachable)
    Code: 3 (Port unreachable) <-- indicates that the port is not listing
                                   for NTP traffic
    Checksum: 0xa7f9 (correct)
    Internet Protocol, Src Addr: 15.50.65.104 (15.50.65.104), Dst Addr:
    15.228.74.53 (15.228.74.53)
    User Datagram Protocol, Src Port: ntp (123), Dst Port: ntp (123)
        Source port: ntp (123)
        Destination port: ntp (123)
        Length: 56
        Checksum: 0xb218 (correct)
    Network Time Protocol
        Flags: 0xe3
        Peer Clock Stratum: unspecified or unavailable (0)
        Peer Polling Interval: 6 (64 sec)
        Peer Clock Precision: 0.000061 sec
        Root Delay:    0.0000 sec
        Clock Dispersion:    0.0000 sec
        Reference Clock ID: Unindentified reference source 'INIT'
        Reference Clock Update Time: NULL
        Originate Time Stamp: NULL
        Receive Time Stamp: NULL
        Transmit Time Stamp: 2005-05-10 17:52:02.9955 UTC
```

Observing a network trace with `ethereal`, we see the exact problem. The destination machine has nothing that is listening on the destination port; therefore, an ICMP error message is returned. Because the `ntpd` daemon does not care about this message, it does not die; rather, it just keeps running, hoping that at some point the `ntp` server will have a time server running on the destination port.

There are times when tracing an application assists in identifying a problem with UDP transmissions. As already demonstrated in this chapter, for hosts to communicate, they must possess an IP. However, most people cannot remember that 64.233.187.99 is one of the IPs for www.google.com. Domain name resolution is left up to the DNS subsystem. This protocol makes use of UDP datagrams to make transfers as fast as possible. As a user, you want the hostname resolution to be seamless and almost instant, and UDP makes this possible.

Scenario 13-3: UDP and Slow DNS Lookups

Suppose your users are having a difficult time communicating on your intranet. All IP communication appears to be slow at times, and the users cannot figure out the reason for the slow communication. All hostnames are resolving; however, this process sometimes takes a few seconds.

A simple test can help identify the problem. We use the `host` command (which replaces `nslookup` on Linux) to see whether a simple name resolution has a problem. If it does not, we can proceed either with `dig` (if we believe the problem is located with the name server) or with performing network traces. See the following example.

```
# strace -f -F -i -r -t -T -v -o /tmp/dns.lookup.trace host \
www.google.com
www.google.com has address 64.233.161.99
```

Notice that the machine did take a second to return. Let us take a look at the application trace.

```
...
22233     0.000040 [ffffe410] socket(PF_INET, SOCK_DGRAM, IPPROTO_UDP \
<unfinished ...>
...
```

```
22233      0.000043 [ffffe410] sendmsg(20, \
{msg_name(16)={sa_family=AF_INET, sin_port=htons(53), \
sin_addr=inet_addr("15.50.7

4.40")},
msg_iov(1)=[{"\310\360\1\0\0\1\0\0\0\0\0\0\3www\6google\3com\0\0\1\0"..., \
32}], msg_controllen=0, msg_flags=0}, 0 \
<unfinished ...>

...

22233      0.000063 [ffffe410] futex(0x805a330, FUTEX_WAIT, 3, NULL \
<unfinished ...>
22235      0.000034 [ffffe410] select(21, [3 20], [], NULL, NULL \
<unfinished ...>
22234      4.999361 [ffffe410] <... futex resumed> ) = -1 ETIMEDOUT \
(Connection timed out) <5.000466>
22234      0.000092 [ffffe410] gettimeofday({1115759285, 549580}, NULL) \
= 0 <0.000024>
22234      0.000074 [ffffe410] futex(0x805a330, FUTEX_WAKE, 1 \
 <unfinished ...>
```

Not shown in the application trace is the fact that the application spawns several processes that simply are waiting on a reply from the DNS server, one such process being PID 22234, which is performing a "fast" user space mutex lock. After 4.99 seconds, the program's timer goes off, and the timeout is reached. The mutex simply is resumed; however, the reply from the DNS server for which we have been waiting returns, waking up the process.

```
...
22233      0.000029 [ffffe410] futex(0x805a2f8, FUTEX_WAKE, 1) = 0 \
<0.000022>
22233      0.000088 [ffffe410] recvmsg(20, \
{msg_name(16)={sa_family=AF_INET, sin_port=htons(53), \
sin_addr=inet_addr("15.50.74.40")}, \
msg_iov(1)=[{"\310\360\201\200\0\1\0\1\0\0\0\0\3www\6google\3com\0\0"..., \
65535}], msg_controllen=20, msg_control=0x8082218, , msg_flags=0}, 0) \
= 48 <0.000025>
22233      0.000385 [ffffe410] fstat64(1, {st_dev=makedev(0, 9), \
st_ino=3, st_mode=S_IFCHR|0600, st_nlink=1, st_uid=1000, st_gid=5, \
st_blksize=1024, st_blocks=0, st_rdev=makedev(136, 1), \
st_atime=2005/05/10-17:08:00, st_mtime=2005/05/10-17:08:00, \
st_ctime=2005/05/10-16:13:47}) = 0 <0.000006>
```

```
22233      0.000122 [ffffe410] mmap2(NULL, 4096, PROT_READ|PROT_WRITE, \
MAP_PRIVATE|MAP_ANONYMOUS, -1, 0) = 0x409b0000 <0.000025>
22233      0.000098 [ffffe410] write(1, "www.google.com has address \
64.23"..., 42) = 42 <0.000348>
...
```

Assume that another trace on the program reveals that the system call was almost instant, taking only a few milliseconds. This causes us immediately to suspect that not all the network traffic is experiencing this slow behavior. After reviewing a network trace, we determine that only the DNS UDP datagrams were taking five seconds, and that even this appeared to occur only after the router device flushed its DNS cache. The following is a small portion of the ethereal trace taken from the previous test.

```
No.    Time        Source              Destination         Protocol Info
    3 2.504490    15.50.74.105        15.50.74.40         DNS
Standard query A www.google.com


Frame 3 (70 bytes on wire, 70 bytes captured)
Ethernet II, Src: 00:12:79:3e:09:ec, Dst: 00:09:5b:24:65:3a
Internet Protocol, Src Addr: 15.50.74.105 (15.50.74.105), Dst Addr:
15.50.74.40 (15.50.74.40)
User Datagram Protocol, Src Port: 33993 (33993), Dst Port: domain (53)
    Source port: 33993 (33993)
    Destination port: domain (53)
    Length: 36
    Checksum: 0x69f0 (correct)
Domain Name System (query)
...
```

Then five seconds later . . .

```
No.    Time        Source              Destination         Protocol Info
    8 7.508797    15.50.74.40         15.50.74.105        DNS
Standard query response A 64.233.161.99


Frame 8 (86 bytes on wire, 86 bytes captured)
Ethernet II, Src: 00:09:5b:24:65:3a, Dst: 00:12:79:3e:09:ec
```

```
Internet Protocol, Src Addr: 15.50.74.40 (15.50.74.40), Dst Addr:
15.50.74.105 (15.50.74.105)
User Datagram Protocol, Src Port: domain (53), Dst Port: 33993 (33993)
    Source port: domain (53)
    Destination port: 33993 (33993)
    Length: 52
    Checksum: 0x7ef8 (correct)
Domain Name System (response)
```

Notice that there are no sequence numbers, so putting together a timeline would be very difficult if this machine were generating a large amount of DNS lookups at the time the trace was performed. Of course, other applications that use UDP, such as NFS, use an addition protocol called Remote Procedure Calls (RPC), which generates a unique number for a sequence enabling the application to place the datagrams back together to service the request. The solution in this case was to simply change the client's name server to a newer system that was not having a problem serving DNS requests.

Scenario 13-4: Under Heavy Load Conditions, the System Experiences UDP Packet Loss

We could see this type of problem with `netstat`, as in the following example.

```
# netstat -us
Udp:
250560 packets received
3318 packets to unknown port received.
8252 packet receive errors
233373 packets sent
```

While still under a UDP load, we rerun the `netstat` command every few seconds to get a good sampling.

```
# netstat -us
Udp:
260175 packets received
3318 packets to unknown port received.
8617 packet receive errors
242987 packets sent
```

Note that about 10,000 requests were sent out, and about 360 have been erroneous. The test generated from another client source results in the same behavior on the server. Notice that when different hardware configurations are tested, we get the same results in the example. Thus, we attempted to increase the network buffer, as indicated here.

```
#sysctl -w net.core.rmem_max=524288
#sysctl -w net.core.wmem_max=524288
#sysctl -w net.core.rmem_default=524288
#sysctl -w net.core.wmem_default=524288
```

Notice that the symptoms remain. We then pursue the following thought process:

* UDP is unreliable, so packet loss is always possible. Is the LAN failing to perform up to specs?
* Confirm with `netperf`.
* It could be that the data simply is not getting read quickly enough. If that were the case, the problem could be with the receiving application.
* UDP cannot ask the sender to stop (TCP has flow control in the form of sliding windows, but UDP does not).
* The application can have delays between `recv()` calls if it does some non-trivial processing (for example, consults a database or does intensive logging). Increasing buffer sizes could alleviate the problem if there were only bursts of activity, but if incoming traffic is steady, we need to `recv()` rapidly enough to enable quick consumption of packets. When the buffer is full, the kernel begins to discard packets.

We then proceed with the following questions and courses of action:

1. Any application using UDP should be designed with the knowledge that UDP is an unreliable protocol and that some datagrams will be lost. Confirm that there are no application-level problems. What are the application's timeout variables?

2. Originally, the problem description was that the datagram loss takes place under heavy loads. Define "heavy load conditions" as to the extent of `%system`, `%user`, and `%WaitIO`. Include CPU run queue.

3. To determine what packet loss can be expected in your configuration, you can run `netperf` (http://www.netperf.org) on client and server boxes. (Note: you should stop all other applications to be sure you are not CPU-limited.) `netperf` should be able to `recv()` quickly enough because it does not do any additional processing.

4. If we see that the server process is not CPU-bound, we can attach to it with `strace` and trace the packets with `tcpdump` simultaneously to see why the server process cannot `recv()` quickly.

5. Confirm that the machine is not disk IO bound by using `sar` and `iostat`.

Solution 13-4

The error was detected at the application level. When the server opened the sockets, it set the buffer receiving size to 4KB with the `setReceiveBufferSize` method in the class `DatagramSocket`. A change was made to delegate this operation to the OS rather than to manual setting of the application. Then the problem subsided.

Scenario 13-5: FTP Slows Down When Transferring from One Machine to Another

In this scenario, the problem is that of all the Ethernet cards on a single machine, one particular interface is slowing down. The slow interface is a virtual interface, `eth1:2`. Furthermore, `eth1`, `eth1:1`, and `eth1:0` are not experiencing the problem. Because the driver is not different between the cards or the hardware, we can rule out a problem with the host immediately.

Note that we've changed the IP addresses from their originals.

Normally, we would not begin with a network trace. Every situation has to have an action plan devised, either in writing (as in our case) or in memory. Do not start with the big guns, such as kernel traces, profiling, hardware packet analyzers, and so on. First of all, it takes years of experience to know what to look for and to become proficient at using all those tools. In this case, an `strace` on the FTP process would not be of much assistance because we know that none of the other interfaces are experiencing the problem and because the issue could not be located at the OS level. Keep in mind, however, that if the user were transferring to a slow disk, it could have been an issue, but we have the user confirm that he was placing the data in the same location at each test.

We begin with a network trace:

```
tcpdump -i interface -s 1500 -w /tmp/trace.out


Frame 48123 (1514 bytes on wire, 1514 bytes captured)
Ethernet II, Src: 00:12:79:3E:09:EC, Dst: 00:12:79:58:E0:5E
Internet Protocol, Src Addr: 4.4.4.131 (4.4.4.131), Dst Addr: 10.3.194.90
(10.3.194.90)
Transmission Control Protocol, Src Port: 40495 (40495), Dst Port: ftp-
data (20), Seq: 3707061465, Ack: 3923484752, Len: 1460
    Source port: 40495 (40495)
    Destination port: ftp-data (20)
    Sequence number: 3707061465
    Next sequence number: 3707062925
    Acknowledgement number: 3923484752
    Header length: 20 bytes
    Flags: 0x0010 (ACK)
    Window size: 24820
    Checksum: 0x3f9c (correct)
FTP Data
```

So, the next seq should be seq 3707062925; however, the machine receives other sequences. Where did the seq go? So the local machine sends an ACK back to the remote machine requesting the data. The remote machine continues to send data, and it must send an ACK saying that it is still waiting on the seq 3707062925.

```
   48123 1.506367    4.4.4.131            10.3.194.90        FTP-DATA \
FTP Data: 1460 bytes
   48124 1.506381    4.4.4.131            10.3.194.90        FTP-DATA \
[TCP Retransmission] FTP Data: 1460 bytes
   48125 1.506423    10.3.194.88          10.3.194.88        TNS \
Request, Data (C), Data
   48126 1.506429    10.3.194.88          10.3.194.88        TNS \
Response, Data (6), Data
   48127 1.506430    10.3.194.88          10.3.194.88        TNS \
[TCP Retransmission] Request, Data (6), Data
   48128 1.506431    10.3.194.90          4.4.4.131          TCP \
ftp-data > 40495 [ACK] Seq=3923484752 Ack=3707062925 Win=57344 Len=0
```

```
    48129 1.506437    10.3.194.88           10.3.194.88          TNS \
[TCP Retransmission] Response, Data (6), Data
    48130 1.506446    10.3.194.90           4.4.4.131            TCP \
[TCP Dup ACK 48128#1] ftp-data > 40495 [ACK] Seq=3923484752
Ack=3707062925 Win=57344 Len=0
    48131 1.506488    10.3.194.88           10.3.194.88          TNS \
Request, Data (6), Data
    48132 1.506494    10.3.194.88           10.3.194.88          TNS \
[TCP Retransmission] Request, Data (6), Data
    48133 1.506531    10.3.194.88           10.3.194.88          TNS \
Response, Data (6), Data
    48134 1.506541    4.4.4.131             10.3.194.90          FTP-DATA \
[TCP Previous segment lost] FTP Data: 892 bytes
    48135 1.506540    10.3.194.88           10.3.194.88          TNS \
[TCP Retransmission] Response, Data (6), Data
    48136 1.506553    4.4.4.131             10.3.194.90          FTP-DATA \
[TCP Retransmission] FTP Data: 892 bytes
    48137 1.506575    10.3.194.88           10.3.194.88          TNS \
Request, Data (6), Data
...
    48416 1.510945    10.3.194.88           10.3.194.88          TNS \
[TCP Retransmission] Response, Data (6), Data
    48417 1.511006    10.3.194.88           10.3.194.88          TNS \
Request, Data (6), Data
    48418 1.511012    10.3.194.88           10.3.194.88          TNS \
[TCP Retransmission] Request, Data (6), Data
    48419 1.511021    10.3.194.88           10.3.194.88          TNS \
Response, Data (6), Data
    48420 1.511025    10.3.194.88           10.3.194.88          TNS \
[TCP Retransmission] Response, Data (6), Data
    48421 1.511032    10.3.194.88           10.3.194.88          TNS \
Request, Data (6), Data
    48422 1.511035    10.3.194.88           10.3.194.88          TNS \
Request, Data (6), Data
    48423 1.511040    10.3.194.88           10.3.194.88          TNS \
[TCP Retransmission] Request, Data (6), Data
    48424 1.511041    10.3.194.88           10.3.194.88          TNS \
[TCP Retransmission] Request, Data (6), Data
    48425 1.511068    4.4.4.131             10.3.194.90          FTP-DATA \
[TCP Fast Retransmission] FTP Data: 1460 bytes
```

Here we go! It is 0.0047 seconds later when we get the seq we were waiting on.

```
Frame 48425 (1514 bytes on wire, 1514 bytes captured)
Ethernet II, Src: 00:12:79:3E:09:EC, Dst: 00:12:79:58:E0:5E
Internet Protocol, Src Addr: 4.4.4.131 (4.4.4.131), Dst Addr: 10.3.194.90
(10.3.194.90)
Transmission Control Protocol, Src Port: 40495 (40495), Dst Port: ftp-
data (20), Seq: 3707062925, Ack: 3923484752, Len: 1460
    Source port: 40495 (40495)
    Destination port: ftp-data (20)
    Sequence number: 3707062925
    Next sequence number: 3707064385
    Acknowledgement number: 3923484752
    Header length: 20 bytes
    Flags: 0x0010 (ACK)
    Window size: 24820
    Checksum: 0xe59e (correct)
    SEQ/ACK analysis
FTP Data
```

The problem is TCP retransmission. This is not to say that the remote machine is wrong in continuing to send data, even though it is getting packets from the local machine saying that it is still waiting for old data. Keep in mind that the remote machine believes the first seq will eventually make it to the local host, or that the local host's ACK of what it has already sent will come back. Only after several retries does the remote machine realize that it needs to resend the packet, which it does. Note that the overall problem here is not how the local and remote host handled the missing packet, but the fact that the packet was missing at all. From what we could tell, this packet loss was causing other issues, including a lot of stress on the ARPA transport software on one or both of the servers.

It is possible that one of the cards or drivers on either the remote or local machine is missing packets; however, this does not stand up against the fact that other IPs on the same NIC are operational. The fact that the problem only seems to happen on certain IPs seems to indicate that the network is the cause of the issue. To test further, we recommend assigning another IP to lan1:3 (to possibly avoid any odd routing entries in the network equipment) and putting sniffers at both ends to see whether they detect these missing packets (eliminating the two servers from being the cause of the issue).

Solution 13-5

In our case, the customer's networking team comes back and informs the end user that a problem occurred with the switch and that it was being replaced. The switch was old and had out-of-date firmware. Instead of upgrading it, they simply replaced it with a newer switch. After the switch was replaced, the issue was resolved.

Troubleshooting at the Application Level: The Final Layer of the TCP/IP Model

This is the layer where we leave the "network" and rely on the application and kernel. Troubleshooting within this layer takes time because each program can have a different characteristic. The TCP/IP model groups three layers of the OSI model into this area. Protocols such as DNS, LDAP, and NetBios-NS, and even FTP, finger, TELNET, X Windows, HTTP, and SNMP reside in this layer.

No one troubleshooting methodology applies to all these protocols; however, understanding where they sit in the grand scheme of the TCP/IP stack assists you in diagnosing and troubleshooting these protocols. All these protocols depend on the lower layers. The application layer, as shown earlier in this chapter, builds a data "bundle." This bundle is passed to the lower layer, transport (TCP/UDP), where it is either broken into smaller chunks or taken as-is and prepended with that layer's header. Then the TCP/UDP layer sends the segment down to the IP layer, where the IP header is prepended, and the result is called a datagram. From here, the kernel passes this datagram down to the link layer, where the MAC header is added, at which point the datagram becomes an Ethernet frame.

Any one of these layers could cause a problem with an application. Always take the easiest approach first. Most of the time, we get lucky and discover that the problem is a simple configuration change. Never start with a network trace because this alone almost never provides a solution or, for that matter, a reasonable explanation for why the application is behaving the way it is.

Summary

As you can see, Linux networking problems can best be resolved by focusing on the networking layers. The different layers have different traits, and an understanding of the basic traits of each layer enables you to more readily isolate networking problems, leading to more efficient resolution. Although the layer structure is a complex one, it can be methodically and systematically approached.

14

Login Problems

User login attempts can fail for many reasons. The account could have been removed or the password changed. Linux provides password aging to force users to change their passwords regularly. A password can have a maximum age after which the account is locked. If a user notifies you that his login attempts fail, the first thing to check is whether he is permitted to log in.

Linux does not provide a meaningful explanation for why logins fail. This is part of good security because few hints are given to would-be intruders. It does make troubleshooting more complex, however. This chapter explains the commands needed to troubleshoot login failures and explains the authentication components. If you follow the steps explained in this chapter, you should be able to understand and correct login failures.

We separate this chapter into the following topics:

- `/etc/passwd`, `/etc/shadow`, and password aging—We explain the structure of `/etc/passwd` and `/etc/shadow`. We demonstrate how to look at and modify the password aging information in accounts. This is important because a login attempt can fail because of the password aging settings for the account.

- **Login failures due to Linux configuration**—Some examples include when the login is disabled because system maintenance is being performed and root login is refused because it is attempted from somewhere other than the console.

- **Pluggable Authentication Modules (PAM) configuration**—PAM provides a configurable set of authentication rules that is shared by applications such as login, KDE, SSH, and so on.

- **Shell problems**—If a user logs in but does not get the shell prompt or the application doesn't start, there may be a problem with the shell configuration. We discuss some common shell issues.

- **Password problems**—Finally, we provide a short program to validate user passwords.

/etc/passwd, /etc/shadow, and Password Aging

One of the first things to do when troubleshooting a login failure is to confirm that the account exists. The `finger` command shows user information, but because `/etc/passwd` has read permissions for all, we prefer just to `grep` for the user name.

```
$ grep bob /etc/passwd
bob:x:515:515::/home/bob:/bin/bash
```

We are only confirming that there is an `/etc/passwd` line for this user to prove that the account hasn't been removed.

/etc/passwd and /etc/shadow

Account information is stored in two files: `/etc/passwd` and `/etc/shadow`. All users can view the `/etc/passwd` file:

```
$ ls -l /etc/passwd
-rw-r--r--   1 root     root         2423 Jan 21 11:17 /etc/passwd
```

The `/etc/passwd` file has seven fields, as shown in Table 14-1.

Table 14-1   /etc/passwd Fields

Field #	Description
1	User name
2	Password
3	User ID
4	Group ID
5	Comment
6	Home directory
7	Login shell

The /etc/passwd file is completely explained in the passwd(5) man page. We are interested in the password field for the purposes of this chapter. The password field does not contain the encrypted password. It should have an "x" instead. The password field did contain the password when UNIX was first released. As computers became more powerful, though, viewable encrypted passwords left systems vulnerable to brute force attacks. Thus, the password was moved to a new file that can only be read by root. This file is /etc/shadow. In Linux, the /etc/shadow file is delivered in the shadow-utils package.

```
$ ls -l /etc/shadow
-r--------    1 root     root          1974 Jan 22 13:30 /etc/shadow
```

Let's look at the /etc/shadow entry for an account. The grep command is an easy way to view /etc/shadow.

```
$ grep bob /etc/shadow
grep: /etc/shadow: Permission denied
```

Right. We must switch to root.

```
#grep bob /etc/shadow
bob:$1$lIDEzDIs$mVFLa6ZVsSolJS8yPc3/o.:12800:0:99999:7:::
```

The /etc/shadow file contains password aging information as well as the password. The fields separated by ":" are explained in Table 14-2.

Table 14-2   /etc/shadow Fields

Field #	Description
1	User name
2	Encrypted password
3	Date the password was last changed
4	Minimum age of password in days before it can be changed (0 by default)
5	Maximum age of password in days after which it must be changed (99999 by default)
6	The number of days before password expiration when user is warned to change the password (7 by default)
7	The number of days after password expiration when account login is disabled
8	The date when account login is disabled
9	Not used

The /etc/shadow date fields are in days since January 1st, 1970. The password expiration date is the result of adding the date the password was last changed field and the maximum age of password field. See the shadow(5) man page for more details.

chage, passwd, and usermod

The chage, passwd, and usermod commands can be used to modify password aging parameters. The usermod command duplicates some but not all the password aging features of chage. The chage -1 *username* syntax is a good way to view the password aging settings for accounts. The following example shows the default password aging information for an account:

```
#chage -l bob
Minimum:         0                            field 4 /etc/shadow
Maximum:         99999                        field 5 /etc/shadow
Warning:         7                            field 6 /etc/shadow
Inactive:        -1                           field 7 /etc/shadow
Last Change:            Jan 17, 2005          field 3 /etc/shadow
Password Expires:       Never                 field 3 + field 5
Password Inactive:      Never                 field 3 + field 5 + field 7
Account Expires:        Never                 field 8 /etc/shadow
```

Let's look at the password aging example. A user tries to log in on January 19, 2005 using ssh, but the term window is disconnected immediately after entering the password:

```
login as: dbadmin3
Sent username "dbadmin3"
TIS authentication refused.
lori@sawnee.somecomp.com's password:
```

The login attempt doesn't identify the problem. The chage -l *username* command shows that the account expired yesterday, preventing logins.

```
#chage -l dbadmin3
Minimum:         0
Maximum:         99999
Warning:         7
Inactive:        -1
Last Change:            Jan 17, 2005
Password Expires:       Never
Password Inactive:      Never
Account Expires:        Jan 18, 2005
```

The `Password Inactive` and `Account Expires` dates prevent a user from logging in. When the `Password Expires` date is reached, the user should be forced to change his or her password during login. However, ssh will just fail the login attempt.

Table 14-3 shows the more useful chage syntaxes.

Table 14-3   chage Syntax

Syntax	Description
chage -l <username>	Display password aging values
chage -m ## <username>	Change minimum password lifetime
chage -M ## <username>	Change maximum password lifetime
chage -I ## <username>	Number of days after password expiration when account login is disabled
chage -E <date> <username>	Set account expiration date
chage -W ## <username>	Set number of days before password expiration to warn user that password will expire
chage -d <date> <username>	Set last password change date

Dates are in YYYY-MM-DD format, 2005-01-19 for example. The ## in the table indicates a number of days parameter.

Here is an example showing a change to the maximum password lifetime. Password lifetime is field 5 of /etc/shadow.

```
#grep dbadmin /etc/shadow
dbadmin:$1$TuCLLDqz$Fc1YnK309QXT6TJMOagdZ.:12841:0:99999:7:::
```

We can use grep to see this information, but chage is nicer.

```
#chage -l dbadmin
Minimum:       0
Maximum:       99999
Warning:       7
Inactive:      -1
```

```
Last Change:              Feb 27, 2005
Password Expires:         Never
Password Inactive:        Never
Account Expires:          Never
```

Now let's set the maximum password lifetime using chage.

```
#chage -M 30 dbadmin
```

We can use grep to see that the password aging field is now 30.

```
#grep dbadmin /etc/shadow
dbadmin:$1$TuCLLDqz$Fc1YnK309QXT6TJMOagdZ.:12841:0:30:7:::
```

Once again, chage -l *username* offers nicer output.

```
# chage -l dbadmin
Minimum:          0
Maximum:          30
Warning:          7
Inactive:        -1
Last Change:              Feb 27, 2005
Password Expires:         Mar 29, 2005
Password Inactive:        Never
Account Expires:          Never
```

A -1 for either a date or days field clears the field from /etc/shadow. Here is an example demonstrating how to reset the Account Expires date, which is field 8. Once again, we look at the password aging information with both grep and chage so that we can clearly see which field is being changed.

```
#grep lori /etc/shadow
lori:$1$cQG1pnOz$UHRmboguvqvOyJv5wAbTr/:12805:0:30:7::12847:
```

```
chage -l lori
Minimum:          0
Maximum:          30
```

```
Warning:          7
Inactive:        -1
Last Change:            Jan 22, 2005
Password Expires:       Feb 21, 2005
Password Inactive:      Never
Account Expires:        Mar 05, 2005
```

Here chage is used to clear the account expiration date.

#chage -E -1 lori

```
#chage -l lori
Minimum:          0
Maximum:          30
Warning:          7
Inactive:        -1
Last Change:            Jan 22, 2005
Password Expires:       Feb 21, 2005
Password Inactive:      Never
Account Expires:        Never
```

Field 8 is empty.

```
#grep lori /etc/shadow
lori:$1$cQG1pnOz$UHRmboguvqvOyJv5wAbTr/:12805:0:30:7::::
```

The usermod command can set the account expiration date and the number of days after the password expires when the account is locked. The syntax is shown for each in Table 14-4.

Table 14-4   usermod Password Aging Syntax

Syntax	Description
usermod -e <date> <username>	Set account expiration date; same as chage -E
usermod -f ## <username>	Set number of days of inactivity before account login is disabled; same as chage -I

The following example is similar to the previous chage example. This time, usermod is used to change the account expiration date, which is field 8 in /etc/shadow.

```
#grep dbadmin /etc/shadow
dbadmin:$1$TuCLLDqz$Fc1YnK309QXT6TJMOagdZ.:12841:0:30:7:::
```

```
chage -l dbadmin
Minimum:        0
Maximum:        30
Warning:        7
Inactive:       -1
Last Change:            Feb 27, 2005
Password Expires:       Mar 29, 2005
Password Inactive:      Never
Account Expires:        Never
```

```
#usermod -e 2006-01-03 dbadmin
```

```
#grep dbadmin /etc/shadow
dbadmin:$1$TuCLLDqz$Fc1YnK309QXT6TJMOagdZ.:12841:0:30:7::13151:
```

```
#chage -l dbadmin
Minimum:        0
Maximum:        30
Warning:        7
Inactive:       -1
Last Change:            Feb 27, 2005
Password Expires:       Mar 29, 2005
Password Inactive:      Never
Account Expires:        Jan 03, 2006
```

Let's remove the Account Expires date:

```
#chage -E -1 dbadmin
```

```
#grep dbadmin /etc/shadow
dbadmin:$1$TuCLLDqz$Fc1YnK309QXT6TJMOagdZ.:12841:0:30:7:::
```

```
#chage -l dbadmin
Minimum:        0
Maximum:        30
Warning:        7
Inactive:       -1
Last Change:            Feb 27, 2005
Password Expires:       Mar 29, 2005
Password Inactive:      Never
Account Expires:        Never
```

The passwd command can change the password aging fields too. The passwd aging options are shown in Table 14-5.

Table 14-5   passwd Password Aging

Syntax	Description
passwd -n ## *<username>*	Minimum password lifetime; same as chage -m
passwd -x ## *<username>*	Maximum password lifetime; same as chage -M
passwd -w ## *<username>*	Set number of days before password expiration to warn user that password will expire; same as chage -W
passwd -i ## *<username>*	Number of days after password expiration when account login is disabled; same as chage -I

The ## in the table indicates a number of days parameter. A -1 for the ## (days field) will clear the field from /etc/shadow like chage.

The usermod and passwd commands can also disable an account. The different syntaxes are shown in Table 14-6.

A ! in the password field of /etc/shadow indicates a locked account. Notice the change in the password field after usermod is used to lock an account.

Table 14-6 Locking Accounts

Syntax	Description
usermod -L <username>	Lock the account
usermod -U <username>	Unlock the account
passwd -l <username>	Lock the account
passwd -u <username>	Unlock the account

```
#grep dbadmin /etc/shadow
dbadmin:$1$TuCLLDqz$Fc1YnK309QXT6TJMOagdZ.:12841:0:30:7:::

#usermod -L dbadmin
grep dbadmin /etc/shadow
dbadmin:!$1$TuCLLDqz$Fc1YnK309QXT6TJMOagdZ.:12841:0:30:7:::
```

The chage -l output doesn't indicate that the account is locked.

```
#chage -l dbadmin
Minimum:          0
Maximum:          30
Warning:          7
Inactive:         -1
Last Change:              Feb 27, 2005
Password Expires:         Mar 29, 2005
Password Inactive:        Never
Account Expires:          Never
```

The account can be unlocked with usermod -U, passwd -u, or by changing the password with the passwd command as root. Why can't the user change the password, assuming he or she is already logged in? Because the user is prompted for the current password before being granted the authority to change the password. The user doesn't know the password anymore because a ! character was added when the account was locked. Root isn't required to enter the current password, which enables the root user to unlock the account with passwd.

The following is an example of a locked account being unlocked with `passwd`.

```
#grep dbadmin /etc/shadow
dbadmin:!$1$8nF5XmBG$Pckwi8Chld..JgP5Zmc4i0:12841:0:30:7:::


#passwd -u dbadmin
Unlocking password for user dbadmin.
passwd: Success.


#grep dbadmin /etc/shadow
dbadmin:$1$8nF5XmBG$Pckwi8Chld..JgP5Zmc4i0:12841:0:30:7:::
```

/etc/passwd and /etc/shadow Corruption

The `passwd` and `shadow` files can be corrupted in numerous ways: `/etc/shadow` might have been restored while `/etc/passwd` was not, incorrect file permissions could cause problems, and so on. Let's look at what happens if someone edits `/etc/shadow` to clear password aging information while a user attempts to change his password. Look at Dave's `/etc/shadow` line:

dave:1dkdAH.dQ$DU1t04WOFGjF4BGymI/ll0:12802:0:2:7:::

The system administrator is using `vi` to edit `/etc/shadow`. Before the system administrator saves the file, Dave changes his password successfully by using the `passwd` command. `/etc/shadow` shows the change to the password field:

dave:1VGCA.Vk8$9u2b8W5eCWjtOdt6ipOlD0:12804:0:2:7:::

Now the system administrator saves `/etc/shadow`. When the administrator tries to save the file, he sees:

```
WARNING: The file has been changed since reading it!!!
Do you really want to write to it (y/n)?
```

Hopefully, the system administrator replies n and tries again. If not, Dave loses his password change. Look at what happens to Dave's password. It changes back to the previous value:

```
#grep dave /etc/shadow
dave:$1$dkdAH.dQ$DU1t04WOFGjF4BGymI/ll0:12802:0:2:7:::
```

Be careful when making changes to /etc/passwd or /etc/shadow. Always try to use a command to make changes instead of editing the file.

pwck

Linux provides the pwck command to look for /etc/passwd and /etc/shadow problems. This command validates field entries and looks for duplicate lines. No output from pwck means it didn't identify any problems. It will not find all problems, so you might need to inspect the passwd and shadow files line by line to confirm the lines are correct. The following error is caused by user rob not having an entry in /etc/shadow. The pwck command didn't catch it.

```
passwd rob
Changing password for user rob.
passwd: Authentication token manipulation error
```

Login Failures Due to Linux Configuration

We saw how password aging can prevent individual users from logging in. Now we show how to restrict where root can log in by using /etc/securetty. Login for every non-root attempt can be prevented with /etc/nologin.

508   Linux Troubleshooting for System Administrators and Power Users

/etc/securetty

The /etc/securetty file is intended as a method for limiting root logins to a list of tty devices. If /etc/securetty exists, root login is permitted only from those devices. For example:

```
console
vc/1
vc/2
vc/3
vc/4
vc/5
vc/6
vc/7
vc/8
vc/9
vc/10
vc/11
tty1
tty2
tty3
tty4
tty5
tty6
tty7
tty8
tty9
tty10
tty11
tty12
```

note

The tty devices are for the KDE virtual console windows. The vc devices are the virtual console devfs devices.

It is common practice to restrict root login to the console. This forces users to su - root after a normal login. This practice makes it easy to track who all those root logins are. The /var/log/messages file shows the su attempts:

```
Jan 19 13:41:28 sawnee sshd(pam_unix)[3008]: session opened for user dave
by (uid=501)
Jan 19 13:41:36 sawnee su(pam_unix)[3043]: session opened for user root
by dave(uid=501)
```

Please note that whether /etc/securetty is honored depends on the PAM configuration for each login method and whether the login application uses PAM. The PAM configuration file for the login application needs the auth (authentication) pam_securetty.so module. See the PAM configuration section for details.

/etc/nologin

The /etc/nologin file gives the system administrator a way to keep users off the Linux system during maintenance. If /etc/nologin exists, non-root login attempts fail, and the contents of /etc/nologin are displayed. For example:

```
#cat /etc/nologin
Sorry.  System Maintenance in progress. System unavailable until 15:00 on
1/19.
```

When someone attempts to log in, he or she sees

```
Red Hat Linux release 9 (Shrike)
Kernel 2.4.20-8 on an i686

sawnee.somecomp.com login: dave
Password:
Sorry.  System Maintenance in progress. System unavailable until 15:00 on
1/19.


Login incorrect

login:
```

A zero-byte /etc/nologin disables non-root logins but prints no special message. Please note that whether /etc/nologin is honored depends on the PAM configuration for each login method. The PAM configuration file for the login application needs the auth "pam_nologin.so" module. See the PAM configuration section for details.

SSH does not look at the /etc/nologin file. A login attempt using ssh succeeds when /etc/nologin exists.

PAM

Linux-PAM is the Linux implementation of PAM. HPUX, Solaris, and other operation systems use PAM. Linux-PAM is a package designed to handle user authentication, which means each application does not need to include a routine to ask for a password, encrypt it with crypt(2), and compare it against the entry in /etc/shadow. PAM does much more than just verifying passwords, however. The access rules can be changed by editing a single PAM configuration file. PAM is a very important part of Linux security. Applications must be written to use PAM.

The heart of PAM is the configuration directory /etc/pam.d or configuration file /etc/pam.conf for older implementations of PAM.

A PAM-enabled application uses a configuration file in /etc/pam.d or a block of lines in /etc/pam.conf. Let's look at /etc/pam.d first because it is the newer and more common method. PAM looks for a configuration file with the name of the application. If one doesn't exist, the file other is used. The login file in /etc/pam.d shows the PAM modules used for the login application. The following is a sample /etc/pam.d/login file from a Red Hat Enterprise Linux AS release 3 system:

```
#%PAM-1.0
auth       required     pam_securetty.so
auth       required     pam_stack.so service=system-auth
auth       required     pam_nologin.so
account    required     pam_stack.so service=system-auth
password   required     pam_stack.so service=system-auth
session    required     pam_stack.so service=system-auth
session    optional     pam_console.so
```

The files in /etc/pam.d have four fields: function, priority, module name, and module arguments. The group of modules in a PAM configuration file is called a module stack. Linux distributions have different authorization modules, but they follow the same format.

Function

Four functions can be configured: account, authentication, password, and session (see Table 14-7). As you can see from the login example, all four can be used by the same application.

Table 14-7 PAM Function Field Values

Field Value	Description
account	Validated user is permitted to use application, password expiration checks, and so on.
auth	Authenticate user identification with a password or some other method.
password	Update authentication mechanisms; for example, the login application authenticates a user and may also request that the user change his or her password.
session	Service management functions done before and after a service is provided.

Priority

The priority field determines what happens if the module fails to grant the function. This field has four allowable values (see Table 14-8).

Table 14-8   PAM Priority Field Values

Field Value	Description
requisite	Failure of this module results in authentication being denied and the rest of the module stack not being executed.
required	Failure of this module means failure of authentication, but the rest of the module stack is executed.
sufficient	Success of this module results in granting authentication even if later modules in the stack fail. If a previously required module fails, authentication is denied.
optional	This module is only used if it is the only module in the stack for the function.

Module Name

This is the full path of the module to be used or the name of a file in /lib/security.

Arguments

Some modules take arguments. These are documented in the module README files. The location of the PAM README files varies, but the files are probably in a subdirectory of /usr/share/doc/. Use rpm -q -filesbypkg pam_ if you are having trouble finding the README files.

/etc/pam.d

The following is from a Red Hat 3.0ES system, and it demonstrates how many applications rely on PAM to perform authorization tasks.

```
# ls -ld /etc/pam.d
drwxr-xr-x    2 root      root        4096 Oct 30 04:25 /etc/pam.d
# ls /etc/pam.d
```

authconfig	printconf-tui	redhat-config-users
authconfig-gtk	printtool	redhat-config-xfree86
bindconf	reboot	redhat-install-packages
chfn	redhat-cdinstall-helper	redhat-logviewer
chsh	redhat-config-authentication	redhat-switch-mail
cups	redhat-config-bind	redhat-switch-mail-nox
dateconfig	redhat-config-date	rhn_register
ethereal	redhat-config-httpd	samba
gdm	redhat-config-keyboard	screen
gdm-autologin	redhat-config-language	serviceconf
gdmsetup	redhat-config-mouse	setup
halt	redhat-config-netboot	smtp
hwbrowser	redhat-config-network	smtp.sendmail
imap	redhat-config-network-cmd	sshd
internet-druid	redhat-config-network-druid	su
kbdrate	redhat-config-nfs	sudo
kde	redhat-config-packages	synaptic
kppp	redhat-config-printer	system-auth
login	redhat-config-printer-gui	up2date
neat	redhat-config-printer-tui	up2date-config
other	redhat-config-proc	up2date-nox
passwd	redhat-config-rootpassword	webmin
pop	redhat-config-samba	xdm
poweroff	redhat-config-securitylevel	xscreensaver
ppp	redhat-config-services	xserver
printconf	redhat-config-soundcard	
printconf-gui	redhat-config-time	

/etc/pam.conf

If /etc/pam.d exists, /etc/pam.conf is ignored. The /etc/pam.conf file lines are identical to those of /etc/pam.d except that they contain one extra field. The lines in

/etc/pam.conf contain the session name as the first field. The session name identifies the stack to which a line belongs.

/lib/security

The libraries supporting the /etc/pam.d authorization modules all have 755 permissions and are owned by root with group root. The following is from a Red Hat 9.0 system:

```
#ls -ld /lib/security
drwxr-xr-x   3 root      root      4096 May 18  2004 /lib/security
#ls -l /lib/security
total 1276
-rwxr-xr-x   1 root      root      9696 Feb 10  2003 pam_access.so
-rwxr-xr-x   1 root      root      6320 Feb 10  2003 pam_chroot.so
-rwxr-xr-x   1 root      root     47584 Feb 10  2003 pam_console.so
-rwxr-xr-x   1 root      root     12964 Feb 10  2003 pam_cracklib.so
-rwxr-xr-x   1 root      root      3404 Feb 10  2003 pam_deny.so
-rwxr-xr-x   1 root      root     11592 Feb 10  2003 pam_env.so
drwxr-xr-x   2 root      root      4096 Nov  6  2003 pam_filter
-rwxr-xr-x   1 root      root     11208 Feb 10  2003 pam_filter.so
-rwxr-xr-x   1 root      root      6048 Feb 10  2003 pam_ftp.so
-rwxr-xr-x   1 root      root     11148 Feb 10  2003 pam_group.so
-rwxr-xr-x   1 root      root      7540 Feb 10  2003 pam_issue.so
-rwxr-xr-x   1 root      root     59508 Jan 30  2003 pam_krb5afs.so
-rwxr-xr-x   1 root      root     57464 Jan 30  2003 pam_krb5.so
-rwxr-xr-x   1 root      root      8468 Feb 10  2003 pam_lastlog.so
-rwxr-xr-x   1 root      root     39080 Jan 25  2003 pam_ldap.so
-rwxr-xr-x   1 root      root     12324 Feb 10  2003 pam_limits.so
-rwxr-xr-x   1 root      root     10740 Feb 10  2003 pam_listfile.so
-rwxr-xr-x   1 root      root      9620 Feb 10  2003 pam_localuser.so
-rwxr-xr-x   1 root      root      9664 Feb 10  2003 pam_mail.so
-rwxr-xr-x   1 root      root     16652 Feb 10  2003 pam_mkhomedir.so
-rwxr-xr-x   1 root      root      4272 Feb 10  2003 pam_motd.so
-rwxr-xr-x   1 root      root      4856 Feb 10  2003 pam_nologin.so
```

```
-rwxr-xr-x    1 root      root        3708 Feb 10   2003 pam_permit.so
-rwxr-xr-x    1 root      root      146336 Feb 10   2003 pam_pwdb.so
-rwxr-xr-x    1 root      root       11372 Feb 10   2003 pam_rhosts_auth.so
-rwxr-xr-x    1 root      root        3936 Feb 10   2003 pam_rootok.so
-rwxr-xr-x    1 root      root        6544 Feb 10   2003 pam_securetty.so
-rwxr-xr-x    1 root      root        5520 Feb 10   2003 pam_shells.so
-rwxr-xr-x    1 root      root       43588 Aug 15   2003 pam_smb_auth.so
-rwxr-xr-x    1 root      root      468260 Apr  5   2003 pam_smbpass.so
-rwxr-xr-x    1 root      root       11132 Feb 10   2003 pam_stack.so
-rwxr-xr-x    1 root      root       10676 Feb 10   2003 pam_stress.so
-rwxr-xr-x    1 root      root       13752 Feb 10   2003 pam_tally.so
-rwxr-xr-x    1 root      root        9752 Feb 10   2003 pam_time.so
-rwxr-xr-x    1 root      root       10544 Feb 10   2003 pam_timestamp.so
lrwxrwxrwx    1 root      root          11 Nov  6   2003 pam_unix_acct.so
-> pam_unix.so
lrwxrwxrwx    1 root      root          11 Nov  6   2003 pam_unix_auth.so
-> pam_unix.so
lrwxrwxrwx    1 root      root          11 Nov  6   2003 pam_unix_passwd.so
-> pam_unix.so
lrwxrwxrwx    1 root      root          11 Nov  6   2003 pam_unix_session.so
-> pam_unix.so
-rwxr-xr-x    1 root      root       48544 Feb 10   2003 pam_unix.so
-rwxr-xr-x    1 root      root        9148 Feb 10   2003 pam_userdb.so
-rwxr-xr-x    1 root      root        4644 Feb 10   2003 pam_warn.so
-rwxr-xr-x    1 root      root        7788 Feb 10   2003 pam_wheel.so
-rwxr-xr-x    1 root      root       13348 Apr  5   2003 pam_winbind.so
-rwxr-xr-x    1 root      root       13860 Feb 10   2003 pam_xauth.so
```

Linux-PAM Resources

The previous coverage is just a brief explanation of Linux-PAM that is needed before we start looking at troubleshooting PAM problems. Detailed PAM information can be found in *The System Administrators' Guide*, *The Module Writers' Manual*, and *The Application Developers' Manual* available from the Linux-PAM home page (http://www.kernel.org/pub/linux/libs/pam/) under the "online documentation" link. There is also a

PAM man page and documentation in `/usr/share/doc`. The `pam(8)` man page is excellent as well.

Troubleshooting PAM

The lab instructor for my first college programming class gave us good advice. He said that we would have bugs in our code that we could not find. We would look very hard and still not find the cause. He said eventually we would decide the problem was caused by a hardware or compiler issue. He said we would be wrong. The point of his lecture was that yes, problems with compilers sometimes occur, and CPUs and memory chips sometimes fail, but it was more likely that our code was buggy. He did not want a bunch of freshman annoying the IT department.

There certainly might be bugs in PAM or a PAM module. Before going there, however, please look over the following questions to confirm that PAM is installed properly. Use `rpm` to verify all PAM packages, modules, libraries, and so on. If a module has been customized, put the default version back and test with it. The same goes for the application using PAM. The problem may be with `sshd` or `login` and not PAM.

- Are PAM modules or libraries missing?
- Have PAM modules or libraries been changed?
- Have PAM directory or file permissions been modified?

Scenario 14-1: Missing Stack Prevents Login

In the next example, the `/etc/pam.d/login` module is missing, and no one can log in.

```
Red Hat Linux release 9 (Shrike)
Kernel 2.4.20-8 on an i686


sawnee.somecomp.com login: root
Login incorrect


Login incorrect


Login incorrect
```

```
Login incorrect

Red Hat Linux release 9 (Shrike)
Kernel 2.4.20-8 on an i686


sawnee.somecomp.com login:
```

The user never even gets an opportunity to enter the password. Because there is no /etc/pam.d/login module, the default module, /etc/pam.d/other, is used. The other file denies authorization outright:

```
#cat /etc/pam.d/other
#%PAM-1.0
auth      required      /lib/security/$ISA/pam_deny.so
account   required      /lib/security/$ISA/pam_deny.so
password  required      /lib/security/$ISA/pam_deny.so
session   required      /lib/security/$ISA/pam_deny.so
```

What happens if other is missing too?

```
Red Hat Linux release 9 (Shrike)
Kernel 2.4.20-8 on an i686
sawnee.somecomp.com login: root
login: PAM Failure, aborting: Critical error - immediate abort

Red Hat Linux release 9 (Shrike)
Kernel 2.4.20-8 on an i686


sawnee.somecomp.com login:
```

PAM does not grant authorization if there is no authorization module. The solution is to create the /etc/pam.d/login file or restore it from backup. If there is an open root session, we can make the fix. If there is none, the box must be booted to single user mode and the fix made from there. Refer to Chapter 1, "System Boot, Startup, and Shutdown Issues," if this subject is not familiar.

Scenario 14-2: Missing /etc/pam.d Prevents Login

A user tries to connect with ssh, but the window closes immediately after the user enters the user name. Again, no one can log in. Login at the console yields the following:

```
sawnee.somecomp.com login: dave
login: PAM Failure, aborting: Critical error - immediate abort
```

This problem has symptoms similar to the missing /etc/pam.d/login example. If there were an open root session, we could troubleshoot PAM. Because there are none, the box must be booted to single user mode. In single user mode, we can quickly see that there is no /etc/pam.d directory. After reading this chapter, the solution should be pretty obvious. We need to create the pam.d directory and one module for system access:

```
#cd /etc
#mkdir pam.d
#chmod 755 pam.d
#cd pam.d
```

Create a file called login with the following entries:

```
auth         required        pam_permit.so
account      required        pam_permit.so
password     required        pam_permit.so
session      required        pam_permit.so
```

Then run init 3 to boot to multiuser mode. No sense trying to start KDE or Gnome because PAM is missing all those modules. Login from the console should be enabled now that we added the login module. Now the /etc/pam.d contents can be restored from backup or whatever else is needed. The temporary login module we show enables any valid user to access the system. This approach doesn't seem secure, but then again, the only place to log in is from the console. There is no ssh or other module. If other access points use login besides the console, though, this might not be the best choice. In that event, it might be better to stay in single user mode and restore the /etc/pam.d from there.

For whatever reason, it might not be possible to use the previous procedure in single user mode. Maybe Linux does not boot at all, or the root filesystem is read-only, and the

/etc/pam.d/login file can't be created. If this happens, boot from a recovery CD or floppy. After the box is booted with this method, the repairs to /etc/pam.d can be made. Chapter 1 explains booting from recovery CDs and floppy disks.

Validate Modules

The rpm command verifies that the files in a package are the same as when they were installed. If an application isn't acting right, and PAM is suspected, try verifying that the module is the same as when it was delivered. For example,

```
#rpm -V -f /etc/pam.d/login
.......T c /etc/pam.d/login
```

The T means the timestamp has changed, and the c indicates /etc/pam.d/login is a configuration file. Please note that the previous syntax verifies the package that delivered the login file and not just the login file itself.

The rpm command is a valuable troubleshooting tool. If you have not read through the rpm(8) man page, you should consider it.

It can be tempting just to verify the PAM packages, but this approach does not prove that the modules are ok. The modules are delivered by the applications that use them. For example:

```
#rpm -q -f /etc/pam.d/login
util-linux-2.11y-9.progeny.1
#rpm -q -f /etc/pam.d/sshd
openssh-server-3.5p1-11.progeny.2
#rpm -q -f /etc/pam.d/samba
samba-2.2.7a-8.9.0
```

Bugs in PAM

After ruling out installation and configuration issues, it might be time to look for known bugs. Search not only the PAM Web site but also the application sites. If you think you have found a problem with the sshd PAM module, check to see what package delivered it:

```
# rpm -q -f /etc/pam.d/sshd
openssh-3.7.1p2-113
```

Look at the documentation supplied with the application to see whether this is a known issue:

```
# rpm -q --filesbypkg openssh-3.7.1p2-113
```
(some lines omitted)
```
openssh                 /etc/pam.d/sshd
```
(some lines omitted)
```
openssh                 /usr/share/doc/packages/openssh
openssh                 /usr/share/doc/packages/openssh/CREDITS
openssh                 /usr/share/doc/packages/openssh/ChangeLog
openssh                 /usr/share/doc/packages/openssh/LICENSE
openssh                 /usr/share/doc/packages/openssh/OVERVIEW
openssh                 /usr/share/doc/packages/openssh/README
openssh                 /usr/share/doc/packages/openssh/README.SuSE
openssh                 /usr/share/doc/packages/openssh/README.kerberos
openssh                 /usr/share/doc/packages/openssh/RFC.nroff
openssh                 /usr/share/doc/packages/openssh/TODO
openssh                 /usr/share/man/man1/scp.1.gz
openssh                 /usr/share/man/man1/sftp.1.gz
openssh                 /usr/share/man/man1/slogin.1.gz
openssh                 /usr/share/man/man1/ssh-add.1.gz
openssh                 /usr/share/man/man1/ssh-agent.1.gz
openssh                 /usr/share/man/man1/ssh-copy-id.1.gz
openssh                 /usr/share/man/man1/ssh-keyconverter.1.gz
openssh                 /usr/share/man/man1/ssh-keygen.1.gz
openssh                 /usr/share/man/man1/ssh-keyscan.1.gz
openssh                 /usr/share/man/man1/ssh.1.gz
openssh                 /usr/share/man/man5/ssh_config.5.gz
openssh                 /usr/share/man/man5/sshd_config.5.gz
```

openssh	/usr/share/man/man8/sftp-server.8.gz
openssh	/usr/share/man/man8/ssh-keysign.8.gz
openssh	/usr/share/man/man8/sshd.8.gz

Finally, search the Internet for known issues. For sshd, http://www.openssh.com/report.html and http://bugzilla.mindrot.org/ are good places to start.

Shell Problems

If a user can log in and get past the password prompt but still has problems, there is a good chance the problem is with the configuration.

User Profile Files

Login shells source several files during login. These files enable a user's environment to be customized. This is where the environment variables such as PATH, PS1 (shell prompt), and MAIL are set. Because these files can be customized, there is a chance that they will cause login problems.

The bash shell is the most commonly used Linux login shell and is the default when adding users with useradd. The files executed at login in order are:

1. /etc/profile
2. *user home directory*/.bash_profile
3. *user home directory*/.bash_login
4. *user home directory*/.profile

All these files do not have to be present. The /etc/profile configuration file is executed by all users. If there is a problem in /etc/profile, it should affect all users. If just a few users are having a problem, /etc/profile is probably not the cause.

The easiest way to troubleshoot this issue is to temporarily replace the dot files with the default versions from /etc/skel and see whether the problem still occurs. If not, move the custom dot configuration files back one at a time until the problem file is found.

The following is from a Red Hat 3.0ES system:

```
# ls -al /etc/skel
total 52
drwxr-xr-x    4 root     root        4096 Feb 11 05:51 .
drwxr-xr-x   72 root     root        8192 Feb 12 06:41 ..
-rw-r--r--    1 root     root          24 Aug 18 13:23 .bash_logout
-rw-r--r--    1 root     root         191 Aug 18 13:23 .bash_profile
-rw-r--r--    1 root     root         124 Aug 18 13:23 .bashrc
-rw-r--r--    1 root     root        5542 Sep 16  2003 .canna
-rw-r--r--    1 root     root         237 Feb  3 10:55 .emacs
-rw-r--r--    1 root     root         120 Aug 24 08:44 .gtkrc
drwxr-xr-x    3 root     root        4096 Aug 12  2002 .kde
drwxr-xr-x    2 root     root        4096 Feb 11 05:49 .xemacs
-rw-r--r--    1 root     root         220 Nov 28  2002 .zshrc
```

note

If you use `ls -l /etc/skel`, you won't see any files. The `-a` option shows files that start with a dot (.).

The configuration files in `/etc/skel` are what `useradd` puts in a newly added user's home directory.

Password Problems

Have you ever had a user call and say she could not log in because the system wouldn't take her password? Is there something wrong, or did she forget the password? You could just reset it, but then your user blames Linux, and you blame the user. Maybe there really is a problem. How do you tell?

The encrypted password is a one-way encryption. The user enters a password when logging in. This password is used along with the two "salt" characters from `/etc/shadow` to encrypt the password. If this encrypted password matches the encrypted password in `/etc/shadow`, the authentication succeeds. This is done with the `crypt(3)` function. There is no method to take the encrypted password and reverse the process to learn the unencrypted password.

We want to offer a short program that takes salt characters and a clear text password as input and outputs the encrypted password. You tell the user her salt characters. She runs the program, passing the salt characters and password as input, and gives you the output. You can compare this to her encrypted password in /etc/shadow. If it doesn't match, the user doesn't know the correct password.[1]

```c
#include <unistd.h>
#include <crypt.h>
#include <stdio.h>
#include <stdlib.h>
#include <errno.h>
#include <strings.h>

main(argc, argv)
 int argc;
 char *argv[];


 {


/* crypt_password.c takes two arguments. The first is comprised of 2 salt
characters. The second field is the password which can be 8 characters.
See the crypt(3) man page for details. */

   if (argc ^= 3) {
       printf(" USAGE: crypt_password  SALT_CHARS PASSWORD  \n\n");
       return 1;
   }

      char salt[3];
      char passwd[80];

      strcpy(salt, argv[1]);
      strcpy(passwd, argv[2]);
      printf("%s\n", crypt(passwd, salt));
}
```

The program can be compiled with the following command:

```
gcc -o crypt_password -lcrypt crypt_password.c
```

Let's say a user calls with the complaint that a password no longer works.

```
sawnee login: dbadmin
Password:
Login incorrect
```

```
sawnee login: dbadmin
Password:
Login incorrect
```

We run chage -l dbadmin to verify that the account isn't disabled:

```
# chage -l dbadmin
Minimum:          0
Maximum:          99999
Warning:          7
Inactive:         -1
Last Change:              Feb 15, 2005
Password Expires:         Never
Password Inactive:        Never
Account Expires:          Never
```

The account is not expired. We may start to think the user just forgot the password. We can use the encrypt_password.c program to check. We need two pieces of information: the salt characters and the password.

The salt characters are the first two in the /etc/shadow password field. For dbadmin, the salt characters are f0. We can also look for a ! as the first character of the password, which would indicate the account is locked:

```
# grep dbadmin /etc/shadow
dbadmin:f0OFhXhLSMWy6:12829:0:99999:7:::
```

The user takes her salt characters `f0` and her password `d9a9mi123` and tries them `with crypt_password`:

```
# ./crypt_password f0 d9a9mi123
f0MugCavWrWaE
```

We can't tell what the password is, but we learned it is not `d9a9mi123`.

Summary

We stated that a Linux login attempt can fail for many reasons. The information provided in this chapter should enable the reader to troubleshoot login problems more effectively:

- If a user can't log in, use `chage` to see whether login for the account is disabled due to password aging settings.

- If login only fails for the root user, try logging in as a normal user and using `su` to switch to root because `/etc/securetty` might exist but contain no devices.

- If at least one user can log in, the global login restriction file `/etc/nologin` is not the trouble. If all users are having login problems, check for `/etc/nologin` and look for PAM module problems.

- If you are still having problems, you could try creating a new user with the default dot configuration files to verify that customization of `.bash_profile` or some other dot file is not preventing successful logins.

Endnote

1. Thanks to Bruce Laughlin in the Hewlett-Packard expert center for contributing this crypt program.

15

X Windows Problems

With today's servers and personal computers, it is hard to imagine not having a graphical desktop. The ability to "point and click" your way around the desktop and configuration menus has made it possible for non-computer geeks to manipulate these machines. In addition, it has made the computer administrator more powerful than ever. Unlike other OSs, under which the graphics are a core part of the OS, Linux, like UNIX, uses an application known as the X server to provide the graphical user interface (GUI). This server process could be thought of as being just like any other application that uses drivers to access and control hardware. With today's desktop environments, a single computer can use multiple monitors along with multiple virtual desktops. Something that makes X stand above the rest is its innate network design, which enables remote machines to display their programs on a local desktop. The X server is a client/server modeled application that relies heavily upon networking. In this chapter, we cover Linux's implementation of X along with some troubleshooting techniques, and we illustrate key concepts using a few scenarios.

X Background

X was originally developed by the Massachusetts Institute of Technology ("Athena Project") in the early to mid '80s. It has since become the standard graphic server on all commercially available UNIX variants. Around 1988, the MIT Group turned the project over to the MIT X Consortium, which took control of the development and distribution of X. Subsequently, in 1993, the members transferred all rights to X Window System to the X Consortium, Inc. And, once again, in 1996, all rights to the X Window System were placed with the Open Software Foundation as the X Consortium shut down.[1] Before closing, however, the X Consortium brought us X11R6 (release 6.3, to be exact). Around that same time (1996), the Open Software Foundation merged with X/Open Company Ltd., creating the organization we know today as The Open Group. The Open Group changed the X Window System license to a fee for commercial distribution in 1998 with the release of X11R6.4.[2] The change caused a shift as developers moved to an already prominent group that did not charge a fee. The group was known the XFree86 project.

Even though the X Window System got its start in 1984, a version for the PC did not come about until a German student ported a version to his 386-based PC. In the early '90s, Thomas Roell ported the X Window System, based on the X11R4, to his 386 PC and called it X386. In 1992, four developers—David Dawes, Glenn Lai, Jim Tsillas, and David Wexelblat—came together to create a free, open source version of an X server for the PC UNIX-like systems. Initially, the project produced a version of the X server derived from Roell's X386. Of course, because the term X386 was already in use, the team came up with the new name, and in 1992, XFree86 was born.[3]

To keep the XFree86 project current with the latest code of the day, the group had to join the X Consortium, which controlled the X Window System source. The group incorporated and joined the X Consortium, enabling XFree86 to be integrated with X11R6.[4] This spurred new versions of the XFree86 product; however, the group did not stay on the same page for long. As mentioned previously, the X Consortium handed all rights to the X Window System over to The Open Group in 1996. However, when the group changed the license with the release of X11R6.4, The XFree86 Project, Inc. stopped referencing the new X11R6 code, which was under the new license. This circumvented the licensing issue for the XFree86 project. Now the XFree86 project was in full swing.

The Open Group did not expect such a backlash of events, so X11R6.4 was rereleased under a "new license." Essentially, the license was the same as the original, so the group created another entity to direct X development. A new spin-off organization that was created by The Open Group in 1999 is called X.org (http://www.X.org), which today's Linux users who are running a recent release of a distribution might recognize.

At that point, two main groups were developing the X Window System: X.org has the official rights to the code, and XFree86 is a free, open source implementation of X. Fast-forwarding a few years, the XFree86 group released several newer revisions of its product. In January 2004, the The Xfree86 Project, Inc. released version 4.4 under a new license.[5] With this new license, which only made a few controversial changes, the X.org Foundation was on the receiving end of developmental input from many X developers. So depending on current affairs, the version of X on any distribution might be quite different from one release to another.

X Components

X can be broken down into two major sections: the server and the client. The client makes calls to the server, instructing the server on exactly how to paint the screen. The server, in turn, handles the communication with the hardware. Both of these components have sub-layers, which we touch on as we discuss each component in detail.

X Server Component

When troubleshooting X, start by determining the version and distribution of the server. This information can be extracted with the rpm or dpkg command if the server was installed as part of a distribution or package. Keep in mind that if the program was upgraded from source, the package manager commands might not reflect the current version. In this case, executing the server and passing the flag -version does the trick. However, it should be noted that "X", in this case, is usually a link to the X server your system has installed.

Server Version

To determine the version of X on your system, try the following command:

```
# type X
X is /usr/X11R6/bin/X
```

The type command (a built-in shell command) is used to find programs in the PATH variable. Now, using a long list, we can determine the file type.

```
# ll /usr/X11R6/bin/X
lrwxrwxrwx    1 root    root    8 May 20 20:56
/usr/X11R6/bin/X -> Xwrapper
```

Note that the Xwrapper is not installed with every distribution. Most distributions link X right to the X server binary. However, when determining the X version on one of our test Linux distributions, we noticed this Xwrapper binary. To determine the X server version, we simply trace the wrapper's execution.

```
# strace -o /tmp/xrapper.trace Xwrapper
# grep exec /tmp/xrapper.trace
execve("/usr/X11R6/bin/Xwrapper", ["Xwrapper"], [/* 45 vars */]) = 0
execve("/etc/X11/X", ["/etc/X11/X"], [/* 45 vars */]) = 0


# ll /etc/X11/X
lrwxrwxrwx   1 root     root         27 May 20 23:42 /etc/X11/X ->
../../usr/X11R6/bin/XFree86*
```

In this case, we find that X is linked to the XFree86 server. To determine the version of X server, simply execute the following:

```
#  /usr/X11R6/bin/XFree86 -version
XFree86 Version 4.3.0
Release Date: 9 May 2003
X Protocol Version 11, Revision 0, Release 6.6
Build Operating System: Linux 2.4.19-36mdkenterprise i686 [ELF]
Build Date: 10 December 2003
        Before reporting problems, check http://www.XFree86.Org/
        to make sure that you have the latest version.
Module Loader present
```

Performing similar steps on a different distribution, such as SUSE, yields the following:

```
# type X
X is /usr/X11R6/bin/X
#  ll /usr/X11R6/bin/X
lrwxrwxrwx  1 root root 16 2005-04-14 06:52 /usr/X11R6/bin/X ->
/var/X11R6/bin/X
#  ll /var/X11R6/bin/X
```

```
lrwxrwxrwx  1 root root 19 2005-04-14 06:52 /var/X11R6/bin/X ->
/usr/X11R6/bin/Xorg
# ll /usr/X11R6/bin/Xorg
-rws--x--x  1 root root 2054641 2005-02-25 11:26 /usr/X11R6/bin/Xorg
```

So, here we find that instead of XFree86, this distribution is using the Xorg version of the X server. To determine the exact version of the X server, we just pass the same argument as shown before:

```
# /usr/X11R6/bin/Xorg -version

X Window System Version 6.8.1
Release Date: 17 September 2004
X Protocol Version 11, Revision 0, Release 6.8.1
Build Operating System: SuSE Linux [ELF] SuSE
Current Operating System: Linux nc6000 2.6.8-24.14-default #1 Tue Mar 29
09:27:43 UTC 2005 i686
Build Date: 25 February 2005
        Before reporting problems, check http://wiki.X.Org
        to make sure that you have the latest version.
Module Loader present
```

Server Hardware

Before attempting to start the X server, it is a good idea to take inventory of the hardware to be configured. This practice enables you to configure the X server correctly with the hardware connected to the machine. Hardware supported by the X server can be found in the release notes for most versions or on the X organizations' Web sites. In addition to these references, the Linux distribution lists all supported hardware, which includes graphic devices. Some "bleeding edge" interfaces might not be supported yet and might not function at their full capacity or at all. Take inventory of the video card (chip set), amount of video memory on the interface, monitor capability, and Human Interface Devices (HID), such as keyboard, mouse, and so on.

To determine the type of video card in the machine, use tools such as lspci. In the next example, we can determine that the machine has a Matrox G400 dual head video card.

```
# lspci

0000:00:00.0 Host bridge: Intel Corp. 82865G/PE/P DRAM Controller/Host- \
Hub Interface (rev 02)

0000:00:01.0 PCI bridge: Intel Corp. 82865G/PE/P PCI to AGP Controller \
(rev 02)

0000:00:1d.0 USB Controller: Intel Corp. 82801EB/ER (ICH5/ICH5R) USB \
UHCI #1 (rev 02)

0000:00:1d.1 USB Controller: Intel Corp. 82801EB/ER (ICH5/ICH5R) USB \
UHCI #2 (rev 02)

0000:00:1d.2 USB Controller: Intel Corp. 82801EB/ER (ICH5/ICH5R) USB \
UHCI #3 (rev 02)

0000:00:1d.3 USB Controller: Intel Corp. 82801EB/ER (ICH5/ICH5R) USB \
UHCI #4 (rev 02)

0000:00:1d.7 USB Controller: Intel Corp. 82801EB/ER (ICH5/ICH5R) USB2 \
EHCI Controller (rev 02)

0000:00:1e.0 PCI bridge: Intel Corp. 82801 PCI Bridge (rev c2)

0000:00:1f.0 ISA bridge: Intel Corp. 82801EB/ER (ICH5/ICH5R) LPC Bridge \
(rev 02)

0000:00:1f.1 IDE interface: Intel Corp. 82801EB/ER (ICH5/ICH5R) Ultra \
ATA 100 Storage Controller (rev 02)

0000:00:1f.3 SMBus: Intel Corp. 82801EB/ER (ICH5/ICH5R) SMBus Controller \
(rev 02)

0000:00:1f.5 Multimedia audio controller: Intel Corp. 82801EB/ER \
(ICH5/ICH5R) AC'97 Audio Controller (rev 02)

0000:01:00.0 VGA compatible controller: Matrox Graphics, Inc. MGA G400 \
AGP (rev 04)

0000:02:05.0 Ethernet controller: Realtek Semiconductor Co., Ltd. RTL- \
8139/8139C/8139C+ (rev 10)

0000:02:0b.0 Multimedia audio controller: Creative Labs SB Live! EMU10k1 \
(rev 07)

0000:02:0b.1 Input device controller: Creative Labs SB Live! MIDI/Game \
Port (rev 07)

0000:02:0d.0 Ethernet controller: Realtek Semiconductor Co., Ltd. RTL- \
8029(AS)
```

We should also determine the amount of memory on the video card. The kernel accesses this memory and creates user-space address mapping. The vender's specifications for the video card would be a great place to determine the exact amount of VRAM on the card. The memory addresses used to access the interface can be found in

/proc/iomem. This file displays the memory map used by the kernel, not only for main memory, but also for memory located on I/O interfaces, which is sometimes referred to as "I/O memory" or "Memory-Mapped I/O". Because the full details of how this memory mapping takes place exceed the scope of this chapter, suffice it to say that having the kernel create a mapping of user-space address to the device's memory increases perform-ance substantially. For example, when the X server reads and writes to the specified address range contained in /proc/iomem, it is actually reading and writing to the video card's memory.

In most cases, the X server detects the memory available on the graphics board. Driver-specific documentation under /usr/X11R6/lib/X11/doc/ or the man pages under /usr/X11R6/man/man4 provide an indication about when the VRAM must be manually specified in the X configuration file. Here is an example of the X server's video driver detecting the VRAM size. This is an example of the XFree86 server using the ATI driver to detect the amount of memory on the ATI Technologies Inc. Rage Mobility interface. Note that when the server starts, it prints a "Marker" legend indicating that "--" stands for probed information.

```
# grep RAM /var/log/XFree86.0.log
(--) ATI(0): Internal RAMDAC (subtype 1) detected.
(--) ATI(0): 8192 kB of SDRAM (1:1) detected (using 8191 kB).
```

Here is an example of /proc/iomem showing the video card and the user-space address range mapped to the device. At address fe000000, the kernel has mapped direct access to the card's memory.

```
# cat /proc/iomem
00000000-0009fbff : System RAM
0009fc00-0009ffff : reserved
000a0000-000bffff : Video RAM area
000c0000-000c7fff : Video ROM
000f0000-000fffff : System ROM
00100000-1ff2ffff : System RAM
  00100000-00306aec : Kernel code
  00306aed-003ca37f : Kernel data
1ff30000-1ff3ffff : ACPI Tables
1ff40000-1ffeffff : ACPI Non-volatile Storage
```

```
1fff0000-1fffffff : reserved
20000000-200003ff : 0000:00:1f.1
f3f00000-f7efffff : PCI Bus #01
  f4000000-f5ffffff : 0000:01:00.0
    f4000000-f5ffffff : vesafb
f8000000-fbffffff : 0000:00:00.0
fd900000-fe9fffff : PCI Bus #01
  fe000000-fe7fffff : 0000:01:00.0
  fe9fc000-fe9fffff : 0000:01:00.0
feaffc00-feaffcff : 0000:02:05.0
  feaffc00-feaffcff : 8139too
febff400-febff4ff : 0000:00:1f.5
febff800-febff9ff : 0000:00:1f.5
febffc00-febfffff : 0000:00:1d.7
  febffc00-febfffff : ehci_hcd
ffb80000-ffffffff : reserved
```

This same address can be found when reviewing the memory map of the running process such as X, as shown in this next example:

```
# X &
[1] 6273

# cat /proc/6273/maps | grep fe000
40b14000-41314000 rw-s fe000000 03:41 7318        /dev/mem
42b28000-43328000 rw-s fe000000 03:41 7318        /dev/mem
43b3c000-4433c000 rw-s fe000000 03:41 7318        /dev/mem
```

Server Configuration

The configuration of the server is controlled by a configuration file stored in /etc/X11/. The file referenced depends entirely upon which server is being used. Older versions of XFree86 use /etc/X11/XF86Config, whereas the newer version 4 uses /etc/X11/XF86Config-4. The Xorg server uses /etc/X11/xorg.conf, and this file is linked to XF86Config. Keep in mind that the server configuration files have changed over the years and will surely change again. The X configuration file needed for your version of the X server should be detailed in the man page on XF86Config. This man page should be used for both XFree86 and Xorg distributions.

To successfully bring the X server online, we must analyze the configuration file and break it down into its sections. The file is made up of several key sections, which include Files, ServerFlags, Module, InputDevice, Monitor, Modes, Screen, Device, and ServerLayout. The full details of the X server's configuration can be found in the man page on XF86Config; however, the following list gives a brief description of each section and its use.

- Files—This section deals with fonts, color (RGBPath), and the dynamic loadable modules path, enabling the X server to display color, render fonts, or install the appropriate drivers for the devices connected to the machine. Section "Files" include the following:

  - RgbPath "/usr/X11R6/lib/X11/rgb"—In today's implementations, this is not contained in the configuration file because it is compiled into the server. You can change the path if needed, but that is rarely the case.

  - FontPath "... fonts, ..."—Older implementations or installations that do not use an X Font Server contain a list of fonts, which enables the graphics engine to render text and other attributes.

    Instead of listing each font, a system administrator could configure the Font Server and instruct the X server to access the Font Server for fonts with the following line:

    FontPath "unix/:-1"

    Note that this requires you to start the Font Server on the UNIX socket "-1" and not a TCP socket so that other machines could not connect to the font server over the network.

  - ModulePath "Path to dynamic loaded modules"—This is a list of comma-separated directories that the server searches for loadable modules.

- ServerFlags—This covers options that can be passed directly to the X server as discussed earlier, such as AllowMouseOpenFail or DontZap.

* `Module`—This is an optional section used to load drivers into the X server. These modules are located throughout the directory of `/usr/X11R6/lib/modules/` on most X implementations. With today's fast computers and graphics cards, drivers such as `glx` and `dri`, along with a slew of other modules, almost always are loaded.

* `InputDevice`—This section is where we would define devices such a keyboard, mouse, or digitizer. There would be an `InputDevice` section for each input device.

* `Monitor`—This is the section in which we would define the monitor's attributes, including sync and refresh ranges. It is also common to define the manufacturer of the monitor or monitor type.

* `Modes`—Some implementations do not use the Modes section. It is just detailed in the Monitor section. In dealing with multiple screens on a device, however, it is common to create a Modes section instead of incorporating it into the Monitor section.

  With today's Linux distributions, these lines are usually filled with hardware scanners, distribution X configuration tools, or both; however, if you seek a challenge and do not mind taking risks with your monitor, you can use `xvidtune` to get the entries. Essentially, the entry can be stated two ways, as shown in the next example:

  ```
  ModeLine "768x576"  50.00  768  832  846 1000  576  590  595  630
  ```

  Here is the equivalent entry stated with three lines:

  ```
  Mode "768x576"

    DotClock   50.00

    HTimings   768  832  846 1000

    VTimings   576  590  595  630
  ```

  It just looks cleaner as one line instead of three.

* `Device`—The Device section identifies the video card(s) being used. Also, any options to the driver, including the PCI bus location of the video card, are identified here.

* `Screen`—This section identifies the screen and labels the monitor and device while also providing a subsection called Display. The Display

subsection is where the color depth is defined. The higher the color depth, the more video memory is required.

• `ServerLayout`—This section uses all the other sections to create a complete configuration layout.

Some Linux distributions, such as Red Hat, SUSE, Debian, Mandriva (formally Mandrake), and others, usually provide tools to aid in X server configuration. However, unless these tools are offered in a TUI version, if the X server does not start, they are not of much use. The Xorg X server has a `getconfig.pl` Perl script that is called when the X server cannot locate the default configuration file. It attempts to use the most generic configuration to bring the server online. The XFree86 implementation does not use such a script, so if the X configuration file is not present, it simply does not start.

The following example illustrates bringing the X server online.

```
# X
X Window System Version 6.8.2
Release Date: 9 February 2005
X Protocol Version 11, Revision 0, Release 6.8.2
Build Operating System: Linux 2.4.22-26mdk i686 [ELF]
Current Operating System: Linux gamer2 2.4.22-26mdk #1 Wed Jan 7 10:47:21
MST 2004 i686
Build Date: 18 August 2005
        Before reporting problems, check http://wiki.X.Org
        to make sure that you have the latest version.
Module Loader present
Markers: (--) probed, (**) from config file, (==) default setting,
        (++) from command line, (!!) notice, (II) informational,
        (WW) warning, (EE) error, (NI) not implemented, (??) unknown.
(==) Log file: "/var/log/Xorg.0.log", Time: Thu Aug 18 22:25:32 2005
(EE) Unable to locate/open config file
xf86AutoConfig: Primary PCI is 1:0:0
Running "/usr/X11R6/bin/getconfig -X 60802000 -I
/etc/X11,/usr/X11R6/etc/X11,/usr/X11R6/lib/modules,/usr/X11R6/lib/X11/
getconfig -v 0x1002 -d 0x4c4d -r 0x64 -s 0x103c -b 0x0010 -c 0x0300"
getconfig.pl: Version 1.0.
```

```
getconfig.pl: Xorg Version: 6.8.2.0.
getconfig.pl: 23 built-in rules.
getconfig.pl: rules file '/usr/X11R6/lib/X11/getconfig/xorg.cfg' has
version 1.0.
getconfig.pl: 1 rule added from file
'/usr/X11R6/lib/X11/getconfig/xorg.cfg'.
getconfig.pl: Evaluated 24 rules with 0 errors.
getconfig.pl: Weight of result is 500.
New driver is "ati"
(==) Using default built-in configuration (53 lines)
(EE) open /dev/fb0: No such file or directory
Could not init font path element /usr/X11R6/lib/X11/fonts/CID/,
removing from list!
```

At this point, the X server should be up and running as indicated by the "weave" pattern, which should be on the screen. By default, the version and configuration file that it uses are displayed as standard output. Because no display or screen number was passed at the command line, the default:0.0 (or local device) is used. Because no desktop environment has been started yet, we can do little in the window except move the mouse around (if one is attached) or issue Ctrl+Alt+Backspace to reset the server, unless someone has inserted the DontZap server option in the configuration file. Of course, if errors are encountered, we can check the X error log file under /var/log.

Figure 15-1 displays the "weave" pattern that is displayed when the X server is online.

With no options passed to the X server, it starts and listens for client communication. All that is presented to the screen is the "weave" background. A client is now needed to instruct the X server on what to draw. Because the X server is a networked application, we simply can execute a client from another machine and direct it to the display on our test machine. Built into the X server are security measures that prevent just anyone from capturing a display or directing clients to a server. The man page on Xsecurity explains all the different implementations of access control. By default, the X server listens for TCP communication; however, it is not allowed access unless the Host is allowed by the access controls. To disable the X server from listening for TCP, use the option -nolisten tcp detailed in the man page on Xserver.

By default, the X server listens on port 600n, where n is the display value. This can be seen by using netstat and lsof.

Figure 15-1 The weave displayed when the X server is online

```
# netstat -an
...
tcp        0        0 0.0.0.0:6000              0.0.0.0:*
LISTEN
...
```

Here is an example of checking the port on which the X server is listening using lsof.

```
# ps -ef ¦ grep X
root      9359    769  0 08:47 ?        00:00:00 X
# lsof  -n -P -p 9359
COMMAND  PID USER   FD   TYPE   DEVICE   SIZE   NODE NAME
X       9359 root  cwd    DIR      3,1    4096 539675 /etc/X11
X       9359 root  rtd    DIR      3,1    4096      2 /
X       9359 root  txt    REG      3,1 2048692 150855 /usr/X11R6/bin/Xorg
```

```
X    9359 root   mem   CHR       1,1             8 /dev/mem
X    9359 root   mem   REG       3,1     80296 637734 /lib/ld-2.3.2.so
X    9359 root   mem   REG       3,1     55448 637782 /lib/libz.so.1.1.4
X    9359 root   mem   REG       3,1    139748 277989 /lib/i686/libm-2.3.2.so
X    9359 root   mem   REG       3,1      9160 637745 /lib/libdl-2.3.2.so
X    9359 root   mem   REG       3,1   1237568 277987 /lib/i686/libc-2.3.2.so
X    9359 root   mem   REG       3,1     34516 637755 /lib/libnss_files-2.3.2.so
X    9359 root   0w    REG       3,1     39041 297910 /var/log/Xorg.0.log
X    9359 root   1u    IPv4    160240          TCP *:6000 (LISTEN)
X    9359 root   2u    CHR     136,0             2 /dev/pts/0
X    9359 root   3u    unix 0xdca2da20          160241 /tmp/.X11-unix/X0
X    9359 root   4u    CHR     10,134            6 /dev/misc/apm_bios
X    9359 root   5u    CHR       4,7            26 /dev/vc/7
X    9359 root   6u    REG       0,2       256  4406 /proc/bus/pci/01/00.0
X    9359 root   7w    REG       0,6       137     4 /dev/cpu/mtrr
X    9359 root   8u    CHR      10,1            85 /dev/misc/psaux
```

This confirms that the X server is listening for connections on TCP port 6000.

X Client Component

The X client is anything that talks to the X server. A prime example is a window manager or simple xterm. Rarely will there be a time when the X server is up and there is no window manager running. Without the window manager, it would be very difficult to manipulate the window frames. This would result in the X window frames overlapping unless we instructed the server exactly where onscreen to place the frame, as is done with point-of-service or single-purpose screens.

In the next example, we execute the xterm command on a remote machine, instructing the command to display on our test machine's display 0.

```
# xterm -display testmachine.atl.hp.com:0
Xlib: connection to "testmachine.atl.hp.com:0.0" refused by server
Xlib: No protocol specified

xterm Xt error: Can't open display: testmachine.atl.hp.com:0
```

The error in the previous example is due to X security controls. Because we do not have an `xterm` running in the screen, we need to instruct the server to allow incoming connections. Of course, if we come from the local host using a different port such as the console, all we would need to do is execute `xterm -display :0`. However, if the client is connecting over the network, we need to grant the client access to our local display. This is achieved through executing the `xhost +` command, which grants the remote machine access to the local display. See the man pages for `xhost` for all options. The + opens the X display up to all hosts; therefore, to minimize security risk, the hostname or IP of the connecting client should be used. However, because we have not started an `xterm` yet, we can create a file called `Xn.hosts` (n = display). The X server reads this file by default and allows any host named in this file to have access to the local display.

In Figure 15-2, the X server is running on a display with two clients (`xterm` and `xclock`) running in the foreground without using a window manager client.

Figure 15-2 Two clients running in the foreground without a window manager client.

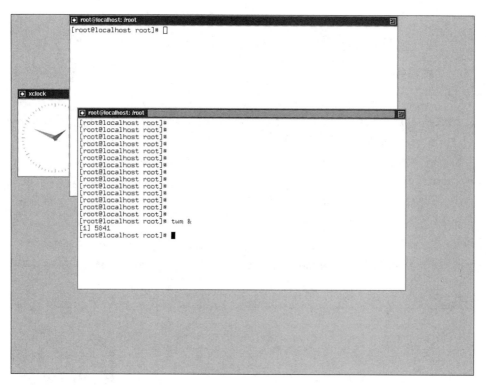

Figure 15-3 With the windows manager running, you can move the window frames around.

As you can see, the clock is sitting on top of the xterm, and we have no way of moving it or defining which window is on top. This is the job of the window manager. After the window manager is started, you can move the window frames around as depicted in Figure 15-3.

X Display Manager

Now that we have touched on the window manager and X server, the display manager is the next logical stop. When troubleshooting the X server, first make sure that the X server even starts. After that has been accomplished, set out to make the desktop usable by enabling a display manager. There are a lot of display managers out there. Although today most distributions default to the K-Desktop Manager or Sawfish, others are available such as fvwm, twm, xdm, and WindowMaker. As mentioned before, these are still X clients, which tell the X server how to paint the screen.

There are several ways to get display managers. If no other desktop managers are installed, the X server itself comes with several ways to get both the window manager and X server started. Commands such as startx and xinit are the most commonly used, followed by xdm. startx is really a front-end to xinit, which has been around since the beginning of X and is found on almost all X server implementations. It uses a configuration file in the user's $HOME directory, which indicates what to start. Because xinit and startx only initialize the server, the configuration file specifies how many terminals to open, along with the window manager to use, normally twm. Although most people use the default, as with everything else in UNIX/Linux, it has a configuration file.

For xinit or startx to initialize the X server along with a couple xterms, an xclock, and the twm window manager, as shown in Figure 15-3, the user's $home/.xinitrc would look like the following:

```
# cat .xinitrc
xsetroot -solid gray &
xterm &
xterm &
xclock &
twm
```

Display managers offer a wide range of features for controlling the desktop. One main feature is X Display Manager Control Protocol, which enables you to use the local X server to display everything from a remote machine. This protocol normally is used with dumb terminals, which "leech" off a more powerful machine. For example, a dumb terminal would have the local video hardware and initialize a local X server, but the terminal normally would not have local resources such as a hard drive or processor. In this case, it would use XDMCP to get the desktop environment from another machine and display it on the local screen. Therefore, when the user is compiling code or doing work, he or she is using the resources of the remote machine. This also can be accomplished with the X -query command. This feature requires some configuration depending on the display manager used the situation with network firewalls. The firewalls must not block the TCP and UDP ports needed for the transmissions. A great resource on configuring the XDMCP protocol can be found in the XDMCP-HOWTO at www.tldp.org.

X Desktop Manager (Environment)

Most modern-day window managers contain desktop managers that create the look and feel of the desktop. Overall, this is referred to as the desktop environment. GNOME originally used the Enlightenment Window Manager, but later revisions moved to the Sawfish Window Manager, whereas the K Desktop Environment uses its own K Window Manager. Essentially, the window manager, as discussed earlier, controls the X server's look and feel, whereas the desktop manager controls the window management.

Troubleshooting the desktop environment can be a daunting task. Each desktop has configuration files stored in the user's home directory. KDE stores users' configuration files under $HOME/.kde, whereas GNOME uses $HOME/.gnome. The best way to troubleshoot the desktop environment is simply to use a new user account to see whether the problem still exists. If the problem does not exist for the new user, then there is something wrong in the configuration files. Divide and conquer. Rename the configuration directory and log back in, and the desktop environment will create a new configuration directory and take the user to default settings. Eventually, you will find the root cause.

X Troubleshooting Scenarios

The following scenarios represent just a small sample of what users can experience with the X server. The overall goal in any X troubleshooting situation is to break down the X server into its individual layers to isolate the problem.

Scenario 15-1: Xauthority

A user uses ssh with the -X option, which is supposed to enable X forwarding. However, when the user connects to the remote machine and issues the command to start his application, he receives an error regarding authentication failure. To troubleshoot the issue, we use the best-known testing program, which in this case is an X native command such as xterm, xclock, xosview, or another located in /usr/bin/x*.

The user connects to a remote machine through ssh and attempts to start his application.

```
[root@local ]# ssh -X -l root remote
Last login: Fri Aug 19 10:43:37 2005 from 15.50.74.102
 [root@remote root]# xclock
```

```
X11 connection rejected because of wrong authentication.
X connection to localhost:11.0 broken (explicit kill or server shutdown).
```

Notice that the connection is to localhost:11.0. With ssh forwarding, it uses display 11 for all X forwarding; however, the problem is not with ssh. The problem is with "authentication." Checking the man page on Xsecurity, the only file that really deals with security at this layer is .Xauthority, which is located in the user's home directory.

Upon using the xuath command to list the contents of the file, we see the problem:

```
xauth> info
Authority file:         /root/.Xauthority
File new:               no
File locked:            no
Number of entries:      0
Changes honored:        yes
Changes made:           no
Current input:          (stdin):3
The file has no entries?
```

After using the command mkxauth -c to re-create the MIT-MAGIC-COOKIE-1 entries for the host, we see the following:

```
xauth> info
Authority file:         /root/.Xauthority
File new:               no
File locked:            no
Number of entries:      2
Changes honored:        yes
Changes made:           no
Current input:          (stdin):2

xauth> list
remote/unix:0  MIT-MAGIC-COOKIE-1   1eb06f066004088c76e619255ac28cfd
remote:0  MIT-MAGIC-COOKIE-1   1eb06f066004088c76e619255ac28cfd
```

When we retry the xclock program, it shows up on our local display.

Scenario 15-2: The X Server Does Not Start on the Second Head of a Dual-Display Video Card

The user tries to get the X server to start and use both heads of the dual-head video card, but she receives an error. When attempting to start the X server, she receives the following message:

```
# X
X Window System Version 6.8.1
Release Date: 17 September 2004
X Protocol Version 11, Revision 0, Release 6.8.1
Build Operating System: Linux 2.6.3-4 i686 [ELF]
Current Operating System: Linux gamer 2.6.3-4 #1 Tue Mar 2 07:26:13 CET
2004 i686

...

 (==) Log file: "/var/log/Xorg.0.log", Time: Mon Aug 15 00:35:19 2005
(==) Using config file: "/etc/X11/xorg.conf"
(EE) MGA: Failed to load module "mga_hal" (module does not exist, 0)
(EE) MGA: Failed to load module "mga_hal" (module does not exist, 0)
(EE) MGA(1): This card requires the "mga_hal" module for dual-head
operation
        It can be found at the Matrox web site <http://www.matrox.com>
(EE) MGA(0): [drm] DRIScreenInit failed.  Disabling DRI.
Could not init font path element /usr/X11R6/lib/X11/fonts/local, removing
from list!
Could not init font path element /usr/X11R6/lib/X11/fonts/CID, removing
from list!
```

Just in reading the standard output from the server, we can see that there are two problems: The dual display is not working because of missing drivers, and hardware acceleration is not working (Direct Rendering Infrastructure).

Because this user is trying to run the latest Xorg X server, we download the latest kernel, kernel source, and X server source. Further research proves that the latest Matrox drivers are included with the Xorg server release. The README file states that we must make modifications to the xc/config/cf/ xf86site.def file. We also install the latest kernel and go to work on compiling the X server.

The following is a small portion of the file that we must uncomment:

```
...
/*
 * If you have the HALlib source code installed in
   xfree86/drivers/mga/hallib,
 * uncomment this:
 */
#define BuildMatroxHal          YES
...
```

Executed:
```
# make World > compiling.out 2>&1
```

Thirty-plus minutes later, with no errors the compile is complete. We perform a `make install`, which installs the latest compiled version of the Xorg server. An example of the new X server follows.

```
# X
```

```
X Window System Version 6.8.2
Release Date: 9 February 2005
X Protocol Version 11, Revision 0, Release 6.8.2
Build Operating System: Linux 2.6.8-24-default i686 [ELF]
Current Operating System: Linux gamer 2.6.8-24-default #1 Wed Oct 6
09:16:23 UTC 2004 i686
Build Date: 17 August 2005
        Before reporting problems, check http://wiki.X.Org
        to make sure that you have the latest version.
Module Loader present
Markers: (--) probed, (**) from config file, (==) default setting,
        (++) from command line, (!!) notice, (II) informational,
        (WW) warning, (EE) error, (NI) not implemented, (??) unknown.
(==) Log file: "/var/log/Xorg.0.log", Time: Thu Aug 18 00:48:59 2005
(==) Using config file: "/etc/X11/xorg.conf"
(EE) MGA(0): [drm] DRIScreenInit failed.  Disabling DRI.
(EE) MGA(1): Not initializing the DRI on the second head
```

The user states that now she has the display on the second head and that she would like to have better performance through hardware acceleration. Taking a look at the log file, we find the answer to why we could not get hardware acceleration to work when running in dual-head mode.

```
# cat /var/log/Xorg.0.log
...
(II) MGA(0): [drm] bpp: 32 depth: 24
(II) MGA(0): [drm] Sarea 2200+664: 2864
(WW) MGA(0): Direct rendering is not supported when Xinerama is enabled
(EE) MGA(0): [drm] DRIScreenInit failed.  Disabling DRI.
...
```

In the current release, direct rendering simply is not supported when operating dual-head display, or Xinerama. To give some idea of how much performance the hardware acceleration would bring, we run the famous test program called glxgears, which runs at around 312 frames per second when Xinerama is enabled. After disabling it and restarting the X server, we enable DRI and the Matrox card, and the user achieves over 750 frames per second. There are other ways to measure X performance. One common way is by using the x11perf command in combination with the Xmark script to inter-rupter the x11perf results.

Summary

When troubleshooting the X server, remember the key components that make up the windowing environment. The X server must be able to start before the window manager and desktop managers take over. Take note of the X server that you are dealing with and check the documentation that comes with the version. The documentation located under the /usr/X11R6/lib directory contains examples including options needed for specific drivers to operate efficiently with certain video cards.

Be mindful of network connections. Clients can connect to the X server from the local host or from over the network. Configuration files such as X0.hosts control this access, along with the Xauthority file covered in the man page on Xsecurity. Remote machines also can connect to the desktop manager to gain access to resources not on their machines. This is controlled through the XDMCP protocol, which most desktop managers support.

When troubleshooting the desktop environment, make sure to take the simplest approach first. Determine whether the problem is with the user or the system. A simple approach is to create a test user account and see whether it experiences the same phenomenon. This is a great data point when it comes to troubleshooting the desktop.

Endnotes

1. man 7 Xconsortium.

2. http://www.opengroup.org/tech/desktop/Press_Releases/x11r6.4ga.htm.

3. man XFree86.

4. man XFree86.

5. http://xfree86.org/legal/licenses.html.

Index

BOOKS ONLINE
ENABLED

THIS BOOK IS SAFARI ENABLED

INCLUDES FREE 45-DAY ACCESS TO THE ONLINE EDITION

The Safari® Enabled icon on the cover of your favorite technology book means the book is available through Safari Bookshelf. When you buy this book, you get free access to the online edition for 45 days.

Safari Bookshelf is an electronic reference library that lets you easily search thousands of technical books, find code samples, download chapters, and access technical information whenever and wherever you need it.

TO GAIN 45-DAY SAFARI ENABLED ACCESS TO THIS BOOK:

- Go to **http://www.prenhallprofessional.com/safarienabled**

- Complete the brief registration form

- Enter the coupon code found in the front of this book on the "Copyright" page

If you have difficulty registering on Safari Bookshelf or accessing the online edition, please e-mail customer-service@safaribooksonline.com.

PRENTICE
HALL

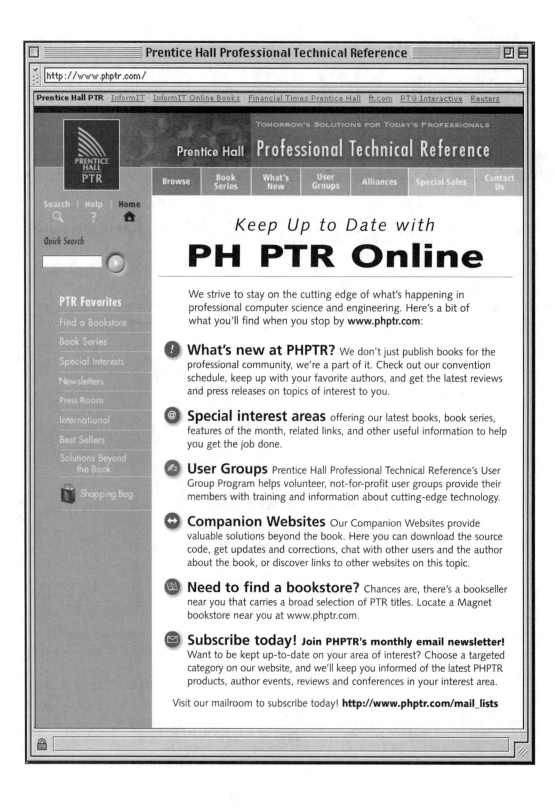

Get the most out of Linux with these essential resources from HP Books!

PHILLIP G. EZOLT

Renowned Linux benchmarking specialist Phillip Ezolt introduces each of today's most important Linux optimization tools, showing how they fit into a proven methodology for perfecting overall application performance.

ISBN 0131486829 • 384 pages • © 2005

ROBERT W. LUCKE

Until now, building and managing Linux clusters has required more specialized knowledge than most IT organizations possess. This book dramatically lowers the learning curve, bringing together all the hands-on knowledge and step-by-step techniques you'll need to get the job done.

ISBN 0131448536 • 648 pages • © 2005

MARTY PONIATOWSKI

A comprehensive guide to administering HP Integrity systems running Linux. HP Solution Architect and Linux/UNIX expert Marty Poniatowski walks you through every essential tool and technique, from installation and bootup, to compiling kernels, to building clusters.

ISBN 0131400002 • 360 pages • © 2005

PRENTICE
HALL